LETECIA STAUCH
TRIAL OF THE WICKED STEPMOTHER

NETTA NEWBOUND, MARCUS BROWN

JUNCTION PUBLISHING

Junction Publishing United Kingdom/New Zealand

Letecia Stauch Trial of the Wicked Stepmother

email – junctionpublishing@outlook.com

www.junction-publishing.com

Ordering Information:

Quantity sales. Special discounts are available on quantity purchases by corporations, associations, and others. For details, contact the "Special Sales Department" at the address above.

LS TOTWSM / Netta Newbound & Marcus Brown -- 1st Ed.

CONTENTS

INTRODUCTION

In a world continually obsessed with true crime investigations, there will always be a case which instantly demands attention. The subsequent trial garners much interest with press and public alike, often opening the floodgates to a furore of horror, especially when the crime committed is against an innocent child.

The trial of Letecia Stauch *is* that case, and one we have been patiently waiting for.

For those following the story will remember watching the security camera footage of poor Gannon Stauch, an 11-year-old boy from Colorado, hobbling to his stepmother's truck never to be seen alive again.

But what actually happened to him?

Did he make it back to the family home that day after their shopping trip as Letecia stated he had?

Letecia Stauch

Letecia told detectives he had gone to visit one of his friends, but he never made it there.

But let's not get ahead of ourselves and go back to the beginning.

Who is Letecia Stauch?

Born Letecia Hardin in South Carolina on the 4th August 1983, she has two half-sisters, Aimee Marie Lowry and Julie Ruby Lowry, as well as one half-brother, Dakota Lowry.

After a dodgy start in life, Letecia had a number of domestic violence, battery, and theft charges laid against her, but she managed to get her act together and, after finishing high school, she went to The University of North Carolina, Pembroke, where she achieved a bachelor's degree in political science. Later she earned a master's degree in curriculum and instruction from Capella University, and a doctorate degree in education from Liberty University.

She was supposedly diagnosed with bipolar disorder in 2009.

Letecia has a daughter, Harley Hunt, from her first marriage.

She married Alfred Stauch in January 2015. He had two children, Gannon and Laina.

The couple lived in Colorado Springs with all three children.

Eugene Albert Stauch, known as Al, was born and raised in Colorado Springs and had met his first wife, Landon Hiott, when they were both serving in the military.

Apparently, Letecia befriended Landon prior to having an affair with Al and breaking the couple up. But Al denies this and claims he and Landon had already separated before he met Letecia.

Al worked away a lot and Letecia found herself responsible for the lion's share of caring for the children.

Did she begrudge this role?

Before we delve into the details of the trial, we will tell you what we know up to now.

CHAPTER 1

BRIEF TIMELINE

Gannon Stauch 29/09/2008

11-year-old Gannon Jacob Stauch was reported missing from his Colorado Springs home by his stepmother, Letecia Stauch, on the 27th January 2020.

Gannon was a typical kid who loved sport and video games.

The police were called at 6:55pm and Letecia told them she'd known there was something wrong when Gannon didn't return home after it started to go dark—it wasn't like him to stay out late.

She told detectives she had last seen him between 3:15pm and 4pm as he left via the side gate of their house. He was supposedly going to visit a friend. Strangely, Letecia didn't know the names or addresses of any of Gannon's friends.

Law enforcement did a preliminary search of the house, and she pointed out a patch of carpet she'd had to cut out as Gannon had burned it with a candle the day before. They didn't find anything of concern, but they did think her behaviour was a little odd.

At first, detectives suspected Gannon was a runaway. However, a few days later they changed the status to missing and endangered. This was due to several reasons; the weather, his age, and the medication he needed. The FBI became involved.

The following morning, Albert Stauch, Gannon's father, who had been away for the weekend training for the National Guard, returned home. Letecia drove her car to the Colorado Springs airport, parked it in the short-term parking lot, and then rented a Kia Rio from Avis.

She picked up Al and drove him back to the house. Her reasoning for renting a car was that her own car was a lease vehicle, and she was getting close to her mileage limit. With Gannon missing she figured they would be doing a lot of mileage driving around looking for him—also, she thought it would be good to look for Gannon in a car he did not recognise.

The car is said to have had 955 miles added to the clock when it was returned the following day.

Al and Letecia were interviewed by detectives. The interview was conducted at their local Starbucks as Letecia didn't want detectives at her house. By now, the entire community is out searching for Gannon.

Gannon's biological mother, Landon, had also arrived from South Carolina to help look for him.

That night, everybody congregated at the house, including Landon.

Al began getting suspicious of certain things Letecia was telling everyone, they just didn't add up and so he asked her to leave the family home.

Lots of people commented that while Al was frantically looking for his son, Letecia didn't seem nearly as concerned.

When detectives discovered Gannon hadn't attended school on the day that he went missing. Letecia told them he hadn't been feeling well as he'd had a stomach ache.

A few days later, a neighbour gave the police some video footage from the Monday showing Leticia backing up Al's red truck into her driveway. The footage showed her going into the house and then two people emerged and got into the truck. Letecia was one of them and Gannon was the other. He was walking very slowly, as though in pain. At 10:15am, the truck drove away and didn't return for four hours. At 2:15pm when Letecia returned, Gannon did not appear to be with her.

Letecia said Gannon had returned with her and got out of the other side of the vehicle that was not covered by cameras. She told the police that she had gone to PetCo on the Monday, and she was shown on CCTV at 1am. but Gannon wasn't seen in the store with her. She went back to PetCo a couple of hours later. She said Gannon was with her when she returned home and then he went out to visit his friend.

Around that time, police began searching several bodies of water in the area.

Al confronted Letecia, wanting to know the truth but she blamed the accident with the candle and the carpet fire. She claimed Gannon had got burns on his arms from it. She said the smoke had been coming up the stairs and she had been scared for their safety. She also told him she'd threatened Gannon he would have to sell his Nintendo Switch and some of their furniture to pay for the damage. Images and video footage from Letecia's phone from the Sunday night, the night before Gannon went missing, confirmed that Gannon had set something alight with a candle, and verified the explanation of the damaged carpet too. The video that was mostly blacked out as though it was taken from inside her pocket, hears Letecia asking Gannon if he was sure he didn't do it on purpose. Gannon can be heard crying and saying he didn't do it on purpose. Letecia then says they will have to sell something to fix the damage 'so the lady don't be mad at us and kick us out of the house'. Gannon is clearly very upset. She indicates this is the reason Gannon ran away.

The next morning, Letecia had called Gannon's school, and also rang her employers telling them she couldn't come in as her stepfather had been killed in a car accident.

After these videos were made public, Al kicked Letecia out of the house. He clearly suspected something more had gone on between his wife and son.

Letecia posted several items regarding Gannon's mother and the conditions the children had been living in before she and Al stepped in to take care of them.

On the 31st January, Letecia gave an interview to 11news.

She said she wasn't allowed to discuss the case but wanted the community to work together and not make false accusations. She said the reason she wasn't out searching for him herself was due to her family getting death threats. She said her husband's ex-wife was living in her home and she was told she couldn't do certain things by the police department.

She said she asked the police several times during her questioning if she could stop the interview and get an attorney, but she was denied. She said she wasn't allowed anything to drink or able to go to the bathroom. She'd asked for an attorney because of the way they treated her during the interview.

She told the reporter there were lots of comments about Gannon being pushed off the hike they'd been on the Sunday prior to him going missing. She said…"I took care of Gannon for the last two years in our home because his mother didn't want to do it. And I would never, never, ever hurt this child, and I know there's some questions out there about 'okay tell me what happened,' that's up to the investigators when they end up letting you guys know, but I have cooperated with them. Even to the point we were held with a gun. And my daughter, a seventeen-year-old who served our country in the United States Air Force, who has never committed a crime or anything in her life, was put in handcuffs over the keys that was in her purse, so they could take her car. They weren't even in her purse. They were in my pocket."

Letecia said she was concerned about her daughter and why she was being detained and in handcuffs when that shouldn't happen to a child who was standing inside of a store, shopping. She said they'd decided to go and purchase clothing because they were no longer able to return home.

She continues… "the rumours had got so bad. I have been told there were at least ten different conspiracy theories that Gannon was dead. He is not dead. We are going to find Gannon. That's the main goal my family has. They have been out searching."

"I am just ready for Gannon to come home. Most importantly for him to see his family, but secondly, I am going to be so ecstatic when I am able to say to people that I hope they have a sincere apology for all these theories that have come out online. For all the things they said people have done or I have done. I just want everyone to know that we're gonna find Gannon. And I love him so much. I have helped take care of him for so long."

She went on to tell the reporter that Gannon is so kind and loves playing video games. "He was always so helpful with the dogs around the house, and he was always a person I could say, Gannon can you go do this, and he would do it right away. He was so sweet and would help anyone…"

She brought Harley, her daughter, in front of the camera to verify Gannon did return home from the hike on Sunday.

Towards the end of the interview, Letecia appeared to become emotional, but it seemed fake.

Law enforcement ramped up the searches but to no avail.

Letecia continued posting on Facebook, in between deactivating, and reactivating her account.

On the 21st February, The EPC Sherriff's *Twitter* (Now known as *X*) page stated all search efforts around Highway 105 had been suspended.

On the 2nd March, Letecia was arrested in Myrtle Beach, South Carolina. The charges laid were:

- First degree murder

- Child abuse resulting in death—

- Tampering with a deceased body

- Tampering with evidence.

This was clearly a shock to anyone who still held out some hope for Gannon to be found alive, but the police were certain he was dead and so they must have found something to back this theory up even though they weren't telling the public at this stage.

Al filed for divorce on the 5th March stating their marriage was irretrievably broken.

Letecia was also accused of assaulting a police officer as she was being extradited back to Colorado.

She appeared in court on 11th March 2020, and she was formally charged with first degree murder. The judge said he believed they had plenty of evidence regardless of not having found Gannon's body.

On the 17th March 2020, Gannon's body was discovered in a suitcase in Florida (21 hours' drive away from his home). The detectives believe his death occurred in Colorado.

During a press conference on the 20th March, it was stated there were several more charges added to the original four. These additional charges included:

- Murder in first degree with intent and deliberation.

- 8 counts of crime of violence—alleged use of a firearm—a blunt instrument—a knife or other sharp instrument for causing the death of Gannon Stauch.

This meant they believed she'd used all three weapons during her assault and murder of Gannon.

A probable cause affidavit released on 2nd April 2020 filled in some of the blanks.

So, let's back up and break it all down...

25th January 2020

According to the affidavit, Letecia made several google searches after Al had left for his trip.

•Find real military singles.

•Parenting should be 4 people not one.

•I'm over doing all the work for my step kids and their mom doesn't help.

•Mom advice from Stepmom.

•If you aren't involved in your kid's life, you are shitty.

•My husband's ex-wife does nothing for her kids.

•I wonder if my husband's ex-wife is sending me a card since I raise her kids.

•I wonder if my husband's ex-wife is sending me a valentine's card since I raise her kids.

•One day some people will wish they treated you differently.

•Why should my husband choose me over family?

•Find me a rich guy who wants me to take care of his kids.

•Find me a guy who wants me to take care of his kids and get paid.

26th January 2020

She made the following searches.

•It's crappy some parents don't care for their kids or buy them presents.

•Parents are those who put their kids before their nails.

27th January 2020

She made the following searches.

•My son burnt the carpet how do I fix it?

•Will humidifier help if exposed to smoke?

•Smoke effects, will humidifier help?

•Smoke from fire effects, will humidifier help?

•Colorado law for kids staying at home.

•School is out, is it okay for my kid to stay home alone?

•My son is sick, but I have to go to work.

•Son is sick can he stay home?

•Suede repair kit for sofa.

•El paso sheriff's office number.

•What is the process for a runaway child?

•Police steps for our runaway.

•Police steps for missing child.

•Can Nintendo find my switch?

•Car net Volkswagen.

•They are asking for our son's toothbrush but said nothing is wrong.

Police also discovered search history that had been deleted.

•Find me a new husband book.

•I feel like a nanny not a stepmom.

•Husband uses me to babysit his kids,

•Are there any free money to move away from bad situation?

•My husband never posts about me but does everything else.

•My husband only cleans up for the army not me.

•I'm just a glorified babysitter.

•Find a new husband.

•Sent my husband sexual messages and he ignores them.

•Make my husband want me more.

•I feel like my husband uses me to babysit his kid.

•Find a guy without kids.

She was clearly unhappy in her marriage, and she took it out on Gannon.

27th January 2020

According to the affidavit, law enforcement believe Letecia and Gannon left the house at around 10:15am. They drove to PetCo, and she was last seen on their cameras at 11:20am. Gannon was not seen at all. Then there was a full 2 hours where neither of them can be located. Letecia returns to PetCo at 1:20pm. A message sent from Al at 12:06pm saying 'Hey buddy,' went unanswered until 1:21pm and the reply was, 'Can I play Zelda at least?' to which Al responded, 'Not today'.

A final search on Gannon's phone for 'can my parent find my cell phone if it's off?' was made, but the police suspect Letecia made the search based on the punctuation being similar to the way she conducted searches on her own phone. It is thought she wanted to know if his phone could be traced before she decided what to do with it. The phone was located at the home address.

At 3:55pm Al sent another text to Gannon, but it wasn't read until 7:40pm.

Letecia is seen returning to the home address, and although it wasn't clear if Gannon also returned, law enforcement believe he was killed in his bedroom that afternoon shortly after 2:15pm.

They had discovered Gannon had lost enough blood to soak through his mattress, through his carpet and pool on the concrete below. There was also blood spatter on the walls. Evidence showed Gannon's body had been taken through the house and loaded into Letecia's car in the garage.

Laina had returned home from school at 3:15pm and Letecia told her that Gannon was asleep in her bed, and she was to go outside to play on her bike.

Harley arrived home from work at 4:42pm and she picked up Laina and took her to the dollar store. Letecia gave her a list of cleaning products to buy for her.

After cleaning the murder scene, Letecia reported Gannon as a runaway. Deputies from the El Paso Sherriff's Office arrived at the home at around 10pm and Letecia gave them permission to search the property. Her story changed dramatically multiple times over the next few days.

She couldn't give deputies any information about Gannon's friends or tell them any addresses where he could be. A limited search of the property was conducted.

28th January 2020

Early the next morning, Letecia drove her car to a short-term parking lot at the airport and rented a Kia from Avis. She then collected Al from the airport. They suspect she did this so Al couldn't find his son's body. Her reasoning for this was she had to be careful putting excess mileage on her lease vehicle and also if they were looking for Gannon it made sense to use a vehicle he didn't recognise.

Al suspected there was more to Gannon's disappearance as Letecia kept telling him different versions of events. He told her to leave the family home.

That night, Letecia returned to collect her car from the airport at just after 7pm, and it is believed she hid Gannon's body off highway 105 in Douglass County, Colorado because Gannon's blood was located at the scene.

At just after 10:30pm, Harley picked up her mother from the area of Powers and Carefree.

29th January 2020

It is believed Harley also picked Letecia up at the airport the next morning after she'd dropped off the Kia at 9am.

At noon that same day, Letecia arrived at the El Paso Sherriff's Office for a voluntary interview. She was initially meant to be there for 10am. They said her statements were untruthful, incomplete, and misleading. Her car was wet when she arrived as though it had just been washed. Detectives seized the vehicle.

She had several pieces of paper on her that contained written notes. During the interview she asked if she could refer to her notes or if they would just read her notes themselves.

During the interview, Letecia changed her initial statement drastically, saying she had been held at gunpoint and raped by a Hispanic male named Eguardo. She said Gannon had been abducted by him after he'd finished raping her. The detectives didn't believe this version of events based on their training and experience dealing with such assaults.

The story went as follows:

After arriving home at 2:30pm, she disarmed her security system, and then went to the basement. According to Letecia, Eguardo was already in the basement, and he attacked her at gunpoint. In the middle of the assault, he allowed her to go upstairs and greet her stepdaughter who had just arrived home from school. Letecia sent her out to play on her bike before returning to the basement where Eguardo raped her between 3:30pm and 4:30pm. She said she must've hit her head during this time and blacked out. However, detectives said there were no injuries to her head.

She said, during the attack, Gannon jumped on Eguardo's back and was thrown across the room. After he had finished his assault, Eguardo held the gun to Gannon and demanded a suitcase which she provided, along with a cardboard box. He attempted to sexually assault her again, but she hit her head once again and blacked out.

After Eguardo left with Gannon, Letecia didn't call the police, and instead she cleaned the area the attack had taken place. She tidied any signs of disturbance in Gannon's bedroom and also in the utility.

Although they thought this story was a total fabrication, the detectives took steps to corroborate it. They checked a neighbour's security camera footage but did not see a Hispanic male either enter or leave the house.

Letecia was offered an examination from a sexual assault nurse, but she refused.

She said she'd first met Eguardo on the 26th January, the day before Gannon's murder. She said he had brown hair and brown eyes but couldn't describe any other specific details. She said Gannon had knocked over a candle causing a burn mark on the carpet (bearing in mind the candle incident didn't occur until the night of the 26th). She said she drove around the area where construction was taking place and met Eguardo working on a house. She asked if he would repair her carpet and, when he agreed, she provided him with the garage door code. He said he would repair the carpet while she was out shopping the next day.

During the times of the supposed attack, Letecia had made a phone call and sent several text messages to Harley and Al.

Detectives obtained details from the motion detectors fitted inside the Stauch home and, during this same time, the back door was opened and closed 10 times.

Towards the end of the interview, Letecia said she wanted to leave, and detectives seized her phone and detained her while they applied for DNA collection. She began stuffing tissues into her pants and said she was having chest pain and shortness of breath. She had made a remarkable recovery once she reached the hospital.

The residence was searched, and they found visible blood in Gannon's bedroom, in the garage, and throughout the house.

31st January 2020

Letecia hired another vehicle and she and Harley drove across country to Florida. It is now believed Gannon's remains were also inside the vehicle.

4th February 2020

Letecia and Harley arrived in Florida and checked into a hotel just three miles away from where Gannon's body is later discovered by a group of construction workers.

Over the next few weeks Letecia's story changed several more times.

- When ESPO came to the residence on the 27th January, the abductor was still inside the house. However, Deputies checked the entirety of the house and nobody else was present.

- Letecia stated she was raped by Quincy Brown, and he abducted Gannon. She knew his identity because she saw a paper and his identification card fell out of his pocket. She sent an image of Quincy Brown to Al she had got from the internet showing Quincy Brown was listed as a *Most Wanted* suspect.

- Quincy Brown followed her from PetCo and was lying in the middle of the road in front of her car. When she stopped to avoid running him over, he jumped into the car and made her take him to the house where he raped her.

- Letecia and Gannon were near County Line Road in Northern El Paso County on the 27th January. Gannon was riding a bicycle and fell off and hit his head. He was then abducted by Quincy Brown. In this version of events, Quincy Brown was being driven around by a man named Terence.

- Letecia stated that the blood in the corner of Gannon's room was a combination of hers and Gannon's. In this explanation, she stated that the abductor anally penetrated her and Gannon with an object. Additionally, she was tied up at some point in the abduction, and the abductor was still present during the EPSO visit that night.

2nd March 2020

Letecia was arrested in Myrtle Beach, South Carolina, for the murder of Gannon.

4th March 2020

Letecia made national headlines after she allegedly attacked a deputy while being extradited back to Colorado.

5th March 2020

Al filed for divorce from Letecia, and said the marriage was irretrievably broken in his filing. He also stated that his wife was in South Carolina awaiting extradition to Colorado charged with first degree murder of his son.

11th March 2020

Letecia was formally charged with first-degree murder in an El Paso County courtroom.

17th March 2020

Gannon's body was discovered in Florida. Inspectors found a suitcase under the bridge and upon opening it found what appeared to be a boy's body wrapped in blankets. Gannon had been shot in the jaw, stabbed in the chest and back, and suffered a skull fracture. He also had defensive wounds covering his arms and legs and a bullet lodged in his skull.

19th January 2021

A mental health evaluation was submitted to the court stating that Letecia is competent to stand trial.

26th February 2021

A Judge granted Letecia's motion to represent herself in court.

30th April 2021

Letecia and Al's divorce was finalized.

3rd May 2021

Letecia was appointed new public defenders.

23rd September 2021

After hearing testimony from law enforcement and expert witnesses, a judge ruled that the case will go to trial.

11th February 2022

Letecia changed her plea to not guilty by reason of insanity.

So, what are your thoughts?

Crazy doesn't even begin to cut it does it?

What Gannon went through in the final moments of his short life doesn't bear thinking about.

The affidavit had been filed before Gannon's body was found, based mainly on the amount of blood discovered in his bedroom, however, there is no evidence Gannon made it back home that day. Could the initial attack have taken place the day before? Would it have been possible for him to lose that amount of blood and still walk to the truck unaided? He did appear sluggish but is this realistic? The truck has something bouncing about in the back, was this the suitcase? She was missing for two hours which is the exact amount of time it would take to get to the spot detectives believe she dumped his body on the 28th. Did she do it that day instead? Maybe she went back to double check the suitcase was properly concealed. It makes no sense her bringing him back to kill him in the house.

What will follow is a blow-by-blow daily account of the trial. We will endeavour to give detailed testimony either by way of summary or transcripts compiled by us which may include repeated or omitted words. In some instances, it may be essential to edit the content or disregard repeated testimony for ease of reading.

CHAPTER 2

Letecia Stauch Trial – Day 1 - 3rd April 2023

The trial begins and Judge Gregory Werner is sworn in, followed by opening statements from both prosecutors and Stauch's public defenders.

Letecia is seated to the side of the room, barely in view of the camera, head bowed, mostly hiding behind her hair. She doesn't look up.

Gannon's parents are both present in the courtroom.

Opening Statements

On behalf of the prosecution - District Attorney Michael Allen is the first to address the jury of eleven men and seven women.

"Well, ladies and gentlemen, here we go. Paramount question you will have to answer as jurors in this case has to do with sanity. Specifically, the defendant's sanity. At the conclusion of the evidence, the court will give you jury instructions, one specific jury instruction will talk about insanity. It will read that as to the question of sanity, the defendant wasn't sane at the time of the commission of the acts if she was so diseased or defective in mind at the time of the commission of the acts as to be incapable of distinguishing right from wrong with respect to that act.

Or she suffered from a conditional mind caused by a mental disease or defect that prevented her from forming a culpable mental state that is an essential element of a crime charged. A culpable mental state is like intentionally or knowingly. Evidence in this case will show that she could distinguish between right and wrong and that she was absolutely capable of forming the specific intent required for these charges.

Those instructions will go on to give specific guidance on what qualifies as a mental disease or defect. Care should be taken not to confuse mental disease or defect with moral obliquity, mental depravity, passion growing out of anger, revenge or hatred, or other motives in kindred evil conditions. Because when an act is induced by any of these causes, the ones that I just listed, the person is accountable to the law. Being that person can be found guilty for committing the crimes charged.

You should consider the evidence you will hear in this case in context with that instruction. This case is about two people. The first is Gannon Jacob Stauch, an 11-year-old little boy, who came into this world premature, weight just one pound six ounces. He proved to be a fighter, overcame the difficulties associated with being born so small. He's survived by his mother Landon Hiott, his father Al Stauch, and his precocious little sister Laina.

On the 26th January 2020, something bad happened inside the Stauch family home. Gannon suffered some burns. You'll learn this from a video recording this defendant made that night. You'll hear her as she manipulated Gannon, putting guilt on him for some mistake that a child made. And in that recording you'll hear Gannon say in his own words, 'I'm just worried about my burns'.

The video of Letecia and Gannon is played in court. It's heartbreaking listening to Gannon knowing what we do now. He was terribly upset and worried about his burns.

The other person in this case is that last voice you just heard. The woman sitting right here, the defendant. 26th January 2020 into 27th January 2020, she was the sole provider for Gannon. Her husband, Al Stauch, Gannon's father, serves in the National Guard. He was in Oklahoma for National Guard training—he left that Saturday night, the 25th. Everything that happened to Gannon from that point forward was her decision, she carried out actions to kill Gannon, to put his body in the suitcase and hide it. To hide evidence of what she did to Gannon. She told numerous stories to investigators to manipulate the course of the investigation. And finally, to discard Gannon inside that suitcase, off of a Florida bridge like garbage.

27th January 2020, Gannon's home located at 6627 Mandan Drive, here in Colorado

Springs, Colorado, turned into the stuff of nightmares. In fact, the one place a little boy like Gannon should have felt the safest, his bedroom, turned into like I said, the stuff of nightmares. That bedroom is in fact where he was brutally murdered.

The defendant attacked him viciously, mercilessly, deliberately, and intentionally. These are exhibit's that you will see from the doctor down in Florida, Doctor Ignacio, who performed the autopsy, will tell you that Gannon suffered 18 stab wounds to his body, his chest, his back, his head, and most importantly his arms and his hands. Why is that important? Gannon was fighting for his life and those were defensive wounds.

Next came a crushing blow to his head that was so strong it fractured his skull like an eggshell. That wasn't enough for this defendant, who retrieved a nine-millimetre handgun, fired it at Gannon three times, two bullets struck the pillow near him and were caught in the fibres of that pillow. That third bullet entered his jaw, travelled through his head, fracturing his mandible, his vertebrae, hitting his spinal cord, and lodged in the back of his head. It was recovered at autopsy.

Gannon's life drained from his body drop by drop.

The photo that's on the screen right now is a picture of his bedroom. The same corner where you will see him in a picture in the bed. Each one of those markers signifies a small blood drop that splattered across his wall. It ran down the corner of his mattress, soaked through the carpet, the carpet pad, and puddled on the concrete foundation below.

The defendant then took very deliberate action. She decided to hide her crimes from the world. She collected Gannon's bloody and broken body, and the blankets and pillow that were near him, and shoved them into a suitcase and hid them in the storage unit in that basement. That basement storage unit is right around the corner from Gannon's bedroom. What she didn't know was that she was leaving clues behind in that storage room. That plastic tub that you see in the bottom left portion of that picture has Gannon's blood on it. There was an *Amazon* box in that storage room that has Gannon's blood on it. The concrete floor in that storage room had Gannon's blood on it.

The defendant next decided to clean Gannon's room. Deliberately, intentionally, knowing what she was doing. She scrubbed the walls, cleaning them off. She scrubbed the carpet with scrub brushes that were later found in the dishwasher. Those scrub brushes have carpet fibres found in them. They have blood on them. They have Gannon's DNA on them. This is Gannon's bedroom when members of the El Paso County Sherriff's Office first came to the house on 27th January during the evening hours. This is what it looked like, no obvious signs of a struggle. No obvious signs of blood as they walked through the house and through Gannon's bedroom, there were no obvious signs of a struggle or murder because the defendant had cleaned them up. She also realised she had Gannon's blood on her person. The clothes that she was wearing, likely containing Gannon's blood, based off how much blood had hit the walls, were never found—her clothing was never found. These shoes, the defendant's shoes, were found on the washing machine, drying. That reddish rust colour that you can see on the soles, Gannon's blood and DNA. You can see just how much blood she was walking through as she was cleaning up that mess.

She then took more deliberate action. She collected and discarded other important clues. I mentioned she stabbed Gannon 18 times, the instrument she used to stab Gannon has never been found. That nine-millimetre handgun that she used to fire three rounds at Gannon, shell casing ejected out of that firearm each time she pulled the trigger, no shell casing was ever found in Gannon's room. She then took more deliberate action when she hid Gannon in the suitcase first in her car, and up north, you know the El Paso County Douglas County line. GPS Location data was used to track her movements and it led to another grisly discovery. A board was found under a tree, that board had Gannon's blood on it. This is miles away from the Stauch family home, which is in the southeast part of the city, close to the airport. You'll learn, through testimony, that this board came from the Stauch family garage.

She then took more deliberate and thoughtful action. She loaded the suitcase containing Gannon into the back of a rented van and drove to Florida, and that's the course of her travels from here to Florida. She rented a hotel room in Pensacola, Florida, on 4th February 2020. She drove a short distance from that hotel room, across a dark bridge, that drives over a river that goes into the Gulf of Mexico, there she acted with determined purpose, she hauled the suitcase out of the back of that van, lugged it to the side of the road, hoisted it up over the railing, pushed it over the side, hoping that Gannon would never be found.

48 days later, 1300 miles away from where Gannon was murdered, the search for answers and Gannon's remains finally ended, on 17th March 2020, when the suitcase that came from that basement storage room, containing Gannon's remains, blankets and the pillow, were found by an unlucky bridge worker checking that bridge for safety. You can imagine the shock that he felt when he realised what was in that suitcase.

Remember the pictures that I showed you just a moment ago of Gannon in bed? These pictures were taken by this defendant on the morning of 27th January 2020 who sent them by text message to Gannon's father, Al, who was in Oklahoma for training. Take note of those blankets that were recovered from the suitcase, the very same blankets and pillow that were in those pictures, they were found 1300 miles away with Gannon underneath that bridge.

The defendant then purposefully, intentionally, came up with numerous different stories about what had happened. Gannon was missing, He went to a friend's house and never returned. Gannon was kidnapped and she was raped by a guy named Eguardo. Gannon was kidnapped and she was raped, but this time by a guy named Quincy Brown. She went to look for a bike up near that Douglas County, El Paso County line, Gannon test rode that bike, crashed, and suffered a horrible head injury, and a guy named Quincy Brown took Gannon and now the defendant doesn't know where Gannon is. Cartels were somehow involved with Gannon's disappearance. And most cruelly, Landon Hiott, Gannon's mother, was involved with Gannon's disappearance. All of her actions were purposely designed by her to distance herself from what she did. Throw off investigators. Buy her time. Escape accountability for what she did to Gannon on 27th January 2020.

At the conclusion of the evidence that we'll be presenting in this case, you'll be asked to determine whether the defendant is guilty or not guilty of the charges that we've levelled against her. You'll also be asked whether she was sane or insane at the time she killed Gannon. All of her decisions. All of her deliberate actions, betray her claims of insanity. She knew what she had done to Gannon was wrong—why hide it? You'll hear her own voice through recorded phone calls and interviews. The evidence itself will prove her sanity.

As jurors, part of your job will be to determine how much credibility, if any, you give to the witnesses. That same rule applies to expert witnesses. You'll get to hear from doctors, you'll get to hear from GPS experts, and when they take the stand and take an oath, you get to judge whether what they are saying makes sense—is it credible or not? And if it's not credible, you get to discard it. If it's not credible, you can use it in your deliberations, but you all get to decide whether that credibility extends to that witness or not. The same will hold true for our expert witnesses and the defence expert witnesses. You'll get to hear from a doctor that will testify that the defendant was insane at the time of the murder of Gannon Stauch. With all expert witnesses, you should gauge what they're saying, measure it against the other evidence that you hear, does it make sense or not? Like all expert witnesses, if it doesn't make sense, you can discard it.

You will also hear from others who know her best. People who have the best opportunity to see how she was acting. Did she understand the difference between right and wrong? Could she form intent? People like Al Stauch, the man who was married to her. People like her brother, Dakota Lowry, who flew out here after Gannon went missing. And most importantly, her very own daughter Harley Hunt, who was in the best position to know the defendant's state of mind, especially as it relates to when this crime occurred. She was the only other older person in the house when Al left to go to Oklahoma. Harley Hunt was working. She was young, 17-years-old at the time, thinking of going into the Air Force but she becomes the defendant's closest confident after the defendant killed Gannon Stauch. In fact, she also rode with the defendant on that van ride from Colorado Springs to Florida. She'll be able to tell you in her own words whether the defendant understood the difference between right and wrong. Whether she could act intentionally or deliberately or not. And she'll tell you that she could on both counts.

Remember, this case is about two people. Gannon had no choice what happened to him that day. The other, this defendant, she held every single decision in her hands. She took deliberate thoughtful action. It ended a precious life and tore a family apart. Your job as jurors will be to listen to all of the evidence because even the most mundane evidence, it might seem inconsequential when you're listening, but is being given to you purposefully so that you can make the determinations you need to make as jurors. Did she understand the difference between right and wrong? Was she able to perform a culpable mental state? Every single piece of evidence that comes from this chair will be used by you to make that determination.

The next time I get to talk with you directly the way I'm doing right now, is when we've concluded evidence and we're giving closing arguments. At that time, both sides will get to ask you to make determinations based on what you all heard. We're going to ask you to hold us to our burden of proof. The criminal justice system doesn't work if you don't hold us to our burden of proof.

Our burden of proof is proof beyond a reasonable doubt. The things we have to prove are the elements of the crimes charged. We also have to disprove that the defendant is insane. Meaning essentially that she was sane. The evidence will do that for you.

We will ask you to get justice for Gannon Stauch. We'll ask you to find this defendant guilty for what she did to him more than three years ago. We'll ask you to find her guilty of murder in the first degree. Murder in the first degree of a child under twelve years of age. Tampering with a deceased human body. For taking Gannon's body from that scene and transporting it across the country. And tampering with physical evidence. I'll ask you to convict her on each, and every one of those charges, and the evidence will guide you towards those convictions.

On 27th January 2020, at 6:55pm, the defendant herself called 911 to report Gannon was missing and had not come home. The call taker you'll hear asks the defendant who was the last person to see Gannon."

He plays her answer... 'Er..., I guess me.'

"Yeah, she was the last person to see Gannon alive. The evidence will show us she was sane on 27th January 2020 when she ended Gannon's life. The evidence will show that she acted intentionally and deliberately when she took Gannon's life. And then we will ask you to convict her.

Thank you."

***

Defence Attorney, Will Cook, steps forward to make his opening statement.

"Good afternoon members of the jury. I talked to some of you during jury selection over the last couple of weeks. I want to reintroduce myself. My name is Will Cook. I, along with Mr Tolini, represent Letecia Stauch.

Now, this is a very tough case. We looked at the jury questionnaires. There was a lot of strong feelings.

Have you formed an opinion about Ms Stauch? And we had a lot of 'she's guilty' and a few 'she's evil'. People forming opinions about this case before they ever heard one shred of evidence.

As a defence attorney, this case is very worrisome. When people have come in and they have preconceived notions of what's going on. With respect to the question on the paperwork that you got about insanity. What do you think about insanity? Is it valid? Something that's legitimate? A lot of people say that insanity is just a way to get out of taking responsibility. It's an excuse. Doesn't exist. It's fake. We got a lot of that.

So why does the defence attorney have two big problems in this case? I represent Ms Stauch, who according to a lot of the jury questionnaires is evil and guilty, and us raising insanity is a bunch of BS. A lot to deal with.

I've been looking at this case for going on three years now. All the photos, I've seen all the reports. Mr Tolini has, and it's a lot. What you saw on the board this afternoon, that's the PG stuff. The rated G information photos. A general audience. Going forward in this case you're going to see the autopsy photos. You're going see the photos of when Gannon was brought out of the suitcase. And they're horrible. Horrible. It was an awful, awful thing that was done to Gannon. And I see Mr Allen get up here and he's emotional, almost in tears talking about it. And I get it. I get it.

What happened to that little 11-year-old boy is beyond description. The facts of this case—awful. You know, it's so bad, this is a lost cause. Ladies and gentlemen, I can't quit. I can't leave this courtroom. I've got to do my job in this case. Mr Tolini does. I can't just... after that opening statement, all the information that I've seen, the photos, the smiling picture of Gannon. Hearing about him being shot, stabbed multiple times. Hundreds of witnesses, and 800 pieces of evidence that are going to come in, I can't check out now and just sit down and ride this out. I can't do it because it wouldn't be fair. It wouldn't be fair to the court system, the process, and it wouldn't be fair to Ms Stauch. And I know people will say, 'well who gives a shit about what's fair for Ms Stauch?' The court systems do. The law does. The constitution. The bill of rights. The war fought over these things that we're dealing with today. Old school laws, the presumption of innocence. The right to remain silent. Stuff that comes all the way back from Old Boston, Paul Revere riding through the streets on his horse, going 'the British are coming, the British are coming'. Old stuff and it matters. And once we decide something in the media, before you have heard one shred of evidence, we judge this case before anything has taken place, then all of that is lost, and we are truly a country that is no longer ruled by law but by the media. I get it, we've lost. Mr Tolini, we've lost. Ms Stauch, we've lost. We have lost in the court of public opinion in the media. She's guilty. I get that.

This is a court of law. As Judge Werner said, when you come through those double doors, this is a special place. This isn't the media. This isn't *Facebook*. Wash all of that away. Don't try to get up and walk out of the courtroom before you start it. Do your jobs. Listen to the evidence. And when the evidence is complete, go back into the jury room and weigh the evidence. All I'm asking of you, just give us a fair shake. I can see it in your eyes, ladies, and gentlemen. A lot of you, as far as you're concerned, I could burn in hell for representing Ms Stauch. A lot of you won't even make eye contact with me. I might as well just be the Devil himself up here running his mouth. But I'm not. I'm no different than those three at that table right there. Paid advocates. They are paid advocates. Amy and I we are paid advocates. They have their side of the story and I just want to be heard. I want our side to be heard. And if at the end—guilty. But you weighed the evidence, you listened. You didn't prejudge the case. Your biases, your sympathies, your prejudices you had at the beginning of this trial, if you didn't let those come in, were fair and impartial but it's still guilty, I'll take that—I'll take that in a case like this. A lot of evidence. A very, very difficult case. But don't quit on me.

Now, Mr Allen is right—he's a good attorney. He's well-spoken. He's been elected DA. This is gonna come down to insanity...

... How do you figure that out? How do you look into the mind of a sick person and divine what they are thinking? Well, evidence, people's statements, observations, supported statements. Phone calls with Ms Stauch talking on. That's good stuff.

What else can you look at? Motive? Somebody's motive. Remember that word? It's come up every day during jury selection for the past two weeks by the prosecution—motive. You were told, and rightly so, by the prosecution that there is no requirement for the prosecution to prove motive. They're right. Does that mean that motive doesn't matter? No, it does not mean that. Even though jury instruction talking about insanity, the prosecution just put up on the board talked about a motive or lack of motive could be a sign that there is insanity or not insanity and it's in the jury instruction there, so it does matter. It's not required, but it matters. And it matters because it's evidence. If you don't have a motive that goes to show a lack of evidence. Say there's a couple of people involved in a shooting and a murder out in the community, paper reports it as a random, senseless act of violence. One person shot to death. Police investigate. They have three people that are suspects that were there at the scene, at the time of the shooting. One problem for the investigators, they don't really have any other evidence. A week later, doing some good police work, they uncover that one of the three people was a drug dealer who was ripped off the week before the shooting by the dead man. A lot of money and drugs were stolen. All of a sudden, with that information, this random, senseless act of violence becomes a murder with a motive. It does matter."

He puts up a photograph onto the screen.

*Letecia, Gannon, and Laina taken the day before
Gannon went missing.*

"All right, we've got a photo here. We've got some familiar looking faces. Gannon and Letecia Stauch. Stepmom, stepson. Gannon's little sister in the back. Look at that. Looks like everybody's doing pretty good, happy sunny day. Ms Stauch is doing a selfie, holding the camera. When, oh when, oh when would have this photo been taken? The day before Gannon died. The day before he was killed. That wasn't a photo of evil. Anger. A photo of someone by all accounts who was a loving stepmother taking care of Gannon. Gannon's father was on a deployment. Stauch worked as a teacher herself in the Whitefield School District, an elementary school teacher. A person that was living what seemed like the American dream. A nice suburban house in Lorson Ranch, the suburbs, Colorado Springs, Colorado.

But behind those photos, those smiles, Stauch was hiding trauma and abuse that had been going on since she was a toddler. The troubled childhood. Her mother wasn't really much of a mother. She had a line of stepdads or boyfriends or whatever. Her mother came in and out, in and out, came in and out of her life. From the time she was three or four years old, until she finally moved out. And she suffered. She suffered horrifically from these stepfathers, these boyfriends of her mother. She watched her mother get beat by the boyfriends, physically abused, until eventually the physical abuse, these men reserved for her mother, eventually trained on Ms Stauch here. First it was just physical beatings, whoopings, emotional abuse, verbal abuse. And then it became sexual, where she was molested regularly from the age of five or six until she was a teenager. Constant. She used to have to sleep in the car out in the driveway to get away, to not have to be sexually assaulted and molested by these men. And because her mom wasn't around a lot, it's kind of an absentee mom, these stepfathers, cared for Ms Stauch exclusively. Mom was out somewhere doing something, gone for several weeks at a time, and Ms Stauch, as a young child and a young woman and a teenager was left in the care of these men.

How do you deal with this? Six or seven years old. What do you do? Physical abuse, sexual abuse, emotional abuse—how does a kid handle that?

Well, a lot of people that have had bad childhoods go on and they're fine. There's some that don't. For some, there's a survival mechanism in these children's personalities—fragment. And why do they do this? Fragmentation of the personalities when there is abuse at a young age. Because, in the case of Ms Stauch, her abuser was also the person who provided her means for survival. A four, five, six-year-old kid does not go out and get a job and work and acquire their own food, pay the electric bill, pay the rent. So, while they're being abused, they also as a matter of survival have to both hate, love, fear and placate their abuser/caretaker.

How does a person do that?

Well, I think in a lot of situations no one person can do that. That's where the fragmentation personality comes in. All the good, and all the bad, all the evil, and the hate can't reside in one place. And I know some of you, based on your jury questionnaires, think I'm telling some fanciful tale about this. I get it. I read the questionnaires. But, as such, you have sworn an oath multiple times to follow the law and the evidence. Don't like vanity, or dissociative identity disorder, that's okay. Joke or an excuse, or not valid, that's okay.

It's okay if you think that outside those doors. In here you've gotta believe it's a legitimate mental health defence. That in fact it exists, and it is scientifically backed. You're gonna hear doctors, sworn experts on both sides, so yeah, it's in the DSM-4 or 5 which is a book of psychological ailments and issues psychologists and psychiatrists use to diagnose things. They're listed, accepted in the scientific community. An issue. A real issue—dissociative identity—or multiple personalities.

Now, whether you believe, or if their experts believe, or what our experts believes about whether it was present in Ms Stauch's case is a different issue. But you must, to be fair and impartial and unbiased, you must believe that it is a possible defence. It is a valid defence. It is a valid defect or a disease of the mind that triggers the insanity provisions under the Colorado laws. Laws that trigger when we bring in some testimony or some evidence that there is insanity causes the rules, the laws to pivot show that the prosecution has the burden of proving beyond a reasonable doubt.

Let's say, circle back around, why all that matters, going back to motive. Motive in the evidence, exhibits, photos, videos. We're gonna be in here for eight weeks. School's gonna be out, making plans for our labour day barbecues, not labour day, barbecues by the time we get done, You know what you're probably not gonna hear? In all that time in all those exhibits, all that evidence. All those witnesses. You're not gonna hear a motive. I'm not gonna be given a motive. The reason is, there is no motive. There is no reason. It doesn't make sense. It's insane.

Smiling photo, next day Gannon's gone. No reason for it. Prosecution may say, oh well, makes it that more tragic that it was such a pointless death of Gannon. I don't know. I'm not gonna speculate on that. But there was some major psychotic crack that went on during this time. To go from teacher, loving stepmother to two children, loving mother to her own child, Harley, a person that Gannon's father entrusted his own two kids, watched and loved by this woman here, to being a killer of an eleven-year-old boy. How do you get there? Big jump. There is no explanation for it. I don't have one. She broke on that day, ladies and gentlemen. She broke. Broke from all that was right, made sense. And the acts, putting Gannon's body in a suitcase and travelling 1300 miles to Florida and throwing the suitcase with Gannon's body in it over the side of an overpass. The different stories she told—she was raped by somebody, the person who raped her kidnapped Gannon, you'll hear all the stories, the prosecution is gonna play it for you, these are all signs and evidence of a mind, a soul, that is broken in the most fundamental and profound way. So broken, it doesn't even know what it was doing.

What was going through that person's head? All the stab wounds, the shootings, the bruises, the beatings, the burns. What was going through that person's head?

I don't know.

I couldn't tell you.

For the person that she was killing that day, attacking, that wasn't Gannon. It wasn't Gannon to her. She didn't wake up that day and go I'm gonna kill him. No. She was killing the demons. Her life from the dark depths of her childhood. You're gonna hear different doctors. We have a Doctor Dorothy Lewis. She's from Yale. She's been at it a long time. An MD—she's got a lot of experience with this. Her legal medical opinion is that on the date of this offence Ms Stauch was legally insane.

Now, the prosecution is gonna have some witnesses from our state mental hospital in Pueblo that I imagine are gonna say, no, she was perfect, she knew what she was doing. It's normal behaviour for a person to do that. Yeah, she's had some mental issues and everything like that, everybody does, but they don't go and kill an eleven-year-old boy. And that is true. A lot of people do have mental health issues. It was talked about in voir dire. People have very severe mental health issues, but they don't go out and kill people. They don't go out and kill eleven-year-old boys, or their stepsons. They had had a nice hike just the day before as evidenced by that photo. They don't stab their stepsons dozens of times, discharge three bullets from a nine-millimetre handgun at the boy, hitting him once, killing him once, beat him, burn him and do all these other things you've heard about. It's wrong, and it's horrible... she will be held accountable.

Not guilty by reason of insanity will get a jury instruction. It's about a paragraph long. It indicates in that case, and I think Judge Werner alluded to it toward a panel of potential jurors in the past couple of weeks. If she's found guilty then it's guilt. She's subject to regular sentencing by the court. But if she's found not guilty by reason of insanity it doesn't mean she walks out of here. She's committed to the state hospital, Colorado Department of Human Services and they take over from there. That's not what we're dealing with here now.

So, I know there is a natural human urge, a real urge when you hear about that little boy with that big bright smile that you saw on the screen, hear about what happened to him, you wanna make somebody pay. You want to make somebody pay dearly. It's not right what happened. Awful. But not providing Stauch constitutional protections for presumption of innocence, the right to remain silent. Placing the burden of proof squarely on the shoulders of the prosecutor, letting bias or sympathy come in and cloud your judgement is not gonna bring Gannon back.

Prejudging the case by what you've heard in the media will do no good. We have a tragedy here and we know it's terrible but just listen to the evidence as I started out with. Don't check out. It's not gonna be easy when into week six during all these witnesses and looking at evidence you're gonna want to check out. You're gonna want to form your decision soon in this case. But you can't do that. For the next six to eight weeks while we're in this trial you can't form an opinion. Werner was telling you that. You are in evidence gathering phase now. You're gathering the facts. When you go back to the jury room when all the evidence is in you start putting the ingredients together, whether you've got a guilty, a not guilty, or not guilty by reason of insanity based on the evidence, the ingredients. When you're in the jury room that's when you start putting it together. Just writing down, taking notes, taking it all in. That's why the judge mentioned several times to you today, 'I don't want you all talking about the case amongst yourselves'. It's kind of a special hidden quiet place this courtroom. Especially you jurors. I don't want you all talking about the case because that leads to deliberating and judgment. That's in the judgement phase, so thank you for your time, thank you everybody for coming back. We'll be spending a lot of time together over the next couple of months so keep an open mind, put a lot of the bad stuff out of your mind for now. As Mr Allen said in his opening statement, he said 'I'm gonna come back in a couple of months and ask you to find her guilty'. I and Mr Tolini in two months are gonna ask you to find her not guilty by reason of insanity.

Now the trial starts. At opening statements, you've had all of that now. What he said and I said it's not evidence. What was up on the board in the videos and audios that he played, it's not evidence. Or what the judge said, if you had to deliver a verdict right now, it's not guilty. This woman right here is not guilty. She's presumed innocent. I'm not telling you to like it. I'm just telling you that's the way it is.

I'm gonna stop now, because I'm running out of steam, but I really, really, really do appreciate your time. I know the judge does too. You're the ones that are making the sacrifice. You're the ones that are losing money because you're not able to go to work. Your workspaces, your offices are idle because you're gonna be here for two months. You're the ones that make the sacrifice in this case, and I do appreciate it. And on behalf on my attorney, Mr Tolini, I know he appreciates you. Thank you."

Judge Werner addresses the jury.

"Alright ladies and gentlemen, I want to give you a little bit of a roadmap as to what you can expect and where we go from here. As I said this morning, opening statements are not evidence. Their purpose is only to help you understand what the evidence will be. Keep in mind, that in this case, as is in every case, attorneys are paid advocates. Their job is to persuade you that evidence proves or does not prove a particular point. And as I said earlier, nothing an attorney says is evidence and they do not take an oath to tell you the truth.

Next the prosecution will offer evidence. Evidence consists of the sworn testimony of the witnesses, the exhibits received in evidence, and stipulated, admitted, or judicially noticed facts. After the prosecution's evidence, the defendant may present evidence in her own behalf, but she is not required to do so. I want to remind you that the defendant is presumed to be innocent. The prosecution must prove the guilt of the defendant beyond a reasonable doubt. The defendant does not have to prove her innocence or call any witnesses or introduce any evidence.

At the conclusion of the evidence, I will tell you the rules of law which you are to use in reaching your verdict. I will read those rules of law to you, and you will be allowed to take them with you to the jury room during your deliberations.

After you have heard all the evidence and the instructions, the prosecution and the defence may make their closing arguments. Like opening statements, closing arguments are not evidence. The prosecuting attorney will have the opportunity to reply to the closing argument made by the defence. You will then go to the jury room to deliberate on a verdict. Your purpose as jurors is to decide what the facts are. And your decision must be based solely upon the evidence. It is my job to decide what rules of law apply to the case. You must follow all the rules as I explain them to you. You may not follow some and ignore others. Even if you disagree with some of the rules you must follow them. You will then apply these rules to the facts which you have determined from the evidence. In this way, you will determine whether the prosecution has proven the guilt of the defendant beyond a reasonable doubt.

At times during the trial attorneys may make objections. That's the part in the TV show or the movie where one lawyer asks a question and the other one stands up and objects. On TV the lawyers start to argue with each other and then sometimes they go up to the bench and they argue with the judge. I know you'll be surprised but that doesn't happen in real life. The lawyers in this room have years of experience. They know that the procedure in this case is governed by a written set of rules that apply to all criminal cases, called the Colorado rules of criminal procedure.

They also know that the evidentiary matters are governed by a written set of rules called the Colorado rules of evidence which apply to all cases proceeding to trial. Watch the lawyers and you will observe what really happens is that if an objection is made, I will ask for an explanation for the objection, something like grounds, and the response from the attorney will be something like hearsay, or foundation, or relevance or 404. And most of the time, most of the attorneys will state an objection in five words or less. There's not a whole lot of arguing going on during that time period. And, regardless, the argument is never directed to opposing counsel, because I'm the one making the ruling, and not opposing counsel. So, in reality, the lawyers rarely come up to the bench to argue a point because all they need to do is reference the rule, case, or principal they are relying upon for their objection. In any event, the objection simply means that the lawyer is requesting that I make a decision on a particular rule of law. It is the duty of a lawyer to object to evidence which they believe may not be properly offered.

Do not draw any conclusions from the objections or from my rulings on the objections. If I sustain an objection to a question, the witness may not answer it. As jurors you must draw no inferences from the question or speculate what the witness would have said if permitted to answer. At other times I may instruct you to not consider a particular statement that was made. You must not consider any evidence to which an objection has been sustained, or which I have instructed you to disregard. Such evidence is to be treated as if you have never seen or heard it..."

There are a few housekeeping issues, but court is done for the day and will resume tomorrow at 9am.

CHAPTER 3

LETECIA STAUCH TRIAL – DAY 2 - 4TH APRIL 2023

Al Stauch (Gannon's father) is the first witness to take the stand. The cameras show only the attorneys and the judge. Letecia is seated at the end of the table trying to avoid the camera.

Mr Allen begins questioning the witness.

Al introduces himself and begins to cry when he is shown a photograph of Gannon. He tells the court how he weighed only 1 pound 6 ounces when he was born four months early, but he soon caught up with other children his age. He loved playing video games and wanted to be a *YouTube* gamer. He'd made one video before his death.

Al tells how he met and began dating Letecia in January 2014. They married in January 2015.

He works for the National Guard as a Missile Defence Officer.

The family moved into the house in Mandan Drive, Colorado Springs in February 2019. It had two bedrooms downstairs in the basement and two up on the main floor. Harley and Gannon had their bedrooms downstairs. There was also a living area downstairs as well as one upstairs. The garage was accessed from the main floor. The kitchen was upstairs.

He goes through a number of photographs of the residence, and they are admitted into evidence.

On the 25th January 2020 he took his mother to the Denver airport and slept in the airport until he caught his own flight the day after.

He heard about a candle spill on the Sunday evening, which damaged the carpet and some spots on the sofa too.

On the evening of Monday 27th January, Letecia told him Gannon hadn't returned home from his friend's house. He had known he hadn't been in school that day as he had been having stomach issues and he was sick. He was puzzled as to why he'd been allowed to go to his friend's house if he was sick.

He contacted several of Gannon's friends himself, but nobody had seen Gannon.

Later that evening when Gannon still hadn't returned home, he arranged to fly home and booked a flight for early the following morning. He was picked up at Colorado Springs airport by Letecia. She had rented a vehicle from the airport which seemed odd to him that she wasn't driving her own vehicle.

Letecia told him they would be doing a lot of driving searching for Gannon and she didn't want to drive her car and put too many miles on the clock with it being a lease vehicle. He thought it strange she would worry about the mileage on her car when it was an emergency and Gannon was missing. She said her car was parked at French Elementary School. She said one of her co-workers dropped her off at the airport. He drove over to the school to look for the car, but it wasn't there.

He said Gannon seemed to love Letecia and he didn't appear to be scared of her. He loved his mom too—he was a typical mommy's boy.

He contacted Landon, and she arrived in the area that same day. Landon stayed at the Mandan Drive property for a couple of nights. This created tension in Letecia's mind and she and Harley moved out of the house because of it.

The children mainly lived with their mother when Al's marriage to Landon first failed and then he applied for custody in 2017 before he moved to Alaska.

During their time in Alaska, Letecia hated it and he felt she manipulated him to move back to Colorado Springs.

Court takes a morning recess.

The questioning resumes, and Al explains how Letecia had raised sexual harassment claims against two of his colleagues to get him to give up his position in Alaska.

Another time she sent him a text telling him she was pregnant with twins, and it accompanied an ultrasound picture. In his opinion, this was another episode of manipulation. She wasn't pregnant with twins.

In January 2019 Letecia filed two burglary allegations and she told Al she believed somebody was squatting in the loft of the house. She told him she had fired one of Al's guns into the window well of the property. He never saw any evidence of the gun being fired. Letecia eventually admitted she had made up the burglary allegations.

While living in Colorado Springs, Letecia was working at Whitefield School District, but she wasn't happy there as she thought she was too educated for the position she held. She decided she wanted to pursue a career as a flight attendant with Spirit Airlines.

He recalls the last time he saw Gannon and he choked up. He remembered it like it was yesterday.

Letecia had told him that Gannon once threatened her with a knife, and she suggested he needed counselling. They arranged this even though Al had never seen Gannon threaten anyone before.

The suitcase Gannon's body was found in had been stored in the storeroom next to Gannon's bedroom. It was in a large green suitcase.

The video of Gannon crying after the candle incident was played again.

Mr Allen admits two more images of Gannon in his bed. They had both been sent to Al on the morning of 27th January 2020.

He remembers searching everywhere for Gannon on the day he returned home. While he was out looking, he found himself at French Elementary School and couldn't see Letecia's car in the car park. That was when he knew she knew there was more to this than she was telling him. He told the police his concerns right away. The next morning, she told him she had been raped, abused, and beaten. Her attacker took Gannon.

After this, he spoke to the FBI, and he was asked to phone Letecia. They told him what to say to her.

Mr Allen asks to add the recordings into evidence.

The court breaks for lunch.

The prosecution plans to play the telephone conversations that were recorded by the FBI as well as text message threads between Al and Letecia.

Mr Allen directs Al to read a text message Letecia sent him on the 27th January 2020 at 2:48am.

> He is in the bathroom again blood coming out butthole and he is crying about going to school tomorrow like this. And he is still upset about the candle accident. I told him it's fine and that as long as he's okay not to worry about something minor we can fix and let's worry about his stomach hurting.

When he got back to Colorado Springs the next day, they met detectives in the Starbucks restaurant. Afterwards, he visited the Sheriff's office, to fill them in with a few details.

Later, after discovering Letecia's car wasn't where she said it was, he headed back to the Sherriff's office. At this point he was freaking out knowing there was something very wrong.

On the morning of the 29th January 2020, Letecia told him the story of the rape by a man named Eguardo. She said the rape took place in Gannon's bedroom.

His mother and sister had spent the night before in Gannon's room. He went to tell them to leave the room as it was potentially a crime scene. He put all the firearms from the house into his truck for safekeeping then he went back to the bedroom with Landon and asked Letecia to go through the story again.

The first FBI phone call between Letecia and Al is played to the court.

They make small talk, and she tells Al she's hungry because she doesn't have any money or cards. She said the police took everything off her from the car. She said she doesn't have a vehicle to get to and from work, a passport to go to the airline job or any money to buy food.

He said the police still have his truck too and he's having problems.

She said it is becoming a witch hunt because they're not listening to everything she's told them.

He asks her to tell him what happened and give him a timeline.

She said Gannon hurt his foot on some boards in the garage on the Saturday. He sat down on the back of the car, and she bandaged it up.

She said Gannon had the key to the side gate, saying he was checking it was locked.

Afterwards, she went downstairs to check on them and Gannon's door was locked to keep Laina out. She heard a loud noise and she knocked on his door. It was just a normal day.

On Sunday, they decided to go on a hike. She heard about the death of Coby Bryant, and she was crying and upset about it. She said she told him about a secret she'd already told Al about, so she didn't need to go through it again. She also spoke to him about the fact she'd lost a lot of babies, and she was sharing a secret with him. Then Harley was called into work. They had everything packed ready to go on a hike, so they decided to take the dogs on a hike to Garden of the Gods. Gannon began complaining his stomach hurt.

Most of the night he had a stomach-ache and he tried to lie down and poop and stuff like that. Gannon had a bath, and everybody was doing their own thing. Gannon lay on the sofa in the downstairs lounge.

She went upstairs getting Laina ready for bed. Then the fire alarm started. She turned the alarm off, but it started again, and she noticed it was saying fire this time. She got Laina and the dogs, ran them outside to the truck and then she ran back inside to Gannon. She was coughing and choking and couldn't get through the smoke part. She ran back through the garage and grabbed a dust mask and ran back downstairs and Gannon was asleep. She jumped on something, (Hard to understand) and Gannon had burns on his arms. They ran outside.

Al asks what time it was so they can look at the footage. She said ADT had an alert for fire, so it was around that time.

They got to the truck and he's screaming and crying. Laina was in the back with the two dogs. They drove off. The smoke had been scarier and more terrifying than the fire. They drove around the block and then returned to the house. She put Laina in their bed. She didn't know Gannon was burned until then when she noticed the inner parts of his arms had bubble spots. He told her he thought she was coming downstairs, and he was playing on the switch when he shouldn't be, so in a panic he knocked the candle over. It had set fire to his cover.

She said she lost her mind because if she hadn't got downstairs when she did, she may not have got to Gannon. That was what had freaked her out. He didn't want to go into his room and so he lay in Laina's bed. He said he was cold and had shivers. She didn't take his clothes off, but she asked if he was hurting. He said it was just his arms. She didn't think it was an emergency as his skin was just bubbly. She said maybe she should have put him in the car and got him checked out to make sure, but he said it wasn't hurting, they put aloe on the burns, and a long-sleeved shirt on him.

He slept in Laina's bed. Laina slept in Letecia's bed and Harley came home. She'd already prepped Harley about what had happened. They both went in to check on Gannon. They gave him water in Laina's bed, and he was more scared because she said they would have to sell the couch. She said she wasn't saying she'd sell the couch to pay for it. She was just concerned he hadn't done it on purpose.

Later that night, Gannon woke up with a bad stomach. She made the decision he could stay home the next day. She said she made the decision he wasn't fit to stay home by himself with his stomach hurting and he was bubbling a little bit here and there...

WHAT? The boy was 'bubbling a little bit here and there...'! He needed to be taken to a hospital, Letecia.

She said he needed to go out with her because she was going to look at a bike for Al.

Gannon started to peel his skin on his arms. Popping it like a blister. She told him if it gets worse, she would take him to the hospital. He also started peeling his fingernails. He had blood on his bed and the side of his wall. She said, 'it wasn't a lot, don't panic'. She rebandaged his arms and headed out to see the bike.

First, they went to find someone to replace the carpet, then she went to the pet store and then to see the guy with the bike.

When they got to PetCo Gannon stayed in the truck playing the switch.

Afterwards, they went towards Douglas County to meet a guy with a bike.

The judge pauses the audio and suggests they take a recess.

After recess, the audio resumes.

Letecia tells Al she had forgotten to tell him about calling in to see a contractor in the neighbourhood to fix the carpet. She asked if he could fix the carpet before they went anywhere – she gave him the garage code to go in and fix it – she had left money on the counter. She said she was trying to get the carpet fixed so the boy wouldn't be so upset.

They got home at around 2:30pm and she noticed she'd set the alarm to alarm away. And somehow it had changed from alarm away to alarm stay. She said she called ADT who said if it was set to alarm away it would automatically go to alarm stay if it sensed movement already in the house.

She said it was a proven fact that the neighbour was paid $5000 to release the video. She told him how tens of thousands of people have investigated the footage, and they can prove Gannon got out the other side of the vehicle. The shadows prove it.

Once home, Gannon went down to his room. Then he told her Al said he could go out with one of his friends. She said he was okay to play in the neighbourhood but not go off with anybody. Then she put her headphones on.

A short while later she heard another loud noise downstairs, and she called Gannon. She heard the noise again and so she went downstairs and saw a guy in the hallway. She thought it was the carpet guy. There was carpet everywhere, boxes etc. And she was knocked out. She hit the back of her head on Gannon's table.

She remembered Gannon jumping on the guy. Then she also remembered Gannon calmly talking to the guy about his mommy. She said there's a piece they're not putting together properly. There is something they were missing. Gannon knew something and he asked the man if he knew where Uncle Matt is at. She didn't even know who Uncle Matt was.

When she woke out of her state of confusion, she remembers Gannon saying he would be back later. She said he'd hit her head twice and had to fight off some guy who she'd given a description of to the police. She thought they were being robbed, she thought they were going to hurt Gannon and she was trying to work out what was happening. She said it's normal to be weak during the first few weeks of being pregnant.

She jumped up saying repeatedly, 'Gannon's gonna be back'.

Al asked her why she didn't tell him she'd been raped this time. She said, 'do you think I wanna tell you what a man done to me?'

She said Gannon jumped on the man's back and was crying. She couldn't see what was going on. She ran upstairs and sent Laina away. Then, when Harley came back, she asked her to go take Laina to the dollar store. She went back downstairs. He had Gannon in his arms, and he attacked her again. When she woke up Gannon was gone. The man had Al's black pistol but when she woke up the pistol had been left there.

She said they left out the side gate but the key to the gate was also inside the house.

She said she cleaned up the area from the night before when she woke up on the Monday morning. She had told Al she'd cleaned up after the attack, so Laina didn't see it when she got home, but then she changed the story.

She said Gannon has huge nose bleeds all the time. He picks his fingers, and he bleeds all the time. Huge nosebleeds at least once a week or two.

Al asked her straight if she killed Gannon. She said she couldn't believe he'd asked her that. She said no, and then she screamed at him.

He asked if something happened that was an accident and she denied everything.

She said people premeditate things and she said there was no evidence of that. She said she works with kids, and she knows how it works. She would never hurt kids. She screams saying 'I can't even believe you're saying Gannon isn't alive'.

Al told her something sounds off to him and he's trying to find the pieces, but he feels she's not being truthful to him.

The call comes to an end.

Al returns to the witness stand.

Mr Allen asks several clarifying questions and then the judge decides to call it a day as there is only twenty minutes left which isn't long enough to play the next phone call.

The court session ends for the day.

CHAPTER 4

LETECIA STAUCH TRIAL – DAY 3 - 5TH APRIL 2023

Al Stauch continues his testimony.

The second phone call between Al and Letecia is being played.

She starts off crying.

Al wishes her a happy Valentines Day.

She asks about Laina and when Al questions why she's asking. She responds with, 'can't I even ask where our kids are at?'

Al asks about Harley and Letecia tells him she had to go to the doctor because she's sick due to malnutrition.

She continues crying, it's difficult to understand what she's saying.

Al tells her he's not interested in social media and people are just looking for a headline.

Letecia says he should've talked to her about all the other stuff. She mentions she had asked him for help, but he turned her down. That she has always been there for him any time he's needed help.

Al tells her she took over $2000 out of the bank account at the beginning of the month and he didn't say a word about it, that he's also offered help and safety and teamwork the whole time, and he's never told her no for anything.

She says she did take $2000 because she needed a place to stay, and she kept begging for help. It costs $125 per night for a hotel, she didn't have a car she had to *Uber* everywhere. She said he's not on her side, and he's talking crap about her.

He said all he wants from here is the truth. They can work through all the other stuff as long as she's honest with him.

She asks what the options were, but he says the options don't come into play until she tells him the truth.

She says if they give her immunity she will help. If they swear she will not be charged with anything she will tell them the truth and she will testify. 'There are more details that we can't discuss because that would incriminate myself... I need immunity, please'.

She said the guy was still there when the police searched the home. 'He's waiting for the reward'. *She is screaming and crying, it's difficult to decipher what she's saying.*

Al asks her to tell him if she knows whether or not Gannon is safe.

Once again, she says that the guy was still in the house when the police searched. He was in the storage room. She also thought Gannon was hiding too. If she was given immunity, she would give them the guy's name. She also told him there was a gang involved.

The call ended.

Mr Allen resumed questioning Al.

He asked several clarifying questions regarding the phone call.

The next call is played.

This call is different from the beginning. Al is angry and demands information. He tells her to start over and tell him who has Gannon and to stop bullshitting him.

She demands immunity.

He says he doesn't believe there is any man--everything she has told him has been lies. He thinks Gannon had a big accident and she panicked and covered it up. He just needs to know where Gannon is.

She says she was there. She'll give the guy's name, but she wants immunity.

She tells him Gannon had been going out every day talking to some dude—asking her weird questions. The dude who was selling the bike followed her. She got to PetCo and was looking in and out of the store because of the guy. All she was trying to do is get him a bike. When she left the store, she realised the dude was following her again. Then she said he was in Al's truck with them.

The call ended.

Mr Allen asked several clarifying questions regarding the call.

The next phone call is played.

She continues what she was saying. That after she had left *PetCo*, somebody was lying down in the road and when she stopped the dude got in the truck with them. Gannon was crying in the back seat until he threw up. He was so scared. He stayed with them all the way back to the house.

Al said he saw the footage of her getting back to the house, he saw her get out and the shadow somebody was talking about on the other side of the truck.

He went inside with them, and he tied her up. Harley and Laina were in the bedroom sleeping. All she could hear was Gannon screaming. She said she didn't know how badly he hurt Gannon.

Al said it's bullshit. He said no guy jumped in the truck.

She said it happened and they were going to kill her. She eventually tells him the guy's name is Quincy Brown. He told her his name was Eguardo, but she discovered his name was Quincy Brown.

This was apparently late that night after the police had left.

Al calls her out again for lying. He said if there really was a man called Quincy Brown, she would've told him three weeks ago.

The phone call ends.

The court takes a break.

Al is back on the stand answering some follow-up questions.

The next phone call is played.

Al asks Letecia if she's ready to talk to him.

She continues with the Quincy Brown story and Al tells her to stop the lies.

She sent him a photograph of Quincy Brown that she'd clearly found from a google search.

They continue arguing but getting nowhere. Al eventually tells her not to contact him until she was willing to tell him where his son was.

The call ended.

Another phone call is played.

Letecia asks if he's still alone.

Al says he is. He says she asked for one more chance, so he is going to shut up and allow her to say what she's got to say.

When asked if he loves her, he says he does.

She asks Al if he knew there had been an accident would he stand by her. He says he would.

She said she's sorry for all the stories, but she didn't know what to do. She starts crying.

'We were going to get your bike and I let Gannon ride it. It was really big though. He fell off it and was hurt bad'. He was bleeding from his head, and the man she was buying the bike off said he would go back to his house and call 911 and get some bandages. The guy was called Quincy Brown, and he took Gannon with him and didn't return.

She had been driving up and down in that direction until they took her car.

The phone call ended.

Letecia is covering her ears while the recording is played.

Al returns to the stand to answer some more follow up questions.

Mr Allen asks to admit some different threads of text messages into evidence. He has no further questions.

The Court breaks for lunch.

Mr Tolini begins cross examination.

Al explains he had been separated from Landon when he first met Letecia, but they hadn't applied for a divorce.

When they first sold the marital home, Landon had the majority of the custody of the children. He and Letecia got married in January 2015.

He had some safety concerns about the person Landon was living with at the time and so he filed for custody. In the fall of 2018, Letecia was the primary caretaker of the children while Al was in Alaska. Al felt his kids were safer to be with Letecia than their mother at that time.

Al had told one of the detectives he got Gannon into counselling right after the custody issue was finalised.

Gannon sent a Mother's Day card to Letecia one year and Al testified that Gannon did appear to have love in his heart for her.

Al had raised concerns about Letecia's mental health with his mother who was a mental health nurse.

He confirmed it was a common occurrence for Gannon to have stomach problems.

When he got home that day, he'd thought it was odd Letecia had picked him up in rental car. He said he never had any negative thoughts about Landon being involved, despite their opinions of her, Landon loved her children.

Al didn't remember Letecia having a mental illness apart from having a little anxiety. She was never diagnosed with having a severe mental disease or defect.

Letecia told him she wished her name was Taylor and she occasionally would call herself this.

There are no further questions. Al stands down.

The next witness called to the stand is Mr Mecon Ponder, a bridge inspector in Pensacola, Florida.

Mr Dave Young for the prosecution begins questioning the witness.

Mr Ponder tells the court that on 17th March 2020 he located a suitcase underneath the bridge he and his colleague Mathew Goins were inspecting in Pensacola. It was lying close to the edge of the bridge in a marshy area. They didn't examine the suitcase right away but made a note to come back to it later on.

When they finished the inspection, they returned to the suitcase and discovered it was very heavy. They suspected whatever was inside was waterlogged as it was tidal underneath the bridge. They pulled the case underneath the bridge and Mr Ponder began to unzip it.

The first thing to hit him was the smell. He told his colleague there's something dead in here. They would often come across a litter of puppies in a bag something like that and they suspected that was the case on this occasion. The smell this day was similar but so strong. They thought about what they would do first before opening it. When they finally unzipped the rest of the case, the smell was so overpowering they took a step back and the first thing he remembers seeing was two little feet that had football socks on them. His colleague dumped the suitcase out and they immediately knew it was a body.

They dialled 911 and they waited for the authorities to arrive.

Several images of the bridge and the suitcase were admitted to evidence.

Mr Young has no further questions.

Will Cook has a few follow up questions for the defence about the bridge and the location of the suitcase.

The witness is released from the stand.

Court breaks for afternoon recess.

Criminal Investigator, Jason Yoder, is called to the stand.

He introduces himself and tells the court he works for Escambia County Sherriff's Office. Escambia borders Florida and Alabama.

He was called to the Escambia Bridge on the 17th March 2020 because the inspectors had uncovered a body in a suitcase underneath the bridge.

Once he arrived at the bridge, he called the crime scene unit and began to process the scene. There was a body that had been rolled out of a suitcase and covered in bedding and pillows.

He is shown several photographs of the bridge and surrounding area including a hotel bordering the area.

He did a state search for missing children. He found nothing locally and then they looked further out from the national database from missing and exploited children, and they discovered a flyer for Gannon. The dental features appeared similar. They were eventually able to positively identify the body as Gannon Stauch.

Detective Yoder was present during the autopsy of Gannon.

He is shown several photographs of the bridge, the suitcase, the body, and the bedding.

The detective contacted El Paso County Sherriff's office to inform them they had found a body and suspected it was Gannon.

He had the pillow x-rayed and found two bullets inside.

Prosecution has no further questions.

Mr Tolini begins cross-examination.

He asks more questions about the bridge and the area. Tolini pointed out there were plenty of longer bridges going over deeper bodies of water in the area. Yoder agreed.

Tolini has no further questions.

Yoder is released from the stand.

Detective Nickolas Brklich from El Paso Sherriff's Office is the next witness called.

Angelina Gratiano for the prosecution begins questioning him.

He is asked if he recognises an envelope that will be admitted as evidence. He says he does and then he proceeds to open it with a pair of scissors provided. It is a toothbrush inside a holder.

He also does the same with another envelope. Inside is a comb.

The detective recognises them as items belonging to Gannon.

He also identifies several items found in the dishwasher at the Stauch residence. There are brushes covered in some kind of carpet fibres.

He identifies envelopes containing DNA swabs he had taken from Landon and Al.

He also identifies Gannon's Nintendo Switch.

She has nothing further.

Will Cook begins cross-examination.

He asks a couple of questions regarding the DNA swabs taken. He has nothing further.

Detective Brklich is released from the stand.

El Paso County Sherriff's Office Patrol Deputy is next to be called.

Ms Gratiano begins questioning him.

The deputy responded to a call for a runaway on the 27th January 2020. He was wearing a body worn camera.

Ms Gratiano admits the camera footage into evidence.

You can hear the audio, but the video is not visible except for the people attending the court.

Letecia's voice is clear and she's explaining to the deputies that Gannon is missing, and he didn't take his bike. One of the officers looks around the house.

Letecia is talking ten to the dozen, but she doesn't appear upset.

She says she was cleaning the carpet downstairs when Gannon left to go to his friend's house.

The body cam only picks up some of it as Letecia clearly goes out of the room with the other deputy.

They ask if he's ever hidden in a car before, she says no.

Letecia tells them Connor's mom came over, but she hadn't seen Gannon. And he took none of his favourite things.

She tells the deputy that she didn't know a lot of Gannon's friends or where they lived as she worked away a lot and Al took care of all that sort of stuff. She said Al had been in touch with a bunch of his friends already.

She tells detectives to contact her husband for his dentist information etc.

The recording ends.

The deputy says Letecia was behaving normal. She appeared calm and was able to answer questions intelligently.

When he looked around the house, he didn't see a man.

Five more images are admitted into evidence.

The deputy was asked if he smelled any strong cleaning odours. He said he didn't.

He said he saw several suitcases when he looked back over the footage, but he hadn't noticed them when he made his initial search.

Prosecution has no further questions.

Defence has no questions.

The witness is released from the stand.

The court breaks until Friday 7th April 2023.

CHAPTER 5

LETECIA STAUCH TRIAL – DAY 4 – FRIDAY 7TH APRIL 2023

Prosecution warns the court that there will be several items admitted today which may be a little graphic.

Kelly Smith, a crime scene technician from the Santa Rosa County Sherriff's Office, is the next witness called.

Mr Allen begins questioning her.

On the 17th March 2020, Ms Smith was called to the Escambia River Bridge for a report of a suitcase with a body in it. She said the suitcase was an olive-green colour. It had a blanket and a body at the side of it.

Mr Allen asks to admit several photographs into evidence.

She could tell it had been there for a period of time due to the colouration and the bug activity, namely maggots.

The witness looks through a number of photographs from the day they found Gannon's body and describes them.

Another group of photographs are added to evidence from the autopsy.

She describes the bullet that was extracted from the victim's head. Also, the pillow that had two defects in it. They later discover the defects were due to two bullets that were inside the pillow.

Mr Allen has no further questions.

Mr Cook has no questions.

Senior Crime Laboratory Analyst, Trevor Seifert, is the next witness called.

Dave Young begins questioning him.

Mr Seifert tells the court about DNA and how DNA analysis works.

He tells how he analysed swabs from Gannon's parents and DNA taken from the rib bone from Gannon's decomposing body and it was a match for the DNA profile already on file for Gannon.

Mr Young has no further questions.

Defence has no questions.

Alexis Pack is the next witness called. She worked at the front desk of a hotel called The Candlewood Suites in Pensacola in February 2020.

Mr Young begins questioning her.

Letecia Stauch checked into the hotel on 4th February 2020.

Mr Young has no further questions.

The court takes a morning recess.

The next witness called is Lieutenant Jason Hess with the El Paso County Sherriff's Office.

Mr Allen begins questioning.

He was involved in the investigation regarding a missing 11-year-old child on the 28th January 2020. He called Letecia with some follow-up questions the day after he had been reported missing. She told him Gannon had not returned home and she had no further information.

Letecia agreed a photograph of Gannon could be circulated to the media.

He was involved in canvassing the area looking for information and CCTV that might help find the missing child.

A few days later he called around to the Stauch residence and saw a white van outside that was being loaded with belongings. Harley, Letecia, an aunt, and Letecia's brother Dakota Lowry were there.

In his experience, Lieutenant Hess believed Letecia's actions were similar to the reactions of other parents in similar situations however most of the time the emotions are a little more heightened. He doesn't believe she appeared to be suffering from any mental health disorder or disease.

Mr Allen has no further questions.

Mr Tolini begins cross-examination. He asks how many people he has dealt with who has dissociative identity disorder? He didn't know.

No further questions.

Leslie Hicks is the next witness called. She works at Mountain Ridge Middle School as assistant principal.

Ms Gratiano begins questioning.

Ms Hicks identifies Letecia as a person she interviewed for a position of resource teacher for children with learning disabilities.

A thread of text messages are added into evidence. Ms Hicks reads them out to the court. Letecia had completed her interview at this point and Ms Hicks was in the process of checking references.

Ms Hicks:Hi Tecia, this is Leslie Hicks at Mountain Ridge Middle School. I left you a phone message yesterday. Would it be possible for you to call me today at this number or email me. I'd like to talk to you about the resource teacher position. Thank you.

Letecia: *I have iMessages, I will email you.*

Ms Hicks: *Hi Tecia, this is Leslie Hicks again. I sent you an email yesterday, is it possible for you to get back to me today.*

Letecia: *I emailed you back.*

Ms Hicks was having trouble getting hold of some of the references and so she asked for some more.

Letecia gave her the number to a Connie Huddle. The caller ID on her phone came up with Eugene Stauch when she called it.

Letecia: *What time do I be there tomorrow?*

Ms Hicks: *Hi Tecia, we're so glad to have you here. The workday begins at 7:30am. You don't need to bring anything in particular. We will have a sub there tomorrow that has been filling in. You will have the opportunity to shadow him and meet the kids as well as get set up with the things you will need. Sherri Fuller, our SPED department leader will be there tomorrow as well. See you soon.*

Letecia: *Good evening. I wanted to ask your guidance about what to do about tomorrow. I had scheduled that interview at the district office before getting hired. I understand they probably have someone in mind, but I don't want to burn any bridges and would at least like to let them know my interest in eventually moving up later or even if it's a year or so. I know we have to all start somewhere. What do you think is the best approach to take? Thank you.*

Ms Hicks: *Hi Tecia. It is your choice if you want to choose to interview tomorrow. Please remember you will need a substitute and sub plans to cover the classes you will miss. Please let us know if you need assistance with that. Thank you.*

Leticia: *Well, they told me to do the fingerprints too, so I was just trying to do the right thing. Okay. I will just try to do the right thing by everyone. I didn't want to stand anyone up and wanted to be loyal to our school too. It's 8am. I mentioned it before in our emails but wanted to make sure to follow the necessary steps. They did say I could do the fingerprints while I'm there so I could get some link to do the paperwork. I haven't done any of that.*

She last saw the defendant in person on Friday the 24th January 2020.

She received a text message on Monday the 27th January 2020 at 3am.

Letecia: I'm sorry for the time of night message but my step-father passed away. Someone hit him with a car while he was walking. I can update you at a later time.

She received the same message again at 4:37am.

Ms Hicks: Oh, my goodness, Letecia. I'm so sorry. Shall we try to find a sub for you today?

Letecia: ? It's apparent. All my family lives on the East Coast. I'm trying to find a way to get there.

Ms Hicks: Okay. I'm just trying to understand your plans so that we can find coverage. And my understanding that you will not be in today.

Letecia:Yes. It's my parent. I can't believe that would not be an assumption in a time like this.

Ms Hicks: I am so sorry for your loss, and we will support you, but I cannot make assumptions, I do need some direction from you. We will get a sub today. Please let us know what else you will need moving forward.

There are no further questions for the witness.

The next witness called is Kevin Clark—the director of crime strategies and intelligence.

Mr Allen begins questioning.

Mr Clark tells the court how on the 1st February 2020, he was asked if he would assist as lead analyst on the investigation.

He told the court the phone number Letecia had given for Connie Huddle was in fact registered to Gannon.

There are no further questions. (Mr Allen says this witness will be called another few times during the course of the trial).

The court breaks for lunch.

Another body cam audio file is submitted as evidence from the night Gannon was first reported as a runaway.

She explains to the officer how she searched the neighbourhood, but she's positive he's with someone he knows because he searched on his phone, *can my parents find me if my phone is off?*

She said he also sent her husband a message saying, do we have any bath salts? He said because his friend said if he gets some, they can play Sonic there on the weekend.

A lot of the recording is the same as the one from day three.

The next witness called is Christopher Ganstine he was Detective Sergeant with the El Paso County Sherriff's Office.

Ms Gratiano begins questioning.

He said one of his tasks was to begin covert surveillance on Letecia Stauch. He began early on the morning of the 30th January 2020. They were using Harley's white Jetta.

While in Harley's car, she sat slouched down in the back seat as though to avoid detection. That afternoon, they were told to move forward and seize Harley's car and the phone.

He coordinated his team and created a multi-person team outside the store Letecia and Harley were in. He planned to do a soft contact approach when she came outside. She tried to get closer to the car when they approached her and then she turned and ran at a full sprint. She threw the keys across the parking lot and continued running the opposite direction.

Afterwards, she was detained and handcuffed although she wasn't arrested. Harley was still inside the store and came out just as Letecia was detained.

Harley was reluctant to hand over the phone, so another officer took it from her.

Letecia was hysterical and screaming.

He had a chat with Letecia and managed to calm her down and then he spoke to Harley, and she also calmed down. They were not arrested and were released soon after.

She made conscious decisions to run and was not in his opinion showing any signs of mental disease.

Ms Gratiano has no further questions.

Will Cook begins cross-examination.

He asks if the detective was ever trained in psychology and if he was qualified to diagnose mental illness. He said he wasn't.

The next witness called is Doctor Leon Kelly, the El Paso County Coroner.

Michael Allen begins questioning.

He became involved in the Stauch case after the remains of Gannon were discovered in Florida. He tells how it was difficult to get a definite identification as the body had begun to break down which makes it difficult to get enough of the material that's still intact to identify them. They received teeth and a femur, the upper portion of the leg bone, to be able to help identify him, which they did.

Allen has no further questions.

Will Cook begins cross-examination.

He asks how long it takes for a dead body to start to smell. He said it depends on the temperature it is kept at for a body to begin to break down and start to smell. 4 to 5 days inside a home at 70 degrees, a few hours at 90 degrees. Freezing will stop decomposition.

Cook has no further questions.

Allen has a few questions on redirect. He asks if the temperature Gannon had been kept at in Colorado would it stop the smell of the decomposition taking place? He said it would dramatically slow it.

There are no further questions for the witness.

The next witness called is Marissa Williams, a detective from the El Paso County Sherriff's Office.

Ms Gratiano began questioning.

On the 28th January 2020, she was present for an interview at El Paso County Sheriff's Office when Mark Riley interviewed Al Stauch.

Soon afterwards, she was assigned in tracking the Stauch's financial records to see what kind of activity they had been taking part in during the time Gannon went missing. She says she would describe Letecia's demeanour as worried but not in the same way a parent would usually be worried. She was more bothered about her own wellbeing than that of her son.

She said there was no indication Letecia appeared as though she was struggling mentally.

Ms Williams contacted Avis regarding the rental car Letecia hired on the 28th January 2020. Avis provided a rental agreement signed by Letecia Stauch for a white Kia Rio 4 door sedan. She used it for one day before being returned to the same location.

Williams also collected various financial documents and reviewed most of them; overall they were able to track movements/charges of Letecia through them.

Gratiano has no further questions.

Defence have no questions for the witness.

The court takes a recess.

The next witness called to the stand is Janine Sanchez. She was a friend of Harley Hunt. They used to work together in Massage Envy, and they went to bible studies together.

Mr Allen begins questioning.

When Gannon first went missing, Harley texted Janine to tell her about it. The last time she worked with Harley was on the 29th January. Harley was a little frantic and crying.

She was with Harley when they picked up Letecia from the hospital. She wasn't crying then. She said Harley acted timid and overwhelmed when Letecia got in the car. Harley appeared quieter than normal.

When Letecia got in the car she said, 'I hope you don't think we're a bunch of murderers.'

Letecia started using Harley's cell phone while seated in the car.

She said she was told the location services had been turned off on Harley's phone. Then the phone was passed back to Harley.

While they were all in the car, Janine received a message from Harley asking if her mother could stay at her home too. She thought this was strange she asked her via a text instead of in person considering they were all seated together.

Letecia said the police had found evidence at the house because the carpet had been damaged in a fire.

Harley said she didn't feel comfortable at her own house. She didn't know why Letecia wanted to stay too.

Mr Allen has no further questions.

Defence has no questions.

The next witness called is Nicole Mobley. She posted an ad on the local *Facebook* page looking for clothes for her niece.

Mr Young begins questioning.

She was contacted by Harley Hunt who said she had some clothing for her, but Letecia arrived instead. She didn't know her and had never met her before. She felt it was weird as she didn't know her, yet Letecia started chatting to her about life stuff. This was in the December before Gannon went missing. She messaged her a few days later and said she was working for an airline and would her niece wanted to go over to stay at the house and watch the dogs. She thought it was odd and didn't feel comfortable letting her niece go to stay.

She saw a post on Facebook saying her stepson hadn't returned home from a friend's house. She had mentioned Harley and the little girl, but she never told her she had a stepson. She expected Letecia to drop off the items and go not stand around talking for twenty minutes.

When she heard about Gannon being missing, she went out with her husband in the freezing cold snow to help search.

They ended up over near the Stauch family's house. There were people out with drones, and dogs. She found it strange everyone was out searching except Letecia. They were out searching until 2am or 3am.

She sent her a *Facebook* message to ask if she could help in any way and asking where they should be looking for Gannon and Letecia blocked her right away.

She saw the interview Letecia gave with her back to the camera, but she found it strange she was only concerned about what people thought of her and not her missing stepson.

Because Letecia had blocked her, she set up a fake *Facebook* page and thought she would be able to get her to start talking. And it worked. She began writing things she had seen in the news. It was clear Letecia had a lot of hate for Landon and so she wrote to her agreeing with her views. She also told her she agreed it was clear there was another person getting out of the truck that day based on the shadows.

They continued communicating initially by Messenger and then via a texting app. Ms Mobley went to the Sherriff's office soon after the string of messages took place.

Mr Allen admits the text messages to evidence.

Nicole begins to read them out.

> Letecia:I didn't hurt my son or kill him, I want you to know that. I also want to know that I can trust you on here.

> Nicole: One hundred percent. If you look up both my real profile and my fake on any of the Gannon pages, you will see that I've been pointing out the shadow and I've not bashed you.

> Letecia: Thank you. I do need some help though, and I could help you in return. Before you think, this isn't anything bad or anything like that.

> Nicole: Just to show you what I've said to my family about all this. (she attached a message she had sent).

> Letecia: If I had done this, I couldn't have gone so far and they would've found him. But they are focusing on me wasting

valuable time.

Nicole: Okay. What do you need help with? I definitely don't think you would ask me to do anything bad so it's okay.

Letecia: So, I want you to tell the truth.

Nicole: Okay.

Letecia: Someone was in the home when we got back. I gave this to the police at my initial interview, but I thought he was being defiant and going against his dad's wishes, leaving. I blacked out.

Nicole: So, you blacked out before he left? Because I'm a mom and I know how that is because I've done it and overreacted with my kids and situations I just did it with my house flooded.

Letecia: I'm beginning to think that the guy is still in the home when police came. Either way, he popped back up with Gannon so I'm assuming they were in the storage room. He threatened me and I put the girls upstairs to protect them.

Nicole: Who was the guy?

Letecia: He took a suitcase and some of our things and Gannon's things and I was crying. Then he hit me across the head.

Nicole: This is why the cops are being the way they are. They knew you didn't do it and that's why they are being so quiet. I knew you were innocent.

Letecia: Someone had to see him leaving with a suitcase and G. I don't know if he was hurt when he did. I was scared. Someone has to be a witness to having seen this guy. Someone had to and is scared.

Nicole: Can I ask you this. Do you think Landon sent this guy?

Letecia: I will do anything to find this person, but I don't know how. She could have and then things may have went wrong.

Nicole: I've been thinking she sent someone to get both kids.

Letecia: But Laina was gone, so he couldn't.

Nicole: How did he get into the house? Did he force his way? Or did he act like he was there for a reason?

Letecia: When we went in through the garage, I went into the bathroom, so either already in there or came later. Maybe G had seen him before that's why he kept checking the gate to make sure it was locked.

Nicole: Do you think the detectives believe you but have to act the way they are so this guy doesn't know they are onto him?

Letecia: Not sure. I think they don't have anything on ring cameras. Someone had to see him leave. I need a witness. Any amount. Do whatever for them if they come forwards. They need to start looking for the guy and posting it on our states.

Nicole: Oh my God, I'm telling you I think Landon did this to try to get her kids back and it went wrong, so now she is using this to get money for her nasty habits. Poor Gannon, I really hope he isn't being tortured.

Letecia: *And get off me. He would've been found close by if I was the killer I couldn't have went far. I think something went wrong now—it's been too long. She would've had him come back and then tried to say we were bad parents by now. Now I think he may be out of state.*

Nicole: *Did Gannon seem like he knew him? Or was he acting scared when he was taking him?*

Letecia: *The guy did say friends with Uncle Matt, but I don't know if that's real. He doesn't have an uncle named that on our side.*

NETTA NEWBOUND, MARCUS BROWN

Nicole: *Oh my God, see, this is what I was thinking, and I told my husband I think bio mom did this. Does Landon have anyone she knows named Matt that she says is like a brother?*

Letecia: *I need a witness. That the guy left. I will do anything. I'm not asking you. I'm asking do you know anyone who will. I will give them my life. A reward, whatever. Anything to get them to expand the search.*

Nicole: *Did he ask where the little girl was? What did he say to you?*

Letecia: *He said, is that your daughter at the door? But I sent her to the mailbox. I'm losing my mind because they need to look for the description of the guy. They need to expand and put up alerts in state. My heart is breaking.*

Nicole: *Okay. Let me think on this on a way to help. I've been on the news, and I know I can't just all of a sudden say that but I will help figure this out or something. Who can help, just give me a little time to think. I will help anything to get him found. I'm so sorry you had to go through that and then get accused, I can't imagine how you feel, I'm here for you.*

Letecia: *You were on the news?*

Nicole: *I did a blue-ribbon thing at the school for Gannon.*

Letecia: *And whatever they need, they're going to have to pay me for defamation, civil rights violations etc. But for now, I need him home. I need my boy home.*

Nicole: *Yes, my husband and I went out the first night till 2am. And then I went out every day for a week looking.*

Letecia: *That's when the guy left. He took a suitcase of things and made Gannon wrapped in his cover. He hit me in the head and then I don't know if they got in a car or what. When I got back up, I was in complete shock and crying. And when I told the police they think I'm crazy that someone could have been there when they arrived. In my questioning they were like, no way, the police didn't know they were there. I mean, heck, I didn't know.*

Nicole: *So, they never even tried to look into any of what you said? WTF is wrong with law enforcement? They could have found him but to me they didn't even try.*

Letecia: *No. They were like it was someone you were cheating with. Dumb stuff. I'm telling you when this is said and done, I will have a heck of a lawsuit. I've already been asked by some attorneys if my innocence prevails then to be the first to see them. I even took a lie detector test. I wouldn't ask if I didn't need the help. I am trusting that you don't say anything about our convo. I am innocent he is my son.*

Nicole: *I did meet a guy that night who freaked me out so bad I had to leave with strangers to get away from him. I wish I could show you what he looked like, but I don't have pictures.*

Letecia: *It may have been him, but he left with a suitcase. And G was walking and took his cover.*

Nicole: *I will never repeat this conversation I promise you. I believe you. This was hours later, and I told my husband about this guy that creeped me out what if he had something to do with it? Then hours later came out to search just to be close to the house and see what was happening. I told him this that night before I knew any of these details.*

Letecia: **(An Image of Gannon's bed).** *This is the cover he left with. This is online now because it showed G back at the house with me time stamped. What if you just said you remembered something suspicious after seeing this picture? And explain the description and you didn't think it was relevant until now because the kid had the same cover. I swear to you I didn't do this. I just need help with someone getting this out there so they can start posting in other states.*

Nicole: *That's a possibility. Do you remember around what time it was?*

Letecia: *After police left, so it was last night. Maybe one or* so. I didn't know he was still there until police had left. And some people were out searching, he could've blended right in. Especially with cars in the area. He had to get in a car at some point.

Nicole: Yeah, there was a lot of cars and people everywhere.

Letecia: I wouldn't ask this if I didn't want to find out. Find our son. I'm cornered because of no ring activity.

Nicole: So, this was before the cops search the house. Not only is this scary but very sick. Do you remember what he looks like? Tall, short, skinny, fat? So I can think of a way to say it when they ask details. So, I was in the field by your house from about 12 to 2 and I could see your house most of the time. So now I need to think really hard about this because I saw a lot of people out and now I'm wondering if I could have seen anything. It was freezing cold and we were exhausted but there was so many people out there.

Letecia: Yes. He's Hispanic. Shorter, five-seven or five-eight. About 175 pounds. He has like either a tattoo or something on his face. Maybe a teardrop or something like that. But a marking. He had on a jacket. I don't remember the colour. But Gannon left with him in that cover so that stuck out to you when you've seen it online just recently. Yes, he stayed in the house, but I didn't know until later, but he took a suitcase with him. Beware, I saw him load it up before he hit me in the head. I'm sure he loaded the suitcase in the car and put Gannon in somehow.

Nicole: I wish I could remember that night better. Like a car in front of your house or close because I parked on your street a few houses down to get out and search the field.

Letecia: At this point I just need the main info out there. Again, I only ask you because it's our child. They're looking in all the wrong places. Most people want to always help but I know this is tricky. I mean, if it's money or whatever, name it. I want them searching right way.

Nicole: *I want to help. Anything to find Gannon. My daughter knows him, and this is destroying her, and I feel broken now that I have been searching and doing what I can. And I met Laina and that made me break down. So I am about to meet with my dad to help him put together a chair, he just got a new house. He is nosy. When I'm on my way on my phone so I only want to message when he is not next to me. So if I'm slow to reply that's why. I don't want anyone knowing I'm talking to you because then people get nosy and like I said anything we talk about is between us. I'm not even telling my husband.*

Letecia: *Okay. I think that's best. You think you could do it? Let me know what you need. Gannon is who I want home and they can turn their searches the right way. They could call me back and take me seriously.*

Nicole: *I'm going to see if my first post is still up from that night, because that will prove that I was right by your house that night and it will help. And no, you don't need to give me anything, I just want to help get him home.*

Letecia: *Okay. I could help with that with what to say and yes, I will. You guys need some help too. I'm desperate to find G.*

Nicole: *You passed the polygraph so why don't they start listening to you? I don't' get it. They're dumb and I know you passed it because they posted that you did.*

Letecia: *Well, I wanted this and then when they call me back in I will take that and they will listen. I will take a witness too. So they say let's call me back in and they will refocus on and search differently. And then I will take results then. The police can keep you anonymous to the public.*

Nicole: *Looking for my first post now.*

Letecia: *Okay. If you could just call Albert and tell him first. He would keep you anonymous except to the police. Besides, it's for Gannon. I can't stop at anything to get them to refocus and find who that was.*

Nicole: *Found it.*

After this Ms Mobley contacted the police and handed over her phone.

Mr Young has no further questions.

The court breaks for the weekend.

CHAPTER 6

LETECIA STAUCH TRIAL – DAY 5 – MONDAY 10TH APRIL

Graphic content warning

Doctor Susan Agnacio, Associate Medical Examiner, Largo, Florida.

Mr Allen begins questioning. He asks the judge if she can be qualified as an expert witness in pathology. Judge Werner allows it.

The doctor tells how she performed the autopsy on Gannon Stauch.

Mr Allen submits several photographs as evidence.

The doctor describes the images as she sees them.

- The first image is Gannon in situ underneath the bridge. She says, 'the whole body looks decomposed, it doesn't look like a normal fresh body. You can see a brown/grey discoloration on the skin, the right hand, you can already see the bones because it's starting to decompose. The skin here is already decomposed and disappeared. Brown discolouration all over. There is a laceration on the left chest. You can't really see it clearly because of the decomposition, the lines are ill-defined. There is a wound here, a wound here'. The doctor corrects herself saying it's not a laceration, it's a sharp force injury. A wound caused by a sharp object like a knife or a blade. Some of the injuries were shallow, superficial and some were deep.

- The next image is a closeup of the previous image.

- The next image is another sharp force injury.

- The next is a closeup of the previous image.

- There was another sharp injury on the left chest.

- A closeup of the previous image.

- Next shows a sharp force injury just above the clavicle on the left.

- Next is a closeup of the previous image.

- A sharp force injury in the left upper arm close to the armpit.

- A closeup of the previous Image.

- Another sharp force injury on the left wrist region.

- A wound on the left upper arm near the axilla.

- The left hand which had another cut on it.

- The back of the right hand had four wounds – consistent with defensive wounds.

- The right hand on the middle finger had another cut.

- The left upper back had a deep wound.

- There were two more wounds on Gannon's left shoulder. Four inches deep.

- Another injury on the inside of the left forearm.

- There was a cut at the back of his right ear.

- A laceration on the back right side of the head that was caused by a blunt object.

- Another blunt force injury to the top of Gannon's head.

- There were several skull fractures that show in the next image. She confirms it would take a lot of force to cause this type of damage to the skull.

She tells the court she counted 18 sharp force injuries and four lacerations from blunt force injury. Then there was a gunshot wound to his face.

She believes the sharp force injuries came first because he was still able to defend himself. However, it is unclear which order the blunt force injuries and the gunshot wound occurred in.

Cause of death was gunshot wound and blunt force injuries to the head.

The manner of death was homicide.

Toxicology reports showed he had Acetaminophen in his system. He also had hydrocodone in his liver tissue, a narcotic analgesic.

Mr Allen has no further questions.

Will cook begins cross-examination.

He asks if the injuries on the top of Gannon's head were postmortem or premortem. She replies they were premortem. They occurred before death.

The doctor agrees this was a violent death and it had no pattern to it.

The blunt force injuries would have been fatal by themselves. The gunshot wound would also have been fatal by itself.

He asks if some of the blunt force injuries could have occurred when the suitcase was thrown off the bridge. She says no.

The sharp force injuries could have proved fatal in themselves, but it was difficult to tell because of the decomposition.

Mr Young has no further questions.

The jury members have a number of questions for the doctor.

Q: **Can you confirm how long the body had been decomposing?**

A: No.

Q: Was there any evidence of burn marks on the arms or bubbling of the skin?

A: I couldn't see that because of the decomposition.

Q: How long does Tylenol and Hydrocodone stay detectable in the body?

A: Usually, the body would metabolise the drug and it would come out in the urine after 12 hours. So, he would have been given the drugs less than 12 hours before he died.

The court takes a morning recess.

Al Stauch (Gannon's father) is recalled.

Mr Allen is questioning.

Al tells the court of an injury to his index finger that occurred in the garage of the house on Mandan Drive. He was prescribed hydrocodone for the pain. The medication was kept in the nightstand beside his bed.

No further questions.

The next witness is FBI Special Agent Andrew Cohen.

Mr Allen is questioning him.

Agent Cohen tells how he was the lead agent in the investigation for the disappearance of Gannon.

He explains how a wiretap works. It was used in this case. They discovered Letecia was using other devices after her own phone was taken into evidence.

Mr Allen adds a disc of wiretap calls from the 18th February 2020 into evidence.

First recording:

Male: How may I help?

Letecia: I'm looking for information about one of the tests that I paid for.

Male: Okay, can I have your name please and I can check if we've got the order here.

Letecia: Yes. Tesha Stauch.

Male: Okay, give me one moment please, let me have a little look. Okay yes, I can see that we've received that, and we have actually sent the test. Have you not received that as yet?

Letecia: What now?

Male: We have already sent the results to your email account.

Letecia: I don't have them.

Male: Okay. Let me try resending that and if you don't receive it give us a call back.

Letecia: Okay thank you.

The FBI traced the call to Fakepolygraph.com.

The next call is played:

Male: How may I help?

Letecia: I was just talking to you. Is there any way you can confirm where you sent those because I still didn't get them.

Male: Yes. So, I'm just gonna get that resent for you so if you could wait for the next 10-15 minutes and let me know if you haven't received it by then.

Letecia: Can you check the email because I just want to make sure.

Male: Okay, yeah, give me a moment. He reads her email address out for her.

Letecia: Okay, so it will be 10 or 15 minutes?

Male: Correct.

The third call is played.

Male: How can I help?

Letecia: Hi, yes, I'm calling again, I still didn't get that email.

Male: Okay, can I ask your name please?

Letecia: Stauch.

Male: Ah, right, yes. Perfect. I can see here...

Letecia: Because you said it would be 10-15 minutes, but I still don't have it.

Male: Unfortunately, it's actually been blocked by my management this order, due to the content of the questions so we're not going to be able to send this report.

Letecia: Okay. So, do I get my money back?

Male: Unfortunately, not on this case, no. Obviously due to our terms and conditions it does clearly state that any illegal activities or anything like that obviously the management do reserve the right not to send the report. We do incur processing fees so that's why a refund wouldn't be due.

Letecia: So, what happens now? Do you just delete it and go on with your life and keep the money?

Male: Yes, we do indeed.

The fourth call is played.

Male: How can I help?

Letecia: I talked to you earlier and you said that the request I did was blocked or something, but I looked at the terms and conditions and it says you can say things about infidelity and stuff like that so I'm not sure how that was blocked.

Male: Say that again sorry, that you can or can't?

Letecia: No, okay, so I did a report earlier and you said when I called back it was blocked, that I wasn't allowed to get the report, but then I clicked the terms and conditions, and it says you can do questions about infidelity and stuff like that.

Male: Yes. Infidelity you can, correct.

Letecia: Right, and that's what I did.

Male: Your report was about infidelity, was it?

Letecia: Yeah, like I put questions in for it and we had to select answers and you said something about it being blocked.

Male: Yeah, so what were your questions?

Letecia: So, it was about during the time that we were away in another state that I talked to that I gave the person's individual name, Ortega. That was one of them. And it said are your eyes blue? And I did a couple of questions on the bottom.

Male: Okay. I'm not sure in that case, unfortunately that's not what came through. I'm not quite sure what's happened there then.

Letecia: Yeah, it says on there that you can do this.

Male: Yeah, you would be able to about infidelity but the questions that were submitted to your order were not to do with infidelity.

Letecia: I didn't submit questions that were not to do with infidelity.

Male: Okay, all right. I'll have to look into that then in that case.

Letecia: You want me to write you the questions down?

Male: No, it's okay I'll just need to have a look into this then to see what can be done. Remind me again what was the name on the report?

Letecia: Stauch.

Male: That's your surname is it? Your last name?

Letecia: Yes.

Male: And your first name?

Letecia: Tecia.

Male: Okay, let me look into it and I'll come back to you.

Can you believe what you are reading? We can't! She was ac-

> ## tually trying to con her way out of the fact she'd asked illegal questions!

Mr Allen has no further questions.

Mr Young has no questions.

The next witness called is crime lab specialist, Christina Cervantez. (she used to be evidence technician at El Paso Sherriff's Office).

Mr Allen begins questioning.

She tells the court she received phone calls asking for her property to be returned. She also had a call from Letecia who was saying she was Harley Hunt.

Mr Allen enters a recording of a phone call into evidence.

The call is played.

A woman who says she's Harley Hunt asks for her book back and several items including her birth certificate and passport. She didn't think it was Harley Hunt as she had spoken to Letecia on several occasions and recognised her voice.

Ms Cervantez tells her she cannot release the items as they had been listed as evidence but if she wants to take it up with the detective in charge of the case that was up to her.

Mr Allen has no further questions.

There are no further questions from the defence nor the jury.

The next witness called is Detective Michael Bauman from the El Paso County Sherriff's Office.

Mr Allen begins questioning.

Mr Bauman explains his main role in his position is to analyse and retrieve data from computers and other devices. He worked on the Gannon Stauch investigation in 2020.

Letecia had a rose gold *iPhone 8*.

Mr Allen admits the contents of two phones connected to Letecia into evidence.

He has no further questions.

Mr Tolini begins cross-examination.

He asks about the process of retrieving the data.

He has no further questions.

The next witness called is Sergeant Kurt Smith from El Paso County Sherriff's Office.

Mr Allen begins questioning.

He worked in the special victim's unit back in 2020 specialising in crimes against children.

Like the last witness, he also performed a data extraction of a device connected to the case (it says the kid's phone on the label attached).

Mr Allen has no further questions.

The defence has no questions.

The court breaks for lunch.

Detective Christina Perry, from the El Paso County Sheriff's Office, is the next witness called.

My Young begins questioning.

She tells how she was involved in the investigation of the Gannon Stauch disappearance.

On the 28th January 2020 Mr Al Stauch contacted the Sherriff's Office regarding the whereabouts of Letecia's vehicle. The detectives went to the school to see if the car was left there initially, then they went to the airport to see if they could locate it. They were not able to locate it. (we now know Letecia had picked up the car already).

She recalls picking up Laina Stauch and taking her to the Sherriff's Office to be interviewed. She also tried to speak to Harley Hunt at the residence as she had refused to speak to officers earlier. Harley chatted about her career aspirations and several other topics but as soon as her brother was mentioned she refused to discuss it. This struck the detective as odd.

She bagged and recorded several items found by other officers:

- A candle that appeared to have carpet fibres, a sock and other things melted into the wax, in the outside trash can.

- Swabs from a woman's right shoe, that had been found in the laundry room.

- Swabs from a woman's left shoe found in the laundry room.

- Swabs of the light switch located in the basement hallway outside of Gannon's room.

- Swabs of the light switch inside Gannon's room.

- Swabs of Gannon's bed.

- Swabs of the east wall of the room.

- Swabs of the outside of Gannon's bedroom door.

On the 29th January 2020, they located Letecia's vehicle when she arrived to be interviewed that day. The car appeared to have just been washed, it was still dripping water. They confiscated the car that day.

A few days later she was told Letecia had rented another vehicle, a Nissan Altima. She applied to obtain a tracking warrant for the vehicle.

She was made aware that a payment of $2600 had been made from Harley Hunt's account into Letecia Stauch's account. They presumed they were planning to leave the area.

She was assigned with reading several social media accounts regarding Gannon. One of them, support T Stauch on Facebook, had a member of Letecia's family posting on it. On one of the groups, a photograph of Gannon in bed had been posted, they were able to see the bedding on Gannon's bed was not located at the residence during any of the searches.

She watched hours of a neighbour's surveillance video to see if any of the information told to the officers actually took place.

Several video clips are admitted into evidence.

The first is Letecia and Gannon leaving the house in Al's truck on the morning of the 27th January 2020.

The second is the truck returning. A close up is done of the video and it is clear there is a second person getting out of the truck. Moments later, Letecia drives her Tiguan vehicle into the garage.

The third is Laina arriving home on the school bus.

Next is Harley arriving home and picking up Laina to go to the store.

The next morning Letecia is seen driving her car out of the garage and moments later Harley drives her car into the garage.

Mr Young has no further questions.

Mr Tolini begins cross-examination.

He asks Detective Perry how many times she searched the crime scene. She replies two times, once on the Tuesday and once on the Wednesday.

He mentions that crime scenes tend to be secured to preserve evidence. However, in this case, Harley and several other parties had unfettered access to the crime scene.

He points out that on one of the videos Laina goes out on her bike, but the footage does not show her returning to the house. She is next seen leaving the house with Harley, so she clearly got home at some point.

The detective agrees.

He asks if any of the footage picks up the sound of gunshots.

She says it doesn't.

Mr Tolini has no further questions.

Mr Young has some redirect.

He asks if there is any way to muffle gunshots.

She says there is.

He has no further questions.

The court takes afternoon recess.

Detective Timothy Farrell from the El Paso County Sherriff's Office is called up next.

Mr Young begins questioning.

He recalls searching the Stauch residence on the 28th January 2020 at around 10pm.

He took photographs of the entire scene and searched the residence for anything that stood out. He didn't see any blood at that point.

Mr Young adds more images into evidence.

There were several images of the laundry room, including a pair of running shoes that appears to have been stained with something red.

There are also images of the family room in the basement. The damaged carpet and also burn marks on the couch. They had been told there had been a fire in the basement involving a candle.

And there are images of the trash cans outside the back of the residence showing melted candle and carpet fibres. Also, there is the 2-foot square of carpet with a hole burnt through that had been removed from the family room.

Just an idea, but could she have been responsible for the fire in the first place? Maybe her plan was to make it look like he'd died in an accident, but Gannon managed to put the fire out foiling her plans and burning himself in the process? It's certainly food for thought.

More images of the guns found at the residence in the master bedroom.

He tells the court about locating Letecia's vehicle on the 29th January 2020 and it was still dripping wet.

More images are added into evidence showing Letecia's car. The detective says it became apparent that whoever had washed the vehicle hadn't washed the top part as it was still covered in dirt and dust.

He was part of the team who followed Harley and Letecia in Harley's car. The were intending to seize Harley's car and cell phone and it was clear Letecia had been using Harley's cell phone.

This is the second occasion we've heard this same story. But this time, Detective Ferrell pulled out his firearm and aimed it at Letecia which caused her to stop and begin complying with their commands. It was never their aim to arrest her at that stage, but they wanted the cell phone because they believed she had something to do with Gannon's disappearance.

On the 3rd February 2020 a more thorough search took place at the Stauch residence. Members of the crime lab attended to collect evidence.

On 9th March 2020 some video surveillance came to light of Letecia entering a Walmart on 1st February 2020.

Mr Young has no further questions.

Will Cook begins cross-examination. He asks if the detective had swabbed the shoes found in the laundry room. He confirms they were swabbed but he didn't know what they were tested for.

The detective says he didn't wear a bodycam back then, but he sometimes does now.

Mr Cook has no further questions.

The next witness called is Detective Pete Vigil for El Paso County Sherriff's Office.

Mr Young begins questioning.

The detective tells the court when he first searched Gannon's bedroom, he could smell an ammonia/bleach smell. That told him there had been cleaning supplies used.

He swabbed two areas of Gannon's mattress with stains resembling blood on it.

Mr Young has no further questions.

The defence have no questions.

The next witness called is Spencer Wilson, a reporter with CBS 4.

Mr Allen begins questioning.

Mr Wilson tells the court how on 31st January 2020 he interviewed Letecia.

(We covered the entire interview in Chapter 1)

Mr Allen asks if Mr Wilson believes she was of sound mind. He said he does believe that.

He has no further questions.

One jury member has a couple of questions.

Q: Did Letecia stop crying immediately?

A: Yes. Quicker than a normal person would stop crying.

Q: Did her demeanour change following the interview?

A: Yes.

The court breaks for the day.

CHAPTER 7

LETECIA STAUCH TRIAL – DAY 6 - TUESDAY 11TH APRIL 2023

The next witness called is Dakota Lowry, Letecia's brother.

Mr Young begins questioning.

As soon as he approaches the stand Dakota begins to sob and calls out, 'Why Tecia?'

The jury are sent back into the jury room while the witness composes himself. It is a highly emotional scene.

Mr Young asks him to focus on him and his wife and together they will get through this.

The jury is brought back.

Dakota tells the court about their other family members. His voice is quivering, and he is barely holding it together. The last time he saw Letecia was in January 2020. They came out to help support her because they felt she was being wrongly accused for something they believed she would never do. They also wanted to help look for Gannon.

Their aunt rented a car for them, and their plan was to support Letecia and Harley. They met Letecia and Harley at a shopping centre just after the police had seized Harley's car and phone.

The next morning, their aunt rented a van and went to the house to get Letecia's things back. They retrieved suitcases and clothes and planned to move back to Myrtle Beach, South Carolina. They went back to the hotel room, and they asked if they could go and help look for Gannon.

Later on, Letecia left the hotel and said she was going to get some dog food.

On 1st February Letecia rented another van because she intended to go back to Myrtle Beach. The family went with her to swap vans and help move the items from one van to another. There was a lot of suitcases. One stood out to him because it looked like Letecia was struggling with it. She said she didn't need help. He didn't feel right about it.

Mr Young put the image of the suitcase onto the screen.

Dakota recognised the suitcase as the one Letecia had been struggling with.

Later that day, they parted. Dakota and his mother went back to the airport to return home and Letecia and Harley headed to Myrtle Beach. That was the last time he saw his sister.

Mr Young asked if he had ever heard anything about Letecia and his father. Dakota said no. He said he believed he would've heard about it had there been anything between them.

He said he'd never known her to behave recklessly. She never called herself by any other names. He believed she must have been insane when she did what she did to Gannon because she wouldn't have done it otherwise.

Mr Young has no further questions.

Mr Tolini begins cross-examination. He asked him to expand on what he meant when he said she wouldn't have done it otherwise.

Dakota said, when he heard about the little boy being found, he immediately knew it had been Letecia and he remembered the suitcase.

He was two years old when Letecia moved out of the house aged 16. He didn't have any active memories of his father's relationship with Letecia.

Mr Tolini mentioned Dakota's dad, James Lowry, had a drinking problem. Tolini said, 'he would get drunk, and he would beat the piss out of your mom'. Dakota agreed this was the case.

He said sometimes when Letecia would visit him, she left him knives so he would be able to protect himself.

Tolini has no further questions.

Mr Young begins re-direct.

He asks if Dakota's dad had been in the armed forces. He said he was, but Dakota couldn't really talk about it because he had been too young to remember the details for himself.

He asks if he had wanted to come out here today to testify? He said 'nope'.

Mr Young asks if he had been subpoenaed and that's why he came out to testify? He said 'yep'.

He asked about what Dakota had said about Letecia having some kind of insanity or a mental break and if he believed that? Dakota said no, too much had gone on for that to be true.

Mr Young has no further questions.

One member of the jury has a question.

Q: **Do you know where the green suitcase was retrieved from when they were getting the belongings from the house?**

A:No.

Mr Young asks when he first saw the green suitcase.

He says when they were swapping the contents of the van.

There are no further questions.

The next witness is Joshua Johnson from Budget truck rental.

Ms Graziano begins questioning.

Mr Johnson goes through the steps required when someone hires a vehicle.

He was present when Letecia Stauch rented a van on 1st February 2020 to the 5th February

2020.

Ms Graziano has no further questions.

One juror has a question.

Q: Where was the van due to be dropped off at?

A: Grapevine, Texas. It was a one-way rental.

No further questions.

The next witness called is Roy Ditzler, a sergeant with the Colorado Springs Police Department.

Mr Young begins questioning.

In January 2020 he was assigned to the Stauch case. On the 31st January, he was asked to affix a GPS tracker to the underside of the silver Nissan Altima that Letecia's aunt had rented for her.

The vehicle was observed while the occupants went to a shopping area and then back to the hotel they were staying at. They were then told the warrant had been signed and they could go ahead and affix the GPS tracker. They came up with a hasty ruse to conceal the GPS tracker.

Mr Young has no further questions.

Defence has no questions for the witness.

The court takes their morning break.

The next witness called is Jacob Abendschan, a deputy Sherriff for the patrol division.

Mr Young begins questioning.

He was the detective sergeant during the Gannon Stauch disappearance in charge of the GPS trackers that were placed on the vehicles. He tells the court that trackers are important during the information gathering stage as they needed to know where Letecia was at all times. He arranged for Mr Ditzler to fix the tracker to the vehicle on the 31st

January 2020.

He was able to access the software that tells them the addresses the vehicle attended during the timeframe.

Mr Young adds a five-page report to evidence. He asks the detective to go through the report for the jury.

2:58pm – The GPS shows the device was parked at the hotel.

3:37pm – Shows the GPS is in motion.

4:41pm – There is a brief stop at the area of 15291 South Perry Park, this location became an area of interest. It was just north of the county line near Palmer Lake.

4:58pm – The vehicle is travelling westbound.

8:23pm – The vehicle is back at the hotel.

On 1st February

10:52am – The vehicle is in Castle Rock heading north.

4:06pm – The vehicle is now in Denver at the rental vehicle return. The detective arranged for someone to retrieve the tracker from the vehicle.

Mr Young has no further questions.

The Defence and the jury have no questions.

The next witness called is Digital Forensics Detective Brian Rogers from Colorado Springs Police Department.

Mr Allen begins questioning. He asks to qualify Detective Rogers as an expert witness and digital forensic examiner.

On 30th January 2020 he was asked to extract data from an *Apple iPhone 8+*. He was not told where the cell phone had come from. The data that was obtained was given to Detective Sirois.

The phone belonged to Harley Hunt.

The next witness called is Detective Robert Sirois. In January 2020 he worked for the El Paso County Sherriff's Office.

Mr Young begins questioning.

In January 2020 he contacted Avis car rental company at the airport and asked for some information and video footage regarding the Kia Rio Letecia had rented.

They were also making efforts to locate Letecia's black Tiguan.

While he was at the Avis counter, one of the employees told him she had just been handed the keys to the Kia Rio he was interested in. She said after handing her the keys she turned and got into a while Jetta and drove away.

He had to look for where the Kia was parked, and they found it in the short-term parking lot. Then he arranged to search the car.

Mr Youngs adds several images into evidence. The images are of the Kia Rio.

A parking ticket was found in the car during the search.

The detective was also responsible for extracting data from a cell phone in this case. The *iPhone* belonged to Al Stauch.

The data is added into evidence.

Mr Young has no further questions.

Mr Cook begins cross-examination. He asks a question regarding the data extraction.

He has no further questions.

The court breaks for lunch.

The next witness called is John Wadden from Avis Budget Group.

Ms Graziano begins questioning.

Mr Wadden explains about the historic GPS tracking of a vehicle. A rental vehicle pings regularly to alert the location and whether it is stationary or in motion. It pings regularly until the truck arrives in Myrtle Beach, South Carolina.

Ms Graziano asks to admit a document into evidence. This is the GPS data from the truck Letecia hired.

Ms Graziano has no further questions.

Defence has no questions.

The next witness called is John Grassel. In 2020 he worked for the Rhode Island State Police.

Mr Young begins questioning.

Mr Grassel was assigned to searching the van Letecia rented to transport Gannon's body to Florida.

Mr Young adds a number of images into evidence. The images show the inside and outside of the van. One of the images showed a portion of the floor mat that had reacted to chemicals indicating the presence of blood.

Mr Young has no further questions.

Mr Tolini begins cross-examination.

He asks how many people had hired the van prior to Letecia.

Mr Gassel didn't know.

Mr Tolini has no further questions.

The next witness called is Catherine Beckel, she worked as a dispatcher in the El Paso County Sherriff's Office in 2020.

Ms Graziano begins questioning.

Ms Beckel explains she receives emergency calls and dispatches accordingly. If somebody calls in on the emergency line but they deem it a non-emergency, they will be asked to call back on the non-emergency line. This happened with the missing person report call from

Letecia.

The calls are played.

Call 1 is poor quality but it's clearly Letecia calling to report Gannon for not arriving home. The dispatcher asks her to call back on the other line.

Call 2 is similar quality. Letecia reports Gannon for not coming home from his friends. She said she's freaking out. He's a good boy, he's never been in trouble—a straight A student. She describes what he was wearing, his description, and tells the dispatcher she was the last person to see him.

Ms Graziano has no further questions.

Mr Tolini asks if panic varies depending on the age of the child to how panicked the parent would be?

She says there is a big difference between two calls if the missing child was a 5-year-old compared with a 15-year-old.

No further questions.

Sergeant Rosario Hubbell from El Paso County Sherriff's Office is the next witness called.

Mr Young begins questioning.

He first became involved with the case on the morning of the 28th January 2020. He was the supervisor over the entire case.

He recalls doing the search on the 3rd February in Gannon's bedroom. During the search they located blood evidence on the wall and plug socket beside Gannon's bed. When he pulled the carpet back, he realised there was saturation through the carpet, and the pad and had stained the concrete below.

On the 25th February he video recorded the entire property so there would be an optical capture of the scene.

My Young adds the video into evidence.

The court takes their afternoon break.

The court is back, and they begin to play the video.

The footage is 22 minutes long and takes a detailed walk through the residence. The detective points out all the areas that reacted to Bluestar, meaning blood was present. A trail of blood was found in the garage, and it went through the laundry, though the living areas and into a storage closet. There was also a large bloodstain in Gannon's bedroom as well as multiple areas of blood spatter on his bedroom walls.

Mr Young has no further questions.

Mr Cook begins cross-examination.

He asks the officer if there was any footage showing the reaction to the Bluestar. Officer Hubbell said they had been having problems filming the reaction.

Mr Cook asks if CSI technicians took swabs of the blood. Officer Hubbell says, 'yes, they did'.

Mr Cook has no further questions.

There are questions from the jury.

Q:Bluestar reacts with blood to make it visible, does Bluestar in any way compromise the subsequent analysis of the collected blood sample?

A:Officer Hubbell doesn't know what the process is so he couldn't answer if they test out the Bluestar or if the Bluestar doesn't affect it at all.

Q:Was the trash bin outside searched for evidence?

A:The night the original search was done, the trash can was looked at.

The next witness called is Amanda Van Nest a forensic nurse examiner from UC Health Memorial Hospital.

Mr Allen begins questioning.

He asks if Ms Van Nest can be added as an expert witness as a forensic nurse examiner.

The witness first became involved in the disappearance of Gannon Stauch on the 29th

January 2020. Letecia had been admitted to the hospital suffering from chest pains and she had reported a sexual assault.

Mr Allen asks to admit several photographs into evidence.

During her examination of Letecia, she filled out a form and asked if she wanted any further physical examination regarding the sexual assault. Letecia declined.

The other two examinations she was required to do was a suspect's exam and a sane exam. These had been requested by the police. Letecia indicated she wanted to proceed. They went to an examination room, and she took specimens from Letecia's body. She took swabs for DNA, fingernail scrapings, and blood.

Letecia left to get her daughter from the waiting room before she did the sane exam, but she did not come back.

Mr Allen asked if Letecia appeared to be suffering from any severe mental disease at that time. Ms Van Nest said no. She believes she was sane and consented to the exam.

He has no further questions.

Mr Tolini begins cross-examination.

He asks Ms Van Nest if she has any training in forensic psychiatry.

She said she doesn't.

He has no further questions.

The court breaks for the day.

CHAPTER 8

LETECIA STAUCH TRIAL – DAY 7 - WEDNESDAY 12TH APRIL 2023

Jessica Bethel is the next witness called. In 2020 she was a detective for the State of Colorado in the investigations division. She is presently a stay-at-home mom.

Mr Allen begins questioning.

In the Stauch investigation Ms Bethel was the lead detective. She says this was not a typical investigation because there were so many agencies involved.

The first police interview with Letecia and Al that was conducted in Starbucks is played first. It is audio only.

She behaves so calm knowing she's just dropped off Gannon's body in her car at the airport.

The audio was hard to follow and would be impossible to transcribe, however, we know everything she says. The next interview might be interesting so stay tuned...

Letecia sneakily rolls something up in her fingers and stuffs whatever it is in her ears. We presume it is toilet paper which we can't see would work too well, but she clearly doesn't want to listen to her own lies.

The next interview is a *Facetime* interview with Letecia. Audio only. She has an attitude and is rude to the detective, demanding to know why she's wasting time talking to her again. She complains that Harley was left at the home with men going in and out and she wasn't allowed to leave.

The detective asks if there is anything more she can tell her that could help to find Gannon. New information? New developments?

Letecia says there isn't. She is clearly angry with the police, and she refuses to speak to the detective without an attorney.

Bethel says she will end the call then if she didn't want to come into the office to talk to her.

When the recording ended, Mr Allen asks several questions about how Bethel felt Letecia's mental state was.

Later that evening, Letecia contacted her again saying she needed to speak to her as there was something she wanted to tell her, but that Al would be angry about it. They arranged for Letecia to go into the Sherriff's office the next morning at 10am.

She also mentioned Gannon had had cuts on him, but she hadn't hurt him. Bethel thought this odd.

She didn't show up at 10am as arranged and when Bethel contacted her Letecia told her she had to put measures in place because her daughter was being stalked and her family was receiving death threats.

She eventually arrived at 12 noon.

The next recording to be played to the court is the next police interview with Letecia that took place at the Sherriff's office.

The recording begins with Letecia being searched.

She says her VW Tiguan is in the parking lot. (We know that is being seized at the same time as this interview).

Bethel asks if she would like anything to eat and drink and she leaves to collect it for her leaving her with another officer.

Letecia tells the officer she knows the interview is being recorded but she is concerned because she needs to tell some personal things. She is concerned the recording would be released.

The detective tells her it wouldn't be released.

She is read her Miranda rights.

Bethel returns to the room.

She begins jabbering about her plans to be a flight attendant, that she doesn't want to be a teacher anymore.

She starts by telling the reason Al doesn't like to be called by his Christian name of Eugene is because his dad was called Eugene, and he was a child molester—he'd raped his sister. So, the name makes him freak out.

The officer asks to go through all details from Sunday through to Monday and to be as detailed as possible.

On Sunday they went hiking to Garden of the Gods.

Gannon started having a stomach problem which cut the hike a little short.

When they got back, they just went about ordinary things. Gannon was still in pain.

Gannon was downstairs and had lit a candle because it was a little gassy down there due to his stomach and the dogs etc.

Laina had fallen asleep after playing with her iPad.

Then an alarm began sounding and Letecia didn't know what it was. She input the alarm code into the keypad, but it didn't go off. Then the alarm started saying fire, fire, fire, fire. Then she saw smoke coming from the downstairs.

She ran back up the stairs woke Laina and gave her the keys and told her to take the dogs to the truck and she ran back downstairs to get Gannon. The fire was on the floor. She smothered the fire with a pile of covers. Gannon wakes up and realised the place is on fire.

They all run out to the truck.

After driving around the block, they drove back to the house and made a plan for the next day to fix the carpet.

Gannon went to bed after that. He had burns on his arms, but they weren't bad. By the next morning she noticed his arms were peeling.

(She's crying as she tells this part). She dressed the burns and she said she feels really bad because she felt she should have taken him to the hospital, and she felt Al was going to kill her.

He had been picking his arms during the night and he had blood on the walls beside his bed.

She knew she needed to fix the carpet and buy some burn cream.

They left the house at 10:15am and headed to the new builds to see if she could find someone to fix the carpet. The guy at the new build said he had some carpet as all the houses were the same. She gave him the garage door code. There is no sensor downstairs.

She had left $50 on the counter for him to take as payment.

They headed to PetCo. Gannon lay in the back of the truck because his stomach was hurting. They went to a gas station. Then she went back to PetCo to get more outfits for the dogs.

After the second PetCo trip they headed home.

When they got inside, she heard something, but she thought it was Gannon.

She begins crying again and says, 'it's all my fault, I gave him the code'.

She walked downstairs and saw Gannon, but she could still hear a sound, so she continued down the stairs and opened the storage closet. The man was there, and he had a gun. He had on a pair of gloves. She tells how he began attacking her. It's all a blur. She remembered Gannon running in and trying to help but it was all a blur from there.

She passed out and when she came to, she couldn't find Gannon. The man was still in the house. She thought Gannon must be hiding. She heard Laina return and so she ran upstairs and there was nobody at the door. She went back downstairs because she didn't know where Gannon was, and she couldn't leave him alone. The man had Gannon when she arrived back downstairs.

Laina arrived home and she went back upstairs and told her to stay outside for a little while.

She returned downstairs and was pleading with him to let them go.

The man asked for a suitcase, and she got him one from the store cupboard.

She was sexually and physically assaulted again, and she passed out once more. When she regained consciousness, the man and Gannon were gone. The gun had been left behind.

When Harley returned home, she didn't tell her what happened. She didn't know how she was going to get out of it and what to do about the fact Gannon wasn't home.

Later that evening, she called 911 who told her to call another number.

A few hours later the police arrived. They searched the house and her car.

The next morning, she left the house to pick Al up from the airport. She rented a small car because she knew they would be driving around everywhere, and she was anal about putting mileage on her lease vehicle. She told Al she had parked her car at French Elementary because she wasn't ready to tell him she didn't intend to return to her job there.

She asks for a bathroom break and then makes a tearful telephone call.

She goes over finding the construction guy again. She said his name was Eguardo. He looked like a legit worker which is why she gave him the code.

She now says there was 10 x $10 notes on the counter. And not the $50 she had mentioned earlier.

She begins crying again when the detective mentions the sexual assault. She said she doesn't really want to go through it. She is getting tetchy about having to go into detail.

She said he wasn't much bigger than her, and they fought. It was after she hit her head for the first time, that's when it began to be a blur.

She says the man raped her the first time but the second time he attempted it, he didn't succeed.

During the assault, Gannon ran in and jumped on the man's back. Gannon was thrown across the room.

She remembers Gannon was bleeding at some point.

Afterwards, she was aware the man had Gannon, while holding the gun.

Laina arrived home and so she went to tell her to go away to keep her safe and then she went back downstairs.

She began reading from her notes.

He told her there would be consequences if she made any noise.

After the second attack she remembers wondering where Gannon was and hoping he was hiding. Once she realized he wasn't there, she went into a mode of, 'okay, I'll fix this'. But even when the officer searched the house, she was still hoping he would find him.

She cleaned up the house and put everything back the way it was. She put the gun away with the other guns.

She mentioned Al checked the guns that morning and made out he was securing them in the truck just in case she decided to harm herself. She said she'd never tried to harm herself or anyone else ever.

Letecia asks if she can leave, and the detective asks her to wait a few moments while she checks it out. But she's arguing and doesn't want to stay there and refuses to be escorted to the hospital. She is not happy.

The other officer comes in and she's obviously stalling trying to make Letecia hang on a while. She refuses to leave the cup in the room, clearly not wanting to leave any DNA behind. They are trying to stop her from leaving.

Letecia's forcing the situation insisting she is to be allowed to leave.

A male detective arrives and asks her to wait because they were applying for a search warrant. She tells them to prove they are legally able to take her phone and keep her there without a warrant.

They tell her she's not free to go. They are going to hold her until they get the warrant.

She tries to leave and demands to make a phone call.

The detective says things have changed since she was first brought in and now she is not free to leave.

The court breaks for the day.

CHAPTER 9

LETECIA STAUCH TRIAL – DAY 8 - FRIDAY 14TH APRIL 2023

The court will pick up where they left off on Wednesday—the police interview with Letecia.

The recording resumes.

Letecia, alone in the room, is going through her bag and it looks as though she's taking pills. She takes a wad of tissues and stuffs them down her pants. She says she accidentally peed a little and now her pants are wet.

The detective comes back and allows Letecia to use the toilet, but they instructed her not to wipe or flush.

When she comes back, she asks if she can sleep. Then she lies down on the sofa and covers herself up with a jacket.

A few minutes later, she begins pacing the room.

She opens the door and tells the officer in the hallway if she can keep the door open as she can't breathe.

The officer says she needs to sit on the couch and if she can't breathe, he will need to call a medic.

The detective returns and asks if she needs to see a medic.

Letecia says she is having chest pains and feels as though she is having a panic attack.

She says she wants medical attention. She's hungry and tired and feels as though she's having a panic attack.

The paramedics arrive to examine her.

She tells them she's having chest pains and can't breathe. She's suddenly confused and can barely make any sense. Her speech is slurred and unclear.

They did their tests, and everything comes back good.

She is able to walk to the ambulance. They take her to the hospital for further tests.

The recording ends.

Ms Bethel returns to the stand.

She says it is common for people when being interviewed for murder that they get panicked.

After being examined at the hospital Letecia managed to leave without further ado.

Letecia wasn't picked up again for a while. However, Bethel received several text messages from her. One said she had done nothing to Gannon and there was no negligence on her part.

After Letecia fled to South Carolina, they decided to go to Myrtle Beach to arrest her as they had obtained a probable cause arrest warrant.

After the arrest, they stopped to pick up another detective. The trip lasted more than 24 hours. During the journey, she ate, sang songs, and played trivia.

The entirety of the trip was recorded, and a portion of the road trip is about to be played to the court.

The video is added into evidence.

In the video Letecia is cuffed at the front of her body when she slips her cuffs and attacks the deputy seated beside her with a can of monster drink to her face, and then she attempted to obtain her firearm. When the car pulled over, Bethel got out to assist the other officer and Letecia also glances at Bethel's gun at her waist.

Letecia says the officer kept threatening her. It takes three officers to restrain her and get the cuffs fastened behind her back.

Bethel calls the incident in and arranges for assistance.

During the phone call Letecia is arguing and struggling. The deputy holds her in a headlock.

The police arrive moments later, and transfer Letecia to the Police vehicle.

The court take their morning break.

Ms Bethel tells how because Letecia slipped her handcuffs, attacked an officer and opened the van door, Bethel believed she intended to escape.

When she was escorting her to the patrol car, Letecia dropped all her weight causing Bethel an injury to her shoulder that needed a surgical repair.

She says she never saw Letecia displaying a different personality during all the interactions they had between them. She says she believes Letecia is sane, manipulative, and very calculated.

Mr Allen has no further questions.

Mr Cook begins cross-examination.

He asks several questions regarding the interviews. He said he believed Letecia had been very cooperative initially.

Bethel says she thought Letecia was apprehensive on occasion. But she agrees she hadn't tried to assault her.

During the first part of the road trip, Letecia had been calm and was singing, doing trivia. It was only the last part she became aggressive.

He asked if she had noticed a change in Letecia's personality during the journey. Bethel says no. He points out Letecia had been singing and doing trivia initially and then she suddenly assaulted an officer, he asks if she would say that was a change in her personality? Bethel says she believes there was a change in her behaviour not her personality.

Mr Cook has no further questions.

Mr Allen begins re-direct.

He asks in her experience as a detective if she ever encountered people with mental disorders.

She says she did, but she never saw anything in Letecia that made her believe she was suffering with a mental disorder.

Mr Allen has no further questions.

The next witness called is Christian Liewer, a crime scene investigator.

Ms Graziano begins questioning. She asks for Mr Liewer to be added as an expert witness.

Liewer tells the court he was called out to the Stauch residence three times in the course of the investigation. Initially he responded on the 3rd February 2020. He said he was looking for bloodstains and latent bloodstains. Latent bloodstains are very diluted and cleaned up to where you cannot see them anymore so additional processing is needed.

Ms Graziano adds several photographs to evidence.

The images show lots of before and after photographs using the Bluestar product. The highlighted areas are clear on the after photographs.

There were also photographs admitted from Gannon's bedroom. The carpet underneath the bed, the underlay below that, and the bloodstained concrete. There was also blood around and inside the plug outlet.

A more detailed examination of the walls in Gannon's room was carried out by another CSI.

A loaded gun was found in the master bedroom which was taken into evidence.

Ms Graziano has no further questions.

Mr Tolini begins cross-examination.

A member of the jury has a question.

Q: **If Bluestar is a pre-emptive test for blood how is testing accomplished to separate Bluestar from an actual blood sample?**

A: So, Bluestar is reacting with the Haem component of the blood whereas when they have a DNA sample, they're looking for DNA within different components of the blood so the Bluestar itself is not overriding the DNA because the DNA component is still present in the sample.

Q: **Does Bluestar impact or affect the actual blood sample?**

A: What would impact the sample is how much we're spraying or diluting the sample. But Bluestar does not negatively affect DNA processing further on down the line.

The witness is released from the stand.

The next witness called is Stephanie Happ, the senior firearms examiner with the Colorado Springs Crime Lab.

Mr Allen begins questioning and asks for her to added as an expert witness.

Allen asks if she examined any firearms involved in this case? She said she examined three firearms—

two x 9 millimetre and one x 380 calibre.

Several items were added to evidence.

Two of the firearms were illuminated as firearms used in this case.

She said she examined two bullets from the pillow found in the suitcase.

She was able to identify one of the projectiles as being fired from the Smith and Wesson firearm, however, although the other one was very similar it was no longer in suitable condition to be able to identify it. The bullet recovered from Gannon's autopsy was also fired from the Smith and Wesson firearm.

Ms Happ explains how each firearm leaves their own unique markings on the bullet when fired.

Mr Allen has no further questions.

Mr Cook begins cross-examination.

He asks several clarifying questions.

The next witness called is Brooke Bell, senior CSI with Metro Crime Lab.

Mr Young begins questioning.

Ms Bell was called to examine the Mandan Drive property on the 29th January 2020.

Mr Young adds multiple images into evidence.

The court pauses for the final afternoon break.

At this point, Letecia is flipping the bird at the witnesses and the cameras. What on Earth is going on in her mind?

When the judge returns, he informs the court that it has been brought to his attention that one member of the jury had recognised the previous witness, Ms Happ. The judge decides they will discuss it closer to the end of the day.

The photographs added previously are still being viewed. Ms Bell points out areas in the home that they witnessed visible blood that was clear from the naked eye and didn't need any chemical processing.

The court breaks for the weekend.

Once the jury had left the courtroom, they needed to address the earlier issue with the one jury member who recognised one of the witnesses.

The judge says he will consider the situation over the weekend and make a decision by Monday.

The prosecution has a further issue they wish to address… the fact Letecia was flipping the bird all afternoon.

The judge threatens to remove Letecia from the courtroom if her bad behaviour continues.

CHAPTER 10

LETECIA STAUCH TRIAL – DAY 9 – MONDAY 17TH APRIL 2023

Firstly, the judge has made a decision to dismiss the juror. He feels if they had known this information from the beginning she would not have been selected.

Secondly, the judge points out the defendant's position has been moved within the courtroom; she is now seated between her two lawyers. He says if there are any further disrespectful displays, he will make life harder for her by either handcuffing her to her chair or banning her from the courtroom entirely.

Ms Bell resumes her seat on the witness stand.

Mr Young has a few more questions. He asks if there were any cartridge cases found at the residence. She says there were not.

He has no further questions.

Mr Tolini begins cross-examination.

He asks how many people had been in an out of the residence the day before the initial search.

Ms Bell says she doesn't know.

Mr Tolini has no further questions.

None of the jury members have any questions.

The next witness called is Harley Hunt (Letecia's daughter).

Mr Young begins questioning.

She tells the court she lived her whole life with Letecia and the last time she saw her in person was on the 3rd March 2020. She tells how Letecia married and moved in with Al and his children. They were all one happy family. Although there was an age difference, she felt she and the children had a good relationship. She says she felt Gannon and Letecia had an okay relationship although there were problems here and there.

She became close to Al after her own father had died when she was 12. He had died of an overdose. She tells the court she had only just found out the truth of how he died. Her mother had told her someone had broken into his house, robbed him and killed him.

Her mother had told her she wished Al was home more, especially when the kids were there. Her mother didn't like being home alone with the kids.

They planned to move to Alaska but there was an incident that happened and so the family chose to move to Colorado Springs instead. They moved in first and then Al met them there a couple of weeks later. This was the first time they all lived together for an extended time. It felt like a family again. Letecia and Al would argue a lot, she would take the kids into her room and turn the TV up, so they didn't have to listen to the arguments.

On the 26th January 2020, Letecia and the two children went on a hike. She recalls Letecia telling her that Gannon had pooped his pants. This hadn't been the first time something like this had happened, he often had stomach issues.

Later that day she got a text message from Letecia telling her that Gannon had set a fire downstairs with a candle. An image showing the damage caused was sent with one of the texts.

She had been confused because Gannon wasn't the type of kid to hang out and light a candle in the basement. Letecia told her he had fallen asleep and knocked over the candle, unless he had been still awake and lied to her.

She finished work around 10:30pm.

When she got home, Letecia and Laina were in the living room, and they began telling her about the fire. Letecia said she thinks Gannon was playing on his Nintendo when he wasn't supposed to be and knocked over the candle accidentally. They had run from the house and Letecia called her fireman friend to make sure it was okay to re-enter the house with the fumes and he said yes. Letecia also said that when they were in the street, Gannon was screaming that he hates his life and things like that. Harley found this odd because she hadn't known him to do anything like that before.

Letecia suggested they go downstairs and tell Gannon goodnight which was not something she would normally do.

They went downstairs and Harley remembers seeing Gannon in his bedroom, but she doesn't recall if he responded to Letecia saying goodnight. That was the last time she saw him. All the windows were open downstairs, and it was cold.

Harley spent the night upstairs that night because Letecia made the comment that Gannon was acting weird, and she didn't know what was wrong with him—she was scared. Gannon was the only one to sleep in the freezing cold basement.

The court take their morning break.

On the morning of 27th January 2020, she texted her mother before leaving for work and asked if she was there.

Later that morning she received a text message from Gannon's phone telling her Letecia had left her phone at home and if she needed her to call Gannon's phone.

When she returned home from work that day, Letecia told her she'd looked up on the internet how remove fire stains from the carpet and she wanted her to go to the store to get the stuff for her. She saw Laina but not Gannon. Letecia told her Gannon was with one of his friends.

She went to the store with Laina and when they got back, time had gone by and Gannon didn't return home, Letecia had said he clearly didn't want to eat sushi. She said Letecia was worried, especially when they went to Gannon's friend's house, and he wasn't there.

At 7:02pm that night, she received a screenshot from Letecia showing a text conversation between her mother and Al.

Harley presumed Gannon had run away.

She was out looking around the school and searching the streets for Gannon.

Letecia told her she wanted to stay home in case Gannon returned home.

Later on, Letecia asked her to search Gannon's backpack and when she did, she found a *Swisher Sweets* cigar inside.

The next morning, 28th January 2020 at 6:21am, Letecia sent her a message telling her not to answer the door to anyone. She was going out looking for Gannon.

Letecia went to pick Al up at the airport.

She sent a message to Harley asking her to put her Jetta inside the garage.

Later that afternoon, Letecia went missing. Harley sent her a message asking her where she was and tried to locate her on the location app they used but it was turned off. Letecia wouldn't tell her where she was for a while. Everybody seemed to be looking for her. She thought Letecia was being treated unfairly by the police.

The court breaks for lunch.

Harley continues recalling the events of the 28th January 2020.

The police called at the house at 7:21pm but Letecia told her not to answer the door. Then she left the house at 10:03pm and the police were still outside waiting. She answered a couple of their questions but didn't want to get into trouble so decided not to answer any more.

The detectives took Laina to from the house and said they were taking her to Al.

Her mom kept telling her the police were trying to set her up.

Letecia told her to meet her at a hotel because they were going to stay there that night. She said she didn't want to be in the house with Al and Landon.

Letecia eventually turned up in the Tiguan. Letecia left her car there and they returned home. She seemed paranoid.

When they got home, she received a string of texts from Letecia during the early hours of the morning asking what the state of the downstairs is like, because the police had been through her things.

On the 29th January 2020, Harley dropped Letecia off at the airport to drop off the hire car. Then Harley dropped her off to pick up the Tiguan.

Harley needed to leave work early because she'd had a call that Letecia was at the hospital. She went with a friend from work to pick her up. She ended up getting a call from a random person telling her to pick her mother up from Taco Bell. Letecia didn't have her phone with her and asked to use Harley's phone. She sent several tests to Al's phone.

The texts between Harley's phone and Al's phone are added to evidence.

They drove to the parking garage to see if her car was still there. Afterwards they went to her friend Janine's house. They had been told they couldn't stay at their own house that night. She asked Janine if her mom could stay there too.

The next morning, they took the dogs out, then they went to the Marshall's store. They went to buy a change of clothes. She was at the checkout when the police came in and took her phone and put her in handcuffs. Outside, she saw her mom had also been handcuffed. They seized her car and her phone.

They walked to the plaza to use the phone and call their family members that were due to arrive. They arranged to be picked up by the family and then they headed to the hotel.

The next day, they went to collect their belongings from the house. Their aunt rented a van for them. The police were at the house when they arrived, and they searched through everything they were collecting. She didn't remember seeing the large green suitcase. It took around an hour to load the van up.

On their way back to the hotel, Letecia saw a reporter and decided to speak to him. At one point, her mom called her over and asked her to tell the reporter she had seen Gannon after the hike.

Back at the hotel, Letecia took the rental car and left to get dog food. She was gone a long time, approximately two and a half hours.

The next morning, she recalls her aunt saying she didn't want to be responsible for the rental of the van, so they went to rent a new one. Later that day, her mom arrived back with a different van. She said the destination kept changing. It was finally decided to be Myrtle Beach. The family headed to the airport to catch their flight home.

They stopped off at several hotels on the way through to Myrtle Beach. On the 4th February they checked into a hotel in Pensacola, Florida at just after midnight. She said Letecia was behaving normally apart from being a little sad. Letecia began being paranoid again and saying the police were following her and knew where she was.

Letecia was arrested in Myrtle Beach on the 2nd March 2020.

When Gannon's body was found in Florida a while later, she thought it was some sort of coincidence because they had been in Florida and thought maybe somebody could have been following them after all. She believed her mother for a while but then she began having a few questions.

She says she never saw her mother behave in a different personality than her own usual personality. She says Letecia had never been an inpatient in a mental hospital. Her mother knew right from wrong all the time. She saw no evidence of her mother showing any signs of mental illness. The only other name she used was Taylor because she didn't like her first name, however she never changed her personality.

Harley told the court she had been scared of being charged as an accessory to murder because of being with her mother during the trip to Florida.

Mr Young has no further questions.

The court take their afternoon break.

Mr Tolini begins cross-examination.

He asks several clarifying questions about her childhood and growing up with her mother.

On the 27th January 2020, she says her mother appeared normal apart from being clearly worried about Gannon not coming home.

During the entire trip to Myrtle Beach, she didn't smell anything strange coming from the back of the van.

She said when her mother changed her plea to not guilty by reason of insanity, she felt betrayed by her.

Mr Tolini asks Harley if she manipulated the truth at times when it suited her. She said no.

He made a statement that she had set up a GoFundMe page and stated she had lost both her parents at age 17, She asked for financial help from people stating she had nobody to assist her financially. She said she made around $800.

Mr Tolini has no further questions.

Mr Young begins re-direct.

He asks why she started the GoFundMe page.

"When this first happened to me, I had literally nothing. You would think that if my mom had done this, she would do something to prepare her daughter or set her daughter up to not have parents or financial help. I had people in the beginning. They were very nice, and they volunteered. I never asked people for anything like I had said in my GoFundMe paragraph."

She tells how her Aunt Brenda cut her off after she had agreed to give a statement against her mother. She suddenly took the car she was using off her and stopped all financial help.

She said she initially didn't believe her mom could hurt Gannon. She's still in shock now. She never questioned if Gannon's body could have been in the van. It never crossed her mind. But now she knows he was in the back of a van stuffed into a suitcase. And believes her mother was capable of picking that suitcase up and throwing it over the side of a bridge.

Mr Young has no further questions.

The jury have questions.

Q: **Did you see a large green suitcase loaded into the second van?**

A: No.

Q: **The night your mom asked you to go down with her to say goodnight to Gannon do you have a specific recollection of seeing any part of his body like his hands, face, or any part of his actual skin?**

A: I remember seeing his head.

Q: **The morning of the first day in Pensacola, Florida when you left the hotel, do you recall if the van was in a different parking spot than where you had parked it when you checked in?**

A: I don't remember.

Q: **During your time living in the Colorado Springs home with the other kids, did it appear to you that Gannon was treated more strict or more unfair than anyone else by your mom?**

A: No.

Mr Young has some follow up questions.

He asks to add an image into evidence. The image shows a large green suitcase. He asks Harley if she recognises the case. She says yes, she remembered it from moving from Alaska, but she had never seen it around the time of Gannon's disappearance up until the 4th February 2020.

Harley is released from the witness stand.

CHAPTER 11

Letecia Stauch Trial – Day 10 - 18th April 2023

The first witness called to the stand is Lieutenant John Sarkisian from El Paso County Sherriff's office.

Ms Graziano begins questioning.

In January 2020 he was assigned as the incident commander for the search efforts regarding the disappearance of Gannon. A lot of people volunteered to help search the areas they were focussing on. They began at the residence and then moved north from there based on snippets of information as they came in.

On 15th February 2020 they located a piece of particle board that was approximately half-an-inch thick and two feet by two and a half feet in diameter. It was off the side of the road under some trees. There had been some heavy snow in the area, but the sun was shining this day and the snow had begun to melt.

Ms Graziano adds several images into evidence. The images show the road and the berm and the board that had been found including the bloodstain on it.

> **If the board had been lying in the back of the car with the suitcase on top of it, there must have been bloodstains on the outside of the case. Why did nobody notice this?**

Ms Graziano has no further questions.

Defence have no questions.

The jury have questions.

Q: **Was the board on the west side of the barbed wire fence?**

A: Yes.

Q: **Was there an opening in the fence?**

A: There were no breaks where the actual board was but there was a gate further up.

Q: **Were there any footprints collected?**

A: The footprints detected were from the searchers and so nobody collected any footprints.

Ms Graziano asks if the board had been moved. He said it was clear it hadn't been moved.

Mr Tolini asks if there were multiple footprints around the board? He said not around it but there was a pathway between the berm and the board.

There are no further questions for the witness.

The next person called to the stand is Kevin Clark, former officer Colorado Springs Police Department. He has already given evidence earlier in the trial.

Mr Allen begins questioning.

Mr Allen asks for several discs to be added into evidence. The discs contains phone records for Letecia's phone, Harley's phone, and Gannon's phone.

Mr Clark was present when the board was located. The data shows GPS in the area from Tuesday 28th January 2020, and the evening of Friday 31st January 2020. It snowed heavily after this date.

Mr Clark tells how, when he was examining Al's phone, he came across an image taken towards the end of 2019. The image shows a broken board in the garage of the residence with a broken corner. The board was very similar to the board found at the side of the road and it also had the same broken corner. There was also a pencilled x on both the image and the board found.

There are no further questions for the witness.

The next witness called is Commander Mitch Mihalko from the El Paso County Sherriff's Office.

Mr Allen begins questioning.

Commander Mihalko had become involved in the case early on. It began as a runaway child and soon developed into much more. Letecia had drastically changed her story when she finally attended the police interview. Mihalko managed to get the phone off her before she left because he suspected she would destroy evidence if she had been allowed to leave with it. So, the phone was seized *before* the warrant was obtained.

The court takes a morning break.

The commander tells the court that on the 7th February they locked down the scene. This means that they changed the locks on the residence and disabled the garage door so nobody could gain access via the garage. It takes a lot more time and effort to prove probable cause when there is a homicide with no body.

Although she wasn't cooperating with officers, she was methodical in the steps taken to misguide them. In his opinion she was not behaving insane at any point.

Mr Allen has no further questions.

Mr Cook begins cross-examination. He asks if the commander had physically taken the phone off Letecia. He said he asked if he could see it and she held it out and so he physically took it from her.

He asks if they had arrested Letecia on the 29th January then she wouldn't have had the chance to transport Gannon to Florida.

The commander said they had no evidence a murder had occurred at that stage, and they had no grounds to arrest her at that stage.

Mr Cook has no further questions.

The next witness called is Alyssa Berriesford. A senior crime scene investigator for Colorado Springs Crime Lab.

Mr Allen begins questioning. He asks for Ms Berriesford to be added as an expert witness.

She specialises in bloodstain pattern analysis.

Ms Berriesford was initially asked to attend to a scene regarding this case on 3rd February 2020. After that she attended the residence on the 5th February 2020.

A large number of photographs are added to evidence. The first image shown is of Gannon's bedroom with the bed removed and a portion of the carpet cut away showing the large bloodstain below. The blood spatter was five feet high and six feet wide. There was more than one event to produce the stains because the spatter was going in different directions.

A bedsheet that had been found in the wardrobe of Gannon's room was also added to evidence.

Mr Allen has no further questions.

Mr Cook begins cross-examination.

He asks her to clarify the meaning of more than one event. She says the blood spatter was indicative of spatter from gunshot wound, blunt force trauma, and sharp force trauma injuries.

Mr Cook has no further questions.

The jury have a question.

Q: **Do the bloodstain patterns at the crime scene suggest a chronological order of events?**

A:Because a lot of information was cleaned away, we couldn't tell a chronological order for it.

The court breaks for lunch.

The next witness called is Tom Griffin, a private consultant specialist in bloodstain pattern analysis, crime scene investigation and reconstruction.

Mr Griffin is added as an expert witness.

He tells the court how he was asked if he could assist in trying to determine the cause of blood spatter at the Stauch residence on the 18th February 2020. The photographs sent to him were not detailed enough and so he needed to attend in person to examine the scene on the 26th February 2020.

There were 54 stickers beside each of the bloodstains on the walls next to where Gannon's bed had been.

DNA results matched Gannon's DNA profile.

He didn't swab every stain because not all the swabs would be analysed. He would expect the other bloodstains found to also have come from Gannon.

The bloodstains on the carpet below where the bed had been measured 20 inches by 20 inches.

Mr Allen has no further questions.

Mr Tolini begin cross-examination.

He asks some clarifying questions.

No further questions for the witness.

The court takes an afternoon recess.

The next witness called is Detective Pete Woods.

Mr Young begins questioning.

He took part in the arrest of Letecia in Myrtle Beach.

Mr Young adds a selection of images into evidence.

Mr Young has no further questions.

The defence have no questions.

The next witness called is Detective Jon Price from El Paso County Sherriff's Office.

Mr Allen begins questioning.

Detective Price became involved in the search for Gannon in January 2020. He was assigned to the searches of the house and also the cars, Letecia's Tiguan and Harley's Jetta.

In the Jetta he found Harley Hunt's passport, her social security card, a passport photo, and a South Carolina school document. He also found Letecia Stauch's passport, a passport photo, a security public library card, a social security card in the name Letecia L Hardin, a social security card in the name Letecia Hardin Stauch, a spending card from a cruise, a marriage certificate between Letecia and Albert, as well as several letters and photocopies.

Mr Allen has no further questions.

Mr Cook begins cross-examination.

He begins asking the witness about cruises and he says he doesn't know anything about cruises. I presume it's because the detective had stated there was no stamps in the passports but I'm unsure why this is so important.

Mr Cook has no further questions.

The next witness called is FBI Special Agent, Amber Cronan.

Mr Allen begins questioning.

The agent was involved in the search for Gannon, she was part of the consensual calls between Al and Letecia as well as several other assignments within the case. She also travelled to South Carolina for the arrest.

There are several recorded phone calls the prosecution wish to play, the first being 46 minutes long from 15th February 2020 at 10:04am. The day is almost over so I can't see they will play the entire recording today.

Recording begins; Al says he doesn't even know what number to call her on, so he told her to call. He says he'll try the one she's texting from.

L: Hello?

Al: Hey.

L: Hey. Why are you moving again?

Al: Why do you think? It's like a week-by-week thing, I told you that. I'm like week by week in these hotels.

L: Why can't you live in the house?

Al: I don't know. I can't even go in without an escort at this point, so.

L: How are you paying for hotels?

Al: I just paid a little week by week and Uncle Jeff paid for this past week, so. I told you that already.

L: Are you by yourself?

Al: Yes.

L: Did you spend last night by yourself?

Al: Yes, who else would I be with?

L: I should've been with you, Albert.

Al: You think I wasn't lonely on freakin' Valentine's Day?

L: I should be with you. I've been begging to be with you.

Al: We can talk about that, but I wanna talk about whatever you've got... you're talking about on this iCloud.

L: I got back into my iCloud finally, because I only had partial whatever, and I couldn't do a backup and I finally got the backup done and a crap ton of messages came through; a text message they should've seen on my phone because it came through on February 5th is like a retarded person or something, but it says money or no boy. I tried to get help; I sent it to the tipline to see if they can check. I've been trying to call all morning to get help but no one –

Al: I can't hear you.

L: I said no one helps me 'cause I'm such a bad person. Can you hear me?

Al: Yeah, I can hear you now but what... I mean, that's all it said, no money no boy or something like that?

L: I'm saying there's a bunch, there's voicemails, I had 30 some voicemails, a lot of them were bull crap and threats and stuff so I went through all of them. Literally all I saw was the first message that said that, and it freaked me out and I started... I had someone to look up the number to try to see where it was at, and it said that it came from or originated from Washington so it wasn't a fake number. It wasn't one of those fake things it was an actual number. I had someone track the number to where it is now, and it said it was outside of Roy Elementary

Al: Where's that at?

L: I don't know if this is people screwing with me, but I tried to reach out to you as soon as I seen it; they should've seen this on my phone it was February 5th.

Al: I know they're like laser-focused on finding Gannon right now and that's kinda the priority right now. I mean...

L: I understand that, but that was why I was saying that. That is about Gannon, why are you trying to make it seem like I wasn't saying that?

Al: I wasn't trying to make it seem like nothing, did you tell them about what we talked about yesterday about Quincy Brown and all that?

L: I sent it in, yes. They keep saying the same thing they keep posting online because no one would write me back on the numbers that –

Al: Well, I guarantee you they're out looking for that dude right now because he is freakin'... I was getting worried about Mike and Landen and all that shit back home, and I looked him up and he's a freakin' sex offender. He's a bad dude, Tecia, and if he's got my son then I'm freakin'. You know how I was about Mike, and he had some criminal stuff, but I mean this is a whole other level so I'm sure they're out looking for him now, so.

L: Did you give them the information?

Al: Yeah, you said you did.

L: Yeah, no I did.

Al: You said you were talking to Bethel, right?

L: I sent a message to her, but she never wrote back so I had that Kate somebody's number, the other lady that was with her that day, so I sent it to her because I was like between them someone would read the messages.

Al: Ok, yeah, I haven't gotten it. Mark hasn't reached out to me this morning but I'm sure they're out, based on this dude being as horrible as he is, I'm sure they're out there looking for him. Can you remember anything else about Quincy Brown other than... I know you said you saw his ID; they had the bike or the SUV right with the bike rack. Anything close to an address at all that would help them?

L: If you would let me come be with you and help, I will walk everybody through everything, but you're refusing that and not standing up for me to do that.

Al: No, I am. I'm trying to get this relevant information that you're providing to them, so that is standing up for you.

L: (Unintelligible) Is also you've got to understand, Albert, and this is not me trying to take away from whatever. Unless I'm like protected completely... this is a whole crazy thing you've got to understand, Albert.

Al: Well, help me understand.

L: I keep begging you to tell me that. I've begged to come stay with you. I've been like, 'Babe let me come stay with you, spend the night, please I will talk to you, please' everything. I've tried everything. They just keep telling me no and I hate being lonely and I hate all this because I'm not... I am not a bad person. I'm innocent. I agreed to even take a lie detector test for you.

Al: Well, that's not for me. I don't have... I'm not gonna give you a lie detector test.

L: It's not permissible in court because it's not. It's for you to believe me.

Al: But who are you... have you talked to them about this lie detector test, or you just told me about it?

L: No, I got recalls from big time attorneys. I got Jose Baez's law firm willing to come and meet me, that's how much they know this is screwed up. Do you know who the Baez law firm is?

Al: You know I don't pay attention to that shit.

L: Do you know who they represented?

Al: No, tell me.

L: A lot of big-time names, and they're... and like People Magazine, People are like pissed that they're not... the way that things are going is not the direction that I think. If you don't want to be on my team to be like against them fucking everything then this People will put it out there.

Al: What are they gonna...?

L: What?

Al: That you're gonna take a lie detector?

L: I will for you. I'll only do it for you.

Al: Well, do it then. Let's do it now. I mean, call the FBI, and tell them you're ready to do it today.

L: I don't know who to call, I don't have the contacts. Nobody will talk to me.

Al: I sent you a number, what was her name from the FBI? Amber maybe? I sent you an email. You look back on your email you got a contact and she, when she called me that one time she reached out and said anything you need, any way we can help anything we can do to help find Gannon, and I think that would qualify as something that would help.

L: What would help?

Al: You were talking about this lie detector test.

L: That will help find Gannon? Me taking a lie detector test when I've already told you...

Al: If you're... listen, listen. I know but listen to me. Walk through this logically, you're smart now, okay. If you're saying they're barking up the wrong tree and that wrong tree is you and a lie detector test will get them off of that tree and on a different tree, don't you think that will help?

L: Yeah.

Al: I mean, it'll... back to what we talked about yesterday, it'll show your innocence. It'll show you didn't do it. It'll show you don't even need immunity. Okay? It'll prove all those things.

L: I'll still have to because lie detector tests are not permissible in court.

Al: Okay, but I'm just trying to... you said you'd do that for me.

L: All a lie detector test does is prove what a person's saying to the person they're trying to prove it to, like people go on Dr Phil and do it, places like that.

Al: Okay, alright, Tecia. Tecia, listen...

L: No, you listen.

Al: I'm willing to take the lie detector test, you brought it up, I mean, I'm willing to work with you or whatever you can contact the FBI and do it and I'm willing to take that result for my peace of mind, but if you're gonna sit here and tell me it's not worthwhile then why even talk about it?

L: I said for you. I said I wanted to do it for you! You're focusing on doing it for someone else, I'm trying to tell you that I wanted –

Al: No, no it's not about me, It's not about you. It's about Gannon. If they're barking up the wrong tree, babe, if they're barking up the wrong tree this'll get them up the right tree.

L: Okay.

Al: So, you need to reach out to Amber whatever her name is, that's the FBI lady that I talked to the one time, and you need to tell her whatever you're willing to do or not do, okay? That's the only way I know to go about it so, but, instead of me waiting on a lie detector test for me and you, I know that'll confirm it, just tell me the truth right now.

L: You won't even help me get the freaking ID so I can go to our doctor's office, and you want me to just keep going over and over and over the same thing.

Al: Tecia, yes, I do, because—

L: Did you kick me off of Tricare or something?

Al: I can't kick you off of Tricare, that only happens... anyway, you're trying to spin this in a different direction, we're talking about Gannon here.

L: I'm just trying to go to the doctor, that's it.

Al: You can go to the doctor any day of the week. I can't kick you off of Tricare.

L: They took all my stuff, I need an ID.

Al: You need the sponsor's social security number and I know you know my social so don't even play me, Tecia.

L: I can't go on base without the ID.

Al: Okay, well if you've gotta go to the doctor that bad, go somewhere else and we'll pay the fee, okay? That's... I'm not gonna say that's irrelevant but we're focused on Gannon right now, okay?

L: Okay, and I'm trying to be with you to focus on Gannon, so I'm asking –

Al: And guess what, we are talking together right now so we are working on this together right now on the phone. Okay?

L: Let me come and stay with you and I'll meet with them to do the test and everything

Al: Listen, I need the truth first and that's what I've said the whole time. Tell me the same, listen, let's just stop. Okay, no, don't 'oh god' me –

L: I said I'll do a lie detector test and it's still not good enough for you, Albert?

Al: No, it is, it's perfect, that's what I want you to do, okay, because there has been multiple stories, but tell me the story right now that you're gonna tell on the lie detector test, that's what I want.

L: You don't tell stories on a lie detector test.

Al: I know, okay, do you want me to put you through that and ask you questions? I'll do it, okay. Is the bike accident a true story? Did he fall and bust his head or was his head already bleeding before you got there? Which one is it?

L: Was he bleeding?

Al: I'm just asking. Was the bike accident true?

L: Why would he already be bleeding?

Al: I don't know, because I've fallen off my bike a hundred times and didn't bust my head bad enough to go to the 911, right? Okay, I'm just trying to sort through this. Is the bike accident true?

L: Albert, I did not hurt Gannon.

Al: I didn't ask you that, Okay? Is the bike accident true? It's yes or no. This is the lie detector test right now. Yes or no.

L: You... somebody has Gannon, Albert. I need protection to help you.

Al: I understand that and I'm trying to help you right now.

L: He will beat me, he will abuse me, he will hurt me, and I keep telling you this and you're not catching the hint.

Al: Is the bike accident true? That's where we're starting.

L: Are you gonna protect me from him?

Al: Yes, once you call Amber, you're gonna get the protection you need. I don't have a gun, I don't have a badge, Amber does and she's the one that's gonna protect you.

L: But you are my husband.

Al: I am and as your husband you need to respect that I'm trying to give you the best guidance I have, okay? And get you to the protection you're asking for. If you call Amber, she'll get somebody with you wherever you're at, to protect you, okay?

L: But why aren't you willing to do that?

Al: How am I gonna protect you against people trying to beat you and kill you?

L: Let me come live with you because you are my husband and you're supposed to provide for a place to stay.

Al: Right, and I've done that from day one so you're not gonna question my ability to protect or provide for you so listen, hey back up, you said you wanted to do something for me.

L: Listen to me, Albert, let me come stay with you.

Al: No, I'm not answering any questions right now because you told me that you'd do something for me and that's answer some yes and no questions, basically a lie detector.

L: I want to be with you, I didn't say like you're gonna put me on... we can talk about this in person why does it have to be over the phone so you can like record people and shit?

Al: So now I'm recording you? What you've done to me for five years is what I'm doing to you? That's projection Tecia and I'm not putting up with that. Okay? Alright?

L: Did you record me yesterday?

Al: No. Why would I record you? I haven't recorded anything. What are you talking about?

L: Was anybody coaching you what to say?

Al: No. I don't need a coach. I've done this for a living for 11 years, Tecia.

L: I said I want to talk to you in person.

Al: Alright, well guess what. Your frickin sister is calling me, tell her to leave me alone.

L: Who? What sister?

Al: Amy whatever her name is.

L: She shouldn't be calling you. I don't even talk to them.

Al: Well, I've been getting calls and texts from all your people, and I don't... I'm sick of it. Listen, I... you know what, if meeting is what it takes to get to the truth, I'll meet with you, but you need to answer some questions first. That's your way of proving to me that a meeting is worthwhile. Okay?

L: Okay.

Al: Number one, I got three or four questions, okay? Number one: Is the bike accident true?

L: No.

Al: No. Is Quincy Brown true?

L: Yes.

Al: Yes. Okay, so what happened? That's my next question. What happened to get Gannon to Quincy Brown? How did Quincy Brown get my son?

L: It doesn't matter how many times I tell you, you're still gonna call me a liar, you're not gonna take it back.

Al: That's not true, now, that's not true. I've given you every opportunity to tell the truth just like I'm doing now, okay? I haven't called you a liar. I've said some pieces of the story have been not true, okay? I'm not sitting here calling you names or putting you down. I'm asking for the truth. You said the bike accident is not true now. Fair enough, we're done with that now. What happened?

L: We were going to get you a bike, though. That was true.

Al: Okay, so you were going to get me a bike, fine. Okay, let's get past the bike if the bike has nothing to do with anything then let's just forget about the bike and the trip to get the bike.

L: I was trying to be a cool mom, okay?

Al: Okay.

L: Gannon wanted to hang out with some friend, and I was just trying to be cool because I'm never looked at as being cool, so I told Gannon he could have a sleepover whatever, whatever, whatever, yadda, yadda, yadda, that was supposed to happen on Saturday or something. He did have this friend who had a car and I told him your daddy said no, on Sunday or whatever day it was, but prior to today he already said something to me about this, I tried to talk through the situation. So, the plan was he was gonna have a sleepover, we planned most of this together yadda, yadda, yadda, yadda, that was just supposed to be the plan. I was just trying to be a cool mom. I just wanted to be accepted by Gannon for him to be like, wow, yes she's always kind of strict on us but maybe she maybe let me do a little bit that I shouldn't probably be doing. Hey, that's all.

Al: Yeah, but that's –

L: It went downhill from there, I'm telling you. I didn't do anything to Gannon.

Al: Okay, so...

L: Listen to me!

Al: I'm sorry, I'm listening.

L: And all these people putting all this stupid stuff up about blood and all this bull-crap, if there was any blood in that house 'cause of Gannon, Gannon bleeds all the time.

Al: Okay.

L: There's no massacre occurred in our home! That's not what people are putting in your head it's nothing like that. Okay? It's nothing. I'm sick of hearing people say, well if he hurt his foot he couldn't be walking. Oh my God! It was just blood from his foot. That's it. There was no like he hit his head or bull-crap like that. I'm tired of all these conspiracy theorists and now it's in your head that you think that I've done something to Gannon in our house because that's what you said yesterday. That is not true. If there was blood it was just simply from what happened to his foot, and I already admitted to you that his arm was burned.

Al: Okay.

L: I already admitted that to you. It wasn't that bad. Did it have blood? Yes. (Unintelligible) candle was. I did everything I could so if you're asking about that part of it... see what you're doing is trying to take two different things. You're trying to think that just because I didn't abuse Gannon emotionally in the video, nothing. The whole point of that was he was so upset, and it wasn't about, it was meaning I was gonna replace the items for him. It was trying to be, okay don't worry about it, it's a secret I'm not gonna say anything. I was trying to be cool. Okay?

Maybe if I let my guard down for trying to be cool, I let him stay up 30 minutes late that night trying to be cool. Just trying to be like we'll start working on hey you staying up 30 minutes later than Laina. So, any of that that you got from some mind that people are trying to say I was abusing him on some video shit, it was not. Gannon was upset because I was sitting there holding him and everybody's saying something about whatever. I assessed the situation. It wasn't a lot of tons and tons of blood, we got it up, it was on his wall a little bit. It was not even a lot.

Al: So, you cleaned his wall up?

L: He did.

Al: Oh, okay.

L: There was blood on the thing, we cleaned it up. It was from his arm and his foot, that's all from helping me outside. There was nobody's head getting hit. I'm sick of hearing all these stories that Gannon's head was hit—he was doing this. No, Albert, if he would've been in that situation, I'd get on the phone and I'd call 911. I'm not stupid. Do you think I'd much rather be sitting here with someone saying that I was irresponsible or whatever and someone accusing me of hurting my child? Do you think that? That's the way I panic at the sight of blood? You would've been freaked out. I'm like oh my god stop peeling it. He peeled it and peeled it and peeled it. If I yell at him for peeling it, it's gonna look like I'm mad at him. You don't understand.

Al: Okay.

L: I told everybody the true story but what they're doing is they're coming in there and saying just because, just because some lady who thinks she's hot shit that's been talking to you apparently, she posts online all this bullshit

Al: Who? Who? What lady?

L: Who knows. Truvia somebody.

Al: Who?

L: She's fucking stupid.

Al: I haven't talked to nobody.

L: Well, she's online saying she's talking to you and Landen, and you and Landen was saying there was blood all over Gannon's room, blood everywhere in the house, blood on the stairs. That is not true.

Al: Who is this now?

L: If it was anything it was from the foot and I stepped, not outside, I stepped in it on the carpet where I frickin picked the carpet up that we walk outside on. But nobody cares that that's how it happened, that's where blood came from. Do you - it was not puddles! If we cleaned it up and smeared it, sorry.

Al: What freaking lady are you talking about?

L: The beds were already pushed together because I told Gannon he could have a sleep-over.

Al: The beds were pushed together?

L: I had pushed them together because I had told him that Sunday he could have a sleepover. I didn't know that his stomach was gonna go start hurting. I had already said he was doing his box.

Al: But who was the sleepover with? Was it Brayden?

L: He just asked me could he have a sleepover even though it was a school night after we were gonna go on a hike? The reason I said yes is he was talking to me about the Kobe thing, and he was talking about the sisters and all he had was his sisters and I said yes, just because I felt so bad because here we are, both in an emotional moment, I'm upset about Kobe, he's upset about him having girls, yadda, yadda, yadda, I agreed. Sorry. I usually don't agree with things. I was trying to be like, okay maybe this is a good chance to maybe bend the rules just a little bit. So yes. I said Gannon, you can have a sleepover. Gannon pushed his beds together, yadda, yadda, yadda. I don't know what happened. Why he didn't go ask about the sleepover I don't know what happened, wherever. I don't know. He didn't ever come say such and such didn't say whatever, I just know his stomach was hurting so I assumed he didn't want to be having a sleepover with the boys, whoever the boy was...

Al: But why?

L: ... just tell me –

Al: Hang on, hang on. Why, so you were gonna let... let me back up.

L: I was gonna let the boy, but he said his brother had a car.

Al: Right, okay, okay fine. But. He's never pushed the beds together for a sleepover before, where did that come from?

L: What do you mean, I do.

Al: No, usually they –

L: Albert, we pushed the beds together 'cause we had all the things lined up around the room and little cardboard box things. They were all lined up around the room and we pushed the beds together. That was it. I mean, me pushing the beds together is not a crime.

Al: I'm not saying it was, it's just weird because to my knowledge he's never done that before.

L: I guess he was gonna build a fort, I don't know. It was just for Sunday, they got pushed back. It was nothing.

Al: Okay, alright.

L: So that is the only reason. That is the only reason when they got pushed back that he would've had back to normal, that he would've peeled his arm after it happened on Sunday. What I would do is to get whoever your friend is and neighbour that knows all this bullshit to give you the video footage of me running out when the doggone fire was going off and you will see all. Was I being whatever...? Was I fussing? Was I doing anything but being loving to children?

Al: Right.

L: I told everybody, it's okay, we're gonna fix it. Nobody was yelling at anybody. Nobody was angry at anybody. Nobody was hurting anybody. Nobody was doing anything wrong.

Al: So –

L: I wasn't even mad, I was scared.

Al: Back up to something you said that really struck me, Tecia. You said it all went downhill. What do you mean? How did it go downhill and then how did this Quincy Brown frickin' dude get involved?

L: You know the story about Quincy! He told me –

Al: Okay, but tell me the part about how did it go downhill? That's what I need to know. You said it went downhill fast and it got out of control, and you know maybe you freaked out whatever but...

L:I never said anything about getting out of control, now you're putting words in my mouth. I never said that.

Al: You said it went downhill, Tecia.

L: I said it went downhill, meaning Gannon was supposed to have a sleepover, his stomach started hurting, that's he didn't get to have a sleepover. That's what it means, it means that.

Al: I got you. I got you.

L: We stayed up late. See how when I talk to you do you see how you already put me as if I'm some criminal?

Al: No. No, I haven't criminalized you at all. I'm asking you questions. That's what you wanted me to do and I'm asking you questions.

L: ... I mean, really? Come on Albert. That is not you saying to me, you know, how many times have you left out of time and my wife just took care of everything. That's not you doing that, that's not you taking my side, that's you picking up on...

Al: Hey, I can't hear you.

L: I said you're saying something about us putting beds together when the child was building a box because you saw it, this is a box for my son. It's a problem if I get involved, and it's a problem if I do it the wrong way. What's the right way?

Al: I'm just trying to –

L: (Unintelligible)

Al: Tecia, babe, listen, okay. I mean, I'm worried to death about Gannon's safety, where he's at, all these things. Yesterday, what you told me the bike story is not true now, okay, but, but you also said he had a head...

L: You know how I feel, if you want me to be honest with you, you know how I feel? I feel like if I just tell you something like that, it's what you wanna hear. That's honestly how you make me feel. You make me feel like if I just tell you there's some... I even sit there and listen to you go, 'Okay, it was an accident okay...' is this what you want me to say?

Al: No.

L: ... because that is not, Albert.

Al: Actually, yes, it is. As a recruiter I did this same shit for 11 years having to dig into people's past and everything to get the truth. Alright, listen, listen you told me you keep telling me what I just wanna hear, I just wanna hear the truth Tecia, okay? Hold on, no, no, listen. Yesterday, and we've passed this point, but you said there was a bike accident with a head injury so is it just the bike accident that's not true or is it the head injury that's also not true?

L: There's no head injury or bike accident. I just told you I felt like you wanted me to say something to you.

Al: Okay, so now what did freakin' Quincy Brown do with Gannon?

L: Can I ask you something? Do you think I...? First of all, why don't you put this in perspective.

Al: Okay.

L: Do you think I even know my way around Colorado first off?

Al: Yeah, we've been here a year now, you go all over the place.

L: Okay. Colorado Springs, right?

Al: Yes, and we've been all over up there, around the outlets and we've been up to Denver a bunch. I think you know a little bit about Colorado so don't play me on that, Tecia.

L: I wasn't, see I wasn't even going there but you see how I said that just to see you jump at me? You see how I said that?

Al: Well, good, you got me. You got me jumpin', alright? My son's out there missing with Quincy Brown, and you got me jumpin', you win. What's your next question?

L: Listen to me? Can you listen to me?

Al: Yeah, sure.

L: Alright.

Mr Allen pauses the recording and the court breaks for the day.

CHAPTER 12

LETECIA STAUCH TRIAL – DAY 11 -19TH APRIL 2023

The court resumes where they left off yesterday with the recorded phone call between Al and Letecia.

L: How many days has it been? I have not... there is nowhere that I could take Gannon that he would just be gone that many days. You have to put that in your brain.

Al: Oh, yeah, it is in my brain. It's in my brain that he's gone and there's nowhere he could be, safely, okay? Because he's with this Quincy Brown guy who's a freakin' sex offender, jumpin' bail, whatever you wanna label him. Whatever, I don't know. You know I don't know all that shit, he's just a bad dude and my son's with him.

L: I told you this.

Al: Okay, alright.

L: I told you what happened. I told you when we came home. I already told you all this. When I told you the truth, this is what you did. You said to me, 'Hey that's not how it happened'.

Al: But you told me the truth? You told me four different versions of the truth, Tecia. That's where the problem is. I want to believe you.

L: The details and you're asking me three weeks later detail for detail.

Al: Yes, absolutely, but in your own words now that you've slept on it and now that you've recovered a little bit you're starting to remember more and more and more so what I wanna know–

L: I've given you everything I remember.

Al: The detail I wanna know is what did Quincy Brown do with Gannon? That's the detail I wanna know, that's the question.

L: I don't know where he took him, I don't know where they went. Don't you think for a second If I knew that, Albert, I would tell you.

Al: Where did he take him from? That's a starting point. where were you at when he took him?

L: At home.

Al: Okay, so yesterday was the bike accident and then...

L: I already told you that. You already talked about...

Al: Fine, but I'm saying yesterday he was taken from Douglas County today he's taken from El Paso County at 6627. Right? Then you changed it and brought it back then you changed it and brought it back.

L: I said that to you because you just want me to say whatever they got you thinking.

Al: I'm thinking what I'm thinking, okay? Nobody... these freaking police have not told me a damn thing other than my son is missing and that they're supposedly looking for him. You're the only one telling me anything about the situation.

L: Albert.

Al: Yes.

L: I told you. He took your gun I couldn't do anything. You talk about how you have to live with that. Do you know how I have to sit here and be like, oh my God, what could I have done to protect him better? Because Albert's gonna turn it and say that I'm a horrible person. You think I want to lose my entire life because I couldn't protect someone 100 percent?

Al: Do you know if Gannon is alive? Or was he alive when he took him? Was he hurt?

L: I don't know, I was out of it. Do you not understand this?

Al: So, you were out... you were blacked out right? And he took him while you were blacked out?

L: No. I just said I was in and out of it from a struggle I hit my head I was in and out of it, he put my arms tied up. You would not listen to me on that. You know what you should've done? As my husband you should've said, 'oh my god this fucker's not only hurt my wife, but took my son,' that's what you should be saying.

Al: I'm trying to believe you, okay? But when I got home Tuesday you had no sign of anything, no marks on your head no marks on your arms, no...

L: Oh, that's a lie, you wanna know why? Because it's all on social media why I have band-aids on my head and my arms? So that's a fuckin' lie.

Al: Okay, alright, fair enough. I ain't seen...

L: It's on social media. It's on social media why all kinds of everything.

Al: Well, it's on social media that you killed him, so you want me to believe everything that I hear on social media?

L: No, because you're... Albert! Why in the world would you think that?

Al: I'm not thinking that. You just told me to believe social media, social media says you're a killer.

L: I said it's on there, meaning they saw it. They saw a picture of me, that's all I meant. I didn't kill anyone.

Al: Social media says you're a killer and that Landen's the hero, do you want me to believe that?

L: Well, if you believe that, you're dumb, you wanna know why? Because you know better than that.

Al: Okay, well.

L: I mean, you're treating her like she's a hero, that's exactly what you're doing instead of being with your wife you've been with your ex-wife.

Al: I haven't been with nobody, I told you, I've been with my family.

L: (Unintelligible) ... you're supposed to be?

Al: You can attack me all you want to, okay, but it really doesn't matter.

L: I'm not attacking you.

Al: Yes, that's an attack.

L: It isn't. You should be with your wife.

Al: Okay, well what's with all this crap you're sending her now. You're telling the world how much of a piece of shit she is, but now you're trying to–

L: I'm not sending her anything. My shit has been hacked, I can't... don't believe nothing unless it's my doggone Yahoo. People have created a fake profile under my name, they've screened the profiles, everything. People were... don't... the only thing I have secured is because I contacted Yahoo is my Yahoo account. Don't listen to anything from anything else.

Al: Okay, fine, but you sent her a message that said the same thing you tried to say to me initially about this ransom and these phone calls from DC so yes, I do believe that you sent her that.

L: Me?

Al: That's what you told me.

L: From DC?

Al: That's what you told me.

L: (Unintelligible).

Al: That's what you told me.

L: Oh. I... do you know why I done that? That's because he sent it from a stupid messenger thing and when I switched up to my phone thing I was trying to write back from, I was like I'm gonna send Landen this too. I was gonna copy both of y'all and because I couldn't get you and I hit draft so if it went through then. I didn't talk to her –

Al: No, no, no, no, no. Landen didn't send anything from DC, you said that the messages came from a DC number or something, that's what you said.

L: Washington, like Washington, Seattle.

Al: Oh, Washington Seattle. Oh, okay. Gotcha.

L: I did tell you that, I said Washington. I said Roy Elementary.

Al: Okay.

L: I haven't said another word to her. Read the emails I sent her when she wrote me, I told her fuck her, she didn't do a goddamn thing for those kids. Don't be playing hero, read 'em. Since you were sitting right beside her.

Al: They went to Texas, I ain't reading shit. I just saw something she forwarded me. She forwarded me something about ransom.

L: She wrote you. I mean, you wrote me that night and as soon as I said something to you about her playing bingo you had to be sitting right beside her, you had to tell her that.

Al: Wait, woah, woah, woah, no. You talking about when she replied to you after that one email you sent when you said fuck her? I was-

L: No–

Al: I'm gonna tell you what happened.

L: (Unintelligible).

Al: No, she didn't, okay. I'll tell you what happened. I was sitting there in the room, they had another hotel room, it was at that time of night that Laina was going to bed and every night I put Laina to bed and the email came through and she read it and that's when she messaged you back and that's the absolute truth and, you know, you can question it all you want to, but that's what happened. I don't show them shit, okay? Because all I...

L: I defended you and I defended myself and said, 'You ain't done no-fucking-thing, don't be coming up in my house you shouldn't be here', did she tell you I said all that?

Al: Listen, I don't get into nothing she said and that's the God's honest truth. She's freaking out every single day and it's driving me nuts so I'm glad they went to Texas, okay?

L: Yeah.

Al: It drives me... between her and Veronica, driving me frickin' nuts.

L: Why do you have to be around them?

Al: I'm not around them, okay? We're looking for our son. We have a shared child in common.

L: The stress on you, if you were listening to them, will drive you nuts.

Al: And guess what, you know me well enough to know I'm gonna get myself out of stressful situations that are not productive. You know that.

L: I know that. So, is this why you wouldn't... you don't want me and Harley to be with you?

Al: I never said that.

L: Or do you have to just keep doing that?

Al: I never said that.

L: I have agreed to do everything you've asked. I've told you whatever. I've agreed to testify, okay? I've agreed to help find him. I've agreed to do everything. I'm tired of being portrayed as the killer of a child that I love. If you wanna know something, I have a better relationship with Gannon than I even do Laina. Gannon and I (unintelligible) with the bike. This is why it's killing me. It's killing me because how it's portrayed is wrong.

Al: Okay, let's pump the brakes here okay. I'm serious, let's pump the brakes. If you give me the truth, and I hate to say it like this, but the whole truth and nothing but the truth and you just lay it on the line for me no matter what the truth is, okay? The absolute truth,

I don't want no more Quincy lying on the road, Quincy bike accident, Quincy hiding in the house, okay? Quincy's secret messages, okay? Ransom. I don't want no more of that, okay. This is driving me frickin' nuts, okay? I just want the truth and then I... no, hey, you listen to me for a second. I want the truth right now and then I'll be willing to meet you.

L: Meet me? Meet me. Like, just meet. That's, that's how... that's all I get is meet you?

Al: Listen, I'm sitting right here, I'm trying to work with you, okay? That's a start, okay? That's a start, I told you yesterday...

L: I want my life. I want my family.

Al: I told you yesterday, the biggest thing in between us right now is the truth, and we have a big gap between us and the truth right now, okay? Alright? I'm not promising you, listen.

L: You're not planning being with me...

Al: I'm not...

L: ... separated.

Crosstalk.

Al: I'm not promising you anything, okay. I want to truth, and I will promise you a meeting.

L: (Unintelligible).

Al:You can come, yes, you're my wife okay. I'm not promising you anything today other than a meeting. You give me the truth, you get your meeting, you get your face to face, you get to see me. All these wonderful things you send me on email about how much you want me...

L: I want to be with you.

Al: Okay, you get to meet with me today that's what you get. You left, and I'm offering you a meeting.

L: Just a meeting? I left? I left? Or I was taken away?

Al: No, you left out of...

L: You can't say about me leaving. No, no, no, no, no, no. You brought your ex-wife to our home and that was wrong.

Al: I didn't bring nobody. She got her ass on a plane and came, and the messages show that you told her that you would support her when you got here so we're not playing this game. She is irrelevant in this conversation.

L: I said I need to ask Albert and then what did I do? I got on the phone with you, and I said I don't agree with this.

Al: Okay, fine.

L: That's exactly what...

Al: You know what? My son's missing, I don't care about stupid petty... you think I'm hooking up with her? It's about Gannon, so you give me the truth and I'll meet.

L: It's not about hooking up with her it's about you (unintelligible)...

Al: But that's all you said. Tecia, stop. Take a break.

L: ... on the damn TV hugging your ex-wife.

Al: Actually, I should because she's the mother of my son and I'm not playing this game with you, okay. Do you want to meet or not?

L: Do you wanna know what?

Al: Do you wanna meet or not?

L: You wanna know something? You should? Then guess what, this wife of yours has done everything that that sorry ass motherfucking mother hasn't done. Okay.

Al: I'm not arguing with you about that, I'm not arguing about anything.

L: Do you think I got a hug from you?

Al: You got plenty of hugs, you got plenty of hugs until you decided to bounce—come and get your shit and bounce.

L: I asked for Valentine's Day, I said, hey let us come stay, do you think you gave me anything? But you can give her conversations every day you could talk to her every day?

Al: Listen, you've been begging me, let... listen.

L: Do you tell this shit to the kids?

Al: Let me tell you something.

L: God, how dare you

Al: You're not making yourself believable to me. You offered the truth, okay? You offered lie detector tests. I don't even believe you're anywhere close to here, that's why you're dodging this meeting, okay? That's the God's honest.

L: I'm not dodging the meeting, I...

Al: Yeah, you are.

L:... I've begged you for days.

Al: Yeah, you are. You're dodging this shit.

L: You call me from your hotel you won't even tell me where you're staying.

Al: Well, I asked you the same question and you won't even tell me where ... you tell me.

L: I gave it to you.

Al: You said the North Inn.

L: The place I was staying.

Al: You said the North Inn, bullshit.

L: I said Extended Stay America. Yes, I did.

Al: Bullshit.

L: Go look at your emails

Al: I know, and its bullshit. You don't think I didn't drive around there? Just like I drove around there looking for other shit.

L: Drive around there? I don't have a car how did you think you were going to find me?

Al: Screenshot me a receipt right now. Send me the receipt from your email 'cause I know you got it cause you always get em, okay? So, don't play me, homie, alright? Send me this shit, and then I'll believe you.

L: Do you think for one second, do you think for one second that I paid for this? Do you think that?

Al: Alright, fine. Alright back up. Back up. You give me the truth and I'll drive to frickin' Extended Stay America right now. Give me the truth.

L:I gave you the truth. I walked you through what happened.

Al: No, you walked me through 27 versions of a fake bullshit lie, okay? Alright? Tell me the truth right now.

L: Now you're, see, you want the truth, but you just told me it was a lie. You're not trying to be on my side.

Al: I am. I'm trying to meet you.

L: You literally just told me it was a fake bullshit of a lie. You told me none of it was true.

Al: Tecia, I got to ask you every day –

L: You just told me that

Al: I got to ask you every day, like yesterday was the bike accident. That was the first time I heard that one after 3 weeks, okay? Now today I call you back willing to work with you for a lie detector test and that's a bullshit story. Okay?

L: I already said I would do a lie detector test. I already told you I would do a lie detector test.

Al: That's completely irrelevant, what's relevant is the truth. You get me, at Extended Stay America... Listen you get me at Extended Stay America, you can do whatever you want to with me, okay? I just want the truth and that's what you get.

L: Okay. Like, yeah, you're really gonna let that happen.

Al: Listen, you give me the truth and we find my son.

L: If you wanted me, you would not be apart from me.

Al: Tecia, watch your interview, you said you left because of Landen. You said that, not me. I didn't say Tecia leave. I said everybody come together, be a team, let's find Gannon, that's what I said. And that's what I've said from day one. And you bounced on me.

L:I left from the house because you had her there in our home

Al: I sure did, and I'll tell every judge and jury in this country that I had my ex-wife, my mom, my two sisters, my uncle, Aunt Veronica, two other freakin' women, Landen's brother, I had a team of like 15 people supporting the family working as a team to do everything we could to find Gannon. That's the truth.

L: I'm sorry if it sounds selfish but I hate that bitch, okay.

Al: Well, guess what, listen to what I just said, listen to what I just said. I had everybody in the house, but you know who wasn't there? You know who wasn't there? My wife and my daughter. They bounced on me, they bounced on me, but me being the good person, I'm still here willing to listen to you.

L: You told my mom we had to turn the keys in to you.

Al: I told her that you can come get your stuff after you said you didn't wanna be there anymore, okay? You left. You and Harley got in Harley's car, packed suitcases, supposedly going to the police station and you never showed up until like the next day or some shit like that okay? So, if you would've done what you were supposed to...

L: (Unintelligible)

Al: No, you listen to me, if you would've done what you were supposed to, we wouldn't be having this conversation right now, okay? So don't turn this on me. I've been a team player this whole time for the entire team.

L:We would be together right now is what you're saying?

Al: If you would've never left, we wouldn't be having this conversation. You got your shit, and you bounced, okay? What we need now is the truth.

L: So, you're saying if I would've never left, we'd be together right now?

Al: I'm saying you bounced, okay? You bounced.

L: Okay see, see that's your point you don't have any... you don't want to be with me.

Al: That's not what I'm saying, it's not about our relationship it's about Gannon and you're dodging me when I keep asking for the truth saying I'm gonna drive to you at Extended Stay America.

Letecia hangs up.

Agent Cronin is called back to the stand.

Mr Allen resumes his questioning. He asks her if she was present for all the calls between Al and Letecia. She says she was.

The main aim was for Al to get the information from Letecia in order to find out the whereabouts of Gannon. She says during this phone call Letecia was in South Carolina and not local as she implied to Al.

She said they didn't believe Quincy Brown was involved in the disappearance of Gannon although they did look him up. The discovered Quincy Brown was a sexual offender who was on the most wanted list that week in the Colorado Springs area. However, they knew he wasn't even in the country at that time.

The next recording was another call between Al and Letecia that occurred on the 15th February 2020 at 12:10pm.

L: Hello?

Al: Hey.

L: Hello?

Al: Hey, can you hear me?

L: Yeah, I can hear you.

Al: So, I just got off the phone with that Amber lady and I don't know, I kinda feel stupid now 'cause she's like no I ain't heard from nobody about nothing like that.

L: I sent her a message.

Al: I'm just telling you what she said to me.

L: Was it a cell phone number or a landline cause I sent it to the number you gave me so if it was a landline maybe she didn't get it but if it's a cell phone then she got it.

Al: Okay, I'm just telling you what the lady told me. I don't know. Like I told you, I don't know what's going on.

L: Is it a cell phone or a landline?

Al: I don't know. I called and she answered, that's all I know. I mean, you wanna hang up and try to call her?

L: I'm telling you it's gotta be a cell phone

Al: Do you wanna hang up and try to call her? I'm just so sick of this, I'm just, listen...

L: (Unintelligible)... hanging up to call the FBI?

Al: You don't have to. I'm just asking do you wanna hang up and try to call her instead of messaging her? What I'm saying is I just want things to go back to like they were like Christmas like right when we got the two puppies, all the kids were there, everybody was so happy, kids were playing their switch, we were playing with the puppies and it's just life was just like happy as could be, and then like... and then here we are. I just wanna go back to that, Tecia, why can't we just get back to that place in our life?

L: Albert?

Al: What?

L: Do you think for a second that's not on my mind every single day and that's not what I want? I - I put it so much effort into Christmas and what you're saying. How much effort I put into Christmas and holidays for everyone? And you think for a second that's not what I want? I go out of my way for all of our children, I have tons and tons of clothing, everything that's (unintelligible)... who do you think bought it? Who do you think did all that? Do you want - don't you think I love doing that? Want to (unintelligible) and I pray every day that's exactly... I wake up every morning looking for you and realise I'm not beside you then realise I'm not helping the kids get ready for school. You think I don't know that and want that? I didn't like, I wasn't going through some turmoil. You know I loved my life. I hate myself. We had a great life, we have a great family, like, really?

So don't bring up Christmas and how you want the dogs. You think that I don't get to be like, oh gosh you know, guess what? It's the 17th so happy anniversary every 17th month by month by month, think that's not coming up, you think I don't want to do that? You think the kids do not think about that every time? All the kids.

You know why Landen pops up and gets to be the saint cause it's the 100th day of school? I got the kids in the school. I kept them in school. I homeschooled them. You think I don't want all that back? Come on now.

Al: Well, how–

L: You think I don't want (unintelligible)... doing all these different things when Gannon finally gets to middle school because maybe just maybe the whole point in us selling (unintelligible)... you know, he might be interested in the sport, so that I can be at the schoolhouse and be a part of. You think I don't miss all this and want it?

Al: Well, how do we get it back? How do we get back to just a month and a half ago? That's what I wanna know. 'Cause a month and a half ago there was five people and two dogs, now it's just me, so how do we get back there?

L: Albert?

Al: Like, I don't even have, listen... I don't even have Laina, she's in Texas right now. I'm frickin'...

L: Hey! That's your fault, let me just go ahead and tell you because you shouldn't have allowed that to happen, that was irresponsible on your part, okay? And you could think that I'm wrong or for whatever reason you want to, don't agree with that, because at the end of the fucking day she's still a drug addict, she still don't take care for her kids, and she still don't have a place to live. I wouldn't have let my child left with her so that's on you, that's not me. I didn't make that decision and would've never made that decision.

Al: So, but... She's coming back, don't get me wrong. She's coming back, I'm just talking about this weekend, okay. She's down there with them but even then, how do we get back to the five of us? The five of us. Me, you, Harley, Gannon, and Laina? How do we get back to that point? How do we have a family and two dogs and a two-story house and all the things that we had, and three cars and you know the American dream. Right now, I'm living the American nightmare. How do I get back to the American dream? I need you to help me get there.

L: Albert. The first step is we figure out... the people in this world are cruel, okay, they are, people are cruel, okay. You in your mind know better most, that American Dream you just talked about, we would have never had it if any of those five people in our home would have been cruel. If any of those five people would have been out to hurt people or do bad things to people, okay. So that's the first step that you need to realise is that this is not me against you. Yeah, of course people always in marriages are gonna have disagreements but you know good and well we literally just got off a cruise for our anniversary. I made sure that the children were in the best care possible with someone staying there not only with Harley, okay, someone, an adult like to make sure that they had everything they needed, not a worry in the world. You know I've always done that.

I've always had security systems installed, checked the ring app, check the alarm. You know me as that person so until you put that in your mind, that's the first step because you can't be against your wife on this. And you can't be thinking what these people are thinking online, that I'm this devil, because that's not true. Without me, without me, and God, the children would not be in our home and without you and God, the children would not be in our home because they were in a horrible situation.

In order to get back to where it is, we need to figure out who can help us. Who can help us figure out the best way to get Gannon? Whether whatever it is. Do you want me to give him my legs? Do you want me to give him my arms?

Al: No, no, no, listen, I'm telling you, I told you this yesterday. I feel like this is all gonna be my fault in the end, okay, because I was gone when this happened so, don't...

L: No-

Al: Don't sit there and offer your legs and arms up when it's my fault.

L: I'm not gonna let you say that and here's why, okay? Let me tell you here's why, because when you were in Oklahoma for 5 months, I had to be the one staying and checking to make sure the kids were okay. I had to be the one driving, making sure of this, that, saving people barely getting time with them. I had to do that for you. I had to drive through the night to Orlando through a hurricane to get them to you in Oklahoma, okay.

Al: But you gotta understand... let me tell you how I feel, let me tell you my feelings. What is one of the most important things to me that I always say? Protection, right? And I failed in that because I couldn't protect my son and I couldn't protect you from getting your head smashed and all these other things, okay? So that's how I'm feeling right now. So how do we get back to what we were with five people in our family?

L: We were! We are that. Why are we saying get back to it? That's what we are.

Al: No, because I'm one person. Gannon's unknown, you and Harley bounced, Laina's with Landen, okay? That's not five people. That's four people somewhere and one person unknown. So how do we get Gannon back, number one?

L: Let me ask you a question, okay? We're gonna sit if we're gonna sit here and we're gonna say okay we're gonna focus on two separate things here. The first thing is we're gonna come back to getting Gannon back and all that. But let me ask you what you just said. Let me answer to what you just said. You can't teach your mind that that's what you wanna get back if, a)... let me just back up and say this. Tecia and Harley didn't leave, this is what happened. Tecia and Harley came back after they took absolutely everything from me. I went in, you were laying on the sofa and I tried to talk to you. I said come to the bedroom let me talk to you, okay? I tried, but then they... you helped them, you did, instead of just calling to say, 'Hey listen they wanna take Harley's car and they wanna take her phone,' you did never say that, okay? You could've been trusting and said that to me. You know good and well I have a lot that I've worked hard for to throw away (unintelligible). You could've called me. You could've said that. Instead, they chased us down and your child that you're saying you want back in your life, and you want, was put in handcuffs when she was buying underwear.

Al: I'll stop you right there. All that's my fault, you're right. I could've stopped it. I could've said, no leave the girls alone. You're right, okay. Keep going, tell me the rest of it.

L: So, when I come back after all this I, we had the most important thing that you knew I needed, the most important thing that means the world to me and all of that, was our items specifically my diamond ring, they were in that car. I tried to reach out to you to say can you please at least ask them can we have those things, you wanted nothing to talk to me because it means the world to me to have my ring on because I took my vows for better or worse with you. And I tried reaching out to you, 'Hey they have my ring they have my ID I don't even have money because they have my card'. You wouldn't even talk to me so then, you wonder why I said if my husband would not even talk to me, he would not even warn me that my child was about to be put in handcuffs, okay? (Unintelligible)... because I was yelling at Harley not to move (Unintelligible)... told them to shoot me right there and this is all on camera.

Al: Listen, I'm sorry. That's my fault too, okay. No, I want you to know, I'm telling you, all this is my fault, okay. I'm acknowledging that. Keep going. I'm just trying to be a team here.

L: So, then you tell everybody I leave, when the truth is you didn't step up in any of that to say (unintelligible).

Al: Okay, alright, I'm gonna stop you there. You told the world on camera you left, I didn't. So, let's clarify that and then you can go on.

L: (Unintelligible).

Al: Okay, go ahead.

L: ... why I wasn't, they asked why I wasn't out there.

Al: Okay.

L: Listen to me. In the situation I'm sitting here getting all my things taken, and I... and people think I don't have feelings. Why this... (unintelligible) ... sitting up in our house when she... (unintelligible) ... she didn't even call Laina on her birthday which is four days before, and you think I weren't angry? You think I wasn't sitting there mad thinking you don't give a fuck about them? Yeah. Call me and I'll take the blame for that. I'll take the blame for being... (unintelligible) ... that you ever let that bitch anywhere near our house the way she did our children.

(Unintelligible) ... that she came to our house drunk and I had to let her stay at Lake Drive. And you locked me out and told me I was on her team? Because she was drunk, and I wouldn't let her lie or whatever? Let her... (unintelligible) ... those kids?

That's why. Because I don't care what the situation was, you should've put her ass in a hotel, but you didn't. You didn't give anything to our children. I don't care what the times were because that didn't do anything but put a wedge between us. So yes, when I came back that night, I had no other choice but to get clothing. I had no intentions of getting but a few things of clothing, but then when I see this bitch Victoria and all these people, I'm not gonna name any names, with my motherfucking clothes on and then I see people using my products you can say what you want to in a time like this you shouldn't worry about that, I'm not worried about the material things, it's the principle in my home. Cause I don't disrespect people's homes, but they disrespected me like that, there's no telling what they did to you or what they did to our children that is why I was angry. So, be mad at me and what you want because I took clothes from there because I didn't want them burned.

When I walked in that house the first time that shit had been moved, that shouldn't have happened, Albert. You shouldn't have let that bitch Veronica walk around and move my shit that was wrong. Where was this bitch at when we needed help? When I needed somebody to help sometimes where was she at, Albert? Where was she at when we needed help sometimes, when you were working? When we needed a babysitter? Where the fuck was she at? And you let her walk around in our home and move my shit and then you let her go downstairs and do what she did to Harley? Oh, that was it.

Al: When? Who did what to Harley? No, I don't know who did what to Harley?

L: Oh. Why don't you ask Veronica about when she walked downstairs and talked to Harley. And then my mother wasn't allowed to say a word to the kids she wanted to make sure we got our things. You ask her that.

Al: No, I'm asking you, I don't know what the hell you're talk-

L: Then you ask Harley Hunt that, man. You let that woman follow that child downstairs and didn't even step in to say a motherfucking word.

Al: Follow her downstairs? Wait, wait, wait, I don't know what happened, Harley can tell me later. I don't know.

L: Yeah. So, my point is, (unintelligible)... I left. I wasn't trying to be apart. You did not step in to help me defeat any of the odds, you sit there and tried to talk to people, to try to remember anything else, to try to go through the steps of it, I immediately had to go into a defence mode fighting for myself when nothing, nothing. I was told... I was and that fricken' bitch in my own home. And you wonder why I was like, well, why I am I gonna be here for? You shouldn't have even let her brother even put his hand on one of our handguns, you had no business with that.

Al: Hey, you better stop right there, because I... hey, no. I was in total control of those weapons the whole time. You will not do that to me. Go ahead.

L: You might have been in total control! But he had no business doing that.

Al: Who gives a crap about that? Come on now.

L: My point is, Albert, you let these people come in during that time, the first few days and you let them control things. And you could say you didn't and maybe you were hurt, maybe you were upset, maybe your focus was on one thing, and I understand that I'm not trying to do nothing but say okay. Thinking about that in my mind and I still want my husband and I still know that he was not in his right mind there and then (unintelligible) ... you could've stepped in and said right then that you are not a Stauch, or you were not related to me by blood... (unintelligible) ... your sisters are, I know your mom is, if you're not a Stauch and you're not related to me by blood you need to leave this house. That's exactly what –

Al: Okay, alright, alright. Tecia, no stop, stop. Listen, I'll tell you. Put all that on me, I don't care, okay. We can fight about all that for the rest of our lives, you're right. I let people come into the house that ain't got no blood relation to me, you're absolutely right, okay. But the bigger issue here, and I've let you go on, I'm trying to be respectful and let you talk and talk and talk but all this is about you and your damn stuff and not a damn thing about Gannon.

L: No, it's not.

Al: Yes, it is. Yes, it is.

L: No, you asked me how, I said we're gonna talk about two separate things, that's what I told you. So that's the first thing. Now the most important thing is Gannon. You asked me how to have everything back, American dream, like you said in December. You just realise where your actions could've been different. So, until we have trust to put those actions back together and bring it back together as one, as one, Albert. As one. You didn't marry me, or I didn't marry you for it to turn our backs on each other in tough times. That's not how it works in life. You know me better. I know you better. You know, you had to live with the past and the things that your father's done. I've never once said to you I don't trust you with my child, and I feel like you're bad around them. Never once

Al: Actually, you have said that. Actually, you have said that which is bullshit, but go ahead, I'll listen to ya.

L: No, I did not. You were both not sober and Landen was trying to get me to turn on you.

Al: Okay, alright.

L: I'm talking about in our home. You know good and well if I went somewhere, and Harley was there I was never worried for a second.

Al: Alright, so stop. You're not, stop, stop. Let me interject because this is supposed to be about Gannon, this part, part one was, no listen please lis-

Crosstalk.

L: ... so we can go get Gannon.

Al: Okay, the problem is here, you said until we have trust, the problem is we're not there yet, okay, we're, because a few minutes...

Crosstalk.

Al: ... no, no, no, listen, listen. I'm gonna tell you why right now, okay? I've given. No.

L: ... want to hear it.

Al: I'm gonna tell you why. I'm gonna tell you why and then I'll let you talk, okay? Please listen. I'm gonna tell you why. Because, okay, I've taken the blame for everything that I'm responsible for in this situation, probably more than I should've but I'll take the blame for all of it, okay? Quincy Brown's got the boy, okay? But the part that I still don't have trust about is when I brought up the fact there's a puddle of blood in the house, you mentioned a head wound, you didn't even say a damn thing about that. Not a peep, Tecia, you blew right past it, so fill in the...

L: What are you talking about?

Al: Fill in the blanks for me.

L: No, n-n-n-no, no, no, no, no. What are you talking about a head wound? I never said to you about any kind of head wound. Now see, this is where –

Al: No, you did, you said in the bicycle incident which you later told me was not true, that you...

L: I already told you I made that up because you would never believe anything I said.

Al: Okay, so how did the puddle of blood get there? Because it wasn't there before we moved in, so. Okay, tell me about the puddle of blood in the corner. No, you said the wall. You said there was something on the wall, who cares what it was, you cleaned it. I don't know anything about that other than what you said.

L: We cleaned everything from when Gannon... okay, I've already told you this.

Al: No, you didn't because we haven't talked about this. There was a puddle of blood the size of like one of those paper dinner platter plates I mean it was, it was significant, and that was on the concrete which means it had to be significantly bigger and more thicker or whatever, I can't hear you

Hello?

I can't hear you.

L: You're talking about something.

AL: I'm talking about something, no it was not already there, okay. That blood was not already there. How did the blood get there? It was a significant amount of blood. How did it get there in the corner of Gannon's room under his bed which you told me the bed were pushed together, so how did the blood get there?

L: Are you done yelling at me?

Al: I'm not yellin'. I'm not yellin'. How did the blood get there?

L: You can tell all your little police people that are listening–

Al: Did Quincy Brown bang Gannon's head up against the wall or something? Did he bust Gannon's head open? Did he hit him with a 2x4? What did Quincy do to Gannon? What did he do to Gannon that put blood on the floor?

L: ... 'cause you were. See, I'm not stupid. I know you have police there. I know you have people there.

Al: You can believe whatever you want, obviously, 'cause I've had so many frickin' stories that you believe that were true to tell me, and then you always back off of 'em okay? So, you can believe whatever the hell you wanna believe. All I believe is what I saw.

L:That's what you've –

Al: All I believe is what I saw - blood on the floor in my son's room and my son is missing, okay? That's the two things I know. Gannon was hurt in my house.

L: I don't know. How many times do I have to say this to you? I don't know.

Al: You don't know how he got hurt? Okay.

L: You asked me fifteen times the same exact question and I'm giving you the same exact answer, I don't know. Then you tried to turn it and you tried to ask me another way and then you tried to turn around and you try to change up nice and sweet like you really care and then you come back and ask me the same question again and I've given you the same answer. If you're so concerned about -

Al: But you had... no, stop no, 'cause you haven't given me the same answer, it's been a different story every time.

L: (Unintelligible) ... to go find him and see what he did to Gannon. You are too busy worrying about something that you think you can solve...

Al: I'm still waiting on the address. You were supposed to give me the address. You were supposed to give me the address from your lawyer's people.

L: Me?

Al: Yes. 'Cause you said they had it.

L: Ask your FBI friends.

Al: Now you're changing your story, you're changing your story. You called the police, not me. I wasn't there. I'll take the blame for not being there, for not protecting you - you called the police. Why did you call the police?

L: I am...

Al: Actually, no stop right there. You called the police and told them that he ran away, not that Quincy Brown took him, what the fuck, Tecia? Answer that for me. You know without a shadow of a doubt Quincy Brown, and I believe you, Quincy Brown has my son. This motherfucker from somewhere up north of here, okay? But you called the police and said he ran away, don't tell me you were freaking out, okay? No, don't give me some bullshit story Tecia. Tell me the goddamn truth right now.

L: If you're not gonna listen to my answer then why are you talking?

Al: I'm listening. This is it. This is the line in the sand. Quincy Brown got my son, and you told the police he ran away and there's blood in his room.

L: If I'm guilty, why would I call the police?

Al: I said Quincy Brown was guilty, I didn't say you. I said Quincy Brown, why are you talking about yourself? Why did you just say if you were guilty? You told me you weren't the whole time, why'd you say if you were guilty? You said Quincy Brown and I said Quincy Brown. You keep bringing it back to you, not me, there's –

L: You are implying...

Al: No, I said there's blood in the room, Quincy Brown took him, you called the police and said he ran away. Explain all those things to me, right now.

[LONG SILENCE]

L: Albert. If you calm down, I'm gonna answer your questions.

Al: Oh, I'm calm. I'm as calm as I can be.

L: Calmer.

Al: I'm as calm as I can be.

L: Because I'm not stupid. Yeah.

Al: I'm not stupid either. You fucking lied to me, and you fucking lied to the police. I'm not stupid either so you better get it right.

L: I told the police when I got there what happened.

Al: Man, you told them he ran away and the whole neighbourhood was looking for a runaway for days and days and days. You're lying. You are now lying and I'm calling you out, you're lying.

L: That is not true. That is not what happened. When they interviewed me, I told them exactly what happened.

Al: I don't give a fuck what you said, you told me he was a runaway, so I called, and called, and I cursed the lady out on the recorded line, told her to get there for my runaway son, okay? You never once told me Quincy Brown had the boy and there was blood in his room, so you better get it straight right now.

L: When you stop yelling at me.

Al: When you start telling the truth. Tell the truth and I'll stop getting upset. You're lying!

L: I told you the truth.

Al: You are lyin', Tecia.

L: You call me back.

Al: Go ahead and hang up. You call me back when you got the truth, you're fuckin' lying.

L: Are you done yelling and cursing at me?

Al: I'm done, go ahead.

L: So, for a second, for a minute, I need you to just breathe, Okay? 'Cause you're yelling at me, and I can't even answer a question when you're screaming and every time I try to open my mouth, you're screaming and yelling at me.

Al: Every time there's a lie. I'm gonna call you out so let's go, let's go, who –

L: There's nothing for there to be a lie.

Al: Okay, I'm just gonna warn you, I'm firing a warning shot right now. You lie, I'm gonna tell you you're lying. Go ahead.

L: I haven't even said nothing and you're still running your yap. You're still running your yap.

Al: Alright, I'm shutting my yap, go ahead.

L: Still running your yap. [silence].

If there was blood in Gannon's room that would have been already from when he cut his foot, I've already told you that. Okay? I told you that his arm from him getting burned was bleeding some and so was his foot, I've already told you that.

Al: Ok, you're lying, you're lying, stop. That's a lie. Change it again because that's a lie. Here's the game we're gonna play. Every time you lie, I'm gonna call you out. You can't bleed that much from a burn. You can't bleed that much from a burn. You can't bleed that much from a cut on your foot from a 2x4. I'm not stupid. You're lying. Go ahead, change it again, you're lying.

L: You said a plate size.

Al: A plate, a dinner plate, that's what seeped through, Tecia. That means there was a puddle of blood on the damn carpet to seep through the carpet, an inch of carpet pad, and onto the concrete pad where it looked like it had been sittin' there for days, okay? That's what I saw, so tell the fuckin' truth.

L: Maybe you should ask the people who were there living, because I never was there with you, that contaminated the crime scene, maybe you should ask them.

Al: Tecia, guess what. Guess what?

L: You got fuckin' asses on the contamination.

Al: Alright, good.

L: Who did that? Who did it?

Al: Guess what, guess what. You just tellin' on yourself now. You're worried about a damn loophole. You're trying to find a loophole, okay?

L: Who contaminated it?

Al: Okay, there's another loophole. Alright, there's another loophole.

L: Who contaminated it?

Al: Okay, there's three loopholes there already.

L: They contaminated it. It sounds funny to me that they left for Texas with a child missing, maybe they contaminated it.

Al: Alright, alright that's fine, so that's.

L: (Unintelligible) ... when I'm talking.

Al: Landen, Lena, Veronica, and me, that's four loopholes right there. Alright, I'm waiting. I'm waiting on you to quit lying. You just told on...hey, between me and you, you just told on yourself 'cause you just said they contaminated a crime scene is what you said.

L: No. I said you, y'all contaminated it, meaning y'all put it in there then.

Al: Oh, we put it in there?

L: You've got nothing to say about that, do you? Do you?

Al: See, here you go, here you go with the spin game. Oh, you were...

L: Maybe your brother did.

Al: ... you were on the cut foot and the burnt arm, now it's a spin game, okay, alright keep going with your spin.

L: You're the one who said you know the answer, so I mean, shit, if you know the fucking answer, that's why am I coming back to you with the bullshit you say to me.

Al: Yeah, that's frickin'... I know what the answer is, it's frickin' Gannon's blood. It's Gannon's blood from a head injury. Now how did he get a head injury? How did he get a head injury over there in the corner? I mean you frickin' told on yourself saying you pushed the beds together. You pushed the beds together, we've never pushed the beds together, you're lying.

L: Let me tell you something, Albert, if you went in somewhere where there was blood and you were allowed to walk in there, maybe you did it.

Al: Oh, maybe I did it huh?

L: You shouldn't have been allowed anywhere to see this.

Al: Wait a minute, wait a minute.

L: You just said you walked in somewhere to see it. Did you do it? Did you do it? If that was the case what you're telling me, you shouldn't have even been allowed in there.

Al: Oh, oh, oh, oh, oh, oh, oh, oh, oh. I was in Oklahoma, that's what I got to say. That's my loophole. Okay. You wanna try to pin it on me, go ahead.

L: You walked in there the other day.

Al: Yeah, I walked in there and saw it after, you told on yourself cause you- hey.

L: Maybe you put it in there because you know why?

Al: Alright, alright, listen, let's calm down. Let's calm down. Let's calm down. Let's calm down, okay?

L: (Unintelligible)... you walk in supposed time.

Al: Listen, let's calm down.

L: Did you walk in? Maybe you walked in the room, huh?

Al: What do you think is gonna happen?

L: Veronica was in there too

Al: What do you think is gonna happen when they solve this crime? Okay? What do you think?

L: Landen and Veronica walked in there too, huh?

Al: What do you think? I don't know who.

L: You look at me and accuse me of stuff, when you said you went somewhere, so who the fuck done it? Did she do it?

Al: Just tell, hey?

L: If this was a crime scene y'all were fucking allowed to be in there.

Al: Tecia, okay.

L: You're telling me... you tell me better than this, 'cause I know you're pretty smart. Tell me better than this. So, you admitted to me that you were allowed to walk into a crime scene?

Al: No, I said I saw it. Don't twist my words, I saw it.

L: Who, who else went in there?

Al: I... Okay, you wanna... Hey, you...

L: (Unintelligible).

Al: You wanna know who else walked in there? You.

L: Yeah.

Al: Gannon with a head injury. Quincy Brown, and a puddle of blood walked in there. That's who walked in there so what do you think is gonna happen when they find that boy and put all these pieces together? Okay. What do you think? What do you think? What do you think is gonna happen?

L: If that's what you think

Al: You can say whatever you want. You can say whatever you want, okay? Maybe this was a freaking accident. Maybe we can fix it, okay? But the... the truth... the truth don't, the truth don't lie.

L: Accuse me! ACCUSE ME! No, no, no.

Al: I didn't accuse you, I accused Quincy Brown and maybe there's a story, or part of this that's an accident, okay?

L: There was no head injury to Gannon Jacob Stauch. I don't know about it, or I didn't do it.

Al: Why is it an or? Why is it an or? Okay, that's why I don't trust you.

L: I didn't do it!

Al: No, you didn't say and, you said or.

L: Why you gonna do this to me?

Al: Listen, listen. All of this stuff doesn't matter because by the time I saw a puddle of blood on the floor, Gannon was already gone, okay? He was already walking sluggish to the truck, okay? And God knows where he is if he's even alive and that's what matters, okay?

L: Walking sluggish to the truck?

Al: Yeah, absolutely. Absolutely. I'm sure he was. Why did you...? Anyways...

L: To the truck, really?

Al: Why would he be walking sluggish to the truck? He never does that when he has a tummy accident.

L: Sluggish. How can you determine sluggish from a video?

Al: The same way you can determine a shadow means somebody getting out of a truck, okay. The same bullshit, okay?

L: Is that any different than walking?

Al: Listen, you claim a shadow means Gannon got out the truck—we never saw him. We saw him walking to the truck, we saw him walking to the truck.

L: (Unintelligible)... against Quincy Brown.

Al: I was walking sluggish when I cut my finger. Gannon was walking sluggish after he had a significant head wound with a puddle of blood on the floor.

L: I've never seen Gannon walk sluggish.

Al: Okay, I'm telling you. I'm telling you he was walking sluggish cause he was hurt and there was a puddle of blood on the floor and it's probably his blood. I haven't seen no frickin' evidence, but I guarantee you it's his blood because it all adds up, Tecia. And he was walking sluggish cause of that, just like I was walking sluggish when I cut my finger off, you hit the nail on the head, honey.

L: I don't even understand... like, you're talking... see this is what's not making any sense. You're trying to say that he got hurt before... (unintelligible). I don't even know that he got hurt at all.

Al: Oh, I'm glad you caught yourself.

L: So, you're saying he got hurt Monday morning?

Al: I'm glad you caught yourself. Yep, I'm glad you caught yourself though. Hey, listen, let's stop, okay? Because this is going nowhere. We can fix this. I want Gannon. I don't want you in trouble. I'm blaming Quincy Brown, okay? I'm blaming frickin' Quincy Brown. I want my son.

L: What you failed to tell me is how, how we were supposed to be back the way in our American dream, and you start screaming at me in the middle of the... (unintelligible).

Al: Because of my son! It's my son's blood all over the frickin' floor, okay? My son's blood. If it was Harley's blood you'd be screaming, too. You're screaming and it's not even your son.

L: You saw this blood and it's Gannon's?

Al: I'm assuming. Who else's blood would be on the floor?

L: You just said assume.

Al: Okay, good. Yeah, you got me, I'm assuming. I'm making a serious, legitimate assumption putting all the pieces together that it's my son's blood. Is Laina cut up? Are you cut up? Is Harley cut up? No. Gannon's the only one and we don't know so yes, I'm assuming. I'm not cut up—I wasn't even there.

L: I'm gonna tell you this, Albert.

Al: You can tell me whatever you want to. Now is the time when we fix this. Right now, okay?

L: Okay, and I'm telling you right now, you listen, instead of yelling back at me.

Al: Alright.

L: Gannon Stauch was not sluggish other than if his stomach might have been hurt and his foot there was nothing wrong with Gannon on Monday morning. He had his Switch—he was playing his Switch and there was nothing wrong with him.

Al: Okay, fine.

L: Maybe he was a little tired because the boy stayed up late at night with his stomach hurting which I messaged you about.

Al: Okay, fine.

L: Maybe he was a little tired for that part of it, but you can't assume that someone's sluggish and hurt on Monday morning that is not true, okay? Gannon was under my care and was fine. If he'd been sluggish and hurt, getting in your truck there would've been blood in your truck. (Unintelligible)... all online talking about he was looking like he was drugged. Really? Gannon drugged? I mean, he only takes his medicine, one, his stomach was hurting he had a lot of MiraLAX in his system trying to clean him out.

Al: So, you did give him... wait, wait, I wanna stop you 'cause you said you didn't give him anything and now you say you *did* give him something. This whole time you said you didn't give him anything.

L: No, you're a fucking liar because I told you I gave it to him on Saturday night.

Al: Okay, I don't remember that, but now you basically say you doped him up on MiraLAX.

L: I already told you this so don't try to correct me and tell me I'm lying when I know for a fact. He was probably very tired. If you go back and look at your phone, I messaged you up until 3 or 4 in the morning 'cause we didn't sleep. I'm sure Laina went to school completely exhausted. So, if he walked out maybe a little bit tired, and you saw that, then blame me, because you know why? We didn't go to sleep.

Al: So, now he is tired and sluggish and a minute ago he's not tired and sluggish?

L: I said if you think that, then that's why.

Al: Okay. Alright. I'm just trying to clarify 'cause you say he wasn't and now he is, okay.

L: (Unintelligible).

Al: I can't hear you. I can't hear you.

L: I said, if he would've had a head injury, that's what you're talking about, okay? He would have blood in your truck, okay? He would have... there would have had to have been something done to him for this supposed head injury you're talking about wouldn't have just stopped bleeding.

Al: I agree with you.

L: Okay? There would have been blood all over your truck, okay? That's just how it would've been if... I understand as a father you are freaked out, okay? I understand at this point you're gonna curse at the world because you're without your child. I understand that. When I thought Harley was lost on that freakin' cruise boat... (unintelligible)... I understand what you're saying when it comes to attack mode, protect mode, attack mode, okay? But you wanna know how do we get back to that, then you have to believe that when Gannon Stauch left that house that day he was not in any shape or form, bleeding, hurt, nothing other than him hurting his foot okay? His stomach hurting and you know what, I was going to leave him at home.

Al: Wait, what about the burns?

L: You already knew this.

Al: Okay, you said… you said. I'm just clarifying 'cause you said in any way shape or form and he had burns on his arms, okay? This is my baby boy now we're talking about.

L: You said his head, I'm trying to clarify.

Al: Alright, so I got you. He didn't leave the house, no, no he didn't leave the house with a head injury alright? So, did you bring him back and then he got a head injury? Or did you bring him back with a head injury, okay? Then he ran away with a… did he run away, or did Quincy Brown take him with a head injury? Okay? What version of that is the truth because the boy was bleeding in the house so how… where did the blood come from?

L: Albert, I'll tell you once again.

Al: Alright.

L: You can say all you want to with the assumptions that you have, okay? Gannon had already been bleeding from his foot, okay? I already cleaned it up outside.

Al: Did he bleed in that corner of the room? Okay. I'm sorry, I'm sorry.

L: Can I talk?

Al: Okay, go ahead.

L: He'd already been bleeding from his foot we then at that point in time fixed the room. The only reason I put the room, cleaned it up or whatever was because, later on, I did that before you got there.

Al: So, you cleaned up the room before I got there, okay.

L: Just fucking listen to me. As far as putting... making the thing back up, fixing his Legos back right, I did that.

Al: Cleaning the wall, right? That was part of the cleanup?

L: Cleaning the wall? Gannon and I had already done that.

Al: Okay, okay. I'm just trying to put a timeline together.

L: You're talking about cleaning something prior, like it was prior to what you're even talking about.

Al: Okay.

L: You're not understanding.

Al: I'm trying to understand because you told me you cleaned up the rape scene in his room initially and now, you know...

L: Yes, my clothing and I've already told you that.

Al: Okay.

L: Okay? I've already told you this, Albert.

Al: What about the corner where the blood was, did you clean that up too? Okay? Was that part of the cleaning? That's fine if that was part of the rape cleanup, but was that part of the cleanup?

L: Now you're trying to go off...

Al: No, I'm trying to understand all of this. You never told me the rape wasn't true and the banging your head wasn't true. You told me the bicycle wasn't true, you didn't tell me this part wasn't true. So, did you clean up the corner too? Is that part of the cleanup? Because that's where the blood was. I mean if that all adds up to an accident to me and that Quincy Brown is responsible, okay? And that you just got scared and freaked out, or was it your blood from when you banged your head? I mean, what happened? How did that...

L: I thought you were sure it was Gannon's blood.

Al: I'm trying to figure it out. I'm assuming it's his, but if you banged your head that hard to pass out you probably were bleeding too, maybe you fell into the corner cause the beds were pushed together, I don't know, alright? I'm just trying to understand, and then you cleaned it up and that was part of the cleanup that you talked about. Just explain to me what's going on here.

L: This is embarrassing to explain to you, Albert. It's embarrassing.

Al: It shouldn't be embarrassing to me, babe.

L: Don't call me babe 'cause you don't really want me as your babe. You're not trying to be loving to me.

Al: I'm trying to find out what happened to my son, all that... everything else is a... is part of the situation after we find Gannon, whatever we decide at that point.

L: (Unintelligible)... Gannon's blood.

Al: In the corner?

L: Wherever it would have been in the room.

Al: Okay, keep going, I just... I'm gonna shut up 'cause this is freakin' me out.

L: Don't even start with the whole freakin' me out like you care.

Al: I care, I don't want nobody to bleed what are you talking about? So, you cleaned up your blood and Gannon's blood in the corner? Why didn't you tell me that?

L: I did. You just said I told you about the cleaning part and whatever about it. You're just like... it doesn't matter what I tell you, you think it's funny, you just wanna laugh at me, that's what you wanna do.

Al: I don't wanna laugh, I don't wanna, no. I wanna know where my son is and what happened. How did your blood get there and how did Gannon's blood get there?

L: Listen to me.

Al: Okay, I'm listening.

L: I already told... I've already told investigators that, okay?

Al: Okay, alright, well tell me, 'cause I don't know.

L: No, no, no, no, no, no. If they let you in on this supposed crime scene that you shouldn't have even been on if it was a crime scene, then they probably let you in on everything, okay? Or they did things illegally whatever they did, my point is it's embarrassing to tell you that, okay? Embarrassing. Okay? Because you know why? You're not gonna take my side so what does it matter?

Al: I am gonna take your side.

L: You're trying to put me on trial. Have you been in the car to go find this dude? Or have you put me on trial?

Al: I... you told me you were getting the address or the phone number something from the attorney's assistant, okay.

L: The reporters were gonna do a whole report on it.

Al: Okay, so why can't I have the address and go there and...

L: It's supposed to be on the TV in a minute.

Al: So, now I can't do anything because I gotta wait for the TV report? The breaking news story when you have the information? Come on, come on.

L: You don't gotta wait for the breaking news report you can... (unintelligible).

Al: Listen, back up.

L: (Unintelligible)... she's protecting you.

Al: No, all I know her is from a voice on the phone. Listen, what I want is what I told you I wanted initially. I want our five people in our family, two dogs...

L: American dream.

Al: ... Christmas presents. Yes, that's what I want, okay? And if this was... I'm just talking about that's the last time we were all together, happy enjoying that I could think of.

L: (Unintelligible).

Al: I'm just talking about good times in our life.

L: What'd you say?

Al: I said that's the last thing I could think of, presents.

L: (Unintelligible).

Al: What?

L: That starts with you. That starts with you. Saying, I want my wife and my daughter here, and Laina here, and we're gonna sit down and we're gonna all go find Gannon.

Al: Right, and we can fix this that's... our family can fix this—all five of us. Maybe it was an accident, I don't know.

L: ... of us.

Al: All five of us can fix this.

L: Talk to Laina. That's how sorry that shit was. Sorry. That's how sorry that shit was. You could've... you could right now fix this. You could right now say listen, my wife, my child and my child we're all gonna be in this one location, because our home has been taken over and we're gonna write it down if we have to wake up every morning and write down every detail as we are pursuing this person.

Al: Okay and that's what I'm trying to do, that's what I'm doing with you, I'm writing down every detail, this adds up to an accident and Quincy Brown.

L: It's not about...

Al: No, you said we can get together and write down every detail, we're on the phone together Tecia, we can write down these details.

L: That's the only way you wanna do it, right?

Al: I offered you a meeting.

L: A meeting?

Al: Yes.

L: Okay, make up your mind, one minute you offered me a meeting, next minute you said how do we have our lives back the way they were.

Al: Alright, and I also told you it starts with the truth. Okay? You still haven't told me.

L: I told you the truth.

Al: Oh, yes, okay, how did the blood get in the corner? Your blood and Gannon's blood, how did it get there? That's the truth that we need, okay? How did it get there?

L: It doesn't matter what I tell you, you're gonna call me a liar.

Al: No, just tell me what the truth is, it does matter.

L: If I tell you you're gonna call me a liar.

Al: Tell me the truth and I won't call you a liar.

L: I've already told you. You called me a liar. I could tell you that I freakin' got hit with a baseball bat and you would still be like. 'you're lying'. I already told you. I could tell you that someone was trying to stick something in my asshole and Gannon's asshole, and you would tell me I was telling a lie. You wouldn't care.

Al: Actually, I would, if you told me the truth, I would absolutely care cause if you got hit with a baseball bat we wouldn't be talking right now, okay? So that's why I just need the truth of how did the blood get there? Now we've established it's Gannon's blood.

L: I just told you, didn't I?

Al:Tell me again, you didn't tell me, you said if I told you this or if I told you that, you didn't tell me anything.

L: You are all over the place, if you're that blind to it then that's on you.

Al: So, somebody hit Gannon with a baseball bat and then molested both of y'all?

L: No.

Al: So, it's blood from his butt?

L:No. I used the baseball bat like as an example how you wouldn't believe nothing I said.

Al: So, somebody raped and molested both of y'all and that's blood from his butt is what you're telling me. And blood from your butt.

L: I'm not telling you anything because I'm not gonna relive it.

Al: Well, Gannon's out there hopefully, reliving it every day. I hope he's out there living.

L: I hope he's not because you know why?

Al: You hope that he's not living? You're hoping he's not living? I said I hope he's out there living.

L: Reliving it every day, oh, my God, do you see what you did?

Al: Yeah, I saw what I did, I took what you said...

L: I said I hope he's not living it every day, like as in living through someone hurting him, and you took that as me saying something different.

Al: But why are you so worried someone did something to you and Gannon, this Quincy Brown guy, you're not gonna be in trouble, you're not gonna be in trouble, but you're talking about contaminated crime scenes, but I'm not telling you you're gonna be in trouble. I don't even know! Okay, you're worried about all this stuff.

L: See?

Al: No, you're worried about immunity, you're worried about contaminated crime scenes, but you didn't do anything.

L: I'm not worried about that, I'm telling you, you didn't like that I came back with you when you said something like that, you didn't like that.

Al: No, you can come back with whatever you want. Okay, it's not a competition, it's not a competition, actually it is a competition to find that boy.

L: (Unintelligible).

Al: I can't hear you.

L: It's the constitution.

Al: What constitution? I can't hear you.

L: It's against the law if someone's been into a crime scene that's not a person allowed to be in there breathing, walking, everything.

Al: But why are you worried about that? Why are you worried about that? You're not on trial here.

L: You don't like when I come at you with the truth.

Al: No. You're not on trial here. The truth is how did the blood get there? Tell me, okay.

L: Now you're asking me again.

Al: How did the blood get there? I'm not saying it's your fault, listen.

L: Same question fuckin' fifteen times.

Al: Because you won't tell me, so I want you to acknowledge for me that, if what you're saying is true, I don't know the constitution like you do, okay, you went to law school and all that stuff, right? So, if the police allowed somebody to go in there that's the police's fault, okay? That's not my fault, that's not your fault.

L: No, no, no, no, no, no, no. Do you ever let people talk and answer you?

Al: Yes.

L: This is what you shoulda been. This is what I told you all the time, you should've been a lawyer.

Al: Right, okay.

L: You asked... (unintelligible)... now I'm out here where I'm trying to tell him. You would not let someone answer you for nothing like you would sit there at work and let people dog your ass, but you would talk shit to me.

Al: No, I'm not talking shit, I'm asking you for the truth.

L: No, it doesn't even make any sense to me. You won't even protect us at freaking *Burger King*, but you'll talk shit to me.

Al: I'm not talking shit. I want my family. I want my son. He was bleeding when he left the house, you told me that.

L: Crosstalk.

Al: You told me he was bleeding.

L: Crosstalk.

Al: You told me he was bleeding when he left the house, you just told me that there's blood all over the floor and he left with Quincy Brown.

L: I don't know where he went.

Al: I didn't ask you that.

L: I know that I'm getting messages. I know that I'm getting whatever, saying something about money. I sent it to you, you didn't acknowledge that, did you?

Al: I did acknowledge that.

L: Why are you attacking me?

Al: But if... you gotta understand.

L: There's no blood.

Al: Okay, fine.

L: If you believed 100%, believed 100%, that I did not hurt Gannon Stauch you would not be interrogating me like you're a police officer.

Al: Okay, I'm not. But I'm gonna go over exactly what I know from what you told me.

L: I don't need you to go over-

Al: I'm going over it.

L: Crosstalk.

Al: You called 911, you reported a missing child, okay? Then when I got home...

L:Crosstalk.

Al: ... when I got home, no, you called. Let me rephrase that because you said he was a runaway you said he left, and the cameras prove he didn't.

L: No, I didn't say that. The police did.

Al: You told me that he went to a friend's house. You told me that, okay? That he went to a friend's house and didn't come home, alright? You told me that.

L: I thought he was hiding.

Al: Then you changed the story to the cops and to me...

L: No.

Al: ... and to everybody.

L: I thought he was hiding.

Al: Okay, fast forward and I see blood, now you've confirmed you also saw blood, okay? And then I asked you to tell me the truth over and over and over again, and you don't. Then I even offer I can help you fix it. It could be an accident. Quincy Brown could be at fault. I could be at fault, okay? But you just keep going down this road and now, how do you expect me...

Crosstalk.

Al: How do you expect me not to blame myself because my son's missing and nobody can find the truth and it's in my household? Okay? How do you expect me...?

L: Do you want me to tell you like... what do you want me to tell you?

Al: Where the blood came from and how it got there, that's what I wanna know.

L: I told you.

Al: You did not.

L: I keep saying it fifteen times.

Al: You didn't say how it got there.

L: If you get hurt you bleed, come on.

Al: What? Say what?

L: If you get hurt you bleed.

Al: Okay, how? You got hurt?

L: It's common sense.

Al: You got hurt? And you bled? And you and Gannon bled in the same puddle? It was one puddle not two, there was one puddle.

L: No.

Al: So, you sat back-to-back and bled together is that what happened?

L: No, that's not what happened. That's where you go again about interrogating me.

Al: I'm not, I'm trying to put together what happened to my son and my wife so tell me where's the second puddle of blood if you were both hurt equally, and you remember all of that now.

L: Equally?

Al: Okay.

L: I'm sitting back here as you try to put words in my mouth.

Al: I'm not, I'm trying to understand. I'm trying to understand. Well, tell me what happened then, tell me where the blood came from. How it got there. Tell me.

There is a long pause.

L: I can only go on what I heard.

Al: Okay, tell me what you heard then.

L: I told you I am not... until you guys can stop trying to make me to be the criminal when I'm not.

Al: I'm not, I told you I'm taking blame for it, no, no, let's clarify.

L: Crosstalk.

Al: I... let's clarify.

L: You got mad and...

Al: Let's clarify.

L: ...for asking to clear your name.

Al: Let's clarify.

L: Why would I be stupid enough to clarify to you?

Al: Cause I'm not blaming you.

L: (Unintelligible)... that I'm clear. I'm not a criminal. I did...

Al: You're right, you're not a criminal for hearing things, nobody is. What did you hear? What did you hear?

L: ... testify this.

Al: Testify to your husband about your son. Our son is missing.

L: Did you just say that? You won't even let you wife and daughter and your other daughter be with you right now...

Al: Because you won't tell me the truth.

L: ... and you're worried about family?

Al: Just tell me what you heard, please.

L: But you better believe Laina was with you but yeah Harley's supposed to be your daughter too right.

Al: You took Harley, I want my family. You and Harley chose to leave, and I never asked you to leave, okay. I wanted it the whole time.

L: She was worrying about you... about you wanting her to pay her car payment and you changed cars on her, why?

Al: I had to do that because I'm responsible for it. Yes, okay, yes. But that doesn't matter right now. You can make the car payment all you want to, that doesn't matter right now, listen.

L: But you want your family, right?

Al: I can't hear you.

L: I said you want your family.

Al: I do.

L: You want your family? A 17-year-old who worked her fuckin' ass off to pay for the car?

Al: Okay, and I worked my ass off to be able to finance the car for her okay, but you need to tell me what you heard because that...

L: Well, then you should've given her the option to get it back herself and finance it.

Al: She can get it back whenever they release it.

Crosstalk.

Al: Alright, you said earlier... listen.

L: Crosstalk... your family treated her in that situation.

Al: Yes, exactly, and a father, and don't tell me how a father is supposed to feel, you're talking about what you said is most important to you, which is things. You said that.

Items, okay? I'm talking about what's most important to me, what's most important to a father is his son. The most important thing to a father is his children. I want my son back and you have the information, and you won't give it to me. You won't tell me what you frickin' heard when he was bleeding to death.

L: You said the most important thing to you was your son.

Al: My son, my children. I said that. My children. My son is missing right now, my two daughters are not missing. My two daughters are not missing.

L: You should've talked to her and said listen –

Al: Laina is safe and sound, Harley is safe and sound.

L: They need love and care. I bet you put Laina to bed last night.

Al: Right. Where's Harley at?

L: You wouldn't let us come.

Al: Exactly, thank you. Thank you. And thank you. You won't tell me where she's at to protect her and keep her safe. She wouldn't tell me that. Tell me, tell me what you heard.

L: Albert?

Al: Listen, listen, you're worried about you now. You're worried about you. This is about Gannon. Gannon's bleeding to death, and you heard it.

L: Gannon's missing and you wanna say something.

Al: No, Gannon's...

L: You think you're the motherfucking FBI but you ain't.

Al: I'm on the phone with you. You want togetherness, I'm giving you that. You said Gannon's bleeding.

L: Get the FBI on the phone.

Al: You said Gannon's bleeding and you...

L: Make this a priority then. You want your family, and you mean that and you're not trying to be... to throw me under the bus.

Al: Hey, you wanna get the FBI on the phone and tell 'em what you heard? I'll call that lady right now. I'll call that lady right now and tell 'em you have the key piece of evidence. Amber. I'll call that Amber lady and tell her you have the key piece of evidence that they're missing.

L: Call her on three-way then.

Al: Call her on three-way? Alright, I gotta go to my message and look up the number or you can read the number to me hold on.

L: What did she say when you called her?

Al: What?

L: What did she say when you called her?

Al: She said that you hadn't–

L: I'm just over this so I'm just trying to understand why the FBI needs to call.

Al: I don't know, okay? I am telling you she reached out to me and said I'm with the FBI, how can I help you? That's what she said. We're to the point now where the FBI is involved so somebody saying they can help me then they can help me and that's what I want so I reached back out to her. You didn't message her. You lied to me.

L: Yes, I did. I'll send you the message right now.

Al: Alright, I'm gonna add her into the call, you ready? And you better tell her what you god damn heard, Tecia about that boy bleeding to death, alright? I'm adding the call right now. Three-way is starting, don't go nowhere.

FBI: This is Amber.

Al: Amber, hey, this is Al again, I got Tecia on the other line, can I merge you in?

FBI: Sure.

Al: Tecia, are you there? Tecia are you there? Tecia?

L: Yes, I'm here.

Al: Amber are you there?

FBI: I'm here, this is Amber.

Al: Okay, Tecia tell Amber whatever it is you got to say about what you heard when Gannon was bleeding to death, because that's what you've been telling me.

L: I did tell you, because Quincy was beating him up and hurting him. Can you hear me?

FBI: Yeah, did you say Quincy was beating him up and hurting him?

L: Yes, I've been telling everybody this for days.

FBI: Mm-hmm. So maybe because obviously I'm FBI and not El Paso County, I'd like for you to go through the story with me. I know it's awkward. I know it's weird. I know it's hard to talk to a stranger telling strangers things like this, but every detail helps us that's why we try to ask you ask many questions as we possibly can, so I'm sorry that you're gonna have to go through it.

L: How many times? I've talked to different people, and no one has ever tried to help me. I haven't tried to not tell you anything. There was three people that already called.

FBI: Okay, well, I'm sorry that I'm another person talking to you. If I'm making you relive something again, and I know it's a very personal situation, but I do wanna get as much information as I can from you because every detail does matter, and it counts. So, I'd like you...

L: Let me just call you back. Can I call you back because I don't have a phone, so I'm gonna walk and get someone's phone if it's gonna be a long conversation.

FBI: Okay.

L: Is it that same number that I text? That 719 number that he gave me.

FBI: Well, the 719 number you guys just called me on is a cell phone, so... and I didn't receive any text messages.

L: Okay. Because I'm on this like text app because they took my phone. In a minute I'm gonna walk and grab another phone and call you right back, okay?

FBI: Okay.

Al: Are we gonna do it three-way again or what?

FBI: Hello?

Al: Tecia? Okay, she hung up.

The court takes a morning break.

Mr Allen resumes questioning Agent Cronin.

She says throughout all the phone calls, Letecia is more focused on herself than trying to help find Gannon. She would often drop nuggets of information that may explain away any evidence that had been found. Some of this evidence had not been publicised so only the person involved would be aware of it.

The next recording to be played to the court is another telephone call, this time between Agent Cronin and Letecia.

Agent: This is Amber. Hello?

L: Hi, I'm calling you back. Hi, I had to get someone's phone.

Agent: Sure. Alright, Tecia. Like I said, I know this this is an awkward thing for you to have to keep going through this over and over again, but I would like you just to start me at the beginning of this whole thing and try to walk me through it as to what happened.

L: So, I mean, am I just supposed to start from Monday because I already went through the whole everything else fifteen times and Monday is when, you know... (unintelligible)... thing, so is that where you want me to start from?

Agent: Yeah, sure start there. I mean, honestly, like I said you know we're in the detail business so it's always every little detail you can think of. It may be a help.

L: Okay. So, on Monday, we were gonna go get a bike. Our agenda was to get a bike.

Agent: Okay, and I'm gonna be one of these annoying people that I'm gonna try to get as much detail from you as possible 'cause like I said, Monday you're gonna go get a bike. Did you get the bike from somebody? Were you talking to somebody? Where were you gonna get the bike? You know, details about stuff like that.

L: I was gonna get to that.

Agent: Sorry.

L: I was just gonna say our agenda before we left home. that's all. The agenda was to get a bike that day that we were gonna trade in some sports equipment and then just you know go shopping a few times, a few places here and there and then come back home but then we set up the day that I was gonna leave Gannon at home because he stays at home sometimes by himself or whatever like if we're at work and yadda, yadda, yadda, but he wasn't feeling well because he had already hurt his foot.

He had some burns from the carpet fire that he accidentally set, so I didn't feel comfortable leaving him by himself. I didn't feel comfortable because I didn't wanna get fussed at about him being at home you know by himself, yadda, yadda, yadda, so I told him, I said, 'hey you have to ride with me'. I decided to stay home with him that day because Albert was out of town, and I said you have to ride with me. He was like, 'okay, can I take my switch?'

He wasn't feeling that well as far as like he was not complaining with any kind of pain or like sickness or anything like that, he just kinda felt down just because he had stayed up the prior night on Sunday, probably until about 3 or 4am because he has a lot of problems using the bathroom when he takes medicine and doesn't take it and he takes Vyvanse.

Agent: Mm-hmm.

L: Sometimes his stomach will get really backed up, it had already gotten that way. So, we stayed up a lot that night after I had put the fire out and he was in there in the bathroom he was kinda tired, exhausted, a little bit whatever, but I was like, 'hey you wanna just ride with me', so he did. It was about like maybe ten o'clock ish or so when I set the alarm to leave.

I think we went to Dunkin Donuts first—we went somewhere to get coffee. I'm not real sure. We got gas because there was no gas in the truck. I don't remember exactly where I got gas, I wanna say Exxon but I don't remember exactly. Then we got gas, you know then we just went on our little way and we went to PetCo which was on Nevada, I don't know the exit I'm not really familiar to give you that detail, I know it was on Nevada.

Agent: Okay, and is it easier for you to just kind of run through the whole story and then I can go back for the details or is it easier if in trying to think about it if you can give me the details on the way? Because obviously we wanna hit all these points like you said you went to Dunkin Donuts so I'd wanna know where that was, to get gas where you stopped there.

L: I mean, yeah, I can, I don't have access to give you exactly...

Agent: You don't have to give me the exact address because obviously I can look that up. The Dunkin Donuts, do you know what the street was?

L: No, it was in Fountain like the one near the house.

Agent: Okay, so Fountain like the one near the house is the Dunkin Donuts and what street was that on or do you know?

L: Mesa Ridge or something like that? Yeah.

Agent: So, you guys get up.

L: I wanna say that the gas store was right across the street first, it was one of the gas stores that was in the area right there the one across from Dunkin Donuts.

Agent: Ok so the Dunkin Donuts near your house on Mesa Ridge then the Costco across the street, then you guys hit PetCo?

L: No, no, I didn't say a Costco, I said the gas store.

Agent: Oh, I'm sorry. I can't read my own handwriting.

L: That's okay. Yeah. And then we went to PetCo. I went in PetCo, he was gonna go inside with me but he was like 'can I stay in the car and play the switch?' and I said, 'yeah' and so I go in PetCo and when I was getting out the car I was like well I probably should make him go with but then I was like you probably don't wanna shop with girls because he never liked shopping with me so I was like, 'yeah okay, he'll be fine'.

I don't ever worry about him in the car or anything but because he wasn't feeling that well I did keep going to look and check and make sure he wasn't looking for me or wanting to go to the bathroom or getting out. He knew that I was in PetCo but at the same time he knows I go somewhere, and I might say I'm in one store and go to the next store too,

Agent: So, did he go in with you at *Dunkin' Donuts* too then?

L: We went through the drive through at Dunkin' Donuts.

Agent: Okay. Alright so he stayed in the car at PetCo?

L: Right.

Agent: Okay.

L: Then we had planned on going to look at some of these bikes so I was like, 'okay, I have the information on my phone so I don't have my phone so it's just in there but...

Agent: So, you said you were gonna go look at these bikes, were you going to a store? Were you going to meet a specific person or...? Where were you gonna look at the bikes?

L: Right, there was that's how I looked up a bunch of things online, so I had the people's information where they said they had emailed back and said just call when you get close, you can come by and look at it.

Agent: Okay, so where all did you search online? Were you looking at... again, was it stores or you looking at was it Craigslist or what was it?

L: Yeah, it was local Craigslist in Colorado Springs, like just Googled Colorado Springs Craigslist or whatever.

Agent: Okay, so you were looking up Craigslist, did you find a lot of them? Just a couple of them?

L: I didn't... I never made... I didn't go to do it yet, that's why I hadn't got to that part to tell you that part.

Agent: Okay, so you're looking up a bunch of places on Craigslist as to where you might do it and then did you arrange to meet somebody?

L: No.

Agent: Okay, so what happened next, you looked on Craigslist?

L: I didn't look on Craigslist that day. I had already looked prior. I was saying that the conversations back and forth was whenever you're route just call and someone could look at it.

Agent: Okay, well.

L: I don't want you to think that...

Agent: No, I got you. So, you had already arranged with somebody to go meet them. Who did you arrange to meet? How were you in contact with em?

L: I said that prior I had looked online on Craigslist to find some different bikes on email when you reply to Craigslist you know how you have like email? I got their information in my phone. I messaged they said when you get close if you plan on coming up, as in up as in north, message whenever you wanted to come by.

Agent: Okay, so you were emailing with them back and forth and they tell you to come when they get close, so they gave you their telephone number?

L: I never told them for certain what day I was coming I just had it all, 'hey we're gonna go on Monday' to me and Gannon, there was no specific person that I was like, this is not even relevant to anything, I just wanted to let you know that was on our agenda.

Agent: Okay, and that's just, we're trying to recreate every moment that you can 'cause you never know what's important. So, you were gonna make this plan to go talk to somebody at Craigslist, you were emailing with them, you're gonna call if you get close, what happens next?

L: So, then we were out of time because we'd already been in town for a little bit, and we had to make sure we were heading back to get Laina.

Agent: Okay.

L: 'Cause Laina would get home from school, so I ended up not meeting with anybody. I just said I would go another day so that's why I said it wasn't really relevant.

Agent: Sure.

L: I just wanted to tell you that was on the agenda.

Agent: And that last thing you had told me was you were at PetCo, so were you just like hanging out in the parking lot doing that or did you drive somewhere?

L: No, I bought things in PetCo.

Agent: Yeah, it's just as you were saying you were out and about, so I didn't know if you made another stop or what was going on there.

L: No, I went to PetCo twice so by the time I was in Dunkin' Donuts, the store, PetCo twice and I don't even remember if I went in another shopping store because it's already been how many days?

Agent: Well, what'd you go to PetCo twice for? I mean, did you go to PetCo and then have to head somewhere else and then come back?

L: I mean, I always do that like go somewhere and then I'm indecisive and I go back.

Agent: Sure, I get that. So, after you left PetCo where'd you head then?

L: Well, I don't know exactly. I just was going to different stores. I don't even know if I did anything else. I feel like I went to the TJ Maxx but I don't remember how to tell you where the TJ Maxx was at.

Agent: Okay, well was it still in Colorado Springs, it's on the North side or...?

L: Yeah, I don't know. I mean, there's only stuff on the north side of us.

Agent: Alright, so you were at PetCo you went probably to somewhere else, maybe TJ Maxx and then back to PetCo again?

L: Yeah.

Agent: Okay, and then you said it was getting to the time you were probably gonna have to pick up Laina?

L: Yeah, we were gonna have to go home to get Laina, so we drove home. I remember I went inside the house, I get out, I walked inside the house, Gannon walked inside the house. I was gonna work out, so I had put like my headphones on 'cause I was gonna work out till Laina got there. I don't remember if we ate or something between there, I'm not really sure exactly what we did between there.

Agent: Okay, but it's the three of you there at the house or...

L: No. Laina hasn't gotten... hadn't got there yet.

Agent: Okay, she hadn't got home yet, okay.

L: Yeah, no. Gannon went to his room, he was doing stuff and playing whatever 'cause he was gonna have a sleepover so he kept you know moving his room around or whatever 'cause he's always wanting to have sleepovers.

Agent: Mm-hmm.

L: I had my ear... my headphones kind of like mash your head a little bit so I kind of pulled them back a little bit and I was listening or doing a thing or whatever and then I heard something really loud. It sounded like something hollow broke, but also you have to remember, you know, upstairs, downstairs, sometimes if you can like just walk loud it'll echo and sound like it was something loud you know so I just... one of the dogs started barking so of course I walked downstairs and Gannon had his door locked. I knocked on it like what are you doing, and... do I need to tell you word for word everything he said or...?

Agent: Well, I'm just trying to get whatever happened, so I mean if... what was he saying to you? You guys are just trying to... I have two boys too, so I totally get that there's the door's locked.

L: Yeah, so he was saying he was trying to keep Laina out, and I was like 'Laina ain't even here yet'. He's been trying to build this memory box 'cause I always told him I kept a memory box for my daughter, and I also had one growing up and I gave it to my daughter as a box. He's been doing everything with these boxes, I mean, he even put pieces of paper and trash in there. He saved the Nintendo thing that's like the cardboard, since you got boys you know, the cardboard box that it come in. He would put it in. So, he was being all secretive about the box and I'm laughing, and then I come back upstairs, and I had the garage open at that time. I think I might've closed it, I'm not really sure. At this point in time, I went back upstairs again and then I hear another loud noise and I was like, oh my god, Gannon, what are you doing again, and Laina hadn't gotten there quite yet and then when I go down, I realized that someone was in our house.

Agent: Okay.

L: And so, they asked me, you know…(unintelligible)… at first, all I remembered was what he looked like or whatever, so I'll get back to that later. I was just gonna tell you that I finally remembered that when I initially called the police, I thought Gannon was hiding.

Agent: Okay. Well, and we've kind of skipped a lot right there. So, you heard somebody, or you found out somebody's in your house, were you downstairs? Were you upstairs?

L: (Unintelligible).

Agent: I'm sorry, I think you're cutting out.

L: I'm sorry, I might've said it was cutting out, it's just hard. I'm just trying to get off the Wi-Fi or whatever.

Agent: Sure.

L: (Unintelligible).

Agent: So, yeah, you were in your story, and you basically had said the last thing I was hearing was you're sitting there, you've heard a loud noise downstairs and then you realized somebody was in the house so…

L: I realized somebody was in the house.

Agent: How did you realize somebody was in the house? Because if you're upstairs and you know that Gannon was downstairs did you go down there and see him?

L: I just told you, what I just told you, I just told you that, I said I went down there and… did you not hear me say that?

Agent: No, I'm sorry, it's probably cutting out. So, you went downstairs and what did you see?

L: Well, I went downstairs immediately, and I saw that this guy was standing at the storage room which is in between Gannon's room and our downstairs basement.

Agent:Okay, and as you're looking at this guy what does he look like?

L: He was dark skinned, like Hispanic, maybe mixed, you know? I'm not real sure like as far as to give you a nationality, more darker skinned complexion, about like 5' 7", and about maybe about 180 pounds.

Agent: I'm sorry did you say 108?

L: In my mind I didn't, in my mind I didn't just go over those originally, I got scared and then I just kinda...

Agent: Yeah, oh I'm sure it's terrifying. I mean, I can imagine it would be terrifying to see somebody in your house. So, you'd said he is about 5'7", 180 or 108? Am I? Did I miss-hear you?

L: 180.

Agent: Oh, okay.

L: I say 180 because my husband is like 200, so like smaller than him, so that's why I would say 180.

Agent: Okay, and do you remember anything else about him, like his hair colour? What he was wearing?

L: Yeah, he was very close-cut, beard, he had a tattoo on his arm, I don't remember what it was, I just vaguely remember that.

Agent: What was he wearing?

L: I don't really remember. I've had so many bad dreams that I've pictured so many different things that I've pictured so many different dreams now that I don't remember.

Agent: And as you're looking at him, which arm was this tattoo on?

L: I don't remember.

Agent: Okay, I mean was he facing you, was he facing away from you.

L: Right, so he was coming out of our storage room which I can assume, I don't wanna make any speculations, that's where he was hiding at, and now, so let me tell you what was weird about that before I finish. When I got there the alarm was... I set the alarm away, when I got there, I mean when I left, but it was armed stay, but it didn't dawn on me at the moment what armed stay meant, that someone there's no...

Agent: Your motion sensors, I know what that means, I got you.

L: So, it didn't dawn on me that I didn't have to put the alarm in when I walked in so none of this went through my mind until in the moment all this is running through my mind, like this is why because I was thinking dogs or whatever, but I was like, this is why all this stuff happened and this is why the alarm didn't...

Agent: So, do you think that somebody reset your alarm? Is that what you're getting at?

L: Do what now?

Agent: I'm sorry, so were you thinking that somebody reset your alarm? Because you said that it was at stay instead of away.

L: No. You don't reset it. If you have, the way that ours is set up because of how that door didn't have a sensor on it, for example if I set it on arm away and I left for the dogs and say one of the dogs got out their crate and moved it would go to armed stay first because there was already motion in there.

Agent: Okay, so when you left the for the day did you set it as stay or away when you and Gannon left at ten?

L: I'm pretty sure I set it as arm away, 'cause this is something I had to show later on so we were talking about it. I'm not a positive if that's why, I'm just saying that was something later on that when we went through everything, that was what we noticed that it went to armed stay.

Agent: Okay.

L: Anyway, at this point in time I was thinking he's gonna like completely rob us because he had one of our guns, so at this point I knew that he had already been in our house somewhere somehow sometime because in order for him to have obtained a handgun he would've had to already be in the house.

Agent: Okay, did you guys normally lock your weapons up?

L: No.

Agent: Where do you normally store 'em?

L: They're all over the house, so prior to this happening my husband and I went on a cruise and we had hired a lady, my daughter was old enough to stay at home with them but we hired a lady to come stay as well on Rover.com and she just kind of stayed in the house so when she came we moved the handguns downstairs and like Albert... we were talking about making sure we weren't just leaving them around the house even though she had been like checked on Rover and stuff like that we didn't want...

Agent: Sure.

L: So, I had took the handguns downstairs so that was the only reason that two of the guns would've been downstairs because we had just got back from our cruise, and we had hidden them down there in the storage room.

Agent: Okay, so he came out of the storage room with one of the weapons you had previously stored in there is that what you're saying?

L: Yeah, and when I say hidden, they weren't like put away somewhere they were just in the storage room they were inside.

Agent: Okay, and which weapon was it that he had with him?

L: One of the black ones.

Agent: Was it a handgun? A long gun?

L: Yeah, a handgun, the big guns were upstairs.

Agent: Okay.

L: So, at first, I was in shock thinking, whatever you want, and I'm not gonna go through screaming what I said, I'm just gonna tell you, you won't understand me if I get worked up on the phone, like four different times telling people so I can't go through screaming and all that again.

Agent: Obviously, you don't have to scream at me, I understand.

L: Yeah, no I just don't want you to think I, you know, word for word, verbatim to tell you what I said and this and that and the other, so I immediately was... Gannon was in the room maybe two feet from his door doing his thing yadda, yadda, yadda.

Agent: I'm sorry, he was... Gannon was in his room or Gannon was outside of his room? So, he saw this guy out there too?

L: No, no, no, no. Gannon was still in his room, I was just giving you a distance of how far 'cause Gannon's door was open at this point 'cause Gannon had I guess opened his door.

Agent: Okay, because you said his door's open, but you could see Gannon in his room?

L: Yeah, yeah, and I could see Gannon in his room.

Agent: Hmm.

L: So, he... I don't remember exactly what the guy was saying to me I just remember I was like yelling and Gannon was yelling and as soon as Gannon saw that I was like freaked out and scared and I told him he could have whatever he wanted all this. So, it went about one hour of us just sitting there, me and Gannon sitting in his room that this guy was asking questions. He was asking did we own this, did we own that, all I remember was about weapons and did we know anything about these people he said somebody named Terrence and I don't even know. I didn't know, have no clue who he was talking about, what he was talking about. My assumption was he had the wrong people that he was looking for because we haven't even lived there that long we don't even know these people.

Agent: Okay, so what kind of possessions was he asking you about if he had? I mean was he asking you about your possessions or somebody else's or what?

L: Yes, he was asking was there a safe, like your typical thief you know like things that a thief would want. If we had a safe, was there any money in the house and I swear to you we don't keep any I swear to God we don't keep any money in the house we barely even keep our card on us. Oh crap, this is at 2%, hold on one second.

The call ends.

Agent Cronin takes the stand again. She tells the court how Letecia's phone and vehicles were being tracked during this time.

A final phone call between Letecia and Al is played.

Al: Hello.

L: Hey.

Al: What is it? I'm freaking beat, Tecia.

L: What?

Al: I'm beat. What, what do you want?

L: So, is it alright if I talk to you?

Al: I'm just beat, I'm just telling you I'm tired, go ahead, whatever.

L: Why are you tired?

Al: Because this is frickin' stressful, my son's out there missing, and I don't know what the hell's going on.

L: We have people who are looking for the guy now.

Al: Okay, the Quincy Brown guy?

L: Why do you keep saying the Quincy Brown guy? Like it's a joke?

Al: I'm not, no I'm not what did the frickin' FBI Say? Are they looking for him now?

L: Well, I gave her my information and I also got a call at the same time which the attorney said he had just talked to El Paso and he was like, 'you do not need to say another word to them so you need to hang the phone up', because I've already clearly gave them this information and at this point in time he was like, 'if they are not reaching out to help you then they're doing nothing to help the investigation', he said so he's getting back on the phone with El Paso and El Paso's supposed to be doing the job because they're the lead agency even though the FBI's taking over, I mean FBI was working, they're not the lead agency so he said to communicate with El Paso and that's exactly what he did.

Al: So, the lawyer's communicating with El Paso?

L: Right.

Al: Okay, alright. I'm trying to keep it all straight. But you did talk to the lady? That's what you've been doing this whole time?

L: Yes, I did talk to her.

Al: Okay. Okay, you talked to her?

L: Right, I talked to her and then the attorney was emailing me back and forth because the lady, this investigative reporter went back out there to this house and he told me, 'do not say another word because El Paso is the lead agency and they could potentially be messing up the investigation', and at the same time, as much as you know he's gonna be wanting to find Gannon, he's also making sure that no one else is interfering because he said something about this person that's who needs to be doing it. He's already sent the information to them.

Al: Okay.

L: He also already forwarded Nicole who went out there to his house, and everything.

Al: Nicole?

L: That's the investigative reporter that we hired Nicole—her name's Nicole.

Al: Okay. You hired an investigative...

L: I didn't hire an investigative reporter, this is whoever the attorney is in contact with, an investigative reporter, yes. I don't know if you hire them, I don't know if you pay them, I don't know what you do, I just know she's an investigative reporter.

Al: Okay.

L: Why do you keep talking to me like that, like okay, like I'm on trial with you?

Al: I'm just trying to listen to what you're saying. So, they went to find this Quincy Brown, did they find him?

L: I don't know if they did. El Paso is in charge they should be communicating with you the father.

Al: They're... I haven't heard anything from these people, have you talked to El Paso too or just Amber?

L: I was instructed by the attorney that everything had been sent to El Paso who is the lead agency, and I did exactly what I said I was gonna do.

Al: Okay. Okay.

L: And I was on the phone with her, and he said, 'do not say another word,' because I made sure that he was on the other line when I called her which is why I told her I'd call her back.

Al: Alright.

L: He said, 'do not say another word'.

Al: Okay.

L: For no reason, so you shouldn't be answering any questions that are not coming directly from El Paso.

Al: Okay, you said you forwarded the information, but have you talked to anybody at the El Paso?

L: If I have an attorney, do you think I talked to them, or my attorney talked to them?

Al: Okay. I'm sorry I'm just trying to piece it all together here you're taking to this lady, you're talking to that lady, you're talking to Bethel, you're talking to Katie, you're talking to Amber.

L: The investigative reporter is for me, like they are on my side.

Al: Okay.

L: The attorney is obviously on my side, so that's who the information will go through.

Al: Okay, what, so...

L: He reported it.

Al: Okay, now that you got people on your side what can I do for you? What do you need me to do to help you get this information or whatever...?

L: Help me get what information

Al: Okay, I mean what can I do to help you? What do you need me to do, just in general, nothing specific what do you need? You tell me.

L: I need you to be with your family so that when Gannon comes home, we can all be together and stop putting me on trial, that's what you can do for me in general. You can show me some love, you can show me everything that I'm showing you. I've showed you love. I told you, hey I miss you, I love you. Oh my gosh I wanna be there to hold you. I wanna hug you. I wanna do all these things with you. That's what you can do in general is to treat me that same way back because I have done that to you. I haven't downed you, talked crap to you. I defended myself, just like I told you. You know good and well, I...

Al: Alright, so.

L: I know what you're going through. I understand the pain.

Al: Right.

L: I don't know what you feel, but I tried to be here for you and that's what I want to continue to do is be here for you.

Al: Okay, well.

L: I also let the attorney know that I would... you have to hire a private person, they said that police don't even do that because it's not admissible, you can hire a private person to administer a lie detector test if I wanted to get those results to you.

Al: Okay, um, so your attorney told you not to answer any more questions, but does that mean me cause what if I have questions, and we can just work through those like we've been working through, does that include me?

L: No, no, no, no, no, you told me if I talked to the lady and if I reported everything, you told me that I will have a meeting with you and your exact words were that we would go from there when we were done trying to find Gannon. That's exactly what you said to me. You said we would move forward when...

Al: Okay.

L: ... and be looking for Gannon. That's what you told me.

Al: Okay, so what about the meeting?

L: Okay? Here I am about the whole meeting part. Either you're in this with me and I'm in this with you or not that's where I'm at with the meeting, because I have done nothing wrong. I am not a criminal. I'm not a monster. I'm not someone that needs to be...

Al: Alright well.

L: ... the way I'm being treated...

Al: All that being said, when can we meet and where can we meet?

L: The meeting will be deciding where we are staying at together to protect each other.

Al: Okay, I didn't say what the meeting was about, I said when and where, Tecia?

L: Okay, that's the meeting where are you staying? Why come we can't come stay with you? If you have a place to stay that you've already paid for, why are we sitting here having to be like, okay, let's stay in this person's house, let's go to this hotel, why?

Al: Okay, alright fair enough, where are you at?

L: You just need to honestly answer, I don't need any more bullshit. You talked about honesty what you wanted from me okay, so honesty is wanted from you.

Al: Alright.

L: Why come we can't get our clothes, I know we can't bring... (unintelligible)... we left them in storage, but why come we can't get together with our clothes where our families is staying, okay? And then we get on a mission, whether we gotta get in the car, whether we need to be doing it ourselves to find him. Whatever, that's the plan I expect to hear from my husband not just... like I'm some side piece that you're gonna meet, that's not who I am.

Al: No, I didn't say side piece and meet, I said meet up to talk about the truth and actually, I mean, I told you initially, no, please listen, please listen. I'm not putting you down, I'm not being mean to you, okay, initially we talked about what the standard was, and you know how I am about my standards. The standard is the truth and a meeting. Okay. In...

L: The truth, Albert, I've already told you the truth.

Al: Okay, that's why I said what about the meeting, that's why I started this conversation, let's talk about the meeting but then there's the truth.

L: You just said the meeting to get the truth.

Al: No, I know.

L: (Unintelligible).

Al: No, listen to me, listen to me I'm trying to clarify for you, okay. There's another part of the truth that you haven't told me, like where you are. You're not in the north end of Colorado Springs, okay? We've established that. Where are you? That's some truth that you can let me know.

L: Okay. I will tell you but if this gets out, I swear it's because you told it.

Al: Okay.

L: Because nobody knew where we are at.

Al: Fair enough and I'll stand by that. If somebody finds out where you are then you can blame me all day long and tell your lawyer that I'm some kind of criminal okay?

L: I'm not gonna tell 'em that you're criminal.

Al: I'm just saying, okay.

L: I stayed in the Extended Stay America in the north end of. We switched to one hotel...
what'd you say?

Al: I said okay.

L: We switched from one hotel to the next hotel then at that point in time I had no more
money, nothing.

Al: Okay.

L: Nothing at all. I had people reach out to me on Instagram and they were like, *hey why
don't you come here why don't you come there?* I don't have a car, I don't have anything, why
do you think people are messaging you wanting to know where we're at? Because nobody
fucking knows. No one knew this. So, Michelle reached out to your *Facebook* she's a girl
that I always talk about when we go to the monument and how we always pass by, I say
'hey my friend Michelle stays there, and she sells cleaning products'.

Al: Yeah right, I remember.

L: Okay, Michelle has a big ass house out here in Monument and she has a building that
is like an apartment over her garage, and she let us come here two nights ago.

Al: Okay.

L: That's why your dog, 'cause she has dogs and we have dogs. I can't stay here forever.
I can't stay here long. We can only stay here just basically for the time being because I've
been trying to work without my husband. And you think I... where do you think I got
money to stay all these places? You act like I'm just living it large staying at all these... Oh,
man, I'm up at the Hilton, I mean...

Al: Alright listen.

L: We haven't had anywhere.

Al: I'll get in my real car, and I'll come to Michelle's house and get you. Just send me an
address.

L: And where are you taking me? Because I know you, you'll try to play me and you'll try to be like, well, you know whatever... so, am I coming to stay with you? Or are you coming to Michelle's house just to play me? And I need the truth.

Al: My intent would probably be just to meet. I don't know if staying together is the right answer now because of all the unknowns, okay?

L: Okay, well if you don't wanna stay with me then that tells me that that's not in the... you don't want to be that picture perfect that you said back in December, that's not what you...

Al: No, no, don't tell me what I want.

L: Then tell me.

Al: I am.

L: Tell me the damn real truth why you don't want me and Harley with you?

Al: Because I want my son. Because I want my son. Because I want my son. The bottom line, and until we get him...

L: Let's not do this. Why would you punish me?

Al: I don't wanna do this. I don't wanna do this. You wouldn't tell me what you heard, you wouldn't tell me the whole truth for days and days, for three weeks now. I'm willing to meet you, to stick out the olive branch as an effort for peace, okay, okay because...

L: Peace?

Al: Yes, peace because you haven't given me the truth until today, you've gotten closer to the truth, okay? Or maybe you gave me the whole truth today, I don't know we'll take it at that, but I'm offering you a moment of peace, a time to meet, a time to talk, we can hug or whatever, okay? But I don't wanna stay together right now because then it's gonna be constantly on my mind, it's gonna be a fight, at least this way we can meet and talk and then we get time to cool down, think about it, that's what I've been doing every day, trying to talk to you and then cool down and then answer you in the email if I can if I feel like it, and then give it another shot the next day. That's exactly the same model I'm trying to teach you, not teach you try to do right now, okay, that's it.

L: It doesn't bother you that, hey, you know, I should be providing somewhere for my wife, daughter and my other daughter and my son to live while we're going through this?

Al: Right, but we don't know where...

L: That doesn't register in your brain?

Al: It does.

L: Don't sugarcoat it.

Al: There is no sugarcoating it. It does bother me that my family got ripped apart when my son was taken away, okay? Yes, it absolutely bothers me.

L: So, if you know that this dude has Gannon, took Gannon, why are you blaming me? Why are you? Why would you...?

Al: I didn't blame you.

L: (Unintelligible)... to lay down beside your wife?

Al: Listen, because the only reason... no. The only thing I blame you for, okay? The only proof I have right now to blame you for anything is you called in a runaway when you knew he wasn't a runaway. That's it, okay? We can move past that, you were scared, you freaked out, whatever, I'm not putting words in your mouth, that's it.

L: True.

Al: Right, you called in a runaway, right? I understand you were scared and freaking out, okay, I'm just saying.

L: I didn't want to hurt anybody.

Al: Right, and I didn't wanna get lied to, but I did. So that's something we gotta work through and that's what I'm saying—we meet, we talk, we hang out, we grab a bite to eat, I dunno, something stupid, and then we take a breath, okay? Just like we've done the past couple days. We're working our way up to a meeting now, we've been talking, we didn't talk for two weeks, okay? It's baby steps here. You've got to understand that my son is missing and I've gotta get through this little by little until he comes home. And that story, okay, the runaway story, the only thing that I know to blame you for right now, the only blame I point in your direction, okay? That caused a gap between us, and I've said that numerous times, there's a gap between us, and the only way to get back is baby steps, and you've got to respect that, okay?

L: You have to also realize that when someone is terrified, they have to do... they act in the moment, do what they think. It's the scaredness. Don't you have compassion for that?

Al: I do. I have compassion for that.

L: (Unintelligible).

Al: Listen, I have compassion.

L: You'd rather sit in your room by yourself and not comfort each other every night, you would rather that and then when Landen comes back, you'll see her every day and not your wife?

Al: But you gotta have compassion for me and a little bit of empathy on my perspective, okay? Because of the runaway story, the cops, the neighbourhood, everybody searching spent days and days and days, and we lost valuable time trying to find Gannon because of that story. And now, three weeks...

L: But I was still...

Al: No, now, three weeks later, I find out Quincy Brown, a sex offender, has my son and the last story you told me was that somebody was trying to stick something up his butt and now I've gotta think about a sex offender having my son, okay? So now you got to have some compassion for me.

L: I do have compassion for you that's why I wanted to be with you to hold you.

Al: No, that's what you want, okay?

L: I know, I just said that.

Al: Having compassion for me is not telling me what you want. Having compassion for me is respecting what I need, and I need baby steps right now, and the next baby step is I'm willing to meet you, okay? I'm willing to meet—that's the baby step but you need to send me an address of where you're at and I'll come to you, and we can meet and if that's unacceptable then...

L: You kicked me off the insurance and you've got a car?

Al: Listen, I'm talking about baby steps to get us closer to Gannon and to family, okay? Meeting me is that next baby step if you can't send me an address where you and Harley are, or at least you're at.

L: (Unintelligible)... and now you've got a car. Why...?

Al: I told you I got a rental car, one of my family members helped me out with a rental car so I could search for Gannon, and I could do what I have to do, okay? But if you can't...

L: Why is there a name on the insurance then, why... (unintelligible).

Al: If you can't, we can talk about all that. That can be part of our meeting, but if you can't meet me, if you can't tell...

L: Why won't you just tell me why is there... (unintelligible).

Al: Alright, here we go. I wanna meeting, you keep changing the subject, so we're gonna have to take three or four steps backwards from this point, okay?

L: No, I wanna do the meeting, I just want to know did you let them take my car?

Al: Who? Who take what car?

L: There's two rental cars.

Al: I don't have two rental cars. I don't know what the hell you're talking about. You got somebody trying to PI me or something? What two rental cars you talking about?

L: No, I just... you said they had a rental car, and you had a rental car.

Al: Who's they?

L: You said Landen had a rental car.

Al: Oh, yeah, Landen. Okay, listen, I don't know what the hell Landen's got going on, her Aunt Veronica's got all that money, and they went to Texas, that's all I know, okay? Whether they still got a rental car or not I don't know, that's all been from her Aunt Veronica. I had to get my family to help me out, okay? And that's all that matters here, so I'm giving you the truth. I'm ready for the truth about where you're at, the address of where you're at so we can have the meeting. If not, like I said we're taking some steps backwards and we'll try again tomorrow, and that's kind of where I'm at right now in this moment.

L: We would take steps backward because I just wanted to be with you. That would be steps backward? When you just told me to have compassion, so I'm just sitting here trying to talk to you.

Al: Okay, Tecia, listen, here we are.

L: You tell me steps backward when I'm just asking... Just tell me, are you trying to be with somebody else? Just tell me.

Al: Am I trying to be with somebody else when my son's out there missing? So here we go changing subject, we change the subject back to Tecia now, alright.

L: No, I just want to know the truth 'cause I want...

Al: Well, I wanna know the truth. You never answered my question about what you heard, okay? So, I wanna know the truth too, but you know what, I bent a little bit, I bent a little bit more, and now I'm bending again... I know you're just not gonna answer my questions so let's meet but that's...

L: Okay, I'll answer your questions if you don't yell at me. Don't yell at me and don't scream at me.

Al: The question of what you heard?

L: If you ask a question, you let me answer it and stop interjecting and treating me like I'm on trial.

Al: Absolutely, you got it.

L: Now go.

Al: What did you hear in the moment that there was bleeding and everything going on. What you heard—that was the question you didn't answer.

L: I'm trying to finish.

The police had left, okay? I put Harley and Laina upstairs in the room, told them don't come out. Nothing terrible, bad—nothing had happened at that point in time. I was still terrified. If I mentioned to the police, if I sent a note, if I did anything, I didn't know what was gonna go wrong.

I told you this seventeen times. I've told them this. You can ask me why didn't I do things differently, I was fucking scared, okay? Scared.

Went back downstairs, okay. I didn't have, we didn't have a safe, we didn't have money. I told him that we didn't have a safe, told him that we didn't have money. I was saying no, we didn't have a safe and I wasn't saying it in this tone like no, whatever, just not gonna be reliving all of it like that—no we don't have a safe, no we don't have this.

I couldn't get your gun upstairs to work. I tried, there were no bullets to the shotgun, and I couldn't get the other gun to work, or I was gonna run back downstairs and frickin' light his ass up. That was my mind. That was what I was gonna do. Couldn't get it to work. Ran back downstairs, girls are upstairs. I knew I had two of our three children safe. And If I would tell you this you'd be like, 'well why was it two of them and not all of them? Why was it not this one and not that one?' People are not realizing that I didn't pick and choose, okay?

Come back in there, plead again about I would do anything, money whatever it may be, okay? Jewellery, I offered every single thing that there was.

He kept saying we had a safe and I kept saying we didn't have a safe.

He grabbed me, pulled me back into the storage room, my hands were tied, I already told you this, seventeen times again, my hands were tied, completely.

Harley, Laina upstairs either sleeping, whatever they were... it was late night at this point in time—11, 12, midnight, whatever it may have been.

I left Harley a note on the counter that said please recall police, gave her the word that we always say is the code word, what is the word that we always say whenever there was trouble?

Al: Desperado.

L: Right. I always said when Harley, you ever heard of that word it means trouble, right? She didn't catch on to what I was saying which I can't blame her, she doesn't, she's sometimes ditzy. Didn't catch on to what I was saying. Nothing.

I called you back. I called you back with him sitting there. You didn't answer, not your phone. I was in my mind thinking if I said to Albert the code word, he might at least think something anything. But no, you could've been on the phone, I don't know.

All I hear is Gannon screaming. He's yelling at me to shut up 'cause he's standing... (unintelligible)...

I did hear a loud noise as if Gannon hit something.

I'm screaming, I'm sitting there trying to make noises because if they're above me then maybe someone will hear it on the wood pieces. Nobody helped. Nothing came. No one. No one came for anything.

When I came back from hitting my head which was hit on that wood piece that's in our storage room, Gannon was gone.

I freaked out. I get in my car which I'm sure they've probably seen on camera. Did I get in my car? Drive maybe once or twice around the neighbourhood thinking you know, what in the hell am I gonna do now? Albert's gonna fucking kill me, everybody's gonna kill me, that's all I kept thinking and Gannon's gone. And I haven't slept in how many days reliving how... if I could have done something. I'm not gonna go fight somebody who has a gun with a knife.

I don't know how they left. I don't know. And the only reason I even know who it was is I told you about the badge. More and more, I'm remembering because I had nightmares every flipping night who it was. Images in my mind. Pictures. Over, and over, and over, and over, and over again. And again, and again.

Can I do anything about it? No. It didn't matter whether I said someone was... something happened. It didn't matter what I said in that moment. My mind immediately went to oh my god. You hear about this. I look on the neighbourhood App all the time. Shit goes down and you don't... like, in your brain you plan if something was to happen what you're gonna do and then you can't, your body don't let you.

I'm not a person who even remotely tried to be a badass with a gun All of it ran through my mind. How am I gonna go find Gannon? How am I gonna go do this? We gotta get help, resources and then if I say, hey you know this fucker was in our home, all they're gonna tell me is I'm fucking crazy and need mental help. I need to see a psychiatrist or some fucking shit. That's all that's gonna be told to me. So, I went the very next day, so no one wasted resources. I went the very next day, that morning, I mean that afternoon. When I talked to them, I explained to them exactly what I told you.

Al: Hey Tecia, Tecia, Tecia, hold on, hold on, hold on listen this is the worst fucking story yet alright, I'm done with this shit.

The call ends.

The court breaks for lunch.

Agent Cronin is back on the stand.

Mr Allen resumes questioning. He asks if there was any actual person called Michelle who lived in Monument and she said no, there was no such person.

Agent Cronin says what Letecia told Al that she planned to do to Quincy Brown was actually what she did to Gannon. Using a gun and a knife and then driving around afterwards thinking, 'Al's gonna kill me,' were all actual events but altered for her story.

Mr Allen has no further questions.

Mr Cook begins cross-examination. He asks the agent why when Letecia had admitted she was aware of the blood in the basement why she hadn't been arrested then.

She said it wasn't her call to make and they had to wait for the DA to inform them when they had enough evidence for an arrest warrant to be issued.

Mr Cook has no further questions.

The next witness called is ex FBI Agent Jonathan Grusing. He had worked for the FBI for 25 years up until his retirement 2 years ago.

A lot of his training was focused on studying behavioural patterns. Letecia was at the centre of her own universe and would try to shift blame to other people including Al, Landon and Landon's husband, Mike.

Another shorter phone call between Al and Letecia is played next.

Al: Hello. So, I just got off the phone with your girl, Nicole, and then I talked to the investigative reporter. Do you know what I found out?

L: What?

Al: I found out where Quincy is, so... we're making progress. His family at the house believes he's been in Mexico for over two years and hasn't been back.

L: Yeah, no, that's not true.

Al: How do you know?

L: Okay, okay, okay, you're not gonna listen to me.

Al: I did, I listened to you.

L: And you think I made up these stories?

Al: I listened.

L: Really?

Al: I listened to you. I listened to your contact, Nicole. I listened to the person she sent, who is the investigative reporter that you were referencing, so all of that was true, so, thank you for telling the truth on that, okay? The part that's not true is Quincy Brown, he's been in Mexico for two years. Quincy Brown is not involved in this.

L: No, he has not! Mexico? Are you that dumb? Mexico.

Al: That's what his family said not... yeah, that's what his family said.

L: Oh yeah, so the family said Mexico.

Al: Yeah, because they've been looking for him too, believe it or not. Go figure.

L: Yeah. Sure.

Al: So why the misinformation? Why are you telling me not true. The news people said this is misinformation that's why they're not running your story.

L: I didn't give them any information.

Al: Yeah, you did, you gave them Quincy Brown. You gave them misinformation. You gave them a story, okay?

L: I didn't give them any news story.

Al: Yeah, Nicole's a news person—you know that. You called her and did an interview with her or statement or whatever, so yeah, you did give her misinformation. That's what they called it. That's what they called it, Tecia, call them back and cuss them out, don't talk to me like this. You gave them misinformation.

L: ... okay? That's what the ID said.

Al: That's what the ID said, and somebody took his ID from two years ago and is now...

L: You need to figure that out because he's not in Mexico.

Al: And that's what I'm doing, trying to figure it out, okay? And you're not working with me here. You said you want to be an involved parent...

L: He has not been in Mexico.

Al: ... I'm just blown away because you say you wanna be an involved parent. You sent me a picture of this dude, okay? What did you get the picture from?

L: Nicole said is this him and I said yes.

Al: Okay. So, Nicole sent you the picture. You've also got messages from this dude, who never says who he is.

L: (Unintelligible) ... the number that they took?

Al: I got it, I got it. But it never said, hey, this is Quincy, send me my money, you know...

L: ... I said that's what he looks like.

Al: Okay.

L: Then he has Gannon in Mexico. Are you stupid? Mexico, that's bullshit, this is what people do.

Al: Okay, but you said he wasn't in Mexico, now you're saying he's in Mexico. They said he was there for two years.

L: People can go back and forth to Mexico. That's an indicator to you right there.

Al: Yeah, but you know what? Check it out, though. He's been wanted for over two years, if he came back and forth across the border in the past month, they would've stopped him because he's a wanted man, okay?

L: No, they wouldn't.

Al: And you just said it's perfect that Gannon's in Mexico? That's one of the worst places in the world right now.

L: (Unintelligible).

Al: For who?

L: You.

Al: What's wrong is my son's missing and you keep lying to me, okay? That's what's wrong, Tecia. That's what's wrong. Okay, fine, give me my son back. Tell the truth, give me my son back.

L: (Unintelligible).

Al: Where's he at then? Who has him? You know, you have not answered one of my questions.

L: (Unintelligible) ... to do that.

Al: Well, guess what? I don't want you to call me back because you're not doing nothing but lying to me and sending me in a different direction to what you know is the truth.

L: Okay, whatever. Good for you, thank you.

Mr Allen continues his questioning of Mr Grusing.

He said it was clear to him during this phone call that Letecia was taking no responsibility for the disappearance of Gannon and that she even appeared relieved that Gannon could actually be in Mexico. But they had already discovered that Quincy Brown was just a fugitive on a wanted page, and he had been in Mexico for two years. This was just another example of misdirection by Letecia.

Another phone call is to be played to the court.

L: What?

Al: Do what?

L: What?

Al: I'm just trying to help get to the bottom of this, Tecia, like you said in the message. I'm just trying to do this for Gannon.

L: Yeah, but this whole time, for three weeks, you've been just like all these people, so you know what? I'm gonna be just like them too, full of speculation, full of lies, full of craziness. I'm gonna be fucking crazy as hell just like this...

Al: So, you're starting that now?

L: ... that's the truth. Huh?

Al: You're starting that now, is that what you're telling me?

L: No, that's how you treated me. And I've been sitting there playing into your game, and all the listening and things—you think I'm ... (unintelligible).

Al: No, I'm just trying to get to the truth and get to Gannon.

L: Do you think I'm stupid?

Al: No. You think I'm stupid.

L: You say you wanted to get to Gannon, and you think I'm not gonna be a fucking crazy ass. You think that for a second? You think I'm not smart enough? Oh, it's invested a lot because, oh, my god, I worshipped the ground you walked on.

Al: Okay, but that being said, why would you give me Nicole's number...?

L: (Unintelligible).

Al: That's fine, that's fine, we're miles away from that, so...

L: Miles away from what?

Al: Miles away from the truth first of all, because this Quincy guy has been gone for two years. The news said that, not me. Okay? The news said that. They also got a confirmation from the sheriff, that this guy was not involved, period. It's misinformation.

L: If that's what they say then they have the answers.

Al: Okay, but between me and you, why can't we just move past Quincy?

L: Because you're not trying to move forward in your fight for your wife and your family. As long as you treat me like that, act like that, I'm gonna be the same damn way.

Al: Okay but hear me out.

L: You treat me like shit, and you think I'm supposed to come be your hero.

Al: Okay, listen. I am trying to get past that point because Quincy being involved in this...

L: You made it so we don't have anywhere to live, and no food and you still can live in a hotel?

Al: Yeah, but you had me believing in Quincy until the news and the El Paso told me it wasn't true.

L: You don't care. We don't even matter to you.

Al: Okay, so you've been telling me stories this whole time, is that what you're telling me? You've been lying to me intentionally?

L: No. (Crosstalk). Why not?

Al: I think you're freaking out because you know that Quincy being not legit anymore is not good for you, and it's not good for Gannon.

L: Okay.

Al: So, listen, I want to start over with this, okay? I wanna start over and...

L: (Unintelligible).

Al: No, I got you, and I want you to ...

L: If you had me you wouldn't have abandoned me for two weeks.

Al: Okay but listen. When I started talking to you on the phone, the most honest you've been to me in this whole frickin' process is when you asked me, and you showed me that you cared and loved me. You asked, Albert, do you still love me? And I answered, and I said, yes, right?

L: Albert, you don't love me.

Al: No, no, no. Listen to me. I said yes, okay?

L: Would you stand by me and tell them all...?

Al: I said yes. And what you said, you said if this was an accident would you stand by me, and I said yes. I said I will stand by you if this was an accident.

L: How many people did you start texting and telling I them I was lying? I just wanna know because this is why I never got trusted through the whole two weeks.

Al: I didn't get on the phone and text no-one about this. And I know you're surprised by that, you can be, okay?

L: Whatever. You ain't told a soul about no names or nothing?

Al: The only person I've been talking about is the fact that Quincy Brown with the whatever Nicole Fiaro told me, okay? That the El Paso County Sherriff's officer you said call, I did exactly what you said. I trusted in you. I got in touch with them.

L: Three weeks.

Al: So, you don't even wanna talk about Gannon? You're not talking about Gannon, you're talking about you, okay?

L: No, this is not about me, it's about Gannon Stauch.

Al: It is. It is about you.

L: You wanna know why?

Al: That's not true because you're somewhere and you're healthy and talking to me. Gannon's not. That's why it's about Gannon, okay? Like I said, I want your honesty. The most honest you've been...

L: You won't even understand any of it if I tried to tell you that your fucking baby mama had something to do with it, you're not gonna believe me, but she did!

Al: Okay. Let's prove it. Give me the proof.

L: For you to fucking laugh at hotels with her?

Al: I'm not. I haven't once, I told you that. I don't care, you can accuse me all you want to like you've done for five years, I don't' have nothing to hide.

L: You won't even tell me anything. You haven't had the decency to tell me anything about nothing. You started kicking me off and kicking me to the curb, but you saw her every day though, didn't you?

Al: Not really, actually.

L: Oh, because she's your children's mother, right?

Al: Yes, absolutely. And you have information that you're not telling me, and you have the chance to show that you're better than her, okay? If she's involved in this, if she's involved in it let's take her down. If she's...

L: You go and make that statement that you're standing by your wife and then see what you get.

Al: Okay. If you sit right here, I will do that, okay? If you sit right...

L: You're a liar.

Al: No, no. Absolutely not. I'm not putting you down at all. You told me, the closest we've been to the truth, I'm gonna keep saying this, is when you asked me if I loved you and I said yes. And then you said if this was an accident and then you said stand by me. So, I think that was the closest to the truth we've been and that something happened. It was an accident and that's the most...

L: If something happened that was an accident where the hell did I put Gannon? What you think? What do the rest of the people think? You think it was an accident and I hurt him and did away with him.

Al: Listen. Hold on, I'm gonna tell you the truth right now. I'm not worried about Gannon right now. I'm worried about you. I'm worried about standing by you.

L: Yeah, you tell me what I want to hear.

Al: I'm not telling you what you want to hear, the only way to move forward with this. This was an accident, which I think is the truth and that you freaked out and I've told you that over and over again. Accidents happen, people freak out with accidents, they will understand that, okay? But the fact that you sent me on a three-day chase of Quincy Brown which is misinformation and not true, that's not good for you. What is good for you is that we can make it through this going down the road of an accident.

Crosstalk.

Al: No, I'm telling you the truth.

L: Ten percent of people don't make it through. If I hadn't saved Gannon's life in the fire, you'd still be treating me the same way.

Al: You saved his life from a fire?

L: I said if I didn't. If I didn't. Because God knows I couldn't figure out where the fire was coming from and Gannon was downstairs... (unintelligible)... for a second, that couch was on fire and Gannon would not be alive.

Al: No, I said that from day one, that you did what you had to do there, but how did you save his life? Was it from the accident with the candle that Gannon did or what? That's what...

L: Had I just laid back down because I'd already put the darn alarm off—I'd already put the alarm off.

Al: Yeah, I know, but you're a good person, you're a good mom, that's what good people do, okay? So that's never been in question. The fact that you're a good person, that just comes natural. The fact that what happened subsequent to that, what happened after that, made the accident... it compounded it ten times and now it's got way out of hand. So that's the only way to get out of this is to figure out what the accident was and go from there.

L: (Unintelligible).

Al: I can't hear you.

L: I'm asking somebody, because we don't have any food.

Al: Okay. Alright.

L: Yeah, gee. Alright. Thanks, that's really great, right. Albert.

Al: Yeah, I'm here.

L: I told you every single day. I woke up every single day and told you I want to tell you that I'm this bad person and something bad. I wanna tell you all that, I do.

Al: Why?

L: Because that's what you think. You have trashed me to everyone.

Al: I have not. Prove it. I have not trashed you to no-one. I have not put anything out in the public intentionally so we can get to the bottom of this, me and you, okay? And here we are trying to get to the bottom of it.

L: Sure, sure, you have your family thinking I'm a murderer.

Al: My family's not even here. I'm all alone again, I told you that. My family just wants to find their nephew, their grandson, their cousin, okay? That's what they want. How about Laina, their brother. Laina's losing her mind because her brother's missing.

L: You think I don't wanna see Laina?

Al: I didn't say see Laina. I said Laina's freaking out because Gannon's missing. What are you talking about?

L: I know, I said I do want to see Laina.

Al: I didn't say you didn't wanna see her, why, where did that come from? I said my mom's worried about her grandson. My siblings are worried about their nephew. Their children are worried about their cousin and then I said Laina's worried about her brother. And you said you wanna see Laina. Everybody wants to see Gannon. Everybody.

L: I know that, Albert.

Al: And I'm trying to get you to understand that if this was just an accident and it got out of hand and you panicked or whoever panicked, okay? That's something we can make it through. You can make it through that.

L: I'm not gonna believe that because you're gonna... (unintelligible).

Al: No, no. I'm not blaming you. I said it was an accident. Accidents really have no-one to blame. If an accident happens...

L: Okay. I was trying to be a cool parent. I already told you that. We placed the beds together, we talked about having a sleepover.

Al: Okay.

L: We were just acting crazy, okay? I already told you that Gannon fell and busted his lip and his toe that's where the blood came from. You all keep thinking there's some crime scene. You kicked everybody out of the house when that's not even... nothing happened to Gannon—deadly, hurtful, anything like that in the home. I'm sick of it. How am I supposed to help people when people won't even move past that? I told you this morning that was the accident I was talking about.

Al: Okay, so there was an accident with Gannon? That's what I'm trying to say, so what next? I mean what...?

L: (Unintelligible)... he was feeling horrible. He's absolutely feeling horrible because we had a fire. We had to run out. He's thinking that whatever you're gonna say, you're gonna be like... oh, my you know whatever, you're not gonna let me just tell you and be genuine unless you just be like maybe how can you even deal with this cause I'm dealing with it hard and comfort each other, you're not gonna do that. You think it's not killing me? Do you think that for a second?

Al: No, I know it's killing you. I know how you are when... because you're a good mom and you're a good person and when things don't go perfect, I know how you are.

L: Albert, do you love me?

Al: Yes.

L: Okay. What is the truth, are you going... don't tell me to make promises... are you going to make this right and stand by your wife?

Al: I told you that the other day, I will stand by you, yes.

L: And I said are you going to make it right?

Al: Yeah, we're going to make this whole situation right.

L: I'm talking about our family.

Al: Absolutely. That's what this is all about, our family. I said that from day one and every day this is about our family.

L: Okay. Because all I keep thinking about... is how he was supposed... I don't know if somebody was supposed to be sending him something online from Amazon. I don't know what promises people had made. I don't know about any kind of promises people had made about coming in March. I don't know about any of that. I just know he was upset...

... He was upset about the whole candle thing, and he kept saying to me that he messes up everything. He said it to me, and I kept saying that's why I didn't let Gannon go to school, he felt troubled with himself. He felt really bad with himself, he was very upset. So, we go on our same trip we've been over everything about the bike, we did all that, all that's true. We did all that. We go to PetCo we did all that. Then, when we leave, we're supposed to meet somebody about the bikes. Then end up and realise that I think somebody was following us, that's the god's honest truth, because when I got over, they got over, I go to turn, they go to turn, I swear to God somebody was following us all the time.

Anyway, I realise that I didn't have a phone for directions, so I turned around—turned back up to PetCo. He's still playing the switch. If you think for a second on some video he might've been whatever, he had busted his nose and his mouth, did you think I'd wanna send him to school like that? Honestly, did you?

Al: I mean, obviously not.

L: Okay, I didn't and then he was feeling so sorry. He didn't have bad burns. It was barely there. They were a little bit bubbly, but I was able to jump on it and put it out. So, then we go back to PetCo, and I say, 'Gannon, hey, we're gonna have to hurry up and get back to get Laina'. Albert, when I got back, Gannon was not in the car. At all. I didn't even know he wasn't in the car.

Al: From when you left PetCo?

L: I feel horrible because I feel like one of those people that didn't realise they'd left their baby in the car. Do you realise how freaked out. People wanna know why I drove around everywhere. Why my GPS went everywhere for days because I tried looking.

Now I have to sit back and have people fuss at me and say, first of all where's Gannon? I don't know. I told you this from the beginning. I don't know. I don't. You think it's not driving me insane? I don't know. You think I don't have to feel like... (unintelligible)... I didn't even pay attention.

He's always so quiet, I wasn't even thinking and then I go into panic mode thinking surely he's gonna be home, surely because he was talking about a friend with his brother had a car. I said, surely maybe he feels horrible, he's gonna call this person to do whatever and he'll be back home. That's it. And you think I don't have to live with this every single day?

Hello?

Al: I'm here. I'm just listening.

L: Now you're just listening. I give you what you want and you're just listening.

Al: Well, what do you want me to do? Do you want me to pick holes in it? I promised you I'd listen. You asked me to listen, and I promised it.

L: Oh, so now there's holes to pick in it?

Al: I can if you want me to. Do you want me to do that?

L: (Unintelligible)... to pick in it.

Al: Alright, listen. Listen, listen, listen, listen. I'm done. Okay? Because we started off talking about an accident, okay. Now basically we've got another Quincy Brown. What's this guy's name, okay? When you come up with the next person's name, you call me back, alright?

The call ends.

Mr Grusing is back on the stand.

He explains the strategy behind the suggestion there had been an accident. They had been able to dismiss the Eguardo story, as well as the Quincy Brown story. Letecia knew both these stories wouldn't go any further with Al and she was desperate for a relationship with him and so they decided to broach the accident scenario and to also remind Letecia she is a good person as well as a good parent to see if she would give them something else, which she did. The story of Gannon now being abducted from outside of PetCo was a new one suggesting nothing happened to him inside of the home.

The next call is played.

Al: Hello?

L: I just got back from the doctor.

Al: What for?

L: Really?

Al: Yeah.

L: I already told you this. I don't have a period and I'm five weeks pregnant.

Al: Okay. How'd it go?

L: (Unintelligible).

Al: Was that you messaging me this morning from another number?

L: Oh, no. This morning is whatever.

Al: No, I'm just asking, that way I know for sure.

L: I don't know, Albert. I don't know. Blame me for whatever.

Al: No, we're not playing the blame game, I just wanted to know because there may have been some details that I wanted to talk about because it was obviously relevant to the things we've been talking about for the past couple of days, so...

L: I would've thought that you would've just called me and said anything nice.

Al: Tecia, you know what my mind's on. My mind's on Gannon, okay? I told you I'd stand by you if we got to the truth so that's what my minds on. My mind's on the truth about Gannon.

L: I've given you the truth. I've given it to you, and I've given you fifteen different things that were not true just to prove a point. Call it what you want. Call it crazy or making up stories, or lying, or whatever you wanna call it and go text people and tell them how horrible of a person I am and I'm just lying and you're backing me into a corner. Know that when you text people, I hope you know that they're posting this stuff online.

Al: When I talk to who?

L: Anybody, unless it's probably legitimately people that you are blood related to then they send it to anybody or anyone... they send it to their best friend... kindergarten... they're posting it online.

Al: Well, I mean, I haven't said nothing to nobody so I don't even know what you're talking about.

L: Well, I'm just telling you that's probably what those people calling you is about. That's probably how they got your number—your number is online everywhere.

Al: I know it is and I mean...

L: People are posting messages that you supposedly sent people. I'm just saying, so, I mean, whoever you be talking to or whatever, people are putting it out there.

Al: Well good for them.

L: I'm just telling you that not to talk bad to you or talk about you or nothing, I'm just telling you that. Honestly, I spent the entire night getting pictures of you or messages made up on Google, all kinds of stuff like anything you could know that you're telling me right, these people are nut jobs.

Al: So, back to what you said a second ago. You told me that you made up all these stories to prove a point? Why would you tell me all these different stories? That doesn't make any sense. I mean, what point is there to prove other than the point of finding Gannon?

L: Because I cannot give you... no matter what I give you... of how Gannon is missing. I can't give you the answer of how did they get him.

Al: Why? No, but you told me...

L: I don't know! If you guys are so... (Unintelligible)... as to question me, you should call the Jose Baez law firm.

Al: I just wanna know why you told me all these different stories but then you told me you'd given me the truth so many times, but then you say a bunch of different stories, so I don't understand what you're trying to say. The only thing I...

L: I'm not walking you through any more stories or truths because it does nothing for me but make me unhealthy—make me stressed and I'm not good with this because I'm not eating, to be like this. I'm just not. It's not healthy and you guys think that you're gonna get me to... (Unintelligible)... myself, or admit to something I didn't do—you guys are all wrong. So, if you're gonna call me, call me, not to stand by my side, not to make any kind of statement to say that these people need to stop threatening your wife, you're not gonna do any of this in your family, of course I'm not just gonna sit there and play your games—if you're treating me like crap, which you've done, why would I treat you with any... (Unintelligible).

Al: I didn't hear what you said, you broke up. Why would you treat me with what?

L: I said, if you're not treating me with compassion, kindness, with any kind of support, with any kind of help, not treating me with any of that, why do I have to owe you any kind of the same respect that...? That's not...

Al: But I've offered that to you, okay? I've offered that to you. I said I'll stand by you once we get the truth, okay? That's what I've said the whole time, and I've told you, you can survive, and you can get through this, okay? It all comes down to the truth, that's the important point.

L: ... to get through something. For you all to think I'm gonna make up something, and it's hard to do something that I didn't even do. I'm not doing that. You called me and said things like oh, you're a teacher—you haven't even said a kind word to me about anything like that—do you think that I didn't think that was all a played-up thing?

Al: Listen, you're welcome to think whatever you want. I mean, you said you've loved me numerous times over the past couple of days and I've replied with the same thing.

L: (Unintelligible).

Al: Yes.

L: ... did you call me when I woke up in the morning to be kind to me? I love you. I miss you, have you said anything to me?

Al: I have but the problem is what you're telling me is finding Gannon is conditional on what you want and what you need. That is what you're saying. The truth is conditional.

L: I'm not... do you not think if I knew for a second how to get Gannon... (unintelligible)... that I would not be waiting on you, like, weeks ago?

Al: Well, I don't know. I don't know the truth on that because I know what you said that an accident happened and that you panicked. And when you panic and bad things... and things get out of control or whatever you said, and they go downhill…

L: I told you… you didn't accept the accident about jumping on the bed… you didn't accept it.

Al: I accepted that there was an accident that happened, you're absolutely right I accepted that, and you panicked.

L: No, that's' not what you accepted. I told you the truth. You asked me about the bedroom, and I've already told you this.

Al: Okay. Let's accept that an accident happened for a moment, but you keep putting somebody else into the picture and that is absolutely bad for you in the context of an accident or the context of anything if somebody else comes into the picture and you keep going down that road if I'm sitting here poking holes in it, which I don't want to do but it just doesn't jive with me. What do you think law-enforcement is gonna do?

L: I'm not worried about what law-enforcement is gonna do because Jose Baez is gonna rip them to shreds—I'm not worried about that. I'm not worried about law-enforcement because I didn't do anything wrong.

Al: Right. We've established it was an accident so how… why would Jose Baez have to rip anybody apart if you were involved in an accident?

L: That is… I never told you that anything was an accident other than what you asked me and I'm gonna keep telling you that 14 times and then you get mad at me and yell at me, scream at me and hang up the phone—tell me it's not a good enough answer.

Al: But you did tell me there was an accident. You told me a fire—that there were burns there was a candle spill—he accidentally stepped on a piece of wood.

L: You already knew all this.

Al: Right. But those are the accidents that you said happened. That he got injured somehow from these accidents. That's what you said. I'm not putting words in your mouth.

L: I've already told you about this. He had a hard time just basically being a boy barefoot-ed.

Al: Yeah, I know, and he freaked out, I got it. He freaked out, after the accidents happened there was a couple of different accidents that happened, he freaked out, got overwhelmed, then what happened?

L: He never had that many accidents.

Al: I agree. That's a lot of accidents in like 12 hours on that one little kid.

L: (Unintelligible).

Al: Okay, whatever. I'm just using that as a random guess, okay? I don't know an exact timeframe.

L: ... me explaining anything to you, it's your picture. Your statements, or whatever, I've listened to you, I have as my representation in a free investigation, let me say that to you. I'm not gonna sit here and walk down 15 more trails again with you for you to hang up, scream, and yell at me.

Al: I'm your husband. I'm not the sheriff, I'm your husband, and it's my son that's missing.

L: (Unintelligible).

Al: Yes, he does, a father does. And once again, I'm trying to do this because I'm feeling the guilt of not being there to help him through all these accidents. So, I'm trying to do all I can outside of the law enforcement because you don't freaking trust them anyways and they've screwed a lot of this up, so I'm sitting here trying to...

L: Do you trust them?

Al: Do I trust them? Not based on what I've seen. So that's why I'm going straight to you—straight to the last person that saw him.

L: I'm not because if I would be the last person that saw him then I would be the person who has him.

Al: Then who was the last person that saw him, that's... this is...

L: I don't know!

Al: Okay.

L: I don't know.

Al: So, you don't know who it was?

L: I don't know anything. I just told you I don't know anything because I've been emotionally kicked out.

Al: By who?

L: Emotionally kicked out.

Al: By who? Who's emotionally beat you down?

Long silence.

Al: Hello?

L: Albert? I understand that as a parent you know that a hundred percent of your mind is focused on someone that God gave you the ability to bring into this world, okay? If anybody knows that, I understand that.

Al: But you're contradicting yourself because you told me.

L: Okay.

Al: No, I'm not even gonna say it. I'm sorry to interrupt you, go ahead.

L: ... I couldn't even finish the second part of my sentence without you attacking me.

Al: Okay.

L: And also know that you should be... under no circumstances be one with me, because that's what God intended you to be. One. One wife. That's what you're supposed to be doing. And that even includes... I haven't even spoken to my husband in weeks. Been there to comfort him, he been there to comfort me in this situation, so I know that God says to put him first and put everything in the order they're supposed to be. And I'm not gonna apologise for that when I've given you information. I've given you a set of information that's the actual truth and it's still not good enough. That's it. Cause, I'm not doing it.

You don't care. You're not gonna be as a parent and accept... (unintelligible)... sometimes our children are gonna make choices that we don't like. You're not gonna accept that. To be a parent and try to tell you to accept something... to keep someone else looking bad. Protect the child, and I'm still the bad person. You should have my back no matter what. You should have my back to the point where we're together, talking to these people and demanding a better answer, but you have not been there, every day. I don't know...

I don't even know where you're at. As far as I'm concerned you might not even be here, I mean, it's online that you're in Texas.

I don't know anything. I don't even... (unintelligible)... I'm not angry from any of it, I'm not listening to... (unintelligible)... tell me exactly where Gannon is right now, or I'm never gonna love you or my family again, that's the condition that you put on me. I don't know where he's at. You've been married to me long enough to know that. Any situation, whether I'm freaked out or not, whatever it might be that I have fought for my family tooth and nail. I'm maybe not the best, being like, you got a cut or whatever, I'm maybe not the best in that aspect but as far as protection...

If I could give you Gannon Stauch, I would.

Al: Alright. Could I talk now?

L: Sure. Thank you.

Al: Alright, so I know you don't wanna hear this, but I'm gonna walk you back through where I'm at and then I'm gonna let you know how I feel, okay? Alright. I fully believe that something happened—it was an accident and you panicked, okay? And that you keep putting somebody else into it and as long as you do that it just doesn't look good for you. I'm trying to... I'm by your side when I say that, okay? And I've said this over and over again, that you can get through this and if you give me the truth, I'll stand by you. But here's where I'm at—here's my feelings on it, okay? You need to hear me out, please, okay? I know that you did something. I know that you're responsible, okay? And I hope there was a good reason for it, but the problem is it's clear to me that I can't get Gannon back through you. Okay? I had a serious hope that we could stand by each other through this, but you know what? I'm past that point now. After all those lies, you just admitted you lied to me for a reason, to prove a point. I don't have hope for us, and you know what I'm worried to death about? I'm gonna have to testify eventually about this and I don't know what I should say. I have no clue what to say about this because now I'm put in a position of the truth or my wife. And I don't know what to say, I don't know what to say when I get called up there to testify eventually.

L: You just said in your conversation that you believe that I did something.

Al: I absolutely said that, and I want to know what you think I should say when I have to testify because I'm gonna get called up there.

L: Called up there for what?

Al: To testify in this situation.

L: For what?

Al: I don't know. I'm hoping it doesn't come down to murder. I haven't' seen my son in three weeks and nobody can find him, okay?

L: Murder?

Al: Or maybe it was an accident, and somebody just panicked but I'm no clo... I'm farther away from the truth than I was when I started talking to you after two weeks. You were the last one to see him and I just don't know what the hell I'm gonna say when I have to sit on that stand and freakin' cry in front of the world about my son. I don't know what I'm gonna say other than you frickin' lied over and over and over and then never told me any element of the truth, so what should I say?

Hello?

L: Hello.

Al: I guess I lost you.

L: So basically, now you're saying someone was getting murdered... that's what you're saying?

Al: No. I said that could be the worst case, okay? I don't know for sure because there's no body, there's no evidence, there's no nothing. I mean, what else do you want me to think in this case? You're the last one to see him. You 're the last one to hear him talk. You're the last person to see anything of Gannon on this earth to my knowledge, okay? No-one else. What else do you want me to say, Tecia? What do you want me to think? I'm as freakin' serious and as freaked out as I've been this whole time, all these freaking injuries in that short time period—accident or not, you had something to do with it, okay? I mean, how else...? All that put together, how else am I supposed to look at it? Just like you're always putting me on the stand and questioning me for stuff you think I do that adds up okay? That's what I'm doing here. There's no other way for me to look at this other than you're involved to some level if not ultimately responsible, so you can tell me what I'm supposed to say or what I'm supposed to think. You can say no, no, all you want to but all you've done is lie to me and make up fake people that are in Mexico right now. Tell me, tell me the truth, Tecia.

L: Yeah.

Al: Tell me what I'm supposed to say. How to stand by you.

L: You've already said what you think is on your mind and what the truth is in your mind.

Al: Yeah. It's not about what I think though, okay? I'm asking how I can stand by you. What the truth is so I can stand by you through this.

L: My husband just said I murdered someone! Listen to what you said.

Al: That's not what I said, okay? You said that not me. I said you're responsible to some degree, that's what I said.

L: You're just worried about you testifying is what you said.

Al: Yeah, absolutely.

L: ... testifying for someone is what you said, against me.

Al: Because I gotta get up there... I'm gonna have to get up there and look you in the eye and tell them that you lied to me and told me 15 stories and when they ask me what I think I'm gonna tell them I think you're responsible. I wanna know what you think I should say. That's where I am right now. I told you that.

L: If that's what you feel in your heart then go with it. That's all I can...

Al: No, that's not. I'm asking you. I'm asking you to convince me otherwise, Tecia.

L: No.

Al: I'm begging you. I'm on my knees, begging you to prove me wrong again. Prove me wrong. Tell me right now—prove me wrong. Give me what I need. Give me the facts of the matter that prove that you had nothing to do with this or that it was an accident and that you freaked out or something. I'm here theorising all these different stories.

L: Why? Are you delusional? It was an accident and I freaked out and then you think I just murder something over an accident?

Al: No, no, that's not what I said. If it was an accident that explains it. If you killed him, that explains it. I mean, that's pretty simple.

L: (Unintelligible).

Al: Okay it was an accident. Okay, an accident.

L: I'm not saying it was an accident. I'm answering your doggone question. Stop yelling at me. I said if you just said... on the stand is what you told me.

Al: No.

L: You said if they ask me what I think... that's a stipulation, okay? You're telling me that you're gonna say what you think happened. You just told me there's no this, there's no evidence, there's no other.

Al: No, alright. You're right. You're right. Back off that. What I will tell them is this... I will tell them this... my wife had the opportunity to tell me the truth, but she chose to lie to me repeatedly. Make up fake people... Uncle Matt, Eduardo, Quincy Jones or whatever his name was in Mexico, okay? She told me all these stories to get me going in 17 different directions that I still don't know the truth and that I know for a fact she was the last one to see him in our home.

L: I'm gonna let you just be like, I'm gonna let you have that opinion because that's...

Al: No, no, no, no. Stop. No that's not an opinion, okay? I stated all the facts, and I dropped the mic and I'm out, okay? That's what that is. I got nothing else to say about it other than you lied to me, and you're the last one to hear my little boy cry, and my little boy say I'm bleeding, and to see him alive and well.

L: Oh, my god. They sent you that video. You're an idiot. That was editing that made that video like that, oh my god.

Al: Okay. Tell me something that's truth. You didn't deny that. You didn't deny...

L: (Unintelligible).

Al: Fine, I'm sorry I said that. Maybe it was edited, but you didn't flip out when I said you were the last one to see him alive, okay? You flipped out when I said that he was bleeding so explain that to me, Tecia.

L: As far as I know, Gannon's alive. I'm not gonna say differently because I'm not gonna be a parent...

Al: Okay. You still didn't answer the question. Now you're telling me your opinion—now you're giving me your opinion. You told me not to give opinion, now you're giving me opinion. Okay, I said you were the last one to see him alive in the house, okay? Because you are. So now fill in the blanks.

L: ... think that.

Al: No, that's not what I think, that's the truth and you haven't denied it one time.

L: Do you think that? I'm not gonna say anything because why would I say anything?

Al: Well, you freakin' jump on me when I say he's in the video, he said he's bleeding. You said they edited that so you can't have it both ways. Are you gonna deny it or are you not gonna deny it? Because you're denying stuff you think is not true.

L: I've already denied to you what you just said.

Al: That you're the last one to see him?

L: That I am not the last one to see him.

Al: Then who is?

L: You know this.

Al: Oh yeah, you told me Quincy Brown, but we proved him false, okay? That was easy. All I had to do was to call a reporter. I didn't have to have any evidence, just call a reporter and she said, yep, he ain't been around for a while. He's been gone a minute.

L: Okay.

Al: Okay, so who was it?

L: You've already said it was no-one, so why does it matter?

Al: But you just said it was, so I'm asking who it was.

L: I'm not listening.

Al: See, here you go again. You can't spin me, Tecia. You can spin Facebook, you can spin the media, but you can't spin me, alright?

L: Facebook? So many times, I ain't even been on there.

Al: Alright, yup. I mean, fine, but you can't spin me. I'm telling you. You should know that by now.

L: I'm not trying to spin you.

Al: Hey, you know what? What about the blood in the corner? How about that? That came from Gannon knocking his nose.

L: What corner?

Al: Yeah, the corner of his bedroom where you pushed the beds together. What about the blood?

L: Oh god. You are just grasping.

Al :I'm not. I saw blood, okay. That's not grasping, I saw it.

L: Tell me again, you saw it.

Al: Saw what?

L:Tell me what you saw.

Al: Oh, you're recording me now? Go ahead, just tell me, I'll say it.

L: No... say this.

Al: I saw it. Blood in the corner of his room. Record me, I don't give a fuck, Tecia. That's my son's blood and I saw it.

L: Okay. You've proved that (a) you saw it and (b) you've proven it's Gannon's blood?

Al: So, how'd it get there, Tecia? You prove that?

L: ... you just said you're going on facts so I'm trying to get this straight. You're going on facts. You're telling me you were able to walk in and they showed you this... crime scene. Is that a fact?

Al: I saw it. You tell me whose blood it was—you were there.

L: Okay. So, there we go.

Al: You were there.

L: What?

Al: You were part of the crime, so you tell me.

L: No, I was not. There was 18 people in that house.

Al: Oh, there was 18 people when Gannon got hurt?

L: No.

Al: Had these accidents happened and then...?

L: No. In the house.

Al: Okay. I told you, you can't spin me, Tecia. But go ahead. I'll listen to your spin. Go ahead, spin it around.

L: I'm not trying to spin you. I'm not trying to spin you at all. I'm saying what you... I'm just trying to get the facts from you... what you're saying. One, you're telling me that all you and whoever else saw blood in the middle of a supposed crime scene.

Al: No. What you're doing is you're not focusing on the crime, you're focusing on the people here, helping to find Gannon, okay? Like that's gonna fly.

L: No, I'm not.

Al: You're gonna go up there and say... no, you're bullshitting, Tecia.

L: They're gonna rip you guy's theory apart because it's a lie.

Al: Okay.

L: Because you contaminated a crime scene, supposedly, is what you said.

Al: Okay, so you... whatever.

L: That's what you said.

Al: But you're... what you said was Gannon's blood so I'm going based off the facts that you told me.

L: You said... I never said that.

Al: Yeah, you did. You said it was Gannon's and your blood, okay? That's what you said.

L: No.

Al: That's exactly what you said. That's what you said.

L: Finding Gannon's blood on any concrete.

Al: You're lying.

L: I never told you about any concrete with Gannon's blood.

Al: Okay, alright, you're lying.

L: You said you saw it.

Al: That's gonna be noted. I'm gonna... I'm writing down these notes right now. You're lying. Tecia lies again.

L: Writing down?

Al: Tecia admitted at the beginning of the conversation she lied 15 times.

L: As long as you and whoever else you had in this home were in the home in the middle of the supposed crime scene, they're gonna rip you to shreds.

Al: But why would you even say that if it's not a crime scene? You told me it was an accident, so was it a crime scene or an accident? You told me it was the scene of an accident. So, was it an accident or a crime scene?

L: Let me ask you this question then. How in the hell is our home a supposed crime scene?

Al: I can't.

L: Okay. If it was a supposed crime scene and then you saw, which you have not come out and said differently, you've done nothing but talk pure shit about okay. So, then your friendly neighbour that fucking got paid money that released the video that says Gannon didn't come home, how the hell is the house a crime scene?

Al: You're the one telling me the house is a crime scene.

L: You told me it was.

Al: You told me it was an accident and now you're telling me it was a crime scene.

L: Answer that question.

Al: What question?

L: How in the hell is our home a crime scene when you guys have done nothing but portrayed...?

Al: Hey, do you want me to tell you what I think? Or what I know? You want me to tell you what I think or what I know?

L: The answer.

Al: I am. Do you wanna know what I think and what I feel or what I know for sure?

L: Whatever you wanna give me.

Al: Okay. What I think is that you did it. What I feel is that you're involved... 'scuse me, what I think, and feel is that you did it. What I know is that you're involved somehow. Okay? That's the bare bones of where I am right now. I have nothing else. You're involved to some extent in Gannon getting hurt whether it was an accident or not. There's blood all over the place down in his room. However, I saw it, who gives a crap at this point because the boy is out there hurt. Okay, what I feel like and what I think is that you did it and you're trying to hide it. And you dumped his body somewhere.

L: I dumped his body?

Al: Yeah.

L: That's your theory that you are saying? Your theory, okay? You're telling me that supposedly you think there was some accident happened that somebody got hurt really bad?

Al: Yep.

L: Inside Gannon's room? Gannon walked outside to the car, okay?

Al: I didn't say you killed him in his room. Why would... I already told you and you told me I was stupid for saying this... I think an accident happened that you're involved with and then we have made... I have made the assessment and everybody who saw the video online made the assessment Gannon was walking kind of sluggish to the truck and you told me I was a fucking idiot for saying that, okay? But it makes sense if he had got hurt, okay? Lightheaded, queasy. I don't know, whatever. And now he's having to walk to the truck so you can take him somewhere, okay?

L: Okay, answer this. Taking him to someone to do what?

Al: You tell me.

L: No, you said you were going on your theory so I wanna hear your theory.

Al: Okay, you wanna hear my theory? Okay, you took him somewhere, yeah, I gonna tell you what I think. You took... you went around town acting all normal. Left your phone at the fucking PetCo on purpose, okay? And took him out somewhere, God knows where, and left him there, maybe whacked him over the head with a 2x4 or something, I don't know.

L: I took him out, why somewhere, you said whacked somebody in the head, so I committed murder? Is that what you're saying?

Al: No, because he could have just been knocked out.

L: Because what?

Al: He could... you could have just knocked him out with a 2x4—not killed him. I mean, if he died, I guess that is murder. I don't know, you're the legal expert here, so actually, let's back up a second, because here's where I'm at, you're lying, okay? Are you lying to cover yourself? Are you lying to cover for Harley? Which one is it?

L: Harley?

Al: Yeah, which one is it?

L: It's already been proved first of all that she had been at work during all y'all's episode.

Al: So, you're lying for yourself?

L: I'm not lying for anyone.

Al: Okay.

L: I'm not lying for a soul.

Al: But you have. This whole time. One of the first things you said this morning was I've lied to you repeatedly. I've lied over, and over, and over again and I had a point to do it. I had a reason. So, what's your reason for lying now?

L: I'm not lying.

Al: But you've been lying the whole time so how do I know that?

L: I told everybody exactly what happened from the beginning.

Al: Yeah, but you just said they were all lies. You said that was a lie, now it's the truth. So...

L: ... didn't like it so therefore you just make up all your stories. So now you got this theory of some 2x4?

Al: No. That's just...

L: (Unintelligible).

Al: You said you told everybody from the beginning... the first story from the beginning was Gannon ran away, okay? Immediately proven false. Second story, you got raped in Gannon's room, also proven false. So, you've been lying from the beginning, not telling the truth and you're still lying. So, what's the next lie, Tecia?

L: I haven't lied.

Al: So now you're lying about saying you were lying?

L: The beginning is what I'm talking about, you just were never gonna believe it.

Al: I know he didn't run away.

L: Why not? Just... then, if that's what you think, that's what you think you know, and your opinion. If you think for a second that your own wife killed your son, then you actually need mental help.

Al: I probably will need to get some after this, you're right. My son's out there missing, my wife's admitted to me today that she's lied to me for three weeks now, okay?

L: No, I did not.

Al: And you did lie to me from the beginning. All these stories you said you had a point, okay? And you still haven't told me what the point is. And now you're lying again, and we've narrowed it down to the other person... it's either by yourself, you and Harley or Harley had some involvement. Who are you lying for?

L: Really? You 're gonna try to...

Al: Yeah, really.

L: So, that's what you think? You think that's what happened when somebody was at work?

Al: Look at you. You're defending your 17-year-old, and all I'm trying to do is defend and find my 11-year-old.

L: You just said that. You said you're defending yours...

Al: Oh, don't even get me started on that because I begged you to let me adopt that child for five years so you can shove that one up your ass right now, okay? You can go ahead and shove that one wherever you want to shove it, but you're disrespecting me. Why don't you just respect me and tell me what happened to Gannon? He's a freakin' 11-year-old out there by himself somewhere. He's with somebody that he don't need to be with and you're the only one who has the truth. You. And you can admitted it, you said you lied over and over again.

L: With somebody he don't need to be with? You just said that but then you told me that no-one else is involved.

Al: So, which one is it? You keep, you keep...

L: You think I have some involvement in killing a child? That's what you think?

Al: Yeah, absolutely because you were there. Gannon's missing, we can't find him, okay? Nobody would stick to the plan this long after the whole world's looking for him. So, it's you. You're the only one sticking to the plan. You're the only one in the spin machine. You're the only one lying. Everybody else is trying to find the truth. Everybody, Tecia. Even Landen, the one that you think I'm hooking up with. She's just trying to find the truth about her baby boy, okay?

L: I'm glad you get to spend the rest of your life with Landen.

Al: Yeah, I mean, whatever. If you think that you're... like you tell me, you're entitled to your opinion because the fact here is that you were the last one to see him. I wasn't there so I don't know anything. You know everything and you're lying repeatedly over and over again. You didn't get raped. Gannon didn't run away. There's no Quincy Brown, Eduardo, Uncle Matt. No high fives, no Gannon jumping on his back, okay? What there is, is blood in his room, okay? And he's gone, and we can't find him, that's what. And you left with him, and didn't come home with him, okay? And you still haven't filled in any of the blanks. I mean, there's facts out there, okay? There's facts out there and you won't even tell me the truth. You keep lying to me, making up some bike bullshit. Gannon fell off his bike and busted his head and needed 911—are you serious? And then as soon as I say that we go back to the house, I mean, I don't even wanna do this, okay? You're just gonna continuously lie to me. Why am I gonna be wasting my time? So, when I testify on the stand that's what I'm gonna say, my wife has all the information she chose to lie about it, I got nothing else to say, okay? That's where I'm at.

L: Alright.

Al: Alright, have a good day.

The next phone call is played.

Al: Hello?

L: I didn't get anything but question marks.

Al: Oh, I said did you wanna talk about... (Unintelligible)... did you set up an appointment for this? How much is it gonna cost?

L: No, my approach is if you don't... (Unintelligible)... in my opinion, and this is how I want it to be so there's no like you know question or anything. If you don't control the aspect of it as far as immunity, checking up, like, you will try to take it, and say that based on what you do or, I just don't, I want to prove 100% to you because I know you're hurt, I know you're upset, but those things are not true what you said. They're just not true. And I don't care about the court of law because you know why my attorney will shred it apart. I'm worried about my husband knowing that I did not do such a thing.

Al: Alright, well.

L: ... because I care about you, and I feel like if you know that that's the truth that I did not then everything could be okay.

Al: Yeah, I...

L: I mean, right? If you know for 100% that I did not, hurt the child, kill our child, hit him with 2x4s, whatever you may say, would it not make you feel a lot different right now?

Al: Yeah, I told you I'd stand by you with the truth, you know? And I pulled up that link and uh and, I mean, it got 5 stars so it looks legit on the surface, yeah, and I mean you hit a good... you hit a great point there, you know, about you know how I am about validating things and looking into things, part of that process would be getting some questions answered that I want answered right. I think you can assume that, right?

L: Okay.

Al: So that being said, I got, as I was waiting on you to get back, I wrote down basically three or four questions and I wanna pose them to you now so that way I'm not surprised when I go in there, okay? Are you willing to do that with me? And then we'll...

L: You're not surprised? Or...

Al: Neither one of us, so you know the questions and I know the questions.

L: Oh yeah okay, I get what you're saying, yep.

Al: Yeah, so I'll ask them, and you just give me yes - it's simple yes or no questions, okay? So, you're not, once again... I'm trying to be fair to you and fair to myself. These are some of the questions that I want answered. Number one, do you know where Gannon is? Yes, or no?

L: Yeah. I mean, but these are the questions I'm gonna prove to you too, right? That's what you're saying?

Al: Right.

L: Okay.

Al: You can answer them now but then you can answer them then as well, okay? Who was Gannon last with?

L: They don't ask you questions like that.

Al: Oh, you're right I'm sorry, it's yes or no... Do you know who Gannon was with last?

L: Okay, so here's what I want you to be careful with on do you know who Gannon was with last? Let me explain to you.

Al: Yeah, go ahead. I'm sorry, go ahead.

L: You have to have a specific approach on that because you need to say do you know a description or have a picture in your mind of who Gannon was with last.

Al: Okay, how about it this way were you the last person Gannon was with?

L: No.

Al: Okay, that leads into...

L: You need to ask the question of someone else with me.

Al: Right, right. Yeah, I know and I'm not gonna probably be the one phrasing the questions I'm just telling you questions I want answered so you answered the question were you the last person Gannon was with, and you said –

L: No.

Al: No. Okay. And I'll leave it at that, I'm not gonna go take that down a rabbit trail, ok. Did you accidentally hurt Gannon?

L: No.

Al: Did you murder Gannon?

L: No.

Al: Okay. Well, so. I mean. That's kinda, that's some of the questions I'm gonna want answered, so when are you gonna be able to do this? I wanna get this done as soon as possible. I'm ready to do it tomorrow. I think it, because of publicity in this case they'll squeeze you in and make an appointment for you tomorrow if we go up there and call 'em and say listen this is the Gannon Stauch case, we need a polygraph ASAP. Let's do it, um, I don't know. When's the earliest you can do it? I'll just take money out of the bank account, and I'll pay for it.

L: So, can you get me just a like two or three times, or days and times that they have available, send them to me and I'll give you exactly which one would work best.

Al: No, Tecia. Tecia, this is...

L: ... talking like I have - I don't have a way around, okay.

Al: Okay.

L: I'm gonna help people out so that I could have food and a place to stay.

Al: Okay. And, but...

L: I'm the one that said to do this.

Al: But I'll even get you tomorrow morning, I wanna do it like 8 or 9 o'clock in the morning. I'll come and get you at Michelle's house, okay? And I'll bring you to this place. It's Michelle, right?

L: I'm not at Michelle's house.

Al: Okay, where you at now?

L: I'm staying with random people, people that reached out online, people that are following the case.

Al: Okay, well send me your location through your phone or send me an address or a ten-digit grid coordinate from Google Earth.

L: You haven't even got a time and you're telling me you're gonna pick me up?

Al: Yeah, because I guarantee you, they will squeeze you in tomorrow because this'll be another star in their cap, another feather in their cap.

L: Why, because it's about some publicity...?

Al: No, no, no, not me. I want the truth and you know what, every minute, every second we sit here and talk about this is another minute that Gannon is in danger.

L: I told you I would do this and... in person.

Al: Alright, well tomorrow's the day, okay? If not, then you're not serious about it. That's just... and I'm not.

L: What are you talking about? I've already told you yes. I've already said yes, yes, yes.

Al: Alright, I'll set the appointment. If it needs to be the afternoon, fine whatever, but we'll do it, okay? Tomorrow.

L: I've already… like, I don't know why you keep saying it, like I've changed it. I've already said yes, I also wanna know, because I need to be because I saw somewhere online it says something about eating and drinking and stuff like that, so.

Al: Alright, I'll answer that for you, but I mean, why don't you plan on like a six-hour window or something, okay? And then –

L: Well, just…?

Al: I'm just going based off generalizations, Tecia, come on now, I don't know the answer to that. You can Google it just like I can. I'll call them and I'll find out. I'm just saying plan on… if you think you're not supposed to eat for a while then don't eat for a while. It's not a big deal, but I'll call them, and I'll set it up for tomorrow afternoon, whatever. You just let me know where to come get you or let me know… just be there if you don't want me to come get you.

L: Now, you had your questions you wanted, and so now I have questions.

Al: So, now I'm taking a polygraph?

L: No, you're not taking a polygraph.

Al: No? Okay.

L: I'm asking you four questions.

Al: Alright, go ahead with them.

L: When you get the results that say I have passed this polygraph test what is your course of action?

Al: These are yes or no questions, please.

L: Okay. Is your course of action to be with your wife and marriage and your daughter and the rest of our family back to normal and figure it out who has Gannon?

Al: No.

L: That's not your... that's not your approach?

Al: You said once you answer some polygraph questions once we find Gannon, okay.

L: That's not what I said.

Al: Alright, alright, okay. I didn't - yes or no questions, I didn't do this to you. I took your yes or no questions.

L: Okay. Once the polygraph test comes back and shows you that I'm telling the truth to the questions that I had nothing to do with Gannon in any kind of way being hurt, murdered, taken, whatever are you gonna be with your wife?

Al: Nope.

L: Really? So, why?

Al: Yes or no questions, please.

L: That's what I'm doing. I just want you to tell me why.

Al: Because the key to standing by you is the truth and Gannon, so.

L: I just told you if I pass a polygraph test and you know I didn't have anything to do with this. I'm trying to understand here, why would you say no to being with your wife if I... if it's proven on the test that I didn't have anything to do with it. I just wanna know the truth on that. I'm still gonna do it so I can clear my name, I just wanna know the truth from you.

Al: I'm waiting for the next yes or no questions.

L: Come on man, just be real with me, this is not the time to play games.

Al: I'm not, Tecia. You gotta understand, there's too... listen, listen, there's a lot of repair...

L: Tell me the truth.

Al: I am, I'm trying to. I'm gonna bend here, again. Gannon is the most important thing but there's a lot of emotions, there's a lot of damage, okay, from this situation and I don't, I'm not here to argue with you, okay. But there's a lot of damage but all the lies that have been told that it's gonna take some time to work through. Okay? I said I'll stand by the truth, and I'll stand by you with the truth. Gannon's the priority, alright? What's your next yes or no question?

L: Do you have any intentions of being back with your wife and family?

AL: No. And it's the same answer, same response as I gave you last time. Gannon's the priority right now. Alright, here's what we're gonna do. I answered your questions and respected you.

L: No –

Al: Hold on, I respected you. I didn't put you through the inquisition. I gave you four yes or no questions and I left it at that. You're not respecting me in that way so I'm gonna go back to question two. You said you were not the last person Gannon was with, so who was? Okay, I answered your questions.

L: ... inquisition questions?

Al: No, you got two or three.

L: You said yes or no.

Al: Alright, what's... see this is why I don't believe you. I'm being straight up with you, if you wanna do this polygraph thing I'm willing to do it and willing to take it at face value, but you're not respecting me and still expecting respect in return. You're expecting to play by the rules and you're not playing by the rules.

L: (Unintelligible)... your wife?

Al: Nope, I said damage.

L: ... telling the truth?

Al: I said there's damage and we gotta repair it, that's all I said. I haven't said anything about anybody to anyone in the media, social media, nothing. And if you got something else then it's false, so.

L: Okay, the next question. Have you filed for divorce?

Al: Nope. See here you go again not playing by the rules.

L: You said yes or no, that's what I said.

Al: Yeah, but you got to put me through the inquisition but you're not answering my question who was the last person Gannon was with if it wasn't you? Because these are gonna be the questions you're gonna have to answer. I mean, I'm just gonna be straight up with you, whether you answer them to me or not.

L: (Unintelligible).

Al: Well, Mr hot-shot Baez will, okay. If you don't, so we might as well do this peacefully between me and you and figure out where Gannon's at.

L: I've already agreed to the... If I, If I'm, agreeing to do this, (a) I'm gonna have to say what happened to him and I have no idea where Gannon's at. Why are you still being adamant that... that's my point I said... you controlling it because you'll still swear up and down.

Al: No, if...

L: (Unintelligible).

Al: But listen, this is pre-polygraph. Polygraph I won't be in the room, probably not even in the building so you're not under any pressure, okay. That's how those things go. It's all you and the guy asking the questions.

L: You won't even be there either because they interview me by myself.

Al: Right, that's what I'm saying, I won't be there. I'll pick you up, take you, drop you off, pay for it but then I'll bounce, okay? But you need to answer me this, as your husband and as the father of the missing child.

L: You have no intentions of being my husband.

Al: But I still am, am I not? Okay? Point is, who was the last person that had Gannon? You said you weren't, so who was?

Silence.

Al: Hello?

L:I'm gonna tell that to the person. Want me to rephrase that in a yes or no question? Because we'll have an issue because no matter what I say to you you're gonna yell at me, scream at me, hang up, act crazy you legit told me the other day I'm a murderer, killer, probably had involvement, you told me this, told me that, then told me you don't have any intentions when you find out your wife is not involved to be with her.

Al: Okay, but did you murder Gannon?

L: That's what your mind is saying.

Al: Hey, did you murder Gannon?

L: What?

Al: Did you kill Gannon?

L: No!

Al: Okay, then back to what we said, it had to be an accident. I mean, so you accidentally hurt him, that's... it's either or—you said that already.

L: Why did you ask that, that's one of your questions ain't it?

Al: Right.

L: Is that one of your questions? Did I murder –

Al: Well, that's two questions but...

L: Here's where I have the problem.

Al: Okay.

L: I will pass it, and then you're gonna come back to square one and still accuse me because you're gonna say there's damage and all this, you're gonna accuse me of somehow still being involved. That's what you're gonna do. Right now, you can't accept... you have the nerve to say to me, I am not gonna be with my wife and family at all, hardly. If Gannon showed up on the doorstep, today, you're still gonna say that to me.

Al: Yeah, yeah, fair enough but you know what I'll...

L: Because you're so fuckin' pissed.

Al: No, I'm not pissed, I'm hurt. My son's missing. I'm hurt because my son's missing and he's hurt, okay, because I saw his blood and I know that if you thought I knew who took Harley and she was missing and hurt and raped and all these things that have been alleged, okay? If you thought I knew that, you'd want me to tell you, too, okay? You admitted you were not the last person that Gannon was with, so that means you know. At least a description, at least a name, or something. And you're not telling me, and you need to put yourself...

L: I gave you a description.

Al: Okay, but that description was Quincy Brown, and 15 different stories and you already told me, you already told me, yeah it was Eduardo the Mexican guy, right? Or uncle Matt? Here we go again.

L: Why don't you ask about legit answers.

Al: Right, did you kill Gannon? That's a legitimate question.

L: No.

Al: Did you accidentally hurt Gannon?

L: You keep asking me like 15 times, like, like you go ahead and get this out your system because I'm gonna...

Al: Okay, fine, fine.

L: Tomorrow, you're gonna be like, wow she passed the test.

Al: Yep. Okay, the bottom line is...

L:Nancy Grace is gonna call my line to do it.

Al: Yeah, let's call her. Let's call Maury Povich too. He'll help.

L: Call 'em. You've already said tomorrow or whenever you're calling this thing, you've already said that... you said you wanted to do it between me, and you because this is for two.

Al: No, you said that. But the truth is, the truth is you won't tell me who because there is no who and the who is you...

L: How? How? Why? Okay, so, here you go again. You are not even trusted and that's why I said you could call who it was because you're not even trusting in a lie detector test.

Al: No, you sent me a link, and you said no to the FBI which is if I had a choice it'd be the FBI like...

L: I don't want the police department.

Al: Okay, then I don't have control. I don't have control and I don't have a say so. See this is where we always get to in our relationship.

L: You said you were gonna call somebody in Colorado Springs.

Al: I did. There's FBI in Colorado Springs and you got her number.

L: You just told me you were gonna call the other people. I'm not doing the FBI because they're police. I'm doing a lie detector...

Al: Okay, so listen.

L: ... no, what you call it.

Al: Listen, if the person who Gannon was last with... if the person was not you, then who is it?

L: You're asking me the same damn question.

Al: Because you never answer it, you never answer it.

L: You already made it clear that I'm not your wife. You already made that clear.

Al: Actually I, and I quote, I said you are still my wife I just said we don't have a relationship right now because of all this. That's what I said. To be clear...

L: But you're telling me, you're telling me, I mean absolutely nothing to you, I'm a piece of crap. That's what you're telling me.

Al: Hey, guess what, so this whole, back to this whole lie detector test bullshit, if you're gonna pass it, who gives a fuck who gives you the lie detector test?

L: I don't want the police involved because...

Al: The police are already involved, what are you talking about? But go ahead, I'm sorry.

L: I'm just trying to prefer you picking anybody else besides the police because I want someone who has no reason at all to be involved or anything so that the validity of the test is complete.

Al: Yeah, okay.

L: That's all I'm saying.

Al: You think the police care about you or me or anything? All they care about is whether they're right or wrong.

L: ... to do it...

Al: All they care about is Gannon.

L: ... is what I'm saying. I'm agreeing like I will do it, I said yes, okay when?

Al: Okay, fine, let's do it, okay? I said let me pick you up, you won't tell me where you are. I told you all these different things, I tried to do one tomorrow, you said three days from now. 9am.

L: I said three times. Three different times is what I said.

Al: Nine, nine-thirty, and ten. Nine, nine-thirty, and ten.

L: That's what they had available?

Al: That's what I'm gonna tell them, okay.

L: Just call me back and tell me what times they have available.

Al: Alright, alright so listen when I call you back, while you're waiting on me to call you back, I want you to think about this, alright, are you ready? Are you ready for this? What happens if you fail this polygraph test? Then what?

L: I'm not gonna fail.

Al: Okay, but you need to think about... what if you fail?

L: I don't need to think about that. There is no doubt in my mind. Trust me.

Al: Okay.

L: I wouldn't be adamant to you, calling you back after you said those things to me. Do you think I'd be wasting my time to try to prove to a man who was fucking just... (unintelligible).

Al: You were adamant about Quincy Brown, remember? Until the news reporter, not the polygraph, the news reporter shot that full of shit.

L: Listen to the person that I care about, the person that I love with everything in me...

Al: Do you care about Gannon?

L: You know that.

Al: Do you care about Gannon or am I the only one you care about?

L: Of course I care about... I have to care about you first in order to care about our children.

Al: Okay so if you truly care about me and all this stuff... No, listen to me, if you truly care about me and want all this stuff that you tell me every day that you want and send me all these pictures, if all that really means anything to you, first of all you sent me a picture without your ring on the other day so that's bullshit, I'm calling bullshit on that.

L: I haven't been wearing my rings.

Al: Second of all... yeah, then you told me you were wearing them and then you sent me a picture without them. anyways, so.

L: No, I said, I haven't been wearing my rings, is what I said.

Al: Oh okay.

L: Because the police have confiscated them, and you won't help me get any of them back because they were in the car that's in your name that you probably already have back.

Al: Yeah, I wish. I'm still paying on it by the way, and I don't have it. So, just so you know.

L: You should be glad to pay on it, it's our car.

Al: And not have it? Right, okay. Anyways, if you really cared about me.

L: (Unintelligible)... like that.

Al: If you really cared about... hey, let's cut this shit off because this is ridiculous. If you really cared about me, you wouldn't have lied to me 15 times and you wouldn't be lying to me now, okay? And that's it.

The next call is played.

The first 6 minutes is unclear, so it is skipped.

L: ... worded it to personally because like basically it was just saying you know if I know someone personally then that conversation...

Al: I don't understand what you mean by that. You had them reworded or he reworded it?

L: No, when you're in there talking to someone that was the question I said. One of the questions that you wanted. I said to you that I would have to say certain... so then he worded it as, do you know personally who's involved with your stepson's disappearance?

Al: Right.

L: ... and I said no, and I was telling the truth.

Al: So, what do you mean by that?

L: Albert, there's nothing I mean by that. What I mean by that is I can come to y'all, which I'm totally fine with, you know, having an attorney, you know showing this to law enforcement, whatever, but at this point I'm just gonna show it, get it verified and not see it, but hear it and that's what I... that's all I can do for now because anything else I've done I've been turned into being a horrible person so nothing else I can do can help because I'm just not a valid source or person that anyone wants to care about, help, information, nothing. That's been proven.

Al: What do you mean by that's been proven? I thought you gave them information that they're using in the search.

L: I did, however...

Al: So that makes you be valid if you gave them information and they're using that.

L: No matter what information that I give them, they would not be searching places they are based on that information. Normal law enforcement agencies, like the little girl in South Carolina, they took those steps immediately. They shut off the neighbourhood. They shut off any cross intersections. They even went as far as... because it was an easy section of crossing over, they shut off a state line.

Al: Okay, but where did you say for them to look if they're not looking where you said?

L: They don't care what I say, Albert.

Al: I care.

L: They wanna hang me.

Al: I care what you say because I don't. I don't wanna hang anybody. I just want Gannon back. So, I absolutely care what you said.

L: It's been a hard, hard month for everybody, right.

Al: Right, right.

L: I mean this time last month we were getting ready to get off a cruise boat, having the time of our lives, right?

Al: Right but, Tecia, yes, I know that. We were on a cruise, and we had a good time but that, you completely skipped past my question like what did you say? Where did you say for them to look?

L: They didn't ask me anywhere specific to look. I'm telling you that the law enforcement in South Carolina took those approaches based on what was told to me.

Al: But what did you tell them? You're telling me what they didn't do, tell me what you did. I don't care about them.

L: I already told them in the witness statement. I'm not gonna go through this again with you.

Al: You're not gonna tell me? The father of the child?

L: You knew, and it wasn't good enough for you.

Al: No, I did not know, you've never told me.

L: Oh, my god.

Al: No.

L: You told me nobody else was involved, you told me I was making up stuff so I'm not going down that route with you.

Al: No, I... I'm not talking about any of that. None of that matters—the other person, none of that stuff matters now. I wanna know where you told them to look that they're not looking.

L: I never said I told them to look where they're not looking.

Al: But you said, yes you did. You said you gave them information that you're not using.

L: Albert, based upon my statement they woulda took the same methods that the police department took in South Carolina in that situation. They would immediately step in and shut off everyone. They... (unintelligible)... for one person and look where we're at. We're at Wednesday February 19th. Wednesday February 19th.

Al: You're telling me, yes, it's 23 days now, you're right. It's 23 days. Where did you tell them? What information did you give them that they're not paying attention to in South

Carolina?

L: That's not what I said. There you go again.

Al:But that is exactly what you said. You said you gave them information, that they're barking up the wrong tree, and they're not doing like they did in South Carolina. That's exactly what you said.

L: I said they're not.

Al: But what does that mean?

L: Day one. They should have shut the neighbourhood down.

Al: Why?

L: Day one.

Al: Why?

L: Okay, see. Never mind.

Al: No, but you're telling me what should have happened but not the information.

L: I've already given it to you, and you haven't supported me. You've told everybody the complete opposite all that happened here. I like how you're sticking by Landen.

Al: I can't, I can't hear you. But why should they have shut the neighbourhood down? What's in the neighbourhood that matters?

L: Nothin'.

Al: Then why should they have shut it down?

L: That's just the process that they should've done.

Al: What about all this stuff they keep finding and asking me about is from the house?

L: What stuff?

Al: Just all this random bullshit, I mean.

L: I don't know. I mean, you keep saying, you keep saying that it's random bullshit, but you won't tell me.

Al: Yeah, but you know what?

L: Ask me a question. I'll tell you if I know what it is.

Al: How do I know somebody's not taping you right now? Yeah, because I've seen all these pictures and all these things that they're asking me is this Gannon's. Is this from the house? If this gets out then I mean, we might never find Gannon.

L: Albert, I never... (Unintelligible).

Al: I can't hear you.

L: People called my Facebook, this guy, they even got one of them, the FBI's got one person who did this already, and they're probably gonna get in trouble for obstruction but the lady that Amy Bolton has been talking to has already been on this and got one person doing it. They're gonna come after a lot more, so I haven't went and posted any of this stuff.

Al: Listen, I'll tell you one thing... I'll tell you one thing that I've seen that is almost absolutely from my house. Remember that board that I was making those foot, or those shoe, compartments out of?

L: Board?

Al: Yeah, that particle board, that big sheets of it that I was gonna make that thing for Harley, for her shoes, remember? That I made the one and painted grey? You know what board I'm talking about? You know that big sheet of board?

L: Particle board?

Al: Yeah, yeah, so they got a piece of that from the house they found somewhere.

L: A piece of particle board? I mean, what does that mean?

Al: That, you, that's what I'm asking you what that means. Why a piece of board from my house is found out in the middle of nowhere and I see a picture of it.

L: In the middle of...

Al: And I see a picture of it, okay. I mean, they didn't tell me where they found it, they just said does this look like it's from your house? Does this look like it might be Gannon's and I'm like yeah it looks like it's from my house. I got all kinds of stuff like that at my house.

L: Albert, I haven't even been there, so I don't know anything about any wood.

Al: Tecia, you know all the wood at the house, all that stuff.

L: I understand. I know the wood, but you guys ought to believe I didn't leave with any wood.

Al: Well, there was wood in the back of the truck. There was a whole pile of wood in the back of the truck.

L: Was there a big sheet of particle board back there like you're talking about?

Al: No, it wasn't a sheet it was a piece of it that they showed me a picture of. Just a piece.

L: Then, I mean, I don't know. I didn't get rid of any wood or any of your board or anything like that.

Al: Did you get rid of anything?

L: No. I didn't get rid of anything. Nothing. If someone has took something from your house since you've been there, someone took it when all these people were there. I haven't even been there to touch board, nothing.

Al: So, okay. If you didn't take anything like that, board, wood anything and get rid of it in that area, why were you in that area?

L: In what area?

Al: The area where the truck was seen at, the area where they're searching. I mean, I'm guessing, assuming this picture that they showed me came from that area.

L: That they're searching?

Al: Right. You talked about that bike accident or whatever? That area, that you went to, and you told me you went to, and you also told me you told them you went to.

L: You gotta say the roads and names of the areas, are you talking about Countyline Road?

Al: Yes, Countyline Road and wherever they're searching at. I don't know the exact areas.

L: Countyline Road.

Al: Yes, why were you there, what purpose do you have to go to PetCo and then Countyline Road and then back to PetCo?

L: Because I was gonna go... Gannon was asking about the castles because remember the time we went riding and there was castles and his grandma who had just left was talking about the castles?

Al: Castles?

L: Remember like we took the back road, and she was with us one time and it was like these old little castles.

Al: No, grandma, my mom, was never with us when we did that.

L: Well, you...

Al: Never.

L: You said something about grandma would like these or something like that.

Al: Alright, okay.

L: So that's what we were talking about. I said, I was taking that road because you can take that road and drop off, because if you go back and look at the traffic cameras... (Unintelligible)... drive was pretty busy so I took that road on that back road, I said something I was like, hey remember we were driving through here one day and he's like oh yeah about the castles and I couldn't find the road with the castles.

Al: Okay, I mean. So, you went to look at castles, then what?

L: I drove up and was going to Castle Rock on that back road I think it turns into like, I don't know, what is that road—45 or something? I couldn't figure out how to get back to 25 from there which wasted a lot of my time.

Al: Why couldn't you figure out to get back to 25?

L: I didn't know how to do that. I didn't know how to get to 25.

Al: You didn't have your GPS?

L: I didn't have my phone.

Al: Right, right. I forgot, I'm sorry.

L: I had my watch.

Al: Okay.

L: But the problem with getting it on my watch is you hardly can't put the words into where you're going. it'll work if you do it on your phone.

Al: Right.

L: I should know this because my watch was with me. People making this big deal about freaking phone or not, the watch is gonna ping the same way a phone does, so I wanna tell 'em get the fuck outta here, duh.

Al: Yeah. Right, right, you're right.

L: I mean, and that's not, like, I'm not stupid, I'm not trying to be like oh my phone, but I got a fucking watch with me, I'm not stupid.

AL: So, you just went out there to ride randomly to look at castles?

L: No, that is not what I did. I was gonna go to Castle Rock real quick.

Al: Okay.

L: I've already said that. So, if anybody put any kind of board or something out there, whatever the hell it was, maybe it was somebody who was in the house, everything...

Al: So, somebody was in the house, and they took the board and took it out there where you were at? Because...

L: I said unless someone did that. I didn't take any boards, unless something fell off the truck.

Al Okay. Why would something fall off the truck if it was all down in the truck?

L: I'm just trying to say to you. I'm just saying to you, I mean, I don't know.

Al: So, did y'all make it to Castle Rock?

L: No. I just told you that I didn't know how to get back to 25.

Al: Okay, but you had to at some point, right?

L: At some point I did, but I don't remember when because it's been freaking how many weeks?

Al: Right, okay so, so...

L: Listen Albert...

AL: No, hold on, hold on one more question.

L: ... you're not gonna do that to me.

Al: You're right, I'm not. I just wanna know where Gannon got out the truck, because...

L: Where he got out the truck?

Al: Yeah, it's not at the house so don't say that, so where did he get out the truck?

L: Can I tell you something?

Al: Yeah, tell me.

L: If you think Gannon got out of the truck, whatever you think of then y'all are over there doing all the searches, keep searching, keep searching, keep searching, okay. Keep searching and understand you've done nothing but make it a witch hunt. You've been in all these areas...

Al: Okay, alright. You're right, you're right so you're saying he never got out the truck, so I need to call them back and tell them to look for him in the truck.

L: That Gannon, what do you mean look for him in the truck?

Al: Well, you said he never got out the truck.

L: Gannon was laying down, playing the switch in the truck. So, I mean, I don't know what your question is. I haven't done anything to Gannon.

Al: Did Gannon throw out that board? Or it may have flew out? Did Gannon throw it out, you think?

L: Albert, if there's a board or something, it coulda been... I don't remember to be honest.

Al: You don't remember how it got out of the truck?

L: If there's a board, I mean, I don't know. Maybe it got thrown out. I don't know.

Al: Okay.

L: I really don't remember, well, I don't remember but I don't understand what's a board got to do with anything?

Al: I don't know, I don't think they'd show me a board if it wasn't relevant. I don't know.

L: You just said they showed you a board, did this come from your house. So, this is where I don't... you talk about you don't, you don't... I'm recording you, or listening or whatever, but then supposedly this is what blows my mind. This is what blows my mind. Okay? The police in this country, and departments do not call people and give them videos and give them evidence. They don't. Because if they do, they know that stuff could be thrown out for that, so I don't believe for a second that police are calling people telling them. I don't believe that unless they're just pictures.

Al: But how would police know if it's relevant or if it's my wood or Gannon's sock or whatever? They gotta ask questions.

L: You're, okay, it was his socks... okay now there's socks being thrown out.

Al: I mean, yeah so, I mean, how did the sock get thrown out? That's another question.

L: Okay, well, I mean, how do you know it's Gannon's sock?

Al:I mean, socks are socks, I mean, you know, I don't know unless they got DNA off it.

L: Okay then, if they... then they should say to you this is Gannon's sock, 100% it's his sock.

Al: What about maybe or maybe not I saw a picture of carpet from the house.

L: Carpet?

Al: Yeah.

L: You saw carpet?

Al: Yeah, the same...

L: You saw carpet?

Al: Maybe.

L: In the woods?

Al: Maybe, yeah. I didn't see no... I saw a picture of it. I mean I didn't say it's in the woods, I'm just saying maybe I saw a picture of the same carpet that's in the house.

L: You saw the same carpet that's in the house in the woods?

Al: I didn't say in the woods, I said I saw a picture that looked maybe, maybe not is the carpet from our house.

L: Okay, so what was it. Was it a big piece of carpet? What?

Al: I mean, I don't know. I don't know, I mean come on I saw a picture of it. There wasn't a ruler next to it or anything, okay. I've seen 20 to 30 pictures, I'm just... maybe even more, I just remember... I mean, I remember a board, I feel like I may have seen but the carpet's been all over the story anyways, so I mean it's, I... I could be putting, like you said... what?

L:You saw the carpet the police were taking out of the garage? Is that the carpet you're talking about?

Al: I don't know, I, I...

L: That's all the carpet that would've been taken out the garage that Gannon got blood on from his foot. And I already told you this.

Al: Oh, and did he cut his foot on the wood or did he...? Your Facebook also said he cut his foot on a tool... I don't know.

L: I don't know if it was a tool, wood, what. He was looking for that doggone thing that you have.

Al: What thing?

L: The thing that has the little holes in it or whatever and you can like slice stuff.

Al: You were looking for something to slice stuff? What do you mean by that?

L: To cut the wood with stuff.

Al: Cut the wood with stuff with something that has holes in it. Say what?

L: Ridges.

Al: Ridges? You talkin' about to make the wood smooth?

L: It has a handle on it, we were looking for that because we thought that that, it has a little handle on it or whatever, you know what I'm talking about?

Al: I think so.

L: Because, you know, the dogs need a piece of carpet, I mean a piece of wood on the side of the thing?

Al: Yeah.

L: I was just trying to shave that down, so we were looking for that thing.

Al: Oh yeah, the little like hand plane or whatever that you make the wood smooth with?

L: The dogs...(Unintelligible)... the side in the kitchen so I was trying... I asked him to email you where the tools were at, we were both trying to figure out... we were trying to get the... (Unintelligible).

Al: Did you ever find it?

L: The piece?

Al: The wood, I mean not the wood, the plane? The thing with the handle on it.

L: No.

Al: But I thought you said that's what he cut his foot on.

L: I did not. I said he was going to get that and stepped on something in there I don't know what he stepped on. He was helping me because I was gonna get it. We were unloading stuff out of the car, I was gonna go sell stuff online—I've already said this. I was gonna sell the Yeti online because I never use it, I was gonna finish selling more clothes and stuff. I mean.

Al: So, are you gonna send me the results of this poly or not?

L: I'm not gonna send them to anyone. I need to meet with you to let you see them.

Al: You'll meet me to let me see them?

L: I have to let you know so when I have this thing with the Nancy Grace people because they're gonna be verifying the validity of it, they're gonna have all that ready so that the public can hear it. So, I tried to talk to you first about it, you didn't wanna talk to me, you didn't wanna say anything and then you whatever... whatever I get it, angry, hurt, you got all this going on. I get it, okay? So, then I think I'll do it this way. I will meet you and go from there. But then I get on the phone with you and now it's like socks and this and that and who knows what.

Al: Right, now you know how I feel.

L: There's all these things. Right? All these things. And it's like, okay, well I mean, what did I do? What did I do wrong?

Al: I didn't ever say you did anything wrong the only thing I've ever come to a conclusion was that it was an accident but, but...

L: You all the way blamed me the other day.

Al: No, I didn't. I asked you. I asked you.

L: Okay, now, listen. You guys, you are still looking for the wrong person, still. And they're not gonna find me putting Gannon somewhere. Or what you guys think. So, whatever you think, you're not gonna find that. Because I didn't do that.

Al: Well, what did you do? Hello?

L: What?

Al: I mean if you didn't do that, what did you do? Or, I mean, who is the person that did something? That's the missing link here to Gannon.

L: Y'all didn't wanna listen the first time.

Al: Listen, I'm all ears now, I'm sitting here at Starbucks making a fool of myself, okay.

L: How are you making a fool of yourself?

Al: Because I'm sitting here trying to hide in the corner so nobody's looking at me, okay. I'm listening now, tell me, what happened? What did you do or who has Gannon? I mean, if you love me like you say, you'll help me stop having to look at all these pictures and hear all these stories and watch the news every night, okay? That's love.

L: Love is also when I tell you and you listen instead of just being like, oh yeah that really happened.

Al:Okay, I'm listening right now.

L: No.

Al: You got my attention right now.

L: Start cursing me out

Al: No, I won't, not at *Starbucks*, I'm not doing this.

L: 95 percent of everybody that takes a lie detector test and lies, fails. The only people who have like schizophrenia and things like that have problems with it, okay. I get it. I clearly answered, and again I know you said I haven't seen this but you're about to because Nancy Grace is having someone verify, so that it can be shown, okay? So, it's coming, alright. She wouldn't even fuckin' mess with it if it was fuckin' bullshit, okay? So, with that being said, that questions were asked. Am I gonna tell the truth? Yes. I told the truth. Did I harm him in any physical way? I told the truth... Did you inflict any harm on him in any way? No. I told the truth. So...

Al: Did they ask you if this was an accident?

L: Did you accidentally, that was the first thing I just said to you, hurt him in any physical way?

Al: Did they ask you did he accidentally hurt himself?

L: No because they only give you a certain... (Unintelligible)... but then... it was then, you gotta go into that and be like are you involved in your stepson's disappearance?

Al: Did they ask you was he injured?

L: They... Albert.

Al: Not if you did it, but was he injured, did they ask you that?

L: Okay, so here's, this is why you're gonna always have a problem with everything.

Al: No, I'm just asking the questions because you won't show me the results.

L: I will show them to you. I've begged you. I begged you to meet me. I begged you to spend one night with your wife and you refused to see everything. I begged you. You're ignoring me like I'm a piece of crap.

Al: Listen, tell me now, I'm listening. Just tell me now. Just tell me everything. You're talking about Nancy Grace and a lie detector test, all that doesn't matter to me, okay? You came up with the idea for a lie detector test and I said yes, do it. But now you won't show me the results, but you said it was for me.

L: No.

Al: Okay, so listen, no, you did, you did. You said it was for me.

L: You won't let... I begged you. You lied to me and told me you were gonna meet me and then I get dressed and everything and then you ignore my emails that night. You think it's not hard on me that I gotta know my husband is fucking another bitch? Do you think that's hard?

Al: You think it's not hard for a father not to know where his son is? I mean.

L: I know it's hard, but you didn't deny that one, did you?

Al: There's no reason to deny it, it's just not true. I'm not playing that game but there is a truth here that you're ignoring that Gannon's missing, and you have information and I'm listening. I'm listening, you said you did.

L: I've given it to you guys. I've given it to you.

Al: I'm sick of... listen, I'm sick and tired of being alone and a way for me to get past that is for me to get the information I need, and I know you have and I'm listening and I'm not gonna judge you. I just want the information. I don't care what happens, okay? I want my son. I really don't care. If you're not... if you're not guilty of anything, then you're not guilty of anything. I... I... that's not what I'm worried about. I really don't care. I don't care who did what. I just want my son home with me, now. That's what matters to me.

And I've even offered to help you, to stand by you if you just tell me.

L: I didn't do it.

Al: I can't hear you. I didn't say you did it I just said tell me the information.

L: ... and I told you that... (Unintelligible)... it's not that.

Al: It's not an accident and I didn't cover it up. So, you didn't do anything and there's no accident so, what? I can't hear you.

L: There's no accident that happened.

Al: I can't hear you.

L: Albert.

Al: I can't hear you.

L: Can you hear me?

Al: I cannot hear you. I can hear you in the background.

L: I said, can you hear me now?

Al: Yes, I can hear you now.

L: I said, there's no accident. So, you think, in your mind that I'm gonna tell you an accident happened, and I panicked and didn't know what to do, and just threw him on the side of the road?

Al: Okay, if that's not the case then, there are kind of two options here, either something happened on accident or something happened on purpose, okay. Either he hurt himself or you hurt him. I mean, you kinda paint the picture for me here, either you killed him, or it was an accident how he got hurt. I mean, those are the things that you gotta decide in how you approach this, okay?

L: I didn't do either of those, do you see what I'm saying?

Al: The part that I'm saying, then fill in the blank, he obviously got hurt, you told me that. Okay, he got hurt somehow but you won't tell me anything else.

L: Albert. I've already told you. This is what's gonna happen. Let me tell you again, but you know what you're gonna do? You're gonna tell me I'm a liar and that's a stupid fucked up story and we're back to blaming it on someone else again. That's what you're gonna tell me.

Al: No, listen, listen. I honestly... let me back up, let me start over. I really don't care if you tell me the truth or not. I'm past that point, I just wanna know how I can get Gannon home.

L: How do I know how you can get Gannon home if someone else is involved? How do I know that? This is where you... this is where you have a disconnect with me.

Al: Tecia, you gotta understand.

L: See, until you can stand there, and you need to be... you should be telling these investigators my wife would not do this. Listen to her.

Al: I've told them that, okay. I've told them that. I've told them that, you're a school-teacher, you've been a babysitter, I mean why would all these people trust you with their kids and then you do something like this? But the problem, the disconnect is you know something if not who and I don't really care who, okay? I just wanna know where Gannon's at and how we can find him. So, you can tell me any, you can throw out any random name, Johnny Tremaine if you want to, whatever kinda name you want to, I just want it to point to where Gannon's at. I mean.

L: Okay.

Al: The truth is.... Okay, go ahead sorry.

L: What's the truth? What?

Al: The truth is so far beyond me right now. The only truth I care about is where Gannon is.

L: Okay, I don't know where Gannon is. So, no matter what I say to you, you're still gonna get the same answer in the end. I don't know where he is.

Al: Okay, so how do we get to who took him?

L: Well, you know, we should've been doing this like three weeks ago.

Al: I've been a week now talking to you and you still won't tell me this.

L: I've told you, Albert.

Al: I don't want, sorry.

L: I told you I went that way, I was, I told the people I went that way. Me. Innocent people don't tell people where they went. They just don't.

Al: Listen, just give me something, just give me a guess. Like I said the only truth that matters is bringing Gannon home, and where he's at.

L: Give you a guess, Albert?

A: Yes, absolutely.

L: Gannon is not in Colorado.

Al: Your guess is that he's not in Colorado.

L: Correct.

Al: Okay, why? What makes you guess that?

L: Because Tecia didn't hurt him.

Al: Okay.

L: Didn't dispose of him.

Al: Okay.

L: Anything like that, okay, so Tecia was in Colorado with nothing, and you guys have ran up all these places where y'all think I've been or whatever, so, and you haven't found Gannon. So, where's the connection with those two together?

Al: So, if you had to guess, where would he be at? Like you said you guessed he's not in Colorado. I don't disagree with that because they've looked and searched and not found a damn thing other than some random pictures of some bullshit, okay? They haven't found Gannon, so if you had to guess where he's at, where do you think he's at?

(There is a long silence).

Hello?

L: Yes.

AL: Answer my question if you if you had to guess where he's at, and he's not in Colorado or you guess he's not, your best guess?

L: Probably somewhere, I mean, as scary as it sounds, probably not even in the United States.

Al: What makes you guess that?

L: I dunno, that's my guess. I don't have a reason for my guess, that's why it's a guess.

Al: I just don't, that doesn't make any sense, especially because, no, no I'm not, I'm talking to myself really, but if that's your guess then that's your guess. I mean, if you think Landen took him to Mexico, or, because you keep saying out of the United States, because you keep saying she's involved.

L: That's perfect. I'm not gonna ever say anything about your wife anymore.

Al: She's not my wife. You're my wife, so I hope you're not talking bad about yourself.

L: Yeah.

Al: You can yeah me all you want, that's the truth, I mean, I just... you guess that he's not in the United States, but you keep saying she's involved, how would she get him out of the United States?

Hello?

L: I don't care what you're gonna tell me, until I'm blue in the face, she's... in my opinion, she's involved, and her deal went wrong and now she is losing her mind and wanting to do everything she can to keep the finger pointed at me. That is what I feel. Because she wanted to plan to get the kids back, for Gannon to come back, oh, you're not being safe by letting them stay at home alone, that was probably gonna be the first thing, you had them home alone, or whatever. That's exactly what happened. And I'm against the world trying to prove it because I don't even have my husband on my side for it.

Al: But I told you all along I'll work with you. I'll stand beside you. Yeah, it is, it's working together to find Gannon. That's the only thing that matters right here.

L: When you work with her?

Al: Yeah.

L: Aren't you staying in the same hotel with her?

Al: Nope.

L: There are pictures and she's all in em.

Al: Well good, because I've been with my daughter to be able to put my daughter to bed doesn't mean anything. I told you the whole time I was in a separate hotel room.

L: (Unintelligible).

Al: Whatever, no that's her daughter too, so we split time, and I don't have to justify myself to you about that. It's her daughter, it's my daughter, and we're splitting time and we're helping take care because guess what. Guess what's going on with Laina, her brother's missing, okay. Have you thought about that?

L: Laina?

Al: Yeah. And Laina, Laina's brother's missing and she gave her statements that said I love you, Bubba, I miss you, come home. Okay, yeah, and it... I mean, I can go, I can take that down a rabbit trail, but I don't really wanna do that right now, because I don't wanna piss you off.

L: Take it down a rabbit trail because you said that. Really? Why would you say that? Why would you take what a child said down a rabbit trail?

Al: No, not what she said, what another child said about it, but I don't even wanna go there because I'm not trying to do that.

L: And look, okay, don't do that. You know why? You're already... you picked... your biological children mean the most to you.

Al: So do yours.

L: Obviously, that's just life, okay. That's just life, okay. So, don't go beating these kids up over this.

Al: Yeah, okay.

L:I did not want Harley to stay there with you with Landen being there.

Al: Oh yeah?

L: I did not. I would've so she could've just stayed in her home, stayed in work, everything.

Al: Yeah, okay.

L: As long as I was able to know she was okay every day, but I was not doing it with Landon.

Al: Okay. Like I said, that's a rabbit trail I don't wanna go on because I don't wanna bring an innocent child into this, you know, like somebody else did, so.

L: Well, that's the truth.

Al: There's a lot of truths involved in that that we're not gonna get into right now, but you know what? Something that's been bothering me from the day Gannon went missing, okay, that text that you, that was sent to me from his phone was complete bullshit.

L: What text?

Al: The text he sent to me about bath salts and all this shit, it sounds like a great story to me but it's not Gannon, okay, yeah so, my question is...

L: Now you'll get Mike's theory, here comes Mike's theory, go ahead.

Al: Mike's theory? What is Mike's theory? Let me hear it.

L: Naw Mike's theory is that I gave Gannon bath salts.

Al: No, I was never even going there. My question here is that absolutely wasn't Gannon sending those texts. I know, okay, so, my question is this, did you send them or did somebody like force you to send them or somebody else was involved and they sent them? Tell me about the bath salts, because that's not Gannon.

L: Okay.

Al: That's just not Gannon.

L: I didn't send them either.

Al: Okay, so who did?

L: I don't know.

Al: Did somebody force you to send them?

L: I don't know, Albert.

Al: You just said you didn't send them, and I asked did somebody force you to send them and you said you don't know.

L: I... listen, you're not getting anything from me...

Al: Yeah.

L: ... until you are on my team.

Al: I'm trying to be but you're not working with me. This is not like every other situation in our marriage where it's like I give in one hundred percent and then you give me a little bit here and there, just like with the money, remember? I had to tell you how much I loved you, had to put your picture on Facebook for you to tell me about the money you took. Not Facebook, Instagram. Remember that eight or nine thousand dollars that you took, but it's the same thing you're trying to do here.

L: My picture on Facebook?

Al: No, Instagram. I said Facebook, but I meant Instagram. You're the only one, when you took the money, it was like, oh you don't love me, you're hiding me, but the point is here you're trying to get me to go all into you without anything from you and that's just not how this works. Okay? It's just not how it works. So, in this situation, it's not money, it's not clothes, it's not an item, it's not a picture, it's a person. So that's the buy in. The buy in is the person. You give me what I need to find Gannon and you've got a little bit of buy in from me.

L: I already took a lie detector test, and you told me you still want nothing to do with me.

Al: No, you didn't, you told me you did, but I haven't seen it. You'll show it to Nancy Grace, but you won't show it to Al Stauch.

L: I've asked you to meet. You wouldn't

Al: I've asked you to meet, I've asked you to show up... hold on, hold on.

L: Could you like at least spend time with your wife? That's what I said. That's all I said. And if you went on this thing because like, you know that it bothers me because I'm like, because I know this is exactly how Landen wanted it.

Al: No, no let me tell you. The buy in here is also that... the poly, that's bullshit. You didn't come to Denver and do a poly. I set it up and my card never got charged.

L: You told me you wouldn't give me the name, so I scheduled my own.

Al: Okay, so now the story's changing, again.

L: It didn't change. I paid $500.

Al: Okay, send me the credit card receipt.

L: (Unintelligible)... did it.

Al: Show me the credit card receipt and show me that you did it.

L: I will see, I will meet...

Al: Listen, Nancy Grace might believe it, but I don't believe it.

L: Okay, fine then. Fine. If Nancy Grace don't believe it and her crew don't verify it and see for herself and now, you're saying she's a liar? Is she a liar? Is she a liar?

Al: I don't know nothing about no Nancy Grace. I don't even know how that's even relevant, okay?

L: Okay here, I have it right here, I'm gonna send it to you.

Al: Let me ask you this while you're sending that to me...

L: Huh?

Al: You want a future with me?

L: Yes.

Al: What is our future gonna look like without Gannon? Answer that for me and think, before you give me some bullshit, think long and hard about what our future looks like without Gannon.

(Long silence).

L: Hello?

I don't have any involvement in Gannon, and I feel like that I've proven it with the polygraph and answering the questions to try to get people on the right track of looking. The future, we'll be together, and it definitely takes a lot of help from Jesus Christ and praying that every single day as hard as it may be that it'll be one of those things where people come home, or whatever.

Al: You say come home? He's not a runaway. Somebody's got him is what you said.

L: Meaning that people have done this, and something happens they take them, they tie them up in basements and all this stuff, there are stories of this. There are.

Al: You're not convincing. I asked you what our future looks like without Gannon, and you just went on some tangent about you didn't do anything.

L: I said that we'd be supportive, and we'd work together to keep every effort in finding Gannon if it means we have to join organisations together to help other people find their children while we're searching for Gannon. If it means that everything we do from building stuff of setting up monuments or things like that for people to come and be like, hey can you help, like we have help. That's our future...

Al: Okay, alright.

L:... because that's a greater plan that God could have.

Al: Okay, so. Okay, so. Fair enough. So, our together starts now, it doesn't start when Gannon doesn't come home, okay? Our together starts now, so start with the bath salts. That was bullshit, wasn't it?

L: No.

Al: So, Gannon sent that to me about bath salts?

L: Okay, so.

Al: No, I want you to think, I want you to understand why I ask you that, because we know the friend was bullshit because he didn't leave to go to a friend's house, okay. And the bath salts were directly involved with the friend, so if there is no friend there is no bath salts.

L: There is, and here's why.

Al: So, there is a friend, or there is bath salts?

L:Oh, my...

Al:Okay, I'm sorry go ahead go ahead, I'm sorry. I'm listening, I'm sorry.

L: The bath salts were involved... when I talked to Gannon, Gannon clearly said that they had talked to him about bath salts at school like during that drug thing, right?

Al: The one that had been weeks before he went missing?

L: Right. He said he already knew about bath salts during this time. He already knew. He knew what they could do, dangers, and things like that. However, someone did tell him that if they could bring bath salts because it's part of the challenge that he would get to play with them. Gannon didn't want to do anything with bath salts. In fact, I even showed Gannon how bath salts can be good, meaning... I said, when you went and did you a bath bomb if you put some bath salts in there it kind of helps you breathe a little, it helps you relax. Gannon didn't have any intentions to go eat or snort or whatever bath salts. Or at least not from my opinion I don't think he did. I think he just sincerely wanted to play with whoever this was.

Al: So, why...? So, this was...? When did they ask him about this?

L: About what?

Al: The bath salts. When did the thing come up with the friend, because another thing about Gannon is he, you know say the puberty class, as soon as he hears something he comes home typically that night and talks about it, so he waited two, three days to talk about it?

L: Gannon talked about...

Al: Him and what?

L: He talked about it.

Al:I can't hear you.

L: He came in immediately and talked about Friday, immediately.

Al: To you?

L: When he came in.

Al: Okay but... and you didn't mention it to me Friday?

L:But he said, when he was talking, that they're not good for you.

Al: Right.

L: Blah blah blah, there was no in... he didn't say anything like, hey I'm about to go do bath salts.

Al: Right, right but you're, you're, okay, you're a good mom why would a good mom not tell her husband, you know, the father of the child that day hey Gannon asked about bath salts? We probably need to address this because you usually do that. So, you...

L: I didn't think about it.

Al: ... so, you waited till he was missing to text me about bath salts?

L: No. I sent you... what are you talking about? I sent you the... you sent me the message about bath salts, and I said to you yes, he came in last night, go read your messages.

Al: Okay, but last night from that message, the message was Monday, okay, so you just said last night being Sunday and then a second ago you told me Friday so.

L: He came home Friday talking about it, yes.

Al: Okay but you said he asked you Sunday, you just said he asked you Sunday.

L: He asked me Sunday do we have any.

Al: Come on.

L: Asking about it and having any are different.

Al: Come on. Tecia, Even, so Friday he comes in and asks you about it, and they're bad, and we all know how he is about bad stuff, okay. He hates it, his mommy does bad stuff he thinks, Mike does bad stuff, okay? So, Friday he tells you, you guys have a conversation of bad stuff, bath salts, and he still comes back Sunday and asks you if you have any?

L: Yes, the bad stuff was not just bath salts it was in general.

Al: But you just said it was...

L:He was telling me about the things that people who were talking about. His class is a halfway decent class, like, good kids, but when they go outside, one of the moms, I know who she is, I could show you a picture, her little boy is in the opposite class that Gannon's in and he's just a nightmare, okay? So, I guess on recess they're outside, they have conversations about this, and all he was talking about is the people that were talking about bad things. That's it. He didn't have any, he didn't say to me hey I'm gonna whatever. I'm telling you, someone peer pressured him that they could hang out and play. That's just the thing—peer pressure. Gannon had no intentions of doing nothing but playing at somebody's house.

Al: Whose house?

L:I've made that clear to you. I don't know.

Al: That's not like Gannon, that's not like Gannon either, to not tell us.

L: Well, that is the truth okay because you can sit here and say some things are not like Gannon, but we've caught him doing certain things.

Al: Like what? When?

L: We will catch children do some things and we have to be like they can't always stay in our life, that's not like them. What we instilled in them and hope that they make the best decisions when crossed with these things, but the bath salts has completely nothing, nothing to do with what Gannon was gonna do. Gannon was not gonna go do anything bad with bath salts.

Al: Well, hey, listen, my battery's getting low, so I just want you to know that if my battery cuts off, I'm not changing my theme here that together, one of the first things together is you give me these polygraph results, okay?

L:And I agreed to meet you and then...

Al: No, you send it to me and then I'll meet you.

L: I am not sending it to you.

Al: Okay then we're not together. We're not together in this.

L: I am not sending a copy.

Al: Tecia, I need you to send me a copy of the polygraph results or it's not clear to me that we're together in this...

The call ended.

Mr Allen informs the court there is one final call to play and the judge makes the decision to play it on Friday.

The court breaks for the day.

CHAPTER 13

LETECIA STAUCH TRIAL – DAY 12 - 21ST APRIL 2023

Mr Grusing returns to the stand. He explains how they had made the decision to change the strategies to see how she would react to certain suggestions.

He pointed out how Letecia left Gannon out of the conversation when she would say things like, you think I killed *someone?* Rather than mentioning Gannon by name.

The final phone call is played.

Al:Hello?

L:Hey.

Al:So, hey, you said there was an emergency that you needed to talk about?

L:Yes. Are you okay, because I sent you the message about stopping searching and I said are you ready to work together with me... yes, I said that to you.

Al:Okay, so what is it?

L:What do you mean what is it? I'm telling you. Oh, my god. I don't know how to clearly say this, do you believe me now that I didn't do anything wrong?

Al:I'm just trying to get... you made it seem like you had some urgent news that you had to tell me.

L:... this is the link you were talking about with the landfill that was old.

Al:So, there wasn't really anything urgent and pressing that would help me find Gannon?

L:I'm asking are you ready to work together with your wife to do it.

Al:Yeah, I'm telling you, I'm going off your list—number one. Gannon. So, let's focus on that.

L:So, you read my list? Why are people sending this about lies and about airports and all this?

Al:I don't know.

L:We can't have a straight goal in common.

Al:I don't know. I don't care about social media, never have. Who cares what people are saying? I rode with my mom to the airport.

L:Okay, where are you?

Al:Where am I? I told you, I just stepped out of work on a lunch break.

L:As in the node?

Al:No. As in the headquarters.

L:Okay. Are you gonna be able to stay with your wife so we can work on this together?

AL:I'm not making any promises.

L:Well, I need to know right now, like, tomorrow.

Al:Well, you're not even here. If you're telling me starting tomorrow...

L:I can't fly the dogs.

Al:Well, how did the dogs get to where you're at if they couldn't fly?

L:In a car with friends. That's all I've been doing—they can't get on an airplane.

Al:What friends?

L:(Unintelligible)... we've been staying everywhere. The dogs cannot get on an airplane.

Al:Okay, fair enough. But I wanna get back to Gannon.

L:I want you to tell me you're gonna work together with me.

Al:That's not a priority.

L:Be together, so we can turn down everything, figure this out, get a plan in place.

Al:But why is the safety of a child contingent on anything other than finding him?

L:I cannot help you if we're not together.

Al:Yes, you can.

L:I can't do any of that if we're not together, we can write it down ten freaking times and work through it. I beg for this.

Al:But I still don't understand how you helping me with Gannon is contingent upon anything else.

L:It's not contingent—I am your wife. Did you file for divorce?

Al:I told you that already—no, do you want me to?

L:No. Are you cheating on me?

Al:Am I cheating on you? No. Listen we need to focus on Gannon, okay? You told me you had...

L:... some big plan.

Al:No, it's not. Yeah, it is, you're right it's a big plan to find my son. Absolutely. Okay, so listen to me. You made this, like you always do in these scenarios, you made it seem like we could fix it immediately—you'd got some big piece of information... listen.

L:Listen to me and be open-minded. (Unintelligible)... you at my side in order for it to be working because if you go against me you be whatever, you try to do all these things, we can get to what you need.

Al:Okay, that's what I wanted you to say, because you just told me that finding Gannon is contingent upon you getting what you want.

Crosstalk.

Al:Yeah, you said if you do I have to buck you or don't be with you and don't sleep with you...

L:I said that?

Al:Yeah. That's what you said in essence is that if I don't give you what you want, we don't find Gannon. So, listen, I'm going back in now, I thought you had some emergency.

L:(Unintelligible).

Al:Listen, if you tell me everything I need to know, like who took Gannon or what happened to Gannon then we talk about these other seven parts of your list, okay? But number one is Gannon. Nothing happens for anybody in the rest of my life period, until I get information about Gannon or find him. I thought you didn't have a car. Sounds like a car to me.

L:(Unintelligible ranting)

Al:Alright I'm sorry, go ahead, I'm sorry.

L:Okay, number one, I need you to tell me that you have confidence and believe in me.

Al:Number one on the list is Gannon, so...

L:Screaming.

Al:Okay, I believe you and have confidence in you that you'll tell me the truth.

L:Number one, finding Gannon. So how come there haven't been any kind of locations, searches, anything, outside of only where I went? It's the most concerning thing to you and the first thing that has to be done, so tell me why that's not happening?

Al:That's a question we need to ask law-enforcement, not me.

L:And that's not something that you have even thought of to ask? Because, I mean, you called me to ask about this landfill that was something... someone was messing around with your hands, being a dick, but this is something. You should've asked them this several times.

Al:Yeah, sure I've asked them this... what? Why are you searching there? *Well, you know, we can't tell you anything.*

L:Okay. Next question. Everywhere I went was searched, acres upon acres, upon acres when I didn't even go to those acres. How do we find Gannon if none of those things... he was in none of the places that I went, does that not make you open up your eyes to say that I'm not involved, someone else is?

Al:Yeah, you're absolutely right, and back to your first question, I believe in you, okay? But I believe you know that someone else is involved and you know who, that's what I want...

L:I don't.

Al:Okay, but then you keep sending me emergency messages, we can fix this right now but then you never tell me anything.

L:Number two—that's the second thing, you know that. Anything I haven't done, so why come, when I gave them the information I gave them, why did they not look into it? Why did they not believe it? Why?

Al:What information? About Quincy Brown?

L:No, I did not.

Al:What information?

L:You just said they don't tell you anything, right? That's what you said...

Al:Okay, yeah, exactly.

L:Which means they would have gotten information from me.

Al:Okay. So what information was there?

L:I told them they have not covered any of the areas except only the areas that I drove.

Al:Okay, but what information are you talking about? Why won't you give me that information? I'm the father of the missing child, Tecia.

L:But I've already told you one time, and it wasn't good enough.

Al:Well, tell me again. Tell me right now. I'm in believe Tecia mode.

L:Okay, how long do you have?

Al:Five to seven minutes, honestly. I've gotta get back...

L:Five to seven minutes.

Al:Well, what do you need? Tell me what you need. An hour? Ten minutes?

L:Are you on lunch? I'm not trying to...

Al:No, I'm working like, four-hour days, so, I mean, I come out because I told you I come out around this time, but I got another hour or some to work and then I'm leaving for the day. Because they're just trying, like I told you this morning they're trying to phase me back in, so I don't wanna be out here for 20-30 minutes.

L:Okay, so then, what time can you sit down and talk with just you, not with you and all your other clan.

Al:Right now.

L:So, you got 30 minutes to give me right now?

Al:Listen, I'll make up some bullshit when I go in there, but yeah, I'll give you 30 minutes right now. Walk me through it.

L:Let me ask you this question. How many of the videos, so you can all make sense of, do you have yourself other than one video?

Al:Listen, this is not Albert answers a bunch of questions, you tell me what I'm missing or haven't seen. That's what this is about, this is not you...

L:Have you seen a video of anyone pulling into our yard after four o'clock?

Al:I'm not sitting here answering questions, okay? I haven't seen other than what's been released to the public. I'm not sitting here getting questioned. You said you had a story to tell me about this...

L:I didn't say I had a story.

Al:Okay.

L:I'm helping you.

Al:Okay, I'm listening.

L:Did you see any of the videos?

Al:I'm listening, I'm not being questioned, okay? Tell me what I'm missing in the video, just tell me.

L:In the video, when Harley comes home, and Laina, I'm sure you had to see this, just tell me where Harley parked her car?

AL:I have no clue Tecia, tell me what you're trying to tell me? Now you're getting me upset.

L:You haven't seen this?

Al:No, I've not seen anything, I told you that. I've seen what is on the internet on the video about the truck. That's it.

L:Okay. So, can you wait by your phone for five minutes?

Al:You said 30 minutes and if you have something.

L:I need you to wait by your phone for five minutes because I have this girl's kids in here.

Al:Yeah. You what?

L:Her kids are in here. I took her car to get some food and I have her kids in here, so I just need five minutes to pull up in the yard for her kids to get out.

Al:Why does that keep you from sending a video?

L:It's not sending a video. I don't want to talk about it with kids around. They can hear me—I'm asking you for five minutes to pull in the yard and they get out.

Al:Just tell me what you gotta tell me. There's no kids in the car, I don't hear a peep.

L:There is a kid in the car.

Al:Listen, tell me now or else I'm going back in work, I'm tired of you jerking me around.

L:I'm literally almost to the street.

Al:I don't have five minutes, the 30 minutes you asked for, I got that. You start telling me whatever it is you got to tell me. Who cares if there are kids in the car. That should be a good thing that you know information that can help you find the missing kid. I'm sure they've heard about it.

L:I don't know if they did, They might not of. Look, I'm turning into her street, just hold on. I swear to you, I'm literally...

Al:I'm not questioning you, I'm in believe Tecia mode, I'm just waiting for some facts that I can believe.

L:... turning on her street.

Al:Okay, I believe you.

L:I'm passing the church right now.

Al:What church?

L:And then I'm going on to this. Church. I guess their church, I guess they go there, I don't know.

Al:Oh, you passed by it, but there's no sign, okay cool.

L:Yes, there's a sign. I'm looking at the road.

Al:I believe you. I believe you. I'm not trying to question you.

L:I'm pulling in. You go inside with your mommy, and I'll be right in.

Letecia begins speaking to someone about the dogs.

L:I need you to believe, Albert. I need you to believe that someone did take Gannon. I need you to believe that I've already given the police department the description. I need you to quit thinking that it's somebody made up, because it's not. Obviously, I didn't do it. There's no way possible that I could've been hours and hours away in a certain window. I need you to help them re-look at that. I'm telling you, Gannon would've left our neighbourhood anywhere between that timeframe and I wouldn't even be surprised if it was like the kid in North Carolina.

Al:What certain window are you talking about?

L:The certain one I'm talking about between three and anywhere that evening, because here's why. There was a lot of people out and about in the neighbourhood everywhere.

Al:So, you weren't home during that certain window? Is that what you said?

L:Do what?

Al:You said you weren't home during that certain window? Or he could've left in that certain window?

L:I'm saying that's when it happened. So, by the time I called, Gannon still could've been in the neighbourhood.

Al:You said when IT happened, what is IT, Tecia?

L:I told you already. You haven't looked at it to see. Okay, go to the rings. See we went out the front door. When we left, we went out the front door, okay? I set the alarm, I went out the front door, I came back in the front door, made sure the alarm was set, went out the garage. You could see that on the ring. When I came out, I think it was like, 10:07, we left out, we were in the garage.

Al:Okay.

L:At that time, there was no more anybody going in and out, and the dogs do not set off the motion in the house.

Al:Right.

L:They don't, okay?

Al:Not when they're in their crates, you're right.

L:They're in their crates. And as sure as heck, if I'm somewhere upstairs they're with me. They're not just roaming around doing their thing. They're following somebody that they love, okay?

When we came back, I told you 15,000 times, about the car following us at PetCo. The reason I left the phone at PetCo, you wanna know why? Why don't you all go and check the alarm on it. I set an alarm for it to go off if I hadn't of came back in the time frame to call the police. I set an alarm on there, Albert. There was no intention, I had my watch on, there was no hiding where I was going or whatever.

Al:But wait, wait, so... you set an alarm to call the police, why?

L:No. Because someone was following us.

Al:From the house, or from PetCo?

L:From the house, to PetCo. Then from PetCo, I was... that's why I kept walking to the door to look, because Gannon was laying down, he was playing the switch, so I knew that they knew nobody was in the car. That's what they thought. Maybe I was being over suspicious...

Al:So, so... help me out here because I'm in believe Tecia mode, okay? Just so you know that. But, somebody's following you from the house and you leave Gannon in the truck?

L:They never knew anybody was in the truck.

Al:But if they followed you from the house didn't they see you get into the truck?

L:It was not from the house as in our house, it was the area.

Al:Okay, help me be in believe Tecia mode, okay? Don't start spinning. Just tell me...

L:I'm not spinning. Just let me go through the whole entire thing.

Al:Okay. Go ahead.

L:Okay, so I get there, I was playing with these period pad things because apparently dogs have periods, so I'm holding the thing, and I set the alarm, just for the alarm to go off. Maybe I was being too suspicious...

Al does a dramatic fake yawn.

L:And now you're yawning?

Al:Listen, I don't sleep good at night. I haven't for years, you know that so go ahead.

L:Albert, I was supposed to, like, deliver papers. I couldn't do it, Albert.

Al:Deliver papers? For what?

Long silence.

Al:Tecia?

L:When I went to Nevada, there was this pregnant lady, so I agreed to help the pregnant lady because she was really pregnant. She gets in the car, which is why Gannon was not in the front seat, he was in the back seat.

Al:Wait, wait, you said you went to Nevada?

L:Went through Nevada going to PetCo.

Al:Oh right. Go ahead.

L:Right. When I realised, she's not pregnant once she gets in the car.

Al:Was this the same lady that was following you?

L:I don't know if they were following us, I just know there was a car following us when I get off... I turn where Harley gets the little eyelashes done because I thought I would lose them, then I saw a pregnant lady. She looked legit like 8 months pregnant.

Al:What kind of car was following you, because maybe...

L:I've told you this 15 times.

Al:Alright, okay.

L:It was like a blue something. Like a blue little car like a cooper or something like that.

Al:So, not a red car, just a blue one.

L:The red earlier today was nothing, it's already been checked out.

Al:Okay.

L:And the reason I know that's been checked out, because I had somebody in Lorson Ranch do it.

Al:Okay, I just wanna make sure I keep these car's straight. So, it was the blue one not the red one?

L:See... you... I'm... I'm...

Al:No, don't get upset. I'm just trying to get it straight, I'm not picking holes in your story, I'm just making sure on the blue car, okay? So, now back to the pregnant lady that gets in the front seat.

L:So, the pregnant lady gets in the front seat, but she's not really pregnant. I don't know that she's not really pregnant, but she says she needs a ride. I felt bad. She looked really, really, pregnant, like, eight months.

Al: Hmm.

L: What?

Al: I said hmm. I'm just listening.

L:You know what, I'm not gonna help if you're gonna do this to me.

Al:I'm listening, don't you believe me?

L: I really came in this to be honest with you.

Al: Okay, and I'm just listening.

L: No, you weren't, you're being a dick, by saying hmm. That's being a dick to me.

Al: I don't know why you're saying that but does the pregnant lady know what happened to G? Does she know where Gannon went?

L: Can I finish?

Al: Yeah. Absolutely.

L: She wasn't really pregnant. She had about I don't even know how much money, inside of this thing that makes her look pregnant. So, you know where my mind immediately goes?

Al: Where?

L: What would you think a pregnant person, disguising as pregnant but money in her belly means?

Al: Probably robbed a bank.

L: Okay, she might have. She could be involved in something crazy, right?

Al:Yeah. I would be scared myself even if it was a woman.

L: Yeah, because that's pretty scary right? You're making fun of this like its...

Al: No, I'm not. If somebody got in my truck with a pregnant belly full of cash I'd be worried to death, you're right.

L: I don't know... I don't know how else to help other than to know we were in the wrong place at the wrong time.

Al: Okay, are you talking about PetCo?

L: Yes, because PetCo... I was just supposed to walk into PetCo, look around, be normal, go drop this lady off somewhere.

Al: Oh, so she told you to walk into PetCo?

L: Yes.

Al: Oh, okay.

L: She forced me.

Al: She forced you, of course, I got ya, okay. Did she have a wea... like a gun or a knife or something to threaten you or what?

L: How do you think someone would force you?

Al: No, you're a tough girl so it's gonna take a lot, that's what I'm trying to say. You're, I mean...

L: A tough girl?

Al: Yeah, yeah. I don't think you'd be scared easy by somebody like that. So, that's just what I'm saying, you'd probably start swinging unless she had a gun or a knife or something.

L: This is a joke to you.

Al: No, I'm serious. I'm trying to...

L: You finally are getting like legit, and it's just a joke to you.

Al: I'm sorry you think that but go ahead.

L: I'm not... forget it, man. You're not wanting to stand by my side, you don't want the help.

Al: I'm right here standing by your side listening to the truth, okay. I'm in believe Tecia mode like I told you.

L: Yeah, and then what you gonna do? Tell me I'm telling a lie and hang up?

Al: Are you telling a lie?

L: No, that's what you're gonna do, you're not gonna believe it, I told you it was beyond your wildest imagination to know we was in the wrong place at the wrong time.

Al: Are you telling me this... I don't' know... you want me to believe you, but I feel you're just telling me something to make me feel better about Gannon being missing. It's kinda like the Quincy Brown thing, but now it's a pregnant lady with cash in her belly. I believe you, what happened next?

L: Now you're...

Al: No, I'm trying to make sense of all of this, okay? You want me to believe you, I'm giving you the benefit of the doubt. Tell me the rest of the story.

L: Albert there's something else. It's just that being at the wrong place at the wrong time with people who are money laundering, wanting me, or whoever they can get, to deliver paper to these Mexican restaurants, and you're supposed to get packages back from them. And I wouldn't do it. So that's why we were on Countyline Road because I was scared to death. I left. So, I was going around and around and around, making sure that no car followed me.

Al: So, was that where they were trying to send you, or you just went there because you knew that was out in the boonies?

L: No, because I got on interstate 25 and it was backed up.

Al: Oh, so you did like we did that one time and took a detour?

L: It was nothing to do with whatever... they'd already searched the entire area. I'm innocent. That's who has Gannon, okay?

Al: The pregnant lady with the cash?

L: No. I've already given you... the Mexican guy. Why do you think I told you that about the Quincy thing? Because... Mexico. We need to be looking at any routes going into Mexico, and I've been telling you this.

Al: No, okay, I'm out of believe Tecia mode now because you told me Quincy Brown was in Colorado Springs. His family told your news reporter that he was in Mexico, okay? You didn't know that beforehand. And of course you have nothing to say about that. I'll talk to you later.

The call ends.

Mr Grusing returns to the stand. He recalls how during the calls she would only agree to help finding Gannon if Al would agree to staying with her, trying to force him to return to the marriage.

Although she was implying she was in Colorado Springs, they knew she was actually in South Carolina.

There had been no indication she was followed from Lorson Ranch to PetCo—she had made two visits to the store two hours apart.

The primary goal during the phone calls was to find Gannon, second, they were looking at building a case against her and working towards an arrest.

The FBI interview is played to the court next.

Letecia is read her rights and asked if she would like an attorney. She declines but suggested if she gets to a point where she changes her mind, she will ask for one.

She seems confused why she is under arrest and Grusing explains to her it is for the murder of Gannon, she scoffs, 'so, Gannon was murdered?'

She says she is happy to tell him all she knows but first she would need to ensure her family was safe and would need new identities for them all. Grusing says the FBI could assist with that if necessary.

He tells her he had been in on the phone calls between her and Al. She says she knew there was somebody listening in, and the reason she gave him all the misleading stories was because she was angry with Al for not standing by her and she'd wanted to punish him.

She says Al was a great dad and although he worked long hours he would always try to be hands on when he was home.

Grusing explains to Letecia about victimology and asks her to tell him everything she knows about Gannon.

She tells how Landon was in a bad place when Gannon first came to live with them. It was difficult to allow the kids to go to stay with their mother and her new husband. He was on medication for ADHD.

She says she and Gannon were very close, and rarely had disagreements. He would often tell her he loved her. She couldn't remember any specific situations but there were rare occasions she would yell at him. He was rarely disagreeable and wouldn't shout back at her or slam doors.

Grusing asks her to tell him about the candle incident.

Gannon had been grounded from the Switch prior to that day, however, he had been so helpful during the hike that she allowed him to play on it when they got home.

Later that evening, she heard the machine beeping and so she put the alarm code in. Then the alarm started saying fire over and over. She grabbed Laina and the dogs and ran out to the truck. Then she went back downstairs, and Gannon was half asleep on the sofa. She smothered the fire with the covers. Then they ran out.

Gannon had little burns on his arms. She didn't think it was bad although on the Monday she did question if he needed to go to the hospital.

When asked what happened the next morning, she says, 'this is where I need help from everybody. But how can I get help before I talk to somebody?'

He explains he needs the information first, and then if she needs protection after that he can assist her, however, if she would prefer to go through the court process first then that is her choice. But he has seen the blood in Gannon's bedroom, and he knows it wasn't caused by him flinging his blood around. There was significant blood loss. He also informs her that even if she didn't cause the injuries, if she allowed someone else to do that to cause them then the charges would be the same.

She denies hurting Gannon or allowing anybody else to hurt him, but she has some information that could help but she would need protection. She tells him the reason there is no evidence on the alarms and ring cameras is because the alarms had already been covered up. If she agrees to tell him what happened in the days leading up to Gannon's disappearance, then she would need protection.

Again, she indicates she knows what happened to Gannon, but she refuses to give any solid information.

He asks her about the searches she made on her phone which she had since deleted.

- Spurting from an arterial bleed.

- I don't like my stepson.

- Should I get a divorce?

- Al Stauch cheating.

- Al Stauch cheating in Colorado Springs.

- Catch Al Stauch cheating.

- How to get blood out of sheets.

- I want immunity because it was gang related.

- Find me a new husband.

- Find me a rich guy who wants me to take care of his kids.

- I'm doing all the work for my step kids and their mom doesn't help.

- Hit and run.

- Traffic accident.

- My husband wants a divorce.

- My husband wants a baby, but I want an abortion.

- One day some people will wish they treated you differently.

- Parenting should be four people not one.

- Quotes a suicidal person might say.

- What to do if you suspect a person swallowed poison.

- You will never forgive me and treat me like a princess.

- You'll never know when it's too late.

She explains a lot of these searches away as though they were just things she had come across and clicked on.

She says the injury to Gannon's foot was real. He cut his foot on a board in the garage.

The burns on his arms weren't that bad.

She says she wants to write the details in the agent's notebook regarding what caused the blood loss in Gannon's room. She wrote Gannon had a head wound. She explains away the blood found in the back of her car as being from the cut foot.

She asks if there is a way someone can pull up some apps but won't tell him what app she is talking about.

She is talking continually yet saying absolutely nothing.

The DA enters the room to discuss offering her protection. She agrees to the recording being turned off and to allow Letecia to speak frankly to Agent Grusing without the discussion being monitored.

They take Letecia to another room to allow her to speak off camera.

While off camera, she tells him the app she had been indicating was connected to a threesome Al had arranged and the person who took Gannon was the third person in the threesome, a female called Angel.

She also told him Gannon had suffered a head injury, a gash to his left temple, when he moved the beds around. However, the injury wasn't too bad and didn't even need stitches.

They returned to the interview room and resumed the recording.

Agent Grusing asked Letecia for more details regarding Angel. She says Angel looks a lot like herself. Gannon was taken to play with Angel's nephew from PetCo, but when he didn't return at 6pm she called the police to report him missing.

Grusing does not believe her and tells her so.

She refuses to talk about it and says over and over that she never hurt Gannon.

The court breaks for the weekend.

CHAPTER 14

LETECIA STAUCH TRIAL – DAY 13 - 24TH APRIL 2023

Former Special Agent John Grusing resumes his testimony.

The remainder of the interview is played.

Letecia is insistent she doesn't know where Gannon is nor what happened to him.

She refuses to tell Grusing when she last saw Gannon. Quoting instead that she has faith in God, and he will make everything right.

Again, she refuses to tell him her last image of Gannon, opting to say it was nothing bad instead.

He tells her that she will have that final image in her brain for the rest of her life. But she insists there is nothing horrible in her mind she has to live with.

He says she has had a way of spinning stories and dodging questions her whole life. But this time it wasn't working for her. He says the best thing she could have done would be to say Gannon just went and I refuse to say anything else, but to describe all the injuries he'd suffered is awful. The blood loss was so significant that Gannon would not have been normal after it.

She scoffs, telling him she had lost a lot of blood before, and she didn't die.

Finally, she says the last image she has of Gannon is him smiling and walking away.

The recording ends after over five hours with her whispering to Grusing that they both should make a trip to North Carolina.

Mr Allen has no further questions.

Mr Cook begins cross examination.

He asks if he found it strange when Letecia spoke about herself in the third person during the phone calls with Al. Grusing said it depends on the person, but he didn't think it was odd at the time.

Grusing agrees that after a 5-hour interview he came away empty handed, however it was as he'd expected.

During redirect, Grusing tells the court that Letecia showed little concern for finding Gannon. Her main concern was for herself. After the interview, he was even more certain something terrible had happened to Gannon.

She was able to recall every detail when what she was trying to convey had nothing to do with Gannon's disappearance, yet she couldn't tell the agent the last time she saw Gannon or what he was wearing. This was indicative to him that the last image of Gannon must have been really awful.

She made the event a three-day ordeal.

Mr Allen has no further questions.

The court take their morning break.

FBI agent David Donati is the next witness called to the stand.

He had been tasked with processing Letecia's Tiguan and to assist in the investigation in the disappearance of Gannon. The car system stored things like GPS coordinates, dates, and times etc.

Several photographs are admitted into evidence.

The images are of the Tiguan, and the infotainment system. The interior is covered in a powdery residue of Bluestar once it had dried.

Mr Allen has no further questions.

Mr Cook has no questions.

The next witness called is FBI automotive forensic specialist Dwight Falkofske.

He is an electrical engineer and specialises in extracting data from vehicles and converting it to a format that is readable. He extracted the data from the electronic modules taken from Letecia's Tiguan.

Mr Allen has no further questions.

Mr Cook has no questions.

The court takes an early lunch break.

The next witness called is Forensic Serologist and DNA Analyst Sherrie Holes.

She specialises in examining biological fluids, blood, saliva, semen, and other biological evidence that may be suitable for DNA analysis.

Several samples were tested against DNA taken from Gannon's toothbrush as well as DNA samples taken from Al Stauch and Landon Hiott, Gannon's biological parents.

- A rolled-up piece of carpet tested positive for the presence of blood. It was forwarded for DNA analysis.

- Three sets of swabs taken from the stairs and floor of the garage tested positive for the presence of blood and were forwarded for DNA analysis.

- Another piece of carpet (carpet 1) tested positive for the presence of blood and was forwarded for DNA analysis.

- A further piece of carpet (carpet 2), as well as foam padding, both tested positive for the presence of blood and were forwarded for DNA analysis.

- Swabs taken from the electrical outlet from Gannon's bedroom were tested positive for blood and sent for DNA analysis.

- A rug tested positive for blood and was forwarded for DNA analysis.

- DNA testing was carried out on swabs taken from Letecia Stauch.

- A pair of shoes were tested for trace DNA on the inside of the shoe. The right shoe reacted positive for the presence of blood on the sole.

- The garage floor and the laundry room reacted positive for the presence of blood and was forwarded for DNA analysis.

- A plastic tub and lid tested positive for the presence of blood and were forwarded for DNA analysis.

- Swabs from Gannon's bed tested positive for the presence of blood and were forwarded for DNA analysis.

- A Brillo scrub brush and a blue and white scrub brush were tested positive for the presence of blood and forwarded for DNA analysis.

- Another scrub brush containing hair and carpet fibres tested positive for the presence of blood and forwarded for DNA analysis.

- Swabs taken from the living room pillow in the basement and area rug tested positive for blood and were forwarded for DNA analysis.

- Swabs taken from the basement stairs and the southeast child's room tested positive for the presence of blood and were forwarded for DNA analysis.

- A pink suitcase found inside Letecia's car when she was arrested, tested positive for the presence of blood on the inside and was forwarded for DNA analysis.

- A blue blanket found inside the pink suitcase, tested positive for the presence of blood and was sent for DNA analysis.

- Two of Gannon's entire fingernails were examined and tested positive for the presence of blood and were forwarded for DNA analysis.

- An empty Heinz vinegar bottle tested positive for the presence of blood and was forwarded for DNA analysis.

- An Amazon box from the storeroom tested positive for the presence of blood and were forwarded for DNA analysis.

- A white bedsheet with blue shark print tested positive for the presence of blood and was forwarded for DNA analysis.

Mr Allen has no further questions.

Mr Cook has no questions.

The next witness called is DNA Analyst and Serologist Donna Manogue.

She did the DNA lab work from the samples collected and submitted to her by the last witness.

Because they had no body initially for Gannon Stauch, she obtained DNA from Gannon's toothbrush and also took DNA samples from Gannon's biological parents. Once his body was found, a bone sample was provided for DNA analysis.

A chart is admitted into evidence showing the results of the DNA testing performed in this case.

- Garage swabs A, B, & C all matched Gannon Stauch's DNA profile.

- Swabs from carpet 1 matched Gannon Stauch's DNA profile.

- The padding matched Gannon Stauch's DNA profile.

- The swab from the electrical outlet matched Gannon Stauch's DNA profile.

- Swabs from carpet 2 matched Gannon Stauch's DNA profile.

- Swabs from the board found matched Gannon Stauch's DNA profile.

- Swabs from the outside of the Nike shoes matched Gannon Stauch's DNA profile.

- Swabs from the outer sole of the Nike shoes matched Gannon Stauch's DNA Profile.

- Swabs from the inside of the Nike shoes matched Letecia Stauch's DNA profile.

- Swabs in the box in the garage matched Gannon Stauch's DNA profile.

- Swabs from the basement stairs matched Gannon Stauch's DNA profile.

- Swabs from Gannon's bed matched Gannon Stauch's DNA profile.

- Two of the scrub brushes matched Gannon Stauch's DNA profile.

- Swabs from the pink suitcase matched Gannon Stauch's DNA profile.

- Swabs from the basement pillow matched Gannon Stauch's DNA profile.

- The cutout burnt carpet sample matched Gannon Stauch's DNA profile.

- Plastic tub and lid matched Gannon's Stauch's DNA profile.

- Swabs from the Amazon box matched Gannon Stauch's DNA profile.

The frequency matched Gannon Stauch's DNA profile by was 1 in 3.4 octillion (27 zeros).

Mr Allen has no further questions.

Mr Cook begins cross examination. He asks if she had Laina Stauch's and Harley hunts DNA profile for analysis and she says she didn't.

No further questions.

Court will end for the day because the witnesses are in transit.

CHAPTER 15

LETECIA STAUCH TRIAL – DAY 14 - TUESDAY 25TH APRIL 2023

FBI Special Agent Kevin Hoyland is the first witness called. He is a cellular analyst.

He explains how the technology works in this day and age to track cell phones and to be able to work out the location of a phone depending on the cell tower ping, or call goes through. A phone is always checking for the best cell tower to use so it is ready when a call or text message comes in.

Mr Allen asks to add Agent Hoyland's report relating to this case into evidence.

Several phone records were added into evidence—three accounts were linked to Eugene Stauch—Eugene Stauch, Letecia Stauch, Harley Hunt. There was a prepaid device purchased in Orlando, Florida in the name of Kylie Britt.

Agent Hoyland mapped the movements between Letecia's phone and the Tiguan's GPS and the Life360 device at the house on Sunday 26th January.

Movement showing Letecia's phone being outside of the house at 9:27pm, then back inside the house at 9:28pm, and 9:35pm.

Harley Hunt's phone corroborated her story that she was in work on that day.

Letecia had a lot of activity on her phone that night and into the following morning hours.

On the morning of Monday 27th January, Harley clocked into work at 8:30am.

A message was sent to Harley saying Letecia had left her phone at home and to contact her on her iWatch that had been paired with Gannon's device.

Albert's truck left the home at 10:13am.

Gannon's phone was picked up twice that morning—once at 10:19am close to their home and once at 11:07am close to the PetCo. And twice more in the afternoon at 1:19pm and 1:20pm at PetCo again.

Letecia is picked up on camera at PetCo at 1:22pm.

Albert's truck returns home at 2:20pm.

Harley clocked out of work at 4:15pm and her device returned to the home at 4:25pm.

That evening between 6:38pm and 6:58pm there were multiple calls from Letecia's phone including the 911 call at 6:55pm all using the cell tower facing the home.

Life360 placed Letecia's device at the home at 6:52pm (the Life360 app is a GPS location app).

Gannon's device placed 2 calls to the same number at 7:31pm and 7:32pm. It was unlikely to be Gannon making these calls.

There was significant vehicle activity.

At 8:05pm Albert contacted El Paso Sherriff's Office.

Harley made three calls at 7:01pm, 7:02pm, and 7:02pm.

That evening between 8pm and 6:19am the next morning, Letecia's phone had 65 different calls or texts connected to it. 64 of them used the tower facing the home, 1 of them at 5am was off the tower south of the home.

Gannon's device had incoming calls and texts as well as outgoing calls utilising the sector at the home.

At 10:09pm until 11:39pm El Paso Sherriff's Office had officers physically present in the home.

At 6:21am Letecia's device sent a text message utilising the tower facing the home.

Camera footage shows the Tiguan leaving the home at the same time, as well as Life360 app 6:24am, 6:25am, 6:27am.

Life360 app heads back south towards the home at 6:28am, 6:30am, and 6:31am.

At 6:40am Letecia's device receives a call through the tower facing the home, and the local ring camera shows the Tiguan backing into the garage at 6:36am.

Between 6:43am and 8:11am both Letecia's and Gannon's phones make and receive calls—2 out of 3 calls on Gannon's device were outgoing.

At 8:13am, there was a Life360 marker west of the house. There was Tiguan data as well as texts and calls at 8:16am, 8:21am, and 8:25am. Then there was an incoming call at 8:34am utilising a tower at the Colorado Springs airport. This is consistent with the device and the vehicle travelling to and arriving at Colorado Springs airport between 8:27am and 8:31am.

At 8:25am Letecia sent Al a text and he replied four minutes later saying he had just landed and asking if she was picking him up. A parking receipt was also found in the Tiguan showing it was parked at 8:28am—this was the last datapoint for the Tiguan on that day.

At 8:45am to 9:02am Letecia's device utilised the tower and sector and also had a number of Life360 hits in the area. She also rented a Kia Rio and picked Al up from the airport at 8:50am. Then her device travels away from the airport and returns to the home address around 9:15am.

Letecia had sent an iMessage to Harley minutes before picking up Al asking her to back her Jetta into the garage.

Between 9:37am to 11:44am a variety of calls, texts, and Life360 data, go from the house and shows Letecia's device travelled to French Elementary. The phone stops at a strip mall for 25 minutes before continuing north.

At 12:07pm, Letecia's device begins to travel south. At 1:30pm it stops near a Starbucks. This is where Letecia ended up being interviewed by the Sheriff's office. At approximately 2:45pm the device is back at the family home.

At 3:06pm, 3:45pm, 4:07pm, 4:17pm, and 4:25pm there is phone activity at the home.

At 4:32pm Life360 data begins to head north towards the airport. At 4:50pm the device was back on route 21 and a call was also made from the device at the same time. At 5pm, the Life360 app puts Letecia's device at the northern section of the airport.

At this time, Al had gone to the Sheriff's office, and he was there when she called him.

Then at 5:18pm and 5:38pm there was a decent amount of activity from the device off the tower facing Massage Envy (where Harley worked).

The device then travels from Massage Envy back towards the family home.

At 6pm, an incoming call put's Letecia's device at the family home, then her Life360 data sees the device head back towards the Starbucks. From there she sent some iMessages back and forth to Albert and Harley before returning home once again.

At 6:43pm, Letecia's device heads back towards the airport. Then at 7pm, Letecia's Tiguan is on the move. It leaves the airport and travels towards Falcon. The Life360 app terminates at 7:14pm so the only data came from the Tiguan at this time.

Harley's phone was using the cell tower down near the residence at this point.

The Tiguan heads towards Palmer Lake close to where the board would eventually be recovered. At 8:34pm, there was a slight deviation off the main path for around half an hour.

The Tiguan began travelling back south towards Massage Envy and arrived in the shopping centre around 11:30pm where it stopped for the night.

Letecia's phone was not reconnected to the network until 12:53am. The most obvious reasons for this would either be the device was turned off or turned onto airplane mode. It is possible the device's battery died.

At 12:34am she made a Wi-Fi call to Al. At 12:53am she reconnected to the network. She headed back to the family home and there was activity from there between 1:23am and 8:29am.

Letecia returned the Kia at 9am and then the Tiguan recorded its first activity for the day at 11am from where it had been parked near Massage Envy.

The Tiguan data, Life360 app, and cell data travelled from Massage Envy to El Paso County Sheriff's Office, stopping off at a carwash on the way. The last outgoing call was made at 11:48am and the car and phone were seized shortly after.

Because of this there was a gap between the data information for two days until Friday 31st January. Letecia's aunt, Brenda Acquard, hired a Nissan Altima as well as a cargo van. There was a tracker affixed to the Nissan that Letecia had been seen driving.

At 3:38pm that day they started to get data. The GPS data showed the Nissan went back to the area where the board was subsequently located. The vehicle spent an hour in that general area.

The van Letecia hired was equipped with a GPS that showed data points twice a day.

Letecia bought a burner phone from Walmart. She made a number of outgoing calls, but she dialled *67 before the number to block her caller ID.

At 6:59pm to 9:59am the next day Letecia's device used the Verizon tower close to the hotel in Amarillo, TX – Candlewood Suites. Financial records also confirmed Letecia had rented a room there for the night.

Over the next few days, Letecia's device continued travelling south towards Pensacola and Myrtle Beach. She made numerous calls to an Amy Lowry, (her sister) one day spending 5 hours talking to Amy, as well as several other calls.

In Pensacola, on 4th February, at 4:15am, the van's GPS marker is 1.8 miles away from where it pings just 55 minutes later which indicates the van was on the move during the early hours of that morning.

Later that morning, the van and Letecia's device left the Pensacola area and travelled south towards Orlando. It arrived in Orlando at 12:10am on 5th February.

Letecia's device stayed in the area until 6:30pm when it starts to travel north. At 10:12am on the 6th February, the van is in Pooler, Georgia. It was dropped off at a Budget Rental in the area.

Mr Allen has no further questions.

The defence has no questions.

The next witness is Doctor Christine Mohr.

She is a clinical program director for a state hospital sexually violent offender treatment program. She typically works in psychiatric hospitals, jails, and prisons. She has worked as a forensic psychologist, conducting sexual and violent risk evaluations, sexual predator and parole evaluations, civil commitment assistance for mentally ill individuals, in a variety of settings.

She has performed clinical evaluations to provide a diagnosis or understanding about what could be concerning about a person. A forensic assessment looks at if there is any violent risk, sexual risk, faking of a mental illnesses. Also, forensic-wise she has conducted pre-sentence evaluations, insanity evaluations, competency evaluations, or looked at somebody's risk in legal setting.

On 5th March 2020 she conducted an initial mental health assessment on Letecia to ensure she didn't have any symptoms they needed to be aware of for her safety and for the safety of others.

Letecia's demeanour was generally very calm and polite. She reported some general symptoms, but she was lucid and maintained fluid conversation. She wasn't in agreement with being on suicide watch but due to the nature of her alleged crime and with it being her first time in jail it was a safety precaution.

She made a diagnosis of general anxiety disorder and put in a referral for a psychiatrist to refer some medication.

Letecia didn't mention any other mental disorders she suffered with. She showed no signs of psychotic disorder.

The court breaks for lunch.

Doctor Mohr returns to the stand. She says Letecia understood why she was being charged and mentioned her husband of 6 years thought she was guilty.

During the next few weeks Doctor Mohr met with Letecia several times and saw no signs of any medical or mental health issues.

When Gannon's body was found Letecia was informed and assessed. She was tearful and overwhelmed. She said she had never been to Florida although she hadn't been told where Gannon's body had been found.

There were still no signs of DID (Dissociative Identity Disorder).

On 29th April 2020, she met with Letecia as one of her weekly follow up visits. She had a normal reported mental status. She asked if she could be taken off the medical ward because she was struggling to sleep.

On 12th May she said she couldn't speak to Mohr because she could be subpoenaed. She offered to speak to her several times, but she declined.

On the 5th June 2020, Letecia raised a concern that she may have multiple personalities. She went into detail of how she was feeling and how being in the jail was exacerbating her traumatic stress. She was missing Harley and her dogs. She told the doctor she had been molested aged 14. However, Doctor Mohr didn't see any signs of DID such as losing gaps of time, or memory loss. There was no change in personalities or voice patterns in any of the meetings.

Letecia spoke about a hiking trip, saying she always used to take a handgun hiking but did not that day. She said I can't cope with it, it's one traumatic situation too many and it was the wrong place at the wrong time.

She said she replays that week of her life over and over and also replays why she didn't ask for more help or provide more information to the police. She was now trying to begin processing everything, meaning Gannon.

She said she needed to talk to someone more than a social worker. That she had been creating stories that weren't true and didn't remember conversations. She said she needed help, and she can't leave January.

She brought up Andrew Wommack and his son dying in Colorado and coming back to life eight hours later. She said, regarding Gannon, she knew that wasn't physically possible, but she'd wanted to fix things and pray his same prayers.

She said she wrote Gannon a letter and that she regretted taking the back road off highway 25, and that she can't relive every situation, every day, and every hour.

On 14th July Letecia reported she was losing weight and claimed she needed a celiac diet. They had done some tests that confirmed she didn't actually need a celiac diet. She said she was going to be so rich one day referring to a civil suit for not having her diet accommodated for or her medical needs taken care of.

On 21st August Doctor Mohr met with Letecia. She recalls seeing her in her bed with a blanket over her head. Letecia said she didn't want to talk.

Letecia had access to a kite system which is an email that is sent to a generic box regarding several different considerations. A kite message was sent from Letecia saying… 'You let them duct tape me and cover the alarm sensors because they came for me in West Palm Beach, then came back and covered alarm with socks. I saw the car on Carriage Meadows so we both left, gun jammed, got shot. They thought I was crazy because I watched Good Girls, but he really had tattoos. You didn't help.'

Another kite was sent saying… 'Being held hostage with camera. People everywhere and no one helps. They took my water from my dog.'

The notes that followed these messages was 'these kites from patient are not consistent with prior presentation of language'.

On 28th August, Letecia refused to be seen by Doctor Mohr once again.

After a competency examination Letecia was assessed for bipolar disorder.

On the 11th September, the psychiatric mental health nurse practitioner determined bipolar disorder was not a consistent diagnosis because Letecia would've had to present with at least a two week bout of depression followed by a four day manic period which she had not.

Letecia stopped taking her anxiety meds although she complained her symptoms were worsening. She also warned staff she would start becoming impulsive, have a different personality, act way out of character, pull her hair out and be manic.

This was the first time Letecia had mentioned she had a different personality. Mohr did not assess her for DID because she said people who have multiple personalities don't tend to inform you, they will change their personality as they have no control over it.

Mohr also says, someone with bipolar disorder wouldn't brag about being manic in the future. With this in mind, Mohr decided to have other mental health clinicians assess Letecia knowing if the case went to court there would need to be several opinions regarding her mental health.

On the 8th September, Letecia told Mohr she was seeing demons. Mohr believes she was faking.

Another progress not stated Letecia told a ward deputy she was going to act out because she wanted to be listed as crazy.

On 17th November 2020, Letecia reported she was bipolar, had multiple personality disorder and PTSD. This was the first time she had ever claimed to have a mental illness.

Mohr found this inconsistent with prior reports. She said Letecia appeared to be at baseline meaning there were no symptoms present during any of the contacts she had had with her.

On 5th January 2021, Letecia mentioned she had been triggered by another inmate. Then she mentioned she spent 90 days in a psychiatric hospital in Canada in 2018. There was never any evidence to support this.

She also told Mohr that her stepfather and her uncle sexually abused her when she was a child. Sexual assault or harassment brought on her hallucinations.

She claimed she was brilliant but that she would start going crazy because she was going stir-crazy in her cell.

Mohr believes the reason Letecia brought up the diagnosis or the symptoms was to help absolve her of the charges she faced or to try to encourage a different sentence.

Mr Allen has no further questions.

Mr Cook begins cross examination.

He said she ended her testimony by saying Letecia only reported she had been molested one time to her, but he believed she had mentioned it earlier.

Mohr agreed there had been mention of it in one of the reports prior to that however this had been the first time she mentioned it to her.

Cook asks if maybe Letecia hadn't been comfortable discussing something so personal in a setting where there are deputies, other inmates etc listening. Also, during times where there wasn't enough staff, Mohr sometimes had to conduct her interview/examination through the door.

Mohr says with sensitive topics like these, most people report them regardless of who is around.

Letecia entered the jail during Covid. Mohr believes she wore a mask during the meetings with Letecia. The staff were made to wear them but not the inmates.

On the day Gannon's body had been found, Letecia had said she has never been to Florida. Mr Cook says Letecia's lawyers had told her earlier that day that Gannon's body had been found in Florida.

The court takes an afternoon break.

Mr Cook resumes questioning Mohr.

He asks when Letecia was first admitted into the jail, Mohr was able to rule out DID fairly quickly. He asks several more questions regarding DID, and the fact Letecia's symptoms may have been overlooked.

The doctor doesn't believe so.

Mr Cook has no further questions.

Mr Young begins redirect. He asks if everyone who has committed first degree murder is put on suicide watch. Mohr says yes, they are.

The only diagnosis Letecia had was for anxiety, and this was consistent with the symptoms Mohr witnessed.

She had no symptoms until competency was raised and then she suddenly had all these symptoms.

Mr Young shows Mohr a document showing when Letecia's attorneys had visited her, and the day Gannon's body had been found there were no such visits.

Mr Young has no further questions.

Mr Cook asks for a chance to re-cross-examine the witness due to the document that was admitted regarding the attorney's visit.

The judge allows it.

Mr Cook recalls that at the time, March 2020 the country had gone into lockdown because of Covid. He asks Mohr if she remembers there were no personal visits allowed for a period of time because of the pandemic. Mohr didn't recall the specifics about this or the dates that were affected.

Cook asks if she knew the visitation record did not include WebEx or video visits between attorneys and clients? She believes so.

Mr Cook has no further questions.

A jury member has a question.

Q: **If what the defendant said is true, that she was sexually, physically, and emotionally abused on an on-going basis from a young age, is it your professional opinion that such a person can still grow up to be sane even if untreated?**

A: Yes.

The court breaks for the day.

CHAPTER 16

LETECIA STAUCH TRIAL – DAY 15 - 26TH APRIL 2023

The next witness called is forensic psychologist Doctor Jackie Grimmett. She is qualified as a specialist witness.

Doctor Grimmett first became involved in the case when she was asked by the court to make a second opinion on Letecia Stauch.

To make a diagnosis she looks at the police reports as well as speaking to the person that is to be evaluated. She does this because in order to assess whether the defendant has a rational and factual understanding of the proceedings of the case, she also needs to understand it.

She met Letecia in December 2020, and the meeting took 3 hours and 40 minutes. She said Letecia understood the context of the meeting, that she was there by the order of the court. Letecia made some complaints about her attorneys and comments regarding a conspiracy.

Grimmett didn't believe Letecia had a severe mental illness.

Letecia did engage in some behaviours. She was humming to herself, hitting her head on the wall. Her expression of emotion didn't seem to fit what was happening—she seemed happier than she should have been. At one point she spoke to someone else and then said she was talking to a vampire.

There had been concerns about prior testing performed on Letecia—MMPI (Minnesota

Multiphasic Personality Interview) and PAI (Personality Assessment Inventory) It was obvious when someone was answering in a way that would appear to be worse than they were, and this is what happened with Letecia.

The MMPI was uninterpretable because of invalid responding.

Grimmett reviewed the jail calls while she was incarcerated to observe her behaviours between people she knew and medical professionals. She would behave incoherently to one person and then call her daughter right after and give clear instructions.

Letecia mentioned she had DID and that she had various personalities—Taylor, Tecia, Jasmine, Jasper. When asked about Victoria, Harmony, Christina, Little Lucia, and Maria Sanchez, Grimmett says Letecia didn't mention them all and there was no indication she was changing personalities either.

Grimmett considered a diagnosis of DID initially based on the information given, however, DID is a very rare disorder, somewhere between 0 and 1% of people have it. It's also a very destructive and disabling disorder, people tend to be very high consumers of mental health services when they have it. It can be very frightening because people don't know what's happening to them, they feel very strange and can't explain what that is and so there's a lot of mental distress that goes along with that. Those people are typically very poor functioning—they can't hold down jobs, hold down relationships, they're not very productive. In Letecia's case, the names she had for the alters, a name for the different personalities, were selected based on the things she liked and aspirations she had. In DID the alters will present themselves to you, you don't create them, and you don't name them whimsically. There was none of the impairment that would be expected to go along with the claims Letecia was making.

Grimmett recalled Letecia telling her about a vampire called Justice. There was supposedly a button in her cell that she could summon Justice, Jasper, and Patrick. She claimed she had been introduced to vampires when she had been in Alaska previously and they used to go door to door like Jehovah's Witnesses. Letecia told her the vampire names were from the movie *Twilight*. The name of the vampire council was also taken directly from the series. This sounded like a fabrication to Grimmett. She says if someone had a mental illness talking to vampires, she would expect them to have their own unique aspects to them.

More tests were performed on Letecia, and they suggested possible feigning of symptoms.

Her diagnosis of Letecia was that she had some personality disfunction both with traits of borderline personality and narcissistic personality disorder but not meeting the threshold for with full disorder. She ruled out PTSD versus an unspecified anxiety disorder. These diagnoses would not reach the threshold of a mental disability.

Letecia told her she felt she could bring Gannon back to life. Grimmett found it was an unusual and delusional belief, but religious beliefs by definition are not delusions if they are commonly held beliefs in a subculture.

Mr Young has no further questions.

Mr Tolini begins cross-examination. He goes over the traits of the different disorders in question.

Grimmett agrees the dysfunctional symptoms in all of the disorders can be minimal or profound. And that a large percentage of people suffering borderline personality disorder and DID have suffered childhood sexual trauma.

The court takes a mid-morning break.

Mr Tolini is pointing out symptoms and suggestions that somebody could have a mild case of bipolar disorder or borderline personality disorder. Grimmett says it's not usual as these disorders are typically serious mental illnesses.

He goes through all the different types of hallucinations and delusions—delusion of grandeur, paranoid delusion, hallucinations, auditory (hearing something that isn't there), visual (seeing something that isn't there), tactile (feeling something that isn't there), olfactory (smelling something that isn't there), gustatory (tasting something that isn't there).

Grimmett says a person would need to have multiple symptoms of psychosis for at least 6 months in order to be diagnosed with schizophrenia.

Mr Tolini states that other mental illnesses can cause transient psychotic features—eg: PTD, DID, and borderline personality disorder. Grimmett agrees.

He says he read in an article that people with borderline personality disorder and childhood trauma have more psychosis than others. Grimmett seems confused with this line of questioning, stating she has already explained her report in this case and didn't understand what he was asking. Each person is different and manifests things in different ways and so it's difficult to narrow it down and say *this* causes *this*.

Mr Tolini asks to admit an article into evidence. He wants to impeach Grimmett for diagnosing Letecia Stauch as having a personality disorder with bordering features, but for saying this is not a serious mental illness. Tolini thinks the article shows how borderline personality disorder can be a serious mental illness.

The judge refuses to admit the entire article and agrees to Tolini reading certain excerpts into evidence only.

Mr Tolini asks Doctor Grimmett where the term borderline personality disorder comes from. She says it is on the borderline between neurosis and psychosis.

Tolini asks if she considered the fact that she thought Gannon could be raised from the dead was delusional. She says not in the context Letecia asked it. She asked it in a religious way that the same belief is followed by other people.

Mr Tolini has no further questions.

Mr Young begins redirect.

He asks if Doctor Grimmett thought Letecia genuinely believed Gannon could be raised from the dead. Grimmett says she did consider if this was a genuine belief.

He asks several questions about Letecia's state of mind after the offence.

Mr Young has no further questions.

Juror questions.

Q: **Can a difficulty or inability to face evidence, or to be rigorously honest, or to hold oneself accountable to consequences of one's questions be indicative of mental disability or past trauma related BPD?**

A: These would not be considered symptoms of a mental disability. It can be indicative of past trauma or BPD but would not reach the level of a mental disability.

Q: **Can compulsive lying indicate a mental disability?**

A: Compulsive lying is usually associated with antisocial personality. It would not be a symptom of a mental illness so it would not reach the threshold of a mental disability.

Q: **What does it take for a theory put for a peer reviewed publication to become mainstream enough to be published as some version of the DSM?**

A: My honest answer is that the DSM is very political. There are groups of people who want to put forth ideas, and there are committees and voting, and agendas and sometimes it can seem a bit capricious as to what gets accepted and what doesn't. With enough people endorsing those ideas and testing out those theories and seeing they they're accurate and gaining momentum and that helps it become more acceptable in the field and possibly to the DSM.

Q: **Is it possible for someone with a great or normal upbringing to have anxiety disorder or develop DID?**

A: Anyone can develop anxiety for a variety of reasons. DID is very highly correlated with trauma.

Mr Tolini has a couple of follow-up questions.

He asks if somebody sincerely thinks that a person would believe them when they have lied about other things would this be delusional? Grimmett responds that it may be irrational, but it would not cross the threshold into delusional belief. If something is irrational it doesn't mean it's delusional.

Regarding the question when does an article become mainstream, Tolini says the DSM-5 actually states that people with borderline personality disorder can suffer psychotic-like symptoms including hallucinations, body-image distortions, ideas of reference, hypogenic phenomena during times of stress. This article had become mainstream enough to be admitted into the DSM-5. Grimmett says she is not familiar enough with the article to comment whether or not it relates to the DSM-5.

The court breaks for lunch.

The next witness called is Doctor Loandra Torres. Clinical director of court services with the office of civil and forensic mental health. She is a licenced psychologist.

The witness is qualified as an expert in forensic psychology.

She became involved in the case in 2020 as one of the evaluators who conducted Letecia's initial evaluation. She conducted a sanity evaluation and a competency evaluation along-side another specialist, Doctor Gray.

Prior to the competency evaluation, Letecia had spent two weeks in a high security forensic unit. This helped to be able to incorporate an observation of her. She had been reported to have past anxiety, past depression, issues with panic attacks, that might be consistent with mania, and bipolar disorder. It was also noted she could have some post-traumatic-stress disorder and bipolar disorder, but it had been self-reported.

During the competency evaluation Letecia claimed she had been sexually abused by her stepfather repeatedly, this abuse had started aged 12. However, two years later, during the sanity evaluation, she told the doctor the abuse had started aged 9.

During the first evaluation Letecia said she had never been psychiatrically hospitalised. However, in the second evaluation she said she had a history of psychiatric hospitalisation in Canada. Letecia couldn't tell them any information of which city or which facility this occurred and so they were unable to request any information.

When Letecia was initially admitted to CMHIP she told mental health staff she had heard voices in the past related to an ex-husband, but she was not currently experiencing hallucinations. She talked about her past trauma, nightmares, visual flashbacks, reported being anxious, having panic attacks several days of the week, and in the past she had had symptoms consistent with a manic episode specifically talking so fast that she did not make sense, rambling about things in a manner that didn't make sense. That she had experienced high energy, brief amounts of sleep, and impulsive and erratic behaviour. However, there were reports from mental health staff and the psychiatrist that she pre-sented as calm, cooperative, pleasant and no apparent symptoms of acute mental illness.

Letecia had asked staff in the state hospital whether they could tell when a patient is faking instability and mental illness.

A competency evaluation focusing the mental state at the current time, but a sanity evaluation involves a more thorough deep dive into past hospitalisations and mental history.

They conducted psychological testing on Letecia. The personality assessment inventory was invalidated due to potentially careless responding or potentially idiosyncratic read on the test (this means it may not have been read in the way the item was written). Because of this the entire profile was not interpretable. A second test, the MMPI2 was given but those results were also invalidated due to exaggeration.

During the competency evaluation, Letecia didn't complain about having multiple personalities.

She was diagnosed with a personality disorder—borderline and narcissistic feature.

Personality disorder is maladaptive personality characteristics evident throughout the lifespan.

Borderline features due to her history of instability in personal relationships, history of mood swings (her public defender at the time reported Letecia could go from zero to a hundred very quickly), her own self-report of impulsivity.

Narcissistic features because she touted her own intelligence and abilities. When she spoke about her treatment in the jail, she told them about how her attorneys should treat her and there was notable entitlement in that which gave them a hint that there might be some narcissistic features in there as well.

Bipolar disorder was ruled out, but post-traumatic stress disorder was not totally ruled out. No psychosis was observed.

In 2022 Letecia pled not guilty by reason of insanity, and then the sanity evaluation was performed. One of the first things they did was consult with both sides—the prosecution and the defence. They also spoke with Al Stauch and Brenda Acquard (Letecia's aunt).

Several videos are admitted into evidence.

The first video is played. It is an interview with Doctor Torres and Letecia Stauch from 24th March 2022.

The video shows Letecia talking about her abuse as a child and how she would use different personalities to be able to cope with the abuse. Harmony was the persona who was abused, Maria was her protector, Taylor is her main personality. Victoria would give advice. Taylor is everything Letecia wants to be, she's married to Tyler, and they have kids—Ariana, Alicia, and Adriano.

Doctor Torres says DID is a complex diagnosis, but the different personalities are not controlled, and the person may not even be aware, hence the blackouts and loss of memory that generally occurs alongside. The emergence of each alter can be random and isn't created by the patient. This is the reason the doctor's thought Letecia was likely to be exaggerating or feigning. Research suggests that there could be some awareness of what alters did.

The next portion of the video is played.

Letecia talks about the relationship between her and Al. She says they didn't officially live together until Colorado Springs because he would work away a lot and she would have the children on his weekends, so he didn't lose his weekend visitation rights. She says she felt as though it was just a marriage of convenience.

She says Al's mom was a nurse practitioner for a psychiatrist. She would tell Al that Letecia needed to be on medication because one minute she's this way, one minute she's that way. She says there wasn't any physical abuse in the marriage but there was mental and emotional abuse. She felt he took advantage of her.

She says she wanted to leave but she worried about leaving the kids because she didn't think they would be looked after. She says she did plan to help Landon get the kids back when she planned to leave. When Al found out about this, he began smashing things up and punching walls etc.

Letecia says the cold weather had an effect on her mood and behaviour as she had her usual strategies to cope with things and she struggled in Colorado.

Doctor Torres says it is helpful to know what led up to the offense and what emotional state they were in.

The court take an afternoon break.

In the next clip Letecia talks about the discrepancies in her personalities. She would be depressed one minute and manic the next.

The doctor thinks this is more likely to be mood swings rather than different personalities.

In the next clip Letecia says she has been psychotic and delusional in her life but not on a regular basis. The devil tells her to do things. He told her to jump off a cliff on the hike.

She switches into personalities when she wants but she cannot switch to Maria without being triggered.

Maria is a sniper. She's for hire and was trained in Russia. She's originally from Mexico and gets paid $1500 per minute. She talks about eliminating this person and that person—paedophiles, people who sexually molest people, people that rape people, they should be eliminated from the planet.

Doctor Torres says this is exaggerated and is not associated with DID. It could be associated with psychosis but there's nothing to corroborate that.

If the devil had been talking to her she didn't listen as she didn't jump off the cliff.

She thinks it's convenient that Letecia can change personalities whenever she likes apart from Maria, the one personality that is important to this situation, yet she doesn't have access to her. Torres thinks its far-fetched.

Torres feels if Letecia had no access to Maria, then she doesn't think she would have an awareness of her. She recalls watching a recording of Leticia as Maria and she was speaking with a Mexican accent.

The next clip played was about the assault on a police officer in the car. Letecia said the officer tried to shoot her with her gun. She says Maria had been the one to take over the situation. And that the officers had it in for her because one of them even had the surname Sanchez and she said Maria's surname was Sanchez (as if this made sense to her).

When Doctor Torres watched the video back of Letecia attacking the officer, she commented that Letecia didn't have a Mexican accent and so the claim Maria had been responsible for the attack was proven false.

In the next clip played Letecia says anytime she feels threatened or in trouble, she has a flashback of trying to protect her mom. One time, her mother's boyfriend, Greg, was beating her and threw her through a glass window, Letecia grabbed a bat, hit him in the legs and knocked him down. She tried therapy but it didn't work for her. She still had flashbacks and sometimes she switches personalities and goes into protective mode.

When she has flashbacks, she'll think she's back in that same time. For example, when she texted her boss to tell her that her stepdad died, she'd had a flashback that morning. When Laina came into her room, she had been having flashbacks and nightmares of the day her stepdad died. She wasn't sure if he was dead or not. One of the triggers is red and black (she acknowledges one of the interviewers is wearing red and black).

She goes on to talk about flashbacks, recalling when the house caught fire and how the smell of burning would give her a flashback.

Another time she was in a Burger King and a man was speaking to Laina about the drinks machine. She had a flashback because the man reminded her of James, her stepdad, and she went into protective mode. She wanted to protect someone first because if Maria does it, she won't remember it and it's going to be bad.

Doctor Torres says the fact she said she couldn't remember what Maria did was interesting. She says that Letecia did suspect that Maria killed Gannon thinking he was Letecia's stepfather.

Torres says Letecia couldn't explain how she has been able to tell them what Maria had done in the past if she wasn't able to remember it.

The court breaks for the day. They will resume on Friday 28th April 2023.

CHAPTER 17

LETECIA STAUCH TRIAL – DAY 16 - FRIDAY 28TH APRIL 2023

Doctor Torres returns to the witness stand.

More video interviews will be played.

In this clip Letecia is asked to talk them through what led up to the event.

She said she had decided to leave and was waiting to get everything in order so she could be mentally okay. She didn't want to have to deal with people who wanted to find out about the car accident. She was looking for a place to stay so she could begin work as a flight attendant.

She left her job. Someone was following her no matter where she was in Colorado. She had an investigator look into it.

She and Albert went on a cruise in January. Her bags were lost at the port, and she was freaking out thinking these people had got her bags. She changed her whole route because she didn't know if they had her itinerary. She told Al she thought she saw the guy following her and he said no-one would go to that extreme.

When she returned from the cruise, Gannon told her some friends had come by in a black car looking for her. She thought it might have been Edgar's car and she started freaking out.

On 22nd January it was Laina's birthday. She picked up Al's mother from the airport because she was afraid to stay home by herself.

She'd been in trouble with the Colorado Sheriff's office for calling 911 and saying somebody was in the backyard. They send officers out, but they didn't find any evidence anybody had been in the backyard. They looked at her alarm status and warned her she could get in trouble for making false reports.

On 26th January, the day basketball star Kobe Bryant died in a helicopter crash. They planned to go to church but decided to go on a hike instead. That's when something started telling her they should jump. She said it had to be a white family to jump as a black family wouldn't make TV because there is a lot of racism in the country.

They decided to go home. Gannon was complaining about his stomach, and he'd had an accident. She went to get dinner with Laina while Gannon had a bath. They got back, had dinner and she felt her mind was trying to tell her something about Michael the Archangel.

They called it a night. Laina was in bed relaxing, and she heard the alarm saying fire repeatedly. The next 30 minutes were a blur. She went into protection mode. She got the dogs, got Laina and took them outside. She came back and got ready to run down the stairs, but she had socks on, and she slipped down the stairwell, banging her head, which is how her blood got on the baseboards.

Then she saw the smoke and went into panic mode. She began having flashbacks of all the fires she had experienced. She ran back out the front door again and then realised Gannon was downstairs.

She ran back down the stairs again. Gannon was on the sofa. The fire was around the sofa. She reached over to grab him, but he was wrapped in the covers. She grabbed the covers and jumped on the fire. She doesn't remember running out, but the doorbell camera shows they did.

They got in the truck, and she began driving. Gannon and Laina were hysterical. She drove around a while then headed back to the house.

She texted Harley about the fire and, when Harley returned home, she began opening all the windows. They all wanted to sleep together but she kept thinking about if she hadn't been able to get to Gannon he would've burned in the fire.

She said she would get a friend called Guam to fix everything. She began recording Gannon because she records everything.

Gannon told her he had set the fire but didn't mean it. She said the video was taken out of context because when she said they would have to sell the sofa she didn't mean it.

She gave Guam the number to the garage and asked him to fix the carpet.

She has gaps in her memory from then. She remembers being in the garage naked.

When Laina came in to have her hair brushed she still thought her stepfather had just died. She didn't snap back until later.

She checked the burns on Gannon's arms and decided they needed to go to hospital.

She kept thinking about Eguardo. He was the person Guam had arranged to fix the carpet.

She told Gannon he could stay off school and they would just go out shopping for the day.

When she got to PetSmart, she saw the black cars driving by.

She left Gannon's phone behind in the PetSmart.

Deciding to go to Castle Rock, she took a back road because 25 was backed up. They were going to drive by an address on the police report and ask them to please stop, offer them money, tell him she wasn't involved in the accident.

Then she saw a man walking along the road that she thought was her stepdad – she realised she wasn't stable enough.

She parked up and she doesn't know how long they were there.

Gannon began tapping her on the shoulder telling her they had to get Laina from school. That was when she snapped back into it.

She asked Gannon to check the mail and then she would buy him a $50 game. She doesn't know if he returned to the car with her or walked back himself but they both ended up back at the house.

The alarm showed there was motion in the house. The dogs were in the crates so couldn't have triggered the alarm. She ran downstairs to see if Eguardo had arrived to fix the carpet.

Gannon said he was going out to play.

Laina came home and then Harley arrived they planned to go eat sushi, but Gannon didn't arrive home by his usual time of 6pm. It was raining. They got in the car and went to ask if the neighbours had seen him—nobody had.

Letecia was pacing the house thinking Gannon was doing a hiding challenge like they do on YouTube.

The police arrived and they were wearing bodycams. She points out there was nothing untoward on the recordings. They asked her if she wanted them to check the house and she said she did.

Later that night she became scared. She knew Gannon's meds would begin to wear off.

After midnight, there was a knock at her bedroom window. She looked out but there was nobody there and so, thinking it was Gannon she got in the car and drove around looking for him. The ring cam shows her driving away and coming back soon after.

Back inside, she kept hearing the same loud noise and she knew Edgar was on his way back over. He hadn't wanted to be there when the police was there, he decided to just go out and look for the black car.

Edgar had planned to be there anyway that morning because he'd already planned to help her move all her stuff to Florida before this happened.

She lay on the sofa and heard the sound again and freaked out because she thought someone was in the house.

She didn't have her handgun on her as it was in the car.

Edgar and Angelica, a member of his family, arrived and she told him she thought someone was in the house. He said she was being paranoid. Angelica lay down.

They heard the sound again and Edgar began going downstairs slowly. She followed him downstairs, and Edgar got the other handgun. Something over the front stairwell looked like a person in a cape.

The person went into the back bedroom. In protection mode, she went to grab the gun from

Edgar. The gun hits her and then hits the person in the cape. She didn't know who the person was at that point, until she sat down with her attorneys, and they realised it was Gannon. She thinks his cover looked like a cape.

She didn't know it was Gannon until she moved the cover.

Laina woke up and found her screaming and crying. Harley stayed asleep.

Laina helped her carry Gannon's body to the car.

Letecia was throwing up at the sight of blood. Gannon was still alive but barely talking. She was in shock. She remembers being on the passenger side of the car, taking Gannon to the hospital. Her leg was bleeding where she had got hit with the bullet.

She remembers waking up in the car and thinking they weren't on the right road for the hospital. She goes back to sleep and the next time she wakes up she hears a howling noise that reminded her of when her grandpa died. She realises she's back in the garage.

The camera footage shows the car does go out for five minutes before returning. She figures the noise must've been Gannon taking his last breath. She was out of it when she returned and parked the car.

Laina and Harley were white like they'd seen a ghost. She kept telling them it was fine, and he was going to be home.

She went into a different personality. It was like it wasn't really happening. She doesn't remember very much about going to the airport. She was just going through the motions for finding Gannon.

She was telling Edgar and another male family member who she refuses to name that it was an accident. She didn't know it was Gannon as he was taller but that was because he was standing on the bed. Her mind had gone into protective mode and Maria could've thought it was her stepdad. She hadn't intended to hurt or murder anybody. She had everything she wanted in her life and had nothing to gain from hurting a child.

She says she had cared for those kids and had to carry Gannon upstairs while he was dying. She couldn't begin to tell anyone what had happened. She couldn't begin to explain to Gannon's mom she thought it was someone in a cape.

What happened next was even worse because she never even moved Gannon's body. She won't incriminate the male in question because there wasn't any intention to harm anyone. She went crazy thinking she could raise Gannon from the dead. She was driving him around trying to get him happy meals and took him to Gamestop to buy him the $60 game he wanted. She was certain he was gonna wake up. She even tried to find Andrew Wommack's house because he had brought his son back from the dead.

An older male person told her mom she had completely lost it. Her mom and brother were all saying she had lost it. They all knew but they hadn't been involved. They were saying she was crazy and needed to go to a hospital.

The male person was the one who tampered with evidence and who tampered with the body. It was not her. He didn't fire the weapon, but he did this part.

She couldn't tell the truth because nobody would understand why she thought he was in a cape. Maria had taken over and was just trying to protect everyone in the house. There was no anger or ill will.

The doctor asks how Gannon's body came to be in Florida.

She says some people helped her to pack her things because she was receiving death threats from people in the neighbourhood. The police said she could leave. There is footage of them filling up the van with her belongings. She kept feeling she was going to wake up from the nightmare any moment.

Another male person, again she wouldn't say who, was trying to protect her and told her she needed help. She planned to go to Florida first to drop her stuff off before going to South Carolina. She intended to meet up with Gannon's grandparents.

Letecia can barely remember driving all that way. At some point Gannon's grandparents called her and told her she was losing her mind and they refused to meet her.

She couldn't pick up Gannon to carry him. Her plan had been to take him to his grandparent's farm to give him a proper burial. She hoped they would know what to do and if not, they could help her bring him back to life. That was when the male person intervened, telling her she was losing her mind.

Gannon's body was never in the van or in the car with her.

When she got to Florida, the individuals who flew on an airplane to Florida helped. She wasn't able to carry Gannon herself.

In South Carolina she kept saying crazy stuff. Telling her friends Gannon was going to come back to life. She knew she was psychotic. Sometimes she checks out of reality.

People make up things about stab marks. They were not stab marks, they were from the fire on his arms and chest.

She refers back to the police bodycam footage and believes she saw something move in the closet with the ornaments. Gannon was hiding in there.

She says she read the autopsy, and it says he was shot in the jaw. If you intended to murder someone you wouldn't shoot them in the jaw.

The doctor says it's been a long day, and they will stop here.

The court takes a morning break.

Doctor Torres returns to the stand. She says as well as this March interview, they interviewed Letecia once again in June.

When asked about the details of Letecia dissociating, the doctor believes because Letecia has no access to Maria's memories or feelings, then she wouldn't be able to recall what happened when she slipped into Maria's personality. She said generally blackouts occur when people are legally insane. She would expect Letecia to report a loss of memory and wouldn't remember Gannon standing on the bed with a blanket wrapped around him like a cape.

Letecia had indicated Maria didn't know it was Gannon and thought he was an intruder. However, Maria supposedly knew who Gannon was and had been there to protect him.

Torres recalls watching the interview with Laina Stauch and she says the last time Laina said she saw Gannon wasn't consistent with Leticia's version of carrying Gannon's body upstairs.

There was also no evidence as far as she was aware that Letecia had been hit in the leg with a bullet.

She says if the events occurred the way Letecia said, then she wouldn't be surprised if Letecia went into some kind of shock. However, if she dissociated, the family members would usually notice if she had changed into another personality.

There was no indication that anybody had helped Letecia move Gannon's body. It is believed he had been taken to the Palmer Lake area first and then picked up and drove to Florida.

The only male relative around at the time Gannon was moved was her brother Dakota Lowry.

The next interview to be played took place on the 29ᵗʰ June 2022.

Letecia is talking about Harley arriving home on the 27ᵗʰ January, and how they had planned to go for sushi. When Gannon hadn't arrived home, they went to ask some of the neighbours if they had seen him. Afterwards, she called the police, and she didn't go out again until the police had arrived.

She suspected Gannon was doing the hiding challenge that had been all over YouTube. The police searched the house and didn't find anything out of order.

Later that night, when she was lying on the sofa, she heard a knocking sound.

She repeats the same version of events that happened after going downstairs, seeing the 'intruder', taking the gun off Edgar and shooting Gannon.

She said she didn't know who the intruder was until she got him to the car and looked under the blanket. Torres asked why she had moved the body if she didn't know it was Gannon.

Letecia said she couldn't answer that as it had been Maria.

She goes over the different personalities again.

Torres asked if she could speak to Maria.

Letecia explains there must be a sense of danger for Maria to take over.

Edgar was supposedly a person Al owed money to, but there is

very little mentioned about him during the trial. Nobody even questions who he is? And although Edgar was said to be present during the shooting, there is no mention of what happens to him afterwards...

Doctor Torres says they did not diagnose Letecia with DID. And if there is no mental disease or defect, then there can't be anything to impair their capacity to form intent or their ability to know right and wrong.

She goes on to explain that to determine whether or not a person has the capacity to form a culpable mental state, they look at the charges. In this case they need to determine, with intent, knowingly, and recklessly, all of which have specific definitions.

With intent - whether the person has a conscious objective to create or have the actual action associated with the statute occur. This is related to tampering with evidence and moving the body. They need to determine what does it mean to be conscious? They need to look at somebody's ability to think, reason, form judgment, they also consider any issues associated with emotions, to see if there is anything making it so that the individual is incapable of forming intent. Torres is unsure if she has ever seen anyone with a mental illness that causes them to lack the ability to form intent. Although intent can be skewed because of irrational thoughts and things like delusions, but that doesn't seem to be the case here.

Knowingly – Do you have an awareness of what is going on? To have an awareness you need to be awake, conscious, have an understanding of what's going on.

Recklessly...

Mr Young stops her from going any further because he says it doesn't apply anymore. He asks her about another culpable state – after deliberation.

After deliberation - not only intentionally but also that the decision to commit the act has been made after the exercise of reflection and judgment concerning the act. An act committed after deliberation is never one which has been committed in a hasty or impulsive manner.

When it comes to the facts, Torres says there's a lot of information in the police reports that outline Letecia's whereabouts. There are varying stories that she told to the police as it pertains to what actually happened with Gannon. They take this into account and whilst conducting a sanity evaluation they tend to focus more on what it is that the defendant is telling them in terms of their perception of what happened. Hopefully what they are being told is in line with what the facts of the case are.

In this situation, Letecia outlined having some paranoia, however Torres would say it was more like being hyper-vigilant or on guard that someone is watching her or tracking her associated with this accident that occurred, and the accident did occur so it's not a delusion, it's a reaction to something that did happen in her life. They were looking to see if there was some sort of mental health issue that was impacting her behaviours, her thoughts, her thinking, her emotions at all of those stages. Usually, the police reports can't tell them the perspective of the defendant which is why they have to rely on what the defendant has to say. They are looking for a mental disease or defect, and if they can identify what that is they are looking at how does that impact everything that is happening at that time.

Afterwards, there is always the question of how does the person respond to the actual crime? Did they call the police themselves? Did they try to hide evidence? Did they run away? But what's even more important is the why if you can get to that. In a lot of murder cases, you don't get to the why.

In this case, Letecia speaks about how the actual act of shooting Gannon, the person in the cape, and how she dissociates, she states it's her personalities that are trying to cover it up. But there is no clear mental illness that is impacting her ability to know right from wrong. Her own version of events imply she has a capacity to form intent.

Doctor Torres' final opinion was that Letecia Stauch was sane at the time of the crime.

No further questions.

Mr Tolini begins cross examination. He brings up issues with the state hospital—staffing issues and several other problems. He asks Doctor Torres if this would've affected the evaluation.

Torres says she wouldn't take the staffing issues into account whilst doing an evaluation.

A video clip is played from March 2022. It is Letecia talking about an occasion when her mother had been attacked by her stepdad when she was nine years old. Because she called the police at the time, her stepdad was demoted, and they lost money and had to downsize their home. She had been blamed for calling the police.

Mr Tolini asks if a trauma like this could affect a nine-year-old girl. Torres agrees that there is a correlation between children suffering childhood trauma and those who develop DID.

He questions Torres on DID, and borderline personality disorder.

Mr Tolini has no further questions.

Mr Young begins re-direct.

He reads a statement from the DSM-5 about antisocial personality disorder.

DID is a rare diagnosis. It is cautioned when used in a criminal setting because of the potential gain. It is easy to blame another personality for being guilty of a crime rather than taking the blame yourself.

The jury have a number of questions.

Q: Would a person with multiple personalities refer to themselves as I when describing the actions a different personality carried out?

A: I don't think so.

Q: We were shown how the defendant performed the clock test well on the first competency test. We were told she performed the same test poorly on a second competency test. Why would the same test be used twice when the first one could train the defendant how to perform or not perform on the second?

A: The same sort of test is given twice depending on the test, sometimes a person might respond different. They administered the MMPI2 three times. It's more sensitive to what is going on with the person right now. You could give it last year and this year and get different results depending on what's happening with the person. Cognitive tests tend to be more stable across time. Someone who is acutely mentally ill in severe psychosis may perform cognitively better after receiving treatment.

Q: Assuming you believe everything she has told you and everything she has said in her story - not looking at correlating information and stuff like that - would you diagnose Letecia with DID?

A: I think I still would not. The way she described creating the personalities, being able to have some sort of control, switching between worlds is inconsistent with DID being something involuntary, overwhelming, and uncontrollable.

The court breaks for the weekend.

CHAPTER 18

LETECIA STAUCH TRIAL – DAY 17 – MONDAY 1ST MAY 2023

The first witness called is the director of crime strategies from the DA's office, Kevin Clark. Mr Clark has testified previously.

He tells how he visited the Stauch home on 27th January 2020. He accessed a week's worth of Ring Doorbell footage from the neighbour.

Several videos are added to evidence.

- Footage shows Letecia and Gannon arriving home on the 27th January at 2:20pm. The footage didn't show them getting out of the truck as they stayed inside for too long.

- At 2:29pm the Tiguan is now in the garage and Letecia is briefly caught just inside the door.

- 6:19am the next morning, Letecia is seen getting into the truck.

- 6:20am the Tiguan pulls out of the garage.

- 6:21am the Tiguan leaves for 10 minutes then comes back. According to the Tiguan data, it drove to Bradley Road then turned back and then returned to the house.

- Letecia backs the Tiguan onto the driveway.

- The garage door is open, and movement is picked up inside.

- The Tiguan is backed into the garage.

Mr Clark says that according to the prior surveillance footage, it was not typical for Letecia to back any vehicle into the garage. This only began on the 27th January.

On Letecia's third cell phone, the search for a fake polygraph test and the subsequent questions that she requested were discovered. Letecia's credit card information was entered for payment.

Mr Clark explains how they can access specific details of a cell phone, when it is charging, if the battery dies, if it is tuned off, if the screen changes from landscape to portrait, if the light goes on. The details are in minute detail, second by second.

When Letecia picked up the Tiguan from the airport on the evening of the 28th January, it shows the phone was on 5% battery and then it was plugged in from 7:04pm until 9:20pm. Evidence shows the Tiguan loitered for 5 minutes around the area the board was found. The phone had been placed in airplane mode at this time.

The timeline from Sunday 26th January 2020 is admitted.

6:55am: Al departs his flight out of DIA.

2pm: The Tiguan leaves the house to go for the hike at Garden of the Gods.

3:15pm: Harley clocks into Massage Envy.

3:36pm: Al texts Gannon, *hey Buddy.*

3: 41pm: A selfie is taken on Letecia's phone of her, Gannon, and Laina.

3:53- 4:11pm: A conversation between Al and Letecia about them having to leave Garden of the Gods early due to Gannon having an accident in his pants.

4:46pm: The Tiguan and Life360 indicate they all return home. Harley is still at work.

5:11-5:12pm: A conversation takes place between Harley and Letecia; Harley asks Letecia to take her some food to work.

9:46pm: A video taken from Letecia's phone; video of Letecia telling Gannon they have to sell items to pay to fix it.

No indication (from ring, etc) that Gannon was in the street yelling on 26th January.

> 9:54pm: A text conversation between Harley & Letecia – *do(n't) panic but Gannon turned on a candle downstairs and set the downstairs on fire.* Harley responded, *the fire was on Chance?*

9:56pm: Letecia took a photo of a candle, spilled wax, and the blue blanket that was in the pink suitcase.

> 9:57pm: Letecia responds, including, *I didn't call the fire department because I put it out right away.*

> They go back and forth clarifying what happened; *dogs are fine.*

9:58-10:15pm: Continuation of that conversation; nothing significant mentioned other than the fire and Letecia portraying herself as a hero for putting the fire out and saving Gannon.

Nothing on video corroborates anyone left the home on Sunday night – There is no evidence that they drove around after the fire.

10:18pm: Harley clocks out of work.

10:24pm: There is more texting between Letecia and Harley; she sends picture of couch with wax on it; no burns just dripped wax.

11:30pm: Harley arrives home, Letecia texts Al,

> *Gannon was on the toilet most of the night upstairs and downstairs, he had a candle on earlier tonight because he said he kept smelling poop from his accidents in his pants that's what he told us afterwards and he went for his headphones and dropped it catching the covers and couch small spot on fire. I got Laina and dogs when we heard fire alarm but once I got down there to get him, I had to throw another cover on it. It was minimal. No need to call for help or anything because nothing*

> *too bad. He is upset and wrote on the notebook he is sorry. He didn't want me to tell you because he was scared and freaking out about getting in trouble and being grounded. It's stuff we can fix, and everyone is okay. I burnt my arm a little but it's all good he was more scared and embarrassed.*

Al does not respond

2:48am:Letecia texts Al,

> *he is in the bathroom again and blood coming out butthole and he is crying about going to school tomorrow like this, he is still upset about the candle accident. I told him its fine and that as long as he's okay not to worry about something minor, we can fix and to let's worry about his stomach hurting.*

Al had not seen this or responded.

4:36am:Letecia texts Leslie Hicks about her stepfather being hit by a car and killed.

4:36-5:02am:Letecia and Al text back and forth.

> *L: I'm just going to give them an excuse at work and stay with him. I don't think he should be here alone. We haven't really slept, and we haven't heard from you by call since you left Saturday night.*

> *Al: Omg is he ok? I texted him too.*

> *L: He just laid down again. I just left from down there with him.*

> *Al: Ok.*

> *L: I love you and miss you.*

> *Al: I too.*

5:03-5:04am: Continuation of the previous conversation.

L: *I'm exhausted. He was so pitiful and freaking out about fixing the carpet but told him to worry about his stomach. I can't sleep because I have coughed nonstop from that smoke.* She attached the candle photo.

Al didn't respond.

5:49am: Letecia received a text from Leslie Hicks about finding a sub for her.

7:21am: Letecia responded with...

?? it's a parent. All my family lives on the east coast. I am trying to find a way to get there.

7:32am:Leslie responds with...

Ok I am just trying to understand your plans so that we can find coverage. Am I understanding you won't be in today?

L: *Yes, that's my parent. I can't believe that would not be an assumption at a time like this.*

Leslie: *I'm so sorry for your loss and we will support you, but I cannot make assumptions, I do need some direction from you. We will get a sub today. Please let us know what else you need moving forward.*

8:09-8:10am: More texts between Letecia and Al.

L: *I keep calling you back.*

Al: *In class now, I'll call on break.*

L: *Ok, it's where he burnt the floor.*

Al: *Burnt?*

L: *He said he was playing his games and wasn't supposed to and thought someone was coming.*

Al: *What?*

L: *Yes, and I sent it to you last night and you said OMG and I explained everything.*

Al: *I was so out of it from not sleeping.*

8:10-8:16am: Letecia resent the same text that was sent at 11:40pm the night before.

Al: *Ok.*

L: *He told me this morning he was playing his game and didn't want to get caught and had to fix the carpet. He said he accidentally knocked it over and couldn't put it out. When I got there, I threw the covers on it and jumped on it.*

Al: *Omg.*

L: *That's the sofa. Carpet I had to cut and add a piece he was freaking out and crying and saying he was going to be grounded for a year. Cut off some with scissors too and you can't tell. and sent the sofa picture.*

Al does not respond.

8:14am: Letecia sent a photo to Al of Gannon in his bed. He had his Nintendo Switch next to his hand.

8:18am: A second photo from a different angle and more zoomed in.

L: *He is sleeping now. He said his stomach was really bad plus he was upset about what he did. I told him you weren't going to ground him for a year and that's replaceable.*

Al did not respond.

8:30am: Harley clocks into work.

8:43-8:50am: A text conversation between Letecia and Al. This is when the idea of an unknown friend with an older brother who drives came up. Also, the first mention of the bath salts. Letecia introduced this idea but there was no indication Gannon sent text messages to anyone asking to hang out with an older friend - they were sent minutes after the last photo of Gannon sleeping in bed.

Bath salts were called the zombie drug at that time and not the same as Epsom salts.

Conversation is just a summation of TikTok challenges and bath salts. Al was against Gannon spending the night with anyone; Al was explaining to Letecia what the drug form of bath salts were.

9:21-9:24am: Letecia and Al had a discussion about TikTok.

> Letecia: *he was watching tiktok hiding it before you left, and I saw him looking at something where people throw quarters in the air and catch them. I told him about my brother Dakota and that he did that years ago and got lodged and no air and my mom rushed him to the hospital. I was wondering why he was saying strange things out of character, so I blocked the Switch from the Wi-Fi and Amazon because he was asking Alexa about it. That's why we went hiking because I told them no technology all day.*

> Al: *Ok, yeah, we're gonna have to keep a close eye cause Laina was watching it and started crying the other day.*

9:27am: Conversation between Letecia and Harley at work. Letecia screenshots the conversation about bath salts between her and Al and sends it to Harley saying, *omg something isn't right.*

Harley did not respond.

9:54-9:59am:

> Letecia:*Left phone at home call Gs on my watch it may stay connected and we will monitor it.*

Al: *K.*

10:12am: Letecia and Gannon leave the home.

10:39am to 2:45pm:

Letecia's phone has no outgoing activity; all incoming calls and texts show phone is at home. It is unusual for Letecia to leave her phone at home, this is the only known instance of that happening.

11:22am: Letecia is at PetCo on Nevada Avenue; she used an American Express card to pay $34.58 for 3 dog outfits.

11:28am: Al: *I have to get a few toiletries from the px.*

Letecia didn't read this until 2:45pm.

Video of Volkswagen Tiguan backing into garage, E213

2:26pm:Al: *You there??*

Letecia does not read this until 2:45pm, she replied, *Ok.* First outgoing activity is her response, there is no more activity for about another hour.

3:10pm:Al: *Where you sleeping?*

There is no response.

3:15pm:Laina gets home from school, and can be seen on CCTV standing outside loitering.

The police beleive Gannon was likely murdered prior to Laina returning home from school.

3:31pm:Al texts Letecia: *Hey I've called a few times.*

3:32pm:Letecia calls Al, they talk for 3 minutes, 35 seconds.

3:35pm:Al texts Gannon, *Hey Buddy.*

The message is not read until 7:40pm after Letecia called to report Gannon missing.

3:40-4:11pm:There are several texts between Letecia and Al.

Al: *I might try to do the headphones from an ATT store.*

L: *How much do you need? Let me look at the banks.*

Al: *Like on the plan.*

L: *I know but I'm saying how much for the ones at the exchange, the ones that go over ear.*

AL: *Don't know, I can look tomorrow. Yeah, like I used to have but wireless.*

L: *Yes, like this?* She attaches a generic earbud image.

Al: *But the JBL were cheaper.*

L: *Do like 69-99.*

4:15pm:Harley clocks out of work.

4:19pm:Harley texts Letecia: *Just got off.*

L: *Yay.*

4:37pm:Harley arrived home in her Jetta.

4:50pm:Letecia attempts to Facetime Harley but it does not go through.

4:51pm: Both Harley and Laina leave the house in the Jetta.

4:52pm:Letecia texts Harley: Carpet powders 2 things baking soda trash bags.

5:07pm:Harley attempts to *Facetime* Letecia, but it doesn't connect.

5:08pm:Letecia's phone had a ten second *Facetime* call with Harley's phone.

5:14pm:A receipt from *Dollar Tree* on Mesa Ridge Parkway, shows Harley purchased the items Letecia had requested along with some candy for Laina.

5:19pm: Harley attempted to *Facetime* Letecia, it doesn't connect.

5:20pm:There was a 10 second *Facetime* from Harley's phone to Letecia's.

5:33pm:Harley and Laina return home.

> 5:34pm: Al texts Letecia: *Have kids Facetime.*

There is no response for one hour.

6:27-6:37pm: Letecia sends the first message indicating something had gone wrong with Gannon.

> L: *Gannon said he was going to his friend's house, and I told him 6. I don't know those people.*

> Al: *Send Laina.*

> L: *Okay hold. I'll stand out and watch her.*

> Al: *If it's the ones on the end of our street then ground him until Thursday.*

> L: *K its pouring rain, can you ask them that may be why, sleeting actually.*

6:38pm:Letecia calls Al but the call doesn't connect.

> 6:40-6:49pm:L: *Taking your truck to look for him.*

> Al: *The truck is low on gas.*

> L: *Laina is running inside to see if he is here.*

> Al: *OK. Where is he???*

> L: *She just went to the door Albert, it's sleeting.*

Al: *Ok.*

L: *Not here, going to Lily's.*

Al: *What???*

They did go to one house and Laina went up to the door.

6:49pm: Letecia calls Al. They have a 3 minute, 50 second conversation.

6:53pm: Al texts Gannon: *Where are you?* It's not read until 7:40pm.

6:54pm: Letecia calls El Paso County Sheriff's for 9 seconds; front desk closed at 5pm.

6:55pm: Letecia calls 911, and has a 2 minute, 50 second call.

6:58pm: Non-emergency call.

6:59-7:08pm: Texts between Letecia and Al.

L: *All the call takers are busy. Omg still on hold, wtf.*

Al: *Where are you?*

L: *In the driveway. Harley has gone to the park. Someone's answered, hold. How tall.*

Al: *4 foot 10 I think.*

L: *Sorry I'm freaking out, asking me if he has tattoos. Asking me if he has alcohol or drugs. 90 pounds. They need his social. I can't think.*

Al: *I don't have it on me.*

L: *Okay.*

7:06pm: Harley tried to *Facetime* Letecia, but it didn't connect.

7:08-7:16pm: Letecia sends messages to Harley:

> L: *Any luck? On call.*

> Harley: *No, I couldn't remember the exact road that the park is on. Usually can just see with my eyes but it's so dark. I am at the school now. Look omg.*

> L: *Ok, anything?*

7:10pm: Call from Letecia to Al lasting 14 minutes 27 seconds.

7:18pm: An incoming call from the sheriff's office to Letecia.

7:24pm: Harley returned home from searching the park and school.

7:31pm: Call to Al lasting 5 minutes, 35 seconds.

> 7:43pm: Al texts Letecia: *Anything? They found some kind of cigarettes in his backpack.*

> L: *Yes. Harley found them.*

7:44-7:45pm: Harley *Facetimes* Al.

> 7:45-7:45pm: Letecia texts Al. L: *Why did you hang up on her?*

> Al: *Because I'm freaking out.*

> L: *We are too. Harley is crying. Laina is crying. I hope he isn't putting the salts in here or using the straws. I'm crying.*

> 7:50-7:51pm: Al texts Letecia: *No police? Did you tell them possible drugs involved?*

> L: *No police.*

7:50-7:53pm: Harley takes the Jetta around the block looking for Gannon.

7:51-7:53pm: Harley and Letecia are texting.

H: *Ask Laina if she remembers any cars, old station wagons, or any old cars and colours.*

L: *No, but don't go there by yourself. Connor's mom is on the way, and she can go with you.*

H: *Ok.*

7:53-8:00pm:Letecia is texting Al.

L: *Connor's mom on the way to start looking. Connor's mom said it's a stupid idea to put elementary at the middle school. Harley has gone to look for Jimmy. I'm freaking out, I can't breathe, how do you let anyone know we're waiting on the police.*

Al: *I texted that lady from SC cause their son is on the same bus.*

L: *Ok. Your mom? His mom?*

Al: *Yes.*

L: *Just in case they asked me, you talked to both.*

Al: *Who.*

L: *Like did you tell his mom, so I know when they ask me if he made contact with her.*

Al: *Yes.*

L: *What is she saying he talked to her?*

Al: *No response.*

L: *Ok because they told me to have a list of people available that we reached out to they need social is it here?*

Al: *I lost them remember.*

L: *Ok are you in your hotel room.*

Al: *Yes.*

L: *Babe you're not saying much I'm losing my mind they aren't here yet.*

8:00pm:Letecia calls Al, 1 min, 24 seconds.

8:05pm:Al calls El Paso Sherriff's Office.

8:06-8:08pm:Text conversation between Letecia and Al.

L: *What did they say?*

Al: *Same BS.*

L: *What did we tell you he wrote I'm sorry for everything last night on his notebook? Just trying to make sure I told you every-thing.*

8:16-8:21pm:Al: *I emailed everything. I emailed the teacher. Anything?*

L: *No. Connor's mom is here, and everyone is going to the fields to look.*

Al: *The fields? Where are the guns?*

Al: *Hello?*

L: *Yes, like to make sure no kids are at some hideout place they have.*

Al: *Where are the guns? Answer me.*

L: *Hold. I'll go check. Green one is there.*

Al: *Black?*

L: *Big one in my closet.*

8:22-8:24pm:Continuation of text conversation between Letecia and Al.

L: *Hold looking because I put it back in your crate later stayed. I didn't check the inside, but it seemed normal it was in there.*

Al: *Ok.*

L: *I don't see your pouch.*

Al: *Really? Are you serious? No one knew they were in there.*

L: *Looked under everything.*

Al: *Yours in there?*

L: *It fell. Pshhhh. All accounted for.*

Al: *Ok.*

L: *It's got to be some older middle schooler.*

Al: *Yes.*

L: *I was panicking for a second about gun but that makes me feel better, so we just need to know where he is hanging out at.*

8:25pm:Letecia calls Al, the call lasts 11 minutes, 47 seconds.

8:33pm: Letecia texts Harley, *Anything yet?*

H: *No.*

8:37pm: *Facetime* from Harley to Letecia lasting 18 seconds.

8:37pm: Outgoing call from Letecia to Al, 19 minutes, 43 seconds.

8:43pm: Letecia texts Harley, *Anything? Still waiting.*

H: *No.*

9:00pm: Outgoing call from Al to Letecia, 15 minutes, 57 seconds.

9:18pm: Al calls Letecia for 2 mins, 7 seconds.

9:23pm: Someone from South Carolina calls Letecia for 4 mins; some numbers are redacted for privacy; Myrtle beach area.

9:26pm: Al calls Letecia but doesn't get through.

9:26pm: Al calls Letecia again, this time the call lasts 4 minutes, 36 seconds.

9:36pm: Al calls Letecia for 17 seconds.

9:39pm: Al calls Letecia for 1 min 23 seconds.

9:45pm: Al calls El Paso Sherriff's Office.

9:46pm: Al calls Letecia for 7 mins 9 seconds.

Al texts Letecia. *Landen said track his Switch through Gmail.*

L: *Tell me how to do that because we looked it up and it said no GPS so how.*

Al: *Any police? No clue.*

L: *Ok, I'll google it.*

9:57pm: Al calls Letecia for 6 mins, 24 seconds.

10:03pm: Gannon's phone calls Landen, the call lasts 4 mins 28 seconds - Gannon was already deceased. Letecia was using the phone.

Letecia texts Al: *She didn't yell she just cried. Cops are here. I* did have to tell her the whole deal. I didn't withhold anything because the cop was right here.

Al: Ok.

10:09pm: EPSO deputies arrive with bodycams.

10:35-10:43pm: Al texts Letecia: Anything??

L: They are calling you.

Al: ??

L: They were asking me questions about dental and the same things I kept telling them and it's frustrating. Where does he go to the dentist?

Al: Fountain. No, no, no.

L: I know but I told them they're overwhelming me with stuff that I don't know or isn't relevant.

Al: But dental records are for ID. OMG.

L: I'm overwhelmed because I'm mad at how long they took.

10:44pm: Letecia calls Al, the call lasts 33 seconds.

10:46pm: Gannon's phone calls Landen's phone, duration of the call is 12 minutes, 6 seconds, again this is Letecia using the phone.

10:53pm: Photo taken with Gannon's phone of a cigar; the one Harley found in his backpack.

11:01-11:09pm: Text conversation between Al and Letecia.

Al: Nothing else? Still talking to police.

L: I feel like I'm having a heart attack.

Al: *Tell the police.*

L: *They had seven people in here asking me irrelevant stuff when I could be going through the rest of the 462 comments.*

Al: *You ok?*

L: *No. Like I do everything I can but none of it matters and now I am asked why he was outside or drill me about other friends when I don't have the first number to one of them. I've walked this house for 5 hours. I haven't eaten. My chest hurts. But it's not about me.*

11:09pm: Al calls Letecia for 11 minutes, 8 seconds.

11:29pm: Letecia calls her mother the call lasts 1 min 12 seconds.

11:39pm: Deputies leave the home. Gannon is entered as missing at 11:48pm.

11:51pm: Harley texts Letecia: *Do you need me to get you anything?*

L: *No, I may need to go to the store.*

11:54-11:57pm: Al texts Letecia. *You ok?*

L: *All these photos are starting to run together. My eyes and head hurt. Someone is bringing me a coke; my head is about to bust.*

28th January 2020

12:09am: Letecia calls Al, it goes to voicemail.

12:40am: She calls Al again, it lasts 8 minutes, 58 seconds.

1:04-1:38am: Letecia texts Al. *Please help me, please talk to me.*

Al: *What's wrong?*

L: *I can't sit on this house Laina on the bike.*

Al: *Did she see him while she was riding?*

L: *That Gannon and he has the hood on he was doing that yesterday the lady has a better image but it's too big to load you can see it's a switch case.*

Al: *What did you say he googled?*

L: *Hold I'll send (she sends ss from G's phone searching if parents can find phone if it's off) Think he was trying to go to his house? The FV family. Sounds crazy but he was looking up their address if that's near here.*

Al: *Don't know anything else being said on that FB page.*

L: *No just people saying to start again in the morning after sunrise. No, she came back as he was leaving.*

Al: *Huh?*

L: *I don't know I was answering something. People brought us food.*

Al: *K.*

1:49-2:06am: L: *The pains are getting worse. Not being insensitive at all just letting you know, please talk are you up? No one has reached out to me but Lorson Ranch. I always give it my all and try to do my best at everything I do.*

Al doesn't respond.

2:46am: Letecia texts her friend Deidre Moss: *Gannon has been missing since he was outside playing yesterday.* There is no response.

2:46-3:00am Letecia texts Al. *No one is ever supportive to step-*

parents like they mean nothing when I've did beyond my part.

Al: *OMG what are you talking about? Gannon is missing and you're worried about what people are saying to you?*

L: *I have no one to talk to. What? No one said anything to me.*

Al: *Dozens of people were out looking, and people brought you food.*

L: *I was telling you how I felt and that all I have here was the Lorson Ranch people.*

Al: *Gannon has no one right now. That's who has no one to talk to.*

L: *Meaning I had other friends here. You totally read it wrong. There was no one putting myself over this. You are my husband I was saying my feelings you completely took it wrong I never discredited anything. You said people were talking to you. Forget I even mentioned having chest pains. I wasn't taking away anything, I was saying they were worse, and I wish I had someone to help. Regardless I'm human, a person too who has pain and worried. What do you mean he has no one? He is talking with his friends. Maybe not good friends. He is coming home once he sees the news. All I'm saying is talk to me like you haven't said anything about yourself.*

Al: *He's in a car long gone.*

L: *And how we can help each other.*

Al: *There is no way he got to that gas station by 4pm on foot.*

L: *Long gone? Like with friends, right? I'm just so lost as to what to say and it's all so sad. I have hurt but you won't talk to me about yours so that's all I'm saying is to talk to me. I can't sleep. I asked the neighbourhood to pray for you on your flight and help you. I'm just so devastated. I run to the door at every sound so I can't imagine you I'm just hurting for you and me too, but I just don't know what to say or do or what to search next. I've been in his life since he was 5 and helped take care of him most of his adolescent years. I don't understand. I think he may be peer pressured, and I don't know about the salt stuff and like I keep imagining salts everywhere and my brain won't stop thinking if he has food. We haven't eaten yet because we were supposed to at 6. Is there anywhere I could go? I have to do something. Please talk to me and tell me.*

3:05-4:42am. L: Babe please, what do you mean long gone? Now I'm freaking out I want to talk to you. I need to be there for you. I'm glad you have lots of people there for you, but we need each other. I need to be there for you most. Are you awake? What time do you leave? I feel so sick. I'm going to help the search people.

Babe, you said your plane was early. I can't sleep.

Babe are you ok? You are supposed to be on the plane, and you have said nothing in hours.

Babe, you have to be up if your flight is at 6 where are you?

Al does not respond.

4:56-4:59am: The South Carolina number texts Letecia: *Any new information?*

L: *No, I keep checking the door every few minutes. Last we heard he was at a store getting food.*

4:59am: Letecia texts Al: *I'm sorry that you feel the need to ignore me checking in, especially my husband getting on a flight with the tragedies that happened with the helicopter this week. I know you're worried, but it doesn't mean to ignore me and not be kind.*

5:16am: Someone from a local number texted Letecia: *Someone posted he wasn't at school either.*

L: *He had to go to the doctor for his stomach, honestly. I don't keep up with friends. Albert lets them walk around the neighbourhood, but he was here in the afternoon.*

5:27am: Letecia texts a 631 area code: *Albert is hurting and taking it out on me.*

5:41-5:57am: Gannon's phone is messaging Landen: *Left every toy.* And sent a photograph of Gannon's room.

> **To call the mother of a missing boy from his own phone is an evil act, but to send messages like this is just twisting the knife, trying to inflict as much emotional pain as possible.**

6:18am: Someone from a local 719 area code texts Letecia: *Is there an AMBER Alert out yet? Is Al home? Someone was saying he was in Oklahoma.*

L: *Yes, Oklahoma and you can't do an AMBER Alert unless you know that someone took them and have to have that person name and tags.*

6:21am: Letecia texts Harley: *Don't answer the door for anyone I'm gonna see if people are out looking.*

Harley doesn't respond.

6:22-6:32am. This is the point where the Tiguan leaves and goes to Bradley Road before coming back.

6:34am: Al texts Letecia: *Just landed in Denver.*

Letecia doesn't respond.

6:35am: Gannon's phone texts Landen: *I'm heading out with the neighbour searches.*

Landen: *Find my baby please.*

6:36am: Letecia backs the Tiguan into garage and door closes.

6:38-6:59am: Phones were in the area of the Mandan Drive residence.

6:36 - 6:55am: Text conversation between Letecia and Al.

> **L:** *Good but why were you ignoring? I was worried you didn't make flight.*

> **Al:** *Not ignoring I laid down at airport, haven't really slept. Flight leaves here at 7:30.*

> **L:** *I understand you are upset but you are my teammate and parents stick together and not take it out on each other. He's coming home today.*

> **Al:** *How's Laina?*

> **L:** *She is tired. Landen said they are coming and that if they could stay. I told her she had to ask you that I wasn't making decisions like that.*

> **Al:** *Yes, in times like this we put our differences aside.*

> (Al forwards a text from Janey Cadenas): *I've been in contact with your wife throughout the night. I am a neighbour in Lorson Ranch. She gave me your info. I wanted to let you know I sent T a FB message that the news sent me with their contact info. They said if you can call their newsroom KKTV they can get a statement released ASAP. We need someone from the family to call our newsroom. If you know them or know someone who does, please pass along our information - phone number - praying for you all. We are currently getting a meal train set up for you all, so you have one less thing to worry about. Please do not hesitate to reach out if you need anything.*

> **L:** *Ok. I don't agree but it's your choice.*

> **Al:** *Just got that* (the text)

L: *Yes, that's Jane, she is out here searching with us.*

Al: *Call the news please.*

L: *It's on 5 stations. Please don't change your plan because I want you guys to be able to be together but I'm probably going to stay somewhere else.*

Al: *Then do that*

L: *Ok. I don't want anyone here cursing and flipping out. Thank you. Well, I'm heading out to the searches.*

Al: *Ok.*

L: *Can you call me?*

Al: *In a minute.*

L: *Well, somebody saw him, but I guess you are too busy talking to someone else instead.*

Back and forth calls between Letecia and Al; he called her. They spoke for 53 seconds. Letecia's phone was in the area of the residence, she never went to search.

6:59-7:15am: Letecia and Al were texting each other.

L: *OMG what happened, Albert?*

Al: *I'm trying not to lose it in the airport.*

L: *Please don't push me about the location. I don't understand things if you don't communicate.*

Al: *Text it.*

L: (forwards a text) **Last night about 6:30pm we saw him running in the rain off Academy and Fountain Road area. The boy was running westbound on Fountain Road. Good**

luck on your search and sending prayers to you and your family. I can't imagine what you guys are going through.

L: *I was telling you to see what you want me to do. We have over 100 people searching.*

Al: *Do what you think is best.*

L: *And willing.*

Al: *If he was in that side of town he was taken and was trying to run.*

L: *Wait, where is that? The bad burger king. Ok a team is going that way. Laina can't go to school, she is falling out crying. What's our plan when you get here?*

Al: *Let me get there and we will make a plan.*

L: *Ok. Landen said she is going to whatever neighbourhood that he was seen last night and knocking. How did Jane contact you? Everyone said she is trying to get me, but I haven't gotten anything.*

Al: *Text. That was the one I sent.*

L: *Ok. Neighbours were asking me.*

Al: *That's all I got.*

7:02am: Gannon's phone makes 6 minute 49 second outgoing call to Landen.

7:17am: Letecia searches *priceline.com find cheap car rentals*.

7:25am: Harley texts Letecia with a KKTV contact request; they reached out over social media.

7:27am: Letecia calls KKTV, the call lasts 1 minute, 30 seconds.

7:27-7:41am: Text messages between Letecia and Al.

L: *Talked to news.*

Al: *Ok.*

L: *Yeah, I tagged a few of them in an insta post. Principal just called ppo do you have the case number? I can't find the card and the news needs it.*

Al: *Deputy Shawn Donahue EPSO, phone number, case number.*

L: *Are you going to be driving a lot?*

Al: *I assume so, why?*

L: *Ok I was going to get a small economy car for miles and for gas, you think that's ok?*

Al: *Sure.*

L: *Have you left Denver?*

Al: *On the plane, airplane mode, only like a 30-minute flight.*

7:36-7:37am: Harley tries to *Facetime* Leticia twice.

7:56-8:13am: Somebody texts Letecia from a local number: *Hey T any updates? How can we help right now? What are police saying? It's Christine Garcia, Jocelyn's mom.*

L: *My coworker has a video of a boy running. Did he have jeans white shoes and a blue jacket?* (she sends a video clip from a Ring).

8:13am: The Tiguan and Life360 start showing movement as Tiguan leaves the residence.

8:23am: Landen messages Gannon's phone: Can you send me the pics of him at the store or anything you have?

Leticia does not respond.

8:26am: Letecia googled *employee parking at COS.*

8:29am: Al: *Just landed, you picking me up?*

L: *Yes.*

8:30am: Receipt in Tiguan shows ticket was pulled.

8:30am: Leticia is at the COS airport renting a Kia Rio and picking up Al.

8:32am: 16 second *Facetime* between Harley and Leticia.

8:33am: Another 15 second *Facetime* between Harley and Letecia.

8:37am: L: *Ok almost inside.*

Al doesn't respond.

8:42am: Harley tries to *Facetime* Leticia, but it doesn't connect.

8:42am: Letecia *Facetimes* Harley, it lasts 47 seconds.

8:44am: Leticia texts Harley. *What shoes are at the front door?*

H: (sends pic of shoes by the front door). Harley tells Letecia she didn't have work until tomorrow.

L Tells Harley to pull the car into the garage.

8:50am: Leticia picks Al up in the Rio.

The Tiguan is left at the short-term parking lot at the airport until 7:02pm that same day. Gannon's body is in the back of the Tiguan.

8:54am: Harley messages Letecia telling her she has parked her car in the garage.

Letecia does not respond.

8:50am: Al and Leticia return home.

Leticia calls a South Carolina phone number and makes two calls to her mother.

9:19am: KKTV calls Letecia, it goes to voicemail.

9:22am: EPSO calls Letecia; it lasts 6 mins 26 seconds.

10:10am: Group message from Harley to her friends about Gannon being missing; she says he had been missing since 4pm the previous day and that he could be anywhere by now as he has been travelling in a vehicle.

11:00am: Life360 shows movement around Lorson Ranch.

11:00am: EPSO does social media release with the first bulletin about Gannon being missing.

> 11:03am: Someone with a 210 area code texts Letecia: *We have hit up all the Fountain businesses and Walmarts.*

> L: *Thank you :)*

> 11:09am: Letecia texts Al. *You inside?*

> Al: *Yes.*

> L: *Any luck? What are they doing babe?*

> Al: *Talking.*

> L: *What are they saying?*

> Al: *They misread the footage. He doesn't think he was here.*

> L: *What? Are you kidding me? OMG.*

11:43am: Letecia texts Harley: she says Albert said to tell Laina to work on her room before everyone gets there.

12:00pm: Letecia's phone leaves residence and travels northwest out of Lorson Ranch.

12:30pm: EPSO does their second neighbourhood canvas; Deputy Hess goes through neighbourhood.

> 12:49pm: Someone with a 210 area code texts Letecia: *There is a family with hunting and tracking canines that would like to assist, would you like me to put them in contact with you?*

> L: *Could you give me their number? I will talk to my husband and add it to my list. We are so overwhelmed, and no one has slept.*

She never followed up.

12:57pm: Letecia googles **Can Nintendo find my Switch?** on her phone.

1:03pm - 2:33pm: Letecia's phone leaves the residence, travels around, comes back southwest of residence.

1:03pm: Letecia has *Facetime* call with Harley.

1:28pm: Initial meet with Letecia and Al at Starbucks.

> 1:40pm: Debra Locklear (Letecia's mother) emails Letecia from work email: *do you think he ran away?*

> It was read at 2:56pm and Letecia responded: *No.*

2:16pm: Letecia sends picture of young man in blue coat to Sergeant Hess with EPSO; this is a tip that was determined not to be Gannon.

> 2:23pm: Harley texts Letecia: *WYD?* (what you doing?) And she sends a picture of one of their dogs.

Letecia does not respond.

During this time Letecia is traveling up to the airport and then further north on Powers.

4:03pm: Al requests EPSO address; Letecia sends it to him.

4:04pm: Letecia and Detective Bethel have a text conversation.

L: *We have a question.*

Bethel: *Ok.*

L: *Want us to look for rags or band aids from our burns from the candle? It may also have DNA to go with the toothbrush it may be in the trash downstairs. Did not want to gross you out.*

Bethel: *A brush or toothbrush should be sufficient for now but if it's readily available bring it. No need if you have to search for it right now.*

L: *Ok no problem. What time do you leave?*

4:25pm: Letecia calls Al, the call lasts 1 minute, 41 seconds.

4:26pm - 4:38pm: Harley and Letecia text; Harley can't find Letecia she says she'll text back and not to open the door; she says police are hiding something.

4:40pm: Al goes to EPSO and does his first interview. He took Gannon's toothbrush and comb.

4:41pm: Al tries to call Letecia; it does not connect; her phone is not on the network - call forwarding not reachable.

4:41pm: COS airport parking ticket showing quick trip through the parking lot; she drives northbound on powers.

4:42pm: Al *Facetimes* Harley for 24 seconds.

4:42pm: Harley texts Letecia about her meeting up with Al.

4:51pm: Letecia calls Al, it lasts 52 seconds.

5:00pm: Harley texts Letecia.

H: *?*

L: *Ok I called them* (she had called Al not law enforcement).

5:04pm: Harley Facetimes Letecia for 56 seconds.

5:18pm: Letecia travels from Powers back to the residence.

5:18pm - 5:23pm: Al texts Letecia: *What did she say?*

L: *She wouldn't answer.*

Al: *Ok.*

L: *I'm about to head that way I need to finish trying to use the bathroom.*

Al: *Ok well I'll see what they say.*

L: *Why are they holding you there?*

Al: *Not holding me just getting all of this recorded I guess.*

L: *Have you started?*

Al: *Done, I think.*

L: *So, you did recording without me?*

Al: *Huh?*

L: *Like they have you separate, and you aren't talking to the lady, and you're done yours?*

Al: *When you get here, I will sit in with you.*

L: *You need to ask for attorney. This doesn't make any sense you should already be finished with your recording. They have lied and treated us like crap.*

5:36pm: Harley tries to *Facetime* Letecia.

5:37pm: Letecia tries to *Facetime* Harley.

5:37pm: Al tries to call Letecia, it doesn't connect, he texts instead. *Hey call.*

Letecia calls and it lasts 12 minutes, 8 seconds.

5:38pm: Harley tries to *FaceTime* Letecia it doesn't connect.

5:45pm: Harley texts Letecia about the pizza delivery and asks if it she's ok to open the door.

5:25pm: Letecia *Facetimes* Harley for 3 minutes, 33 seconds.

6:00pm - 6:56pm: Letecia is at the residence and then ends up back at the airport in the Rio.

6:00pm: SVU calls Letecia for 34 minutes 57 seconds.

6:12pm - 6:15pm: Letecia and Harley text.

L: *What's going on there?*

H: *Albert came and left and is back now.*

6:15pm - 6:22pm: Letecia texts Al:

Where are you?

Al: *Home.*

L: *What questions did they ask you??*

6:24pm: Letecia texts Harley.

L: *What is Al doing?*

H: *Talking to the news. They are here.*

6:25pm: Al: *Same ones.*

L: *Same ones how?*

6:31pm - 6:34pm: Letecia texts Harley about Al being with the news and asks who is there.

6:35pm: Letecia texts Al after trying to call. *I need to talk to you and why is Laina still with Harley? Hello? This is important.*

Al doesn't respond.

6:37pm - 6:38pm: Letecia calls Al twice; no answer.

6:39pm - 6:48pm: Letecia calls Al 3 more times; no answer.

L: *You're supposed to be my teammate and we need to talk and where are you? I don't know what's going on with you, but Harley is going to need to leave, and she said you came out and left. Albert they were asking bad stuff about you that's why I said a lawyer. Where are you? Did you do those things?*

6:56pm: Letecia calls Harley, the call lasts 3 minutes and 38 seconds.

The Kia Rio is not returned properly at rental car return, it was found the next day in short term parking. She parks the Rio and leaves the airport in the Tiguan.

7:00pm - 7:26pm: Letecia, her phone, and the Tiguan leave the airport, goes north on Powers, northeast on 24, then stops at the strip mall at Meridian and Woodman.

7:00pm: Letecia calls Al, it doesn't connect.

7:01pm - 7:08pm: Letecia texts Al: *Why are you ignoring me and going to get Landen? I've been home to meet you like you said. I've called and called. I called the lady and told her you are now missing off the face of the earth and was supposed to be going to get Landen and you were supposed to take Laina and then Harley said you left, and I went there, and you weren't there.*

7:02pm: The Tiguan leaves the short-term parking lot.

7:03pm: Letecia calls Bethel the call lasts 3 minutes, 52 seconds.

7:17pm: Letecia texts Al: *Well Harley was supposed to help me meet this team. I do know where you are and got worried. I'm sorry I just wanted to be with you afterwards.*

There was no response.

7:21pm – 7:23pm: Harley texts Letecia telling her people with badges were at the house.

Letecia told her not to open the door.

7:25pm: Letecia texts Al: *I'm looking for you, are you ok?*

There was no response.

7:26pm - 7:34pm:Letecia and Harley text about the detectives, knocking on the door, calling her phone and peering in the windows.

7:33pm: Al is doing 2nd interview with EPSO.

7:37pm: L: *Well, I'm going back home.*

No response from Al.

7:37pm: Letecia calls Harley, the call lasts 10 minutes, 15 seconds.

7:45pm: Letecia calls Harley, the call lasts 2 minutes, 55 seconds.

7:48pm: Harley calls Letecia, the call lasts 6 minutes, 48 seconds.

7:59pm - 9:28pm: Letecia drives the Tiguan with Gannon in the back to the S curve up in Douglas County.

7:59pm: Letecia places phone on airplane mode; Harley and Al try to call

multiple times, but the calls don't go through.

8:16pm: Al texts Letecia. *Call me.*

Letecia reads the text at 9:54pm.

9:54pm: Letecia's phone is no longer in airplane mode.

8:24pm - 8:29pm: Al texts Harley: *I've been calling.*

H: *People are here.*

Al: *Who?? Answer me please. Who is there?* (Al tries to call but she doesn't answer)

H: *Detectives.*

Al: *Where's Laina? Is Landen there?*

H: *Here and no.*

Al: *Ok.*

9:15pm: Landen calls Leticia; it does not connect.

9:22pm: Al texts Harley: *Harley?*

She doesn't answer.

9:49pm - 11:30pm: The Tiguan leaves S curve, makes way back down to shops at Briargate and I25. It connects to the Wi-Fi at Starbucks.

9:51pm: Letecia's phone connects to the Hilton across the street briefly before connecting to the Starbucks Wi-Fi.

9:55pm: Letecia *Facetimes* to Harley for six minutes, 33 seconds.

10:02pm: Letecia searches: **CBI Amber Alert** and looks at current active Colorado Amber alerts.

10:03pm - 10:12pm: Harley and Letecia text about detectives talking to her, they took Laina for questioning, and Letecia asks if her mother knows the detectives were trying to set her up. Letecia tells Harley to call the police if they won't let her leave.

10:16pm: Letecia texts Al: *Why? Tell them one of their own met me and told me what was going on and how you turned on me. I can't believe you. I'm not stupid. They said for you to say that. It*

> *will come out. I'm being set up. I knew you were lying the whole time this afternoon. It has already been leaked to me. Makes me thankful there are crooked people in the blues who are working just as hard pushing back secretively.*

Al did not respond.

10:17pm - 10:20pm: Letecia texts Harley about her not liking Harley being at the house by herself; Harley did not read it until 1:36am.

10:23pm: Letecia *Facetimes* with Harley for 16 minutes, 15 seconds.

10:24pm: Al meets with EPSO.

> 10:45pm: Letecia texts Bethel: *What do you want from me? Because I have nothing. One of your own leaked to me what you guys were doing. I did nothing and I'm being set up. I'm not really even sure, other than being told that by another blue with El Paso. I was told I couldn't go home to sleep and on top of that men were sent to a home with a minor female and she was forced to stay there, not to even leave for food. Every conversation that said even at this moment I can hear inside. What do you want from me?*

Harley tries to call Letecia several times but there's no answer - Letecia is moving and is not connected to Wi-Fi.

11:26pm - 11:31pm: Harley tries to *Facetime* Letecia twice.

> 11:39pm: Detective Bethel responds to texts saying: *Come in to talk to me. I would just like information to find Gannon.*

> 11:42pm - 11:50pm: Letecia logged back onto Wi-Fi and sent a message to Bethel saying: *My life is being ruined am I unable to go to my home? I have nowhere to sleep. You said you asked me questions already. I tried to call.* Her phone was connected to Holiday Inn's Wi-Fi next to Massage Envy.

11:51pm: Letecia Facetimes Bethel, the call lasts 3 minutes.

12:00 - 12:22am: Letecia and Al text.

L: *Are you able to talk now? Harley would like to get all her things because she has to work and start school and she has nowhere to go. And she was left there with men. I tried to talk to you forever tonight and you ignored me. You have all this wrong. You told some dude what I was driving. For what? I have talked to everyone. You left her with Laina there and wouldn't even tell her anything. Wouldn't talk to me. I thought something was wrong now you bring your ex to our home and refuse to talk to me. This is all wrong and you have this wrong I have paid for my share of things at my home this is stupid.*

Al: *I'm not refusing anything this was the plan. There is so much you are withholding from me, and I see that now. Please do not come back here tonight or at all until you are ready to talk.*

L: *It is my home and I am. You can't kick us out. I have nowhere to go. Harley has nowhere to go. The utilities are in my name.*

Al: *Do not come here and cause problems. Where are y'all then? Where is Gannon?*

L: *I'm not coming there to cause problems I own over half the stuff there.*

Al: *Take it.*

L: *So, you don't want to be my husband? Why? Why are you doing this? I will talk to you and only you. Call me first.*

Hello? Albert it's cold. It's not what you think. I don't know where he is I am your spouse, and you have your ex-wife in our home. It was not the plan I said I would talk to you.

Al: *My missing child's mother is here. Come talk then.*

L: *I have every right to be in that home.*

Al: *But it better start with the truth or I'm calling the detectives.*

L: *What are you talking about? Truth about what? You can't* call detectives on me for speaking or not. I did nothing wrong talking, call me.

Al: *I'm home. That's all I'm worried about right now and my boy. Mom is on the way.*

L: *I have sympathy, but you are turning on me and the other guy who told me what they said to you. I want to sleep in my bed with my dog and Harley wants to sleep in her bed. It's my home there is no law that prevents me from sleeping in my home.*

Al: *Yup.*

L: *So, can we sleep in our home? We are outside with our dogs with nothing. This is ridiculous.*

12:50 - 12:52am: L: *Hello?*

Al: *Where?*

L: *Where is everyone going to be? I want to sleep in our bed?? Hello?*

Al: *I don't care.*

L: *Our dogs need to go out. You said to talk to you, and I asked where is everyone going to be? I need to sleep.*

Al: *Landen is with Laina. Brandon is on the couch. Harley has her suite, and you get the bed.*

L: *And your mom?*

Al: *Her and Becky are in G's room. I need the truth.*

L: *What time are they getting there? Is anyone going to say anything to me.*

Al: *Nope. I need the truth.*

12:53 - 12:56am:

L: So, what exactly are you doing if I come in and go to bed and don't bother you?

Al: I'll be on the couch.

L: Ok and everything is all good and no one is bothering anyone?

Al: You need to tell me the truth.

L: See how you don't accept the truth so I can sleep.

Al: Sleep all you want, I need the truth.

L: Where's everyone going to be while we are walking in?

Al: In bed. Stop dodging. I need the truth.

L: I am asking you is everyone in bed so we can come?

Al: Yes, except mom isn't here yet. Truth?

L: What time is she getting there?

Al: 20.

L: Ok, so how long before they will be in bed too?

Al: Whatever.

1:04am: Letecia connects to KFC south of the Massage Envy and the Holiday Inn's Wi-Fi.

1:04am - 1:12am: L: *We will be there. Please don't let anyone bother our dogs. Will you let me know when she is there? We can wait close by? Albert, I have to work I'm not getting paid out??*

Al does not respond.

> 1:15am: Letecia texts Deidre Moss: *I came back home because they said they were doing that to see, but it's still sketchy I can be here I have to leave soon. I can't take being a punching bag anymore. I should've left last week when I said it.*

> 1:17am - 1:18am: Letecia texts Al: *I'm trying to talk to you I asked one simple request to let me know where everyone is in bed because its cold and the dogs need to go out.*

No response.

1:23am - 8:25am: Letecia's phone is using a tower near the home.

> 1:23am: L: *We are outside if you want to talk.* She calls him twice; but there's no answer.

1:36am - 1:40am: Letecia and Harley are texting each other. They are now inside the residence.

> L: *Is Chance ok?*

> H: *Yes*

> L: *They tore up my clothes and went crazy in here and threw stuff everywhere.*

> H: *Wow.*

> L: *Your stuff?*

> H: *It's fine.*

> L: *And what did the downstairs look like?*

> H: *idk (i don't know) its dark*

> 1:42am: Letecia texts Al: *You felt the need to destroy my closet?*

No response.

> **1:46am: Harley texts Letecia:** *Should I lock my door?*

> L: *Yes.*

> H: *Ok.*

> **1:50am: Letecia forwards a voicemail to Al:** *So, this was on purpose that I have a few voicemails with her talking crap about you working all the time and the kids not getting love.*

The voicemail was not relevant to the investigation; when Letecia's phone was in airplane mode, Landen called her and accidentally left a voicemail.

> **1:51am - 1:54am: Harley texts Letecia:** *You and Sadie can come sleep down here with me if you want.*

> L: *I honestly don't want to walk around them. Sadie has to go out so bad she is at the door begging.*

> **2:08am - 2:54am: Letecia texts Detective Bethel:** *Can we talk soon? I appreciate all your hard work. I have information. Gannon was upset about the candle. I didn't know that he had cut himself with it because he had on a blue undershirt and long sleeves and he had a small burn area, I did too. When we came back inside from the smoke there was blood on both of us. I didn't know what to do. I was scared I would get fussed out about it and I didn't know if he should go to the doctor. I kept trying to add the candle thing, but Albert kept saying it was small and minor. I was scared the basement was smoky and when I threw the covers on everything, we both had blood. You don't understand how hard it is to be a stepmom. I get judged for everything and he was scared for being grounded so then the next day, this is where I need to talk to you.*

> **Bethel:** *Ok can you come in to talk?*

> L: *Yes, I'm sorry I wasn't ever hiding anything from you. You don't understand the pressure I get put under about not doing*

enough. Could you trust in me and let me meet you in the morning? I am so tired I still haven't slept yet?

Bethel: *We can talk in the morning. Is there anything I should know since we are still looking tonight?*

L: *I did not hurt Gannon. I did not put him in harm's way.*

Bethel: *Is he hurt?*

L: *I don't think he is because I'm keeping faith, but I really need your help to make sure everyone knows I would never hurt him and did not in any way.*

Bethel: *What time can you come in today after you sleep?*

L: *I don't want you upset with me for all your hard work and everyone else's and I ask that you please protect our house and us from anyone that may be dangerous too from me giving extra info. And as soon as I wake.*

Bethel: *What information do you have? I can't protect anyone from anything if I don't know what it is. Come in at 10am at the OTS.*

L: *Ok, I will be there. Can you please not get me for not giving all the details that I knew to you at first? I know people do it a lot and it gets frustrating for you, but I am a victim as well and didn't want to be forced to take a test at some doctor's office.*

Bethel: *We can talk more about that when you come in.*

L: *Do you have to release personal info to the media and online like as in with me? Say, for example, a friend of mine had an abusive spouse and so she had to cover up everything—asking for a friend.*

Bethel: *I don't release information.*

L: *Ok, thank you. My husband wouldn't ever look at me the*

same knowing what happened to me and I couldn't tell you in front of him and I know he would act in a violent manner. Thank you see you tomorrow I mean today.

Bethel: *Ok see you soon we will talk later today please get some sleep.*

L: *And so I don't forget let me add this on here so I can remember to tell you. Gannon and I were working together because Albert always works so I'll explain things that you may have had concerns together we had a plan because even though she wasn't the best it was more than what Albert did because he was working or sleeping and didn't spend any time with them kk.*

2:56am: Letecia texts a 360 number a photo of a SkyWest application along with, *I never sent you what I'd received.*

3:20am: Letecia drafted a message and didn't send it to Debra Locklear: *No just upset because they keep freaking out on me and everyone in his family acts like I know where he is and won't tell.*

7:04am: Letecia received message from 910 number: *Hey Tecia how are y'all doing?*

L: *Oh, sorry I'm at home. I'm doing ok.*

7:19am - 7:24am: Letecia texts Al: *My chargers are in your car can I please have them?*

Al: *Sure.*

L: *Could you get it? I don't have any battery and Sadie needs to go out really bad.*

Al: *No.*

L: *Please, I'm not trying to cause any trouble.*

Al: *I need the truth.*

L: *I already did what you asked, you are the one who would not wake up.*

Al: *Wake up? I haven't slept in days and that's manipulative to say you told me when I was sleeping.*

L: *I wasn't knocking you about sleeping I'm sorry. I was saying I did what you asked, and you were tired.*

Al: *What? I asked you to tell me the truth.*

L: *Albert I'm not getting yelled at by a bunch of people. I told you I would speak to you in person. I went in there and said, 'hey are you ready now' last night and you told me no.*

Al: *I was asleep let me in now and tell me.*

L: *The door is unlocked.*

7:50am - 7:59am: Letecia texted Al: *Can you please come here? Can you please take Sadie out? Can you tell Landen to come here? Can you please take Sadie out? Please, I'm ashamed.*

No response.

8:15am: Al calls EPSO and reports that Letecia is at the house, and someone raped her and kidnapped Gannon.

8:25am: Letecia texted Harley: Please come get Sadie my phone is about to die.

No response.

8:35am: EPSO arrives, Letecia is in the basement.

9:50am: Harley and Letecia get in the Jetta. Harley is due to go to work. They stop at the airport first and Letecia hands the Rio keys to an employee, and they drive away.

10:21am: Harley clocks in at Massage Envy.

> 10:25am: Letecia texts Bethel: *I'm on the way.*

> Bethel: *Ok.*

> L: *Here shortly. Sorry, had to handle some things because my family is getting harassed and threatened and my daughter's safety is now in danger. She's getting threatened online and my family.*

> Bethel: *Ok we need to talk about that. Where is she now? Are you ok? Just checking to see.*

10:57am: Letecia's phone connects to 1st and Main near the Massage Envy.

11:00am - 11:51am: The Tiguan and Life360 leaves the Massage Envy area and goes to the EPSO.

> 11:00am - 11:02am: Letecia texts Bethel: *Resend the address please.*

> And then, *I found it.*

> Bethel: *Ok how long until you're here?*

> L: *10.8 miles.*

Bethel: *Ok, great.*

11:03am: Letecia calls her sister, Aimee Lowry, the call lasts 19 mins, 36 seconds.

11:26am: Bethel asks where she is and would she like a coffee or soda.

Letecia does not respond for 10 minutes.

> 11:36am - 11:40am: L: *Diet. Parking. Thank you.*

> Bethel: *Ok, where are you parked? Do we need to make sure a meter gets fed or do I need to validate parking?*

L: *I'm not sure that's what I'm trying to figure out where to go.*

Bethel: *You can park in the garage behind the building, and I will validate for you.*

11:57am - 11:58am: L: *What's the name again?*

Bethel: *Office of the Sheriff.*

L: *I'm here. They said you would be out shortly.*

12:00pm: Letecia does the interview with EPSO, and her car is seized.

2:18pm: Harley texts Letecia saying uncle wants you to call him.

L: *Ok, love you.*

The phone is seized after this message.

4:20pm: Towards the end of interview Letecia complained of shortness of breath and chest pains on top of rape story. She is transported from the sheriff's office to memorial hospital.

5:30pm: Harley clocks out of work.

7:52pm: Letecia leaves the hospital.

8:31pm: Janine and Harley pick up Letecia at Taco Bell near the hospital; and head to Janine's house.

8:48pm: Harley's phone texts Aimee Lowry: *We have to take location off and get another number. We will call you back.*

9:16pm - 9:19pm: Harley's phone texts Al: *I need to be able to get all my belongings tomorrow with my grandma so that I have a place to live my family please.*

Al: *Call me.*

H: *No, I don't want to. I do not want to live there. I just need to know that I can do that privately with my grandma present.*

Al: *Ok whatever you need I will support you. You taking Chance and Sadie?*

H: *Will that be ok to load up all of my things alone?*

Al: *Harley I will be there to help you. Obviously, I want you to stay, and you know that, but I understand your feelings.*

H: *I need their supplies too. They were left with no way to go out and I feel I will give them a better care.*

Al: *Not true the deputies took them out and fed them. I made sure of that and went home once to check.*

9:19pm - 9:24pm: H: *They need love not just going out.*

Al: *We all do.*

H: *Again, is it ok that my grandma and I load up my things?*

Al: *Yes. I will be there to help and support you.*

H: *I asked you could we be alone. I do not want your things.*

Al: *I will not bother you, but I have a responsibility to you and that isn't changing.*

H: *I will get my cell changed tomorrow thank you. My family would like to be with me and I'm asking that you understand that and let me get them. I want my mom's things too because we wear a lot of the same things and I have all my memory boxes. What day can I get everything alone?*

Al: *Is momma not coming home? Do you know something because we know nothing.*

H: *That's funny because the lady showed me your thread.*

9:25pm - 9:30pm: H: *Please tell me I can get my things privately so my family can spend their money on a ticket and a rental truck. I have to tell them.*

Al: *Tell them what?*

H: *I asked could I arrange a time to come privately with my family to get belongings?*

Al: *Tell who?*

H: *My grandma.*

Al: *Anyone can come but I will be there, and a cop can be there too.*

H: *No one would take anything of yours.*

Al: *Harley, I'm not worried about that. I have a responsibility here and this is the right way.*

9:30pm - 9:33pm: H: *Ok, could it be just you and no one else?*

Al: *Yes.*

H: *And no one wants to talk so we ask that as well.*

Al: *Ok.*

H: *Thank you I will let you know when.*

Al: *Ok. Still can't find Gannon btw.*

Thursday 30th January

Letecia and Harley spent the night at Janine Sanchez's house.

4:38am: Harley texts her supervisor at Massage Envy and quits her job: *I wanted to say that I thank you for being supportive and for our time at work. I know I provided an initial date that was for me leaving for BMT but due to safety concerns with my family situation I need to take care of myself and make sure I am safe at this time. I hope you understand that this was an extenuating circumstance and hope that I can leave the company with a great relationship and future references. Thank you.*

It is believed Letecia wrote this.

7:57am – 8:57am: Harley texts Al.

H: *My life was threatened on social media and told how people are looking for me. My grandma has been threatened so I do understand the pain and scaredness, but my mom did not do anything to harm Gannon you should know that. I can come this afternoon to get my things.*

Al: *None of that is by me. You are always safe with me, and you know that.*

H: *Not by you but you could stop it.*

Al: *Social media is stupid you should be with me. Your grandma and them should not have gone on there either. Call me.*

H: *I did and you didn't answer.*

Al: *No, I just called you and it went straight to voicemail. Harley you are 17 and you are my responsibility. I know you are scared and confused about all of this, but I am making this very clear. I am asking you and Aimee to come see me I need to verify your safety. If you leave without seeing me first, I will fear for your safety and will have to report it to police as missing runaway. If your mom signed consent like you said I must see it ASAP and have a copy and it must specify who you're allowed to leave with. This is the issue I was trying to avoid by sending you to safety yesterday, but you chose to not do that. Either way maintain constant contact with me and keep me informed of your location. I will not come and try to bother you, but I have* to know you're safe at all times. Love you.

H: *I'm not scared. Why would you do this when I don't want to be around you? Be with Landen. You turned on my mom I want to be with my grandma my uncle and my aunt. I'm not your child nor will I ever be.*

Al: *I disagree but I respect your opinion. I have to visually confirm your safety. After that if you decide to leave with your family, we'll work through that. Where can we meet? I'm about to go to Laina's school so we can meet there or close to the house.*

H: *You promised I could get my things with my family, and you said no one would be there but you.*

Al: *Yes, but you're not working with me.*

H: *I'm not. You will do me like you did mom. Please stop. You have your car. Give it to Landen. I paid for it all this time. Stop trying to force me to do something.*

Al: *I'm not getting into a text battle I need to confirm your safety and then what you do from there is your decision. Someone is influencing you wrongly.*

H: *Influencing me to go with my blood family? We have the same blood so how is that wrong. I'm safe so please let me come with my family to get my things.*

Al: *I have to visually confirm.*

H: *I'm not meeting you what is wrong with you? I do not want to be around you. I'm afraid to be around you if my mom is not there.*

Al: *10:30 at the house to get your stuff.*

H: *I've been asking for confirmation because we need to get a rental truck to transport. We could never get that from you, so we have to make the plans.*

AI: *That means nothing to authorities please meet at 10:30.*

H: *Why are you trying to take me? What do you get out of forcing me when I hate you now? No one is influencing me. I hate you.*

AI: *Not forcing you only confirming your safety.*

H: *You mean nothing to me. None of you. You set my mom up so you could be with your ex-wife. I hate you.*

AI: *Well, I love you and I'm sorry you feel that way.*

H: *If you don't wanna be with me and my mom then you can't have me. She's the best mom ever and she would not harm anyone. You are doing this for control. Mom's attorney is coming to get her things. He will have an order.*

11:06am: Letecia's family arrive in Colorado, and they hired a 2020 Nissan Altima.

1:24pm: Letecia and Harley go to Marshall's; this is where Harley's phone and car are seized.

9:44am: The family goes to Enterprise - Letecia, Harley, Brenda, Debra, and Dakota; they hire a 2019 Ford transit van – (van #1)

11:19am: Van #1 and the Nissan Altima with Letecia driving arrive at the Stauch home to pick up their belongings.

12:10pm: KKTV do an interview with Letecia and Harley. Letecia said Gannon 12 ish times during the interview, and I, me or my over 100 times.

3:26pm and 3:38pm: The family with the two vehicles return to the *Extended Stay America* on Corporate Drive – after they arrive, law enforcement place the tracker on the Altima.

3:45pm: The Nissan Altima departs the ESA and travels north on I25. Letecia was driving.

4:41pm: The Nissan Altima pings at the S curve. She was travelling in that area for an hour. It is believed Gannon's body was picked up and is now in the Altima.

5:37pm - 5:41pm: Nissan went through Starbucks drive through.

5:56pm - 6:19pm: Nissan goes to PetCo; same one she went to with Gannon; she spent $32.

6:23pm - 6:26pm: The Altima arrives back at ESA and parked up for the night.

Saturday 1st February.

8am: Van #1 departs ESA and drives to Budget on Garden of the Gods Road; Letecia hires another van, Van #2 – she pays $679 using American Express. Van #1 has windows – Van #2 does not have windows.

10:10am: Van is outside of Pueblo at Love's gas station; there is a coinciding purchase for $8.34 at the same time the van gives a ping.

11:56am - 12:27pm: Letecia and Harley go to Walmart in Trinidad; Letecia purchases prepaid Verizon phone with 407 area code: $89.03; the numbers on the back of the prepaid card found in the van in Rhode Island match this prepaid phone.

Time zone change: from Mountain time to central time,

7:49pm: Phone #2.

11:10pm: The van pings in the parking lot of Candlewood Suites in Amarillo Texas; charge earlier for $91.

Sunday 2nd February 2020.

The van is at Candlewood still at 5:10am and 11:10am.

7:38pm: $25 charge on Amex - Candlewood Suites in Decatur, Texas.

11:10pm:GPS ping at the Candlewood Suites.

Monday 3rd February 2020.

3:14am - 5:10am: The powerup and 6-hour ping show the van at Candlewood Suites in

Decatur.

Tuesday 4th February 2020.

12:22am: $106 Amex Candlewood Suites Pensacola Florida. There was no video from the Pensacola Candlewood Suites; it had been overwritten.

4:15am: A powerup event occurred; the van had moved less than 2 miles from powerup ping to where Gannon was found and less; 1.8 miles from hotel to ping. According to the two pings, from when the van arrived at 12:22am and the powerup event at 4:15am, the van had moved.

5:10am, 11:10am: Scheduled pings, in the Comfort Inn parking lot (back of the Candlewood Suites).

11:44am: Harley buys breakfast at McDonalds about a block from the hotel.

Time zone change: from Central to Eastern.

11:32pm: Holiday Inn $315.70 charge in Orlando Florida.

Wednesday 5th February 2020.

Letecia and Harley arrive in Myrtle Beach and return the van before 6:10pm.

8th February 2020.

Letecia gets her 3rd phone while in South Carolina. This phone was seized when she was arrested.

15th February 2020.

The board is found at the S curve with Gannon's blood on it.

Letecia makes a post on FB, Exhibit 50: the video of Gannon in Hawaii, waving and saying goodbye and jumping off a dock into the water.

18th February 2020.

The 1st fake polygraph Letecia tried to obtain but it violated policy.

19th February 2020.

Note created with 5 altered questions.

21st February 2020.

Letecia texts Nicole Mobley (this is the series of texts where Letecia was asking for a witness these messages were previously admitted).

The 2nd fake polygraph was done on SC phone.

2nd March 2020.

Letecia is arrested and charged with murder. She is interviewed by agent Grusing.

4th March 2020

Letecia attacks Deputy James; no Spanish accent or reference to herself as Maria.

17th March 2020

Gannon's body is found.

The focus now turns to the internet searches on Letecia's devices, and she had made over 6000 of them. 4500 had been deleted but they still had the date and time.

Grusing confirmed that the searches with no date were not taken into account.

21st January 2020

- 9:05pm: Landen Marie Hiott.

- 9:10pm: Uhaul truck rental.

- 9:12pm: Uhaul trucks rates Colorado Springs to Orlando Florida on 22nd January 2020.

- 9:14pm: Uhaul truck rates Colorado Springs to Orlando Florida on 6th February 2020.

24th January 2020

- 7:32pm: Jobs employment in Myrtle Beach South Carolina.

- 8:01pm: Sometimes you just leave and take nothing.

Saturday 25th January 2020

- 8:48am: Jobs employment in Los Angeles, CA.

- 12:16pm: Find real military singles.

- 12:16pm: Military dating and singles.

- 1:40pm: Parenting should be four people not one.

- 1:40pm: I'm over doing all the work for my step kids and their mom doesn't help.

- 1:48pm: If you aren't involved in your kid's life you are shitty.

- 1:49pm: My husband's ex-wife does nothing for her kids.

- 1:51pm: I wonder if my husband's ex-wife is sending me a valentine's card since I raise her kids.

- 1:54pm: One day some people will wish they treated you differently.

- 7:57pm: Find me a rich guy who wants me to take care of his kids.

- 7:58pm: Find a guy who wants me to take care of his kids and get paid.

- 9:11pm: Apartments for rent in Fort Lauderdale FL.

- 9:13pm: 1 bed 1 bath apartments for rent in Fort Lauderdale.

- 9:15pm: Craigslist south Florida jobs apartments for sale services community and events.

- 9:15pm: South Florida rooms and shares.

- 9:20pm: South Florida jobs.

- 9:47pm: Orlando jobs.

27th January 2020

- 12:09am: My son burned the carpet how do I fix it?

- 1:03am: Son sick can he stay home?

- 2:42am: Craigslist Orlando FL jobs apartments for sale services community and events.

28th January 2020

- 4:15am: What is the process for our runaway child?

- 4:16am: Police steps for our runaway.

- 4:16am: Police steps for our missing child.

- 7:17am: Find cheap rental car deals.

- 8:17am: 37 dollars a day compact car.

- 12:57pm: Can Nintendo find my Switch?

29th January 2020

- 2:34am: I want immunity because it was gang related.

- 2:34am: She downloaded an article about be careful about being granted immunity and not testifying; this later came up in the phone calls.

Phone #3 SC phone:

19th February 2020

- 1:22pm: Crime online.

- 3:49pm: Palmer Herald - a newspaper in the Palmer Lake area.

- 7:22pm: Does textfree show location?

- 7:43pm: How can I make my phones IP address hidden?

- 8:11pm: Send a fake email.

20th February 2020

- 6:52am: How long will fingerprints stay on an object?

- 8:49pm: I need a fake ID that's legit.

21st February 2020

- 6:43am: Children trafficking to Mexico from Colorado.

- 6:54am: I need a criminal polygraph.

- 7:08am: I need a fake criminal polygraph.

- 7:21am: I need a fake polygraph test.

- 7:35am: Can you get away with fake lie detector website?

- 9:52am: Gannon Stauch, El Paso, searching in landfill.

- 11:26am: Search efforts for Gannon Stauch.

- 6:46pm: I need to change my look to hide.

- 6:47pm: Face disguise.

- 6:49pm: Full face change.

- 6:51pm: First face transplant woman.

- 6:51pm: Full face transplant.

- 6:51pm: Face transplant near me.

- 6:53pm: Full face plastic surgery.

- 6:56pm: Full face plastic surgery Atlanta.

- 7:23pm: Need a guy who wants me to move in.

- 7:24 PM: Find a man with a place to let me move in.

22nd February 2020

- 9:50am: Change my facial appearance.

- 9:50am: Drastic ways to change your appearance.

- 9:52am: See what my face will be with plastic surgery.

- 9:52am: Plastic surgery Myrtle Beach SC.

23rd February 2020

- 3:08am: Gannon Stauch found.

- 8:24am: Replacement passport.

- 3:15pm: Shock from watching someone get shot.

- 5:13pm: Face mask that looks real to disguise.

24th February 2020

- 9:14am: GoFundMe Tecia and Harley support.

- 1:23pm: How long does it take to get DNA?

- 1:24pm: How long does it take to get DNA from crime?

- 1:24pm: How long does it take to get DNA results from a crime scene?

- 1:26pm: How long does it take police to get DNA results?

- 1:29pm: How long does it take police to get DNA results in Colorado.

- 1:39pm: How long does it take police to get DNA results in Colorado Springs?

25th February 2020

- 5:49am: Make a security video.

- 5:49am: Make a security video past tense.

- 4:12pm: I need a new social security number to hide.

- 4:28pm: Apply for a social if I lived on an Indian reservation.

- 6:56pm: Cadaver dog.

26th February 2020

During this entire segment, Letecia and her attorney have been behaving appallingly – they are looking at something on the laptop and blatantly laughing.

- 6:18am: Do they check in ditches under bridges?

- 6:18am: Maintenance under ditches under bridges?

- 6:57am: Can I get a plea with no jail time?

- 7:00am: Criminally negligent homicide in Colorado.

- 7:30am: Can I find a rich guy.

- 8:10am: Can they search Snapchat?

- 8:30am: Colorado closed case.

- 8:30am: Colorado Springs closed murder cases.

- 8:33am: Drug cartels in Colorado Springs.

- 8:48am: Make my phone get a call from Mexico.

- 8:51am: Fake a call from Mexico drug cartel.

- 8:51am: Fake a call from Mexico drug cartel.

- 8:53am: Bluff my call app.

- 8:54am: What are some Mexican drug cartel phone numbers?

- 9:13am: What do they do when they find a person's body in another state?

- 9:13am: How do they identify bodies found in another state?

- 9:33am: Make a fake snapchat video.

- 10:45am: Can the FBI go to los canos?

- 10:53am: Create a recording of someone's voice and change the words.

- 10:55am: Add someone's voice in a video.

- 10:56am: Change someone's words in a video.

- 2:38pm: Bahamas marriage certificate.

- 2:40pm: I need a fake marriage license.

27th February 2020

- 7:03am: How do police tell whose body has been found?

- 7:58am: Can God help me escape jail time?

- 8:05am: How do they identify who's blood is at the scene?

- 8:35am: Find people who want to go to jail.

- 8:58am: Spanish girl names.

- 9:04am: Petco Nevada Colorado Springs.

- 10:00am: Find an immigrant who will admit to a crime.

28th February 2020

- 7:02am: How long does a body start to decompose in a bag?

- 7:03am: What does a dead body look like after a month?

- 7:04am: What does a dead body look like after a month?

- 8:12am: Active drug cartels in Mexico.

- 8:23am: Bluff my call free.

- 8:33am: Address of drug cartels

- 8:36am: Current drug cartels in Colorado Springs.

- 7:44pm: How does the FBI find people?

- 7:49pm: How does the FBI find fugitives?

- 7:49pm: How fugitives avoid capture?

29th February 2020

- 6:27am: Casey Anthony.

- 6:29am: Casey Anthony and Patrick McKenna.

- 1:30pm: When does FBI take over a case?

1st March 2020

- 3:58pm: How to make my fingerprints not scan?

- 4:03pm: Fingerprint rubber.

- 4:03pm: Fingerprint rubber to make fingerprint.

Prosecution have no further questions.

Mr Cook begins cross examination.

He asks a few questions about Torres interview.

He also asks about the meaning of bath salts. Mr Clark says he believes it's a slang name for a type of drug.

Cook asks about the searches Letecia made and that wanted confirmation that Mr Clark only read out the ones he believed were relevant to the case. Mr Clark agrees this was the case.

Jury questions.

Q - To clarify, were the messages saying she left her phone at home sent from defendant's phone or Gannon's phone?

A - It was sent on the defendant's phone telling him to call her watch because it might stay connected to Gannon's phone; they left the house 15 minutes later.

There are no more questions for the witness.

The judge asks council and Deputy Robinson to approach him. We are not party to what they say but can only assume it was because of the behaviour from the defence table,

Prosecution says they are prepared to rest.

The court breaks for the day.

CHAPTER 19

Letecia Stauch Trial – Day 18 - Tuesday 2nd May 2023

Once the jury are settled, the prosecution rests.

The defence calls their first witness, clinical psychologist Ronda Niederhauser. She tells the court of her qualifications. She met Letecia twice in December 2019. She was having constipation, and she was also having some anxiety. Niederhauser recommended therapy and hydroxyzine, an antihistamine that helps with anxiety and sleep.

Mr Cook has nothing further.

Mr Allen begins cross examination.

He asks if Niederhauser examined Letecia and got a list of symptoms. She said there was no disorientation observed no memory issues, no delusions, her judgement wasn't impaired, normal speech, no abnormalities stated at all. She had anxiety but her mental health was not impaired, and she believed there was no danger to herself of others.

Mr Allen has no further questions.

Juror questions.

Q: Did you or the defendant set the second appointment on 13th December?

A: I asked for Letecia to set another appointment.

The witness is released from the stand.

There is an issue with the next witness and the judge send the jury out until 1pm.

Psychiatrist, Doctor Dorothy Lewis is the next witness to be called. She tells the court how she met with Letecia in November 2022.

Doctor Lewis says DID often goes together with schizophrenia, brain damage and epilepsy. Often brain injuries can cause impulses like violence and lack of control.

She believes Letecia was brought up in an extremely violent household. One of her mother's partners beat Letecia and pushed her into a shower naked. Apparently, she was given enemas daily by her grandfather which is a form of sodomy. Leticia also gave enemas to Gannon, but she said this was what he had wanted her to do, but the doctor feels this was a form of sexual abuse.

She recalls Letecia speaking in a Russian accent and it seemed Letecia had switched personalities. Letecia told her about her alters, Maria was physically abusive, and she was harsh and angry. When she spoke to her she thought she may have just met the aspect of Letecia's personality that killed Gannon.

She says Letecia is an amazing and intelligent young woman, yet she makes up the darnedest stories that no person of below average intelligence would expect to be believed. This puzzled Doctor Lewis. She came to the opinion that Letecia didn't actually know for sure what happened.

She recalls after the candle fire she had several psychotic episodes where she had hallucinations.

The way Maria spoke to her was disorganised and confused. She spoke about people shooting out of windows, needing people to guard funerals. She had a chaotic quality and as Maria she was more aggressive and had a scary persona.

Aspects of her behaviour was consistent with certain types of brain damage. She was close in terms of dissociation and neurologic impairment. She had wanted EEGs f=done as it would show that Letecia couldn't stop what happened.

Her expert opinion for the time Gannon was killed was that Letecia was psychotic. She wasn't in touch with reality.

Mr Tolini has no further questions.

Mr Young begins his cross examination. He asks her the legal definition of insanity in Colorado.

In her report she said she believes Letecia was insane at the time of the homicide and the days following. She believes she was also psychotic, and she also believes she doesn't know she even did it.

She had wanted neurological exam, an MRI and EEG done before she would diagnose insanity, however the court would not finance the tests and so she made the diagnosis without the tests.

The judge tells the court that the defence withdrew their request for an EEG and an MRI in October 2022. Doctor Lewis says this is news to her.

Mr Young quotes the doctor's own book where it states it is easy to fake DID and so further testing would be required. If the testing had been carried out it could have shown there was brain damage or brain dysfunction and then they could look in another area. Without it, all she had to go on was Letecia's word.

She will be paid $350 per hour but she's unsure of how many hours she will be billing them for in total.

Mr Young asks why Mr Tolini contacted her in the first place. She responds that she assumes it was because she was reputable and experienced in this particular field. She advised Mr Tolini she felt there was enough evidence to plead not guilty by reason of insanity based on the fact she did not know the nature of what she had done, and/or that it was wrong. Also, that she did not have control over what she was doing. She could not conform her behaviour to that which the law required.

Mr Young questions how she knew that back in February 2022 when she hadn't even interviewed the defendant until November 2022? She says she would need to look over the information she had been given before she could comment on that. She didn't know Mr Tolini had changed the pleas from not guilty to not guilty by the reason of insanity.

She has tried not to take a political stance on the death penalty in general. She says it depends on the offense and what the person did.

She first diagnosed multiple personality disorder in the 80s this is what DID used to be called.

There is usually evidence of DID going back to childhood if you are able to examine different sources: writing styles, diaries, names, school reports, family interviews. If there is no evidence leading up to a crime, then she would be very suspicious of the defendant.

She says there are lots of disorders that make a person crazy but not necessarily insane. And in her opinion, the doctors from the state hospital that did the first evaluation had been requested by the state and she thinks this would be slanted in their direction because they both get paid by the state. He says she's getting paid by the state also. She stutters and says she doesn't know who's paying her.

They discuss more about DID and the different alters. Doctor Lewis is asked why Maria couldn't be called up at will for Doctor Torres and yet she was for her. He asks her why. Doctor Lewis says, *Magic*.

The court breaks for the day.

CHAPTER 20

LETECIA STAUCH TRIAL – DAY 19 – WEDNESDAY 3RD MAY 2023.

Doctor Lewis returns to the stand.

She is waffling and slips in that she was looking through her notes the previous evening and found that some family member had told her that Letecia used to call herself Maria Sanchez when she was 12 years old. Mr Young does not accept this and accuses her of adding this information because she doesn't have anything to corroborate her diagnosis. She denies this is the case.

She speaks about the clock test and says Letecia failed it. She said everything was crowded into one area. This is common in dementia patients. The second time she attempted it was much better than the first. She also changed hands which had puzzled Doctor Lewis.

Mr Young asks if he considered she could be faking it? She didn't think this because the second time she had done a better job. If she had been faking it, she feels it would not have improved.

Mr Young gives several examples of symptoms and asks her if she felt that was possibly insanity. She says I'll go along with it because that's your story, that's what you made up and it is possible. However, the diagnosis of insanity is far more complex than looking at one thing.

The fact that Letecia called into work to say her father had been killed puzzled her. She says it could be that Letecia was psychotic. Mr Young asks couldn't she just be trying to get some time off work. She responds unlikely but possible.

WHAT IS WRONG WITH THIS WOMAN?

She clearly didn't watch the videos showing Letecia and Gannon leaving in the truck and returning later that same day.

He asks her if she had seen the autopsy report. She says she did and although there were 18 stab wounds, she thinks it's a stretch to say it was intentional and that the defendant may not have formed the intent to kill.

They go from the stab wounds to the blunt force trauma. He asks if she thinks if Letecia could have formed the intent to kill. She again says she doesn't know what was going through Letecia's head and that she may have felt she was in danger.

He said a little boy has received 18 stab wounds while lying in his bed, and then she takes and object and crushes his skull. Does that indicate he's fighting back at that point?

She says, I don't know what was going through her mind at that point. Was she defending herself? Was she attempting to kill him? The puzzle is all other data says that she loved him and that he loved her.

Mr Young says, yeah, she loved him quite a bit. The next thing she does is get another object. Does the fact she gets a gun tell you she has the capacity to use it and the capacity to form the intent to kill?

She didn't know. When she spoke to Letecia, she told her she could see a gun in her hand, but Doctor Lewis didn't know what was going through her mind. But this was a child she loved, and so did she wish to kill him? I don't know that it was even him that she wished to kill.

Mr Young says, 'well let's go forward then, because what does she do after she does all that? She drags his body to the storage room, and stuffs it in a large green suitcase. Do you think she had the capacity to know right from wrong when she did that?'

She says it would certainly seem she knew that this was something that should not have happened.

The court takes a morning break.

The questioning resumes and Mr Young is listing everything Letecia did to try to get Doctor Lewis to admit she must have had the capacity to know right from wrong, but she's not having it.

She put Gannon's body in the Tiguan, drove to and left it at the airport, then hired another car. Then, later that day she went back, drove to Palmer Lake, and found an isolated spot to hide the body. Doctor Lewis says this could be evidence of psychosis.

All this time, Letecia was texting Harley, telling her to stay inside, not open the door to the police—she was multi-tasking.

Then a few days later, Letecia made the trip to Pensacola, Florida, and dumped Gannon's body over the side of a bridge.

A video of Doctor Lewis interviewing Letecia is played. The audio is terrible.

Mr Young asks a few questions regarding the interview. It was more of the same—him asking if each of her actions proved she had the capacity to know right from wrong and her saying she couldn't be sure what was happening in Letecia's mind at that moment in time.

Court breaks for lunch.

Doctor Lewis is once again back on the stand. Mr Young tells her she can only refer to her report from here on in because the notes she has been referring to have not been submitted as evidence.

He then asks her to look at an email she had supposedly sent to Mr Tolini requesting he drop the EEG request. After several attempts to stutter an explanation, the judge asks her if she recognises the email thread yes, or no. She says yes.

The next video clip is played.

It shows Letecia writing something using her left hand. It is unclear which personality Letecia is meant to be at that moment.

As the clip progresses, it is clear she's meant to be Taylor. She says she is good. She never does bad things. She's being very smiley. She says she tries to be the mediator and make everybody get along. She says she casts herself as Taylor if anyone comes to visit and that helps her deal with the situation.

She says she reported Gannon missing, not Letecia. She didn't think anything was wrong and thought he was doing the hiding challenge and that he was okay.

When it started to rain, she began to panic because it was cold outside. She found his body but can't remember where and tried to bring him back to life. Gannon was not supposed to die. It wasn't supposed to be him. She says she's not a monster, but people are thinking she's a mass murderer.

She begins speaking fast, maybe Russian or gobbledy-gook.

She says she had to protect everybody in the house. She was trained to kill. That's what she does. She kept saying 'I'm trained to kill, okay. That's what I did'.

She begins speaking in what sounds like Spanish. She says she did what she was supposed to do—killed a guy. She had to protect Letecia's family. She was upset, everyone's upset, the little baby girl is crying—that's what she is trained for. She is staring at the doctor with a hard expression on her face, no longer smiley.

The audio is very distorted.

She says she had to protect her before in Mexico. She is 28 years old. She says she's always 28 although Letecia is 39.

She is staring intently at the doctor and making a tight fist.

As the video ends it shows a man leaving the interview room. Doctor Lewis says it was her son. Mr Young asks if that is usual to have a member of her family in this type of interview. She says he was helping with the cameras.

Mr Young asks why Lewis ended the interview considering she had been trying to get Maria to come forward and when she had they ended the interview. Doctor Lewis says she was tired.

The next video is played.

It begins with Doctor Lewis attempting to read a signed confession in Spanish/Latin/? from Maria.

Letecia begins talking about flashbacks.

Doctor Lewis asks her to tell her about the cape. Letecia shrugs and says she just saw a person in a red and black cape. It was a man.

The court takes an afternoon break.

The video resumes.

Letecia asks Doctor Lewis, 'What do you want from me?'

Once again, the audio is terrible. They are talking about Harmony, one of Letecia's alters. She says Letecia's dad molested Harmony when she was 10 years old. She says Gannon was also molested.

She says she shot the man who was wearing the cape, but it didn't turn out to be Gannon until later.

A lot more unintelligible audio.

Letecia, or her alter, goes on to tell of someone hitting James (her stepdad) with a board. He had tried to sell Letecia for drugs.

Doctor Lewis asks, did he die?

She says no, but he did not... (unintelligible)... anymore. She gives a creepy high-pitched giggle.

Letecia says, 'James wore a lot of capes'.

The recording continues but it's so difficult to work out what's being said. Letecia apparently falls in and out of several personalities, accents, and mannerisms but we will just have to take their word for it.

The video ends.

Doctor Lewis says the Latin confession that was at the beginning of the recording had been lost.

Mr Young asks if she still thinks it was a good idea to have Mr Tolini in on the interview. The fact he asks if she thought Gannon was James helps his theory. She doesn't agree.

He says the fact she says Gannon has a knife and she thought it was James and so she shot him was now pointing to self-defence.

Doctor Lewis argues with him.

Mr Young has no further questions.

Mr Tolini begins redirect.

He asks if he had been trying to feed Letecia a story, would it make sense to do it in a situation where it was recorded? She said no.

He asks if there are similarities between borderline personality disorder and DID? She says yes.

Would it be possible if someone was diagnosed with that kind of mental illness that her daughter may or may not be aware of it.

There are no further questions.

Juror questions.

There are six juror questions, but the judge forgets to turn the microphones back on so sadly there is no audio.

We received the questions from another source however we did not hear them in person.

Q: In what way would the defendant giving Gannon enemas impact her relationship with him?

A: Lewis said that enemas, especially performed regularly on a child, can be a form of child molestation and sexual assault. However, Lewis cautioned that this claim from the defendant may not be true.

Q: Did the number of cases drop at Bellevue (the hospital Lewis used to work at)

after Lewis's dissociative identity disorder clinic opened?

A: Lewis said there was no actual research conducted on this, as far as she knows, but she would bet money that the answer is yes.

Q: How do you determine if someone is faking or exaggerating their mental illness or not?

A: Lewis repeated what she had already mentioned during her testimony, you have to look how someone acts in an interview and at evidence of it existing in the past.

Q: Did you perform any tests to help determine if the defendant was faking or exaggerating DID?

Answer: Yes.

Q: Earlier, you said people with DID are more susceptible to believe what people say to them, if this is true, why do you openly talk about potential theories and explanations in front of the defendant during the interview.

A: It's often good to run theories and questions by defendants to see their responses, even if their answers can't necessarily be trusted, as the response can still inform on sanity.

Q: If the EEG and MRI weren't provided, how can you issue a final sanity report?

A: Lewis said that basically she can still conduct the sanity exam with interviews and background research and be confident in her findings, but that the EEG and MRI would have just (potentially) helped prove her findings.

There are no further questions.

Letecia makes her decision not to testify.

The court breaks for the day.

CHAPTER 21
LETECIA STAUCH TRIAL – DAY 20 - 5TH MAY 2023

The defence rests and there is no rebuttal from the state.

The judge speaks to the jury explaining the rules and instructions. He goes over all the charges.

Mr Young begins his closing arguments for the prosecution.

He starts by thanking the jury for being so dedicated and attentive during the trial.

"Every homicide case evolves to talk about the defendant, and then when you add a defence of insanity, we spend even more time talking about the defendant. I want to come back to Gannon a little bit.

Gannon's been in a box back here for the whole trial (he holds up a photograph of Gannon). This is what the trial should be about. I'm not doing this to get sympathy from you. I'm doing this to tell you that what Gannon had to tell you in this trial through the autopsy. All you need to know. And when the defendant did what she did to him, she was sane at the time she did it.

Not only do we know how he was killed and the effort and determination it took to kill him. We also know that his body was found in Florida. If his body wasn't found in Florida, do you think we'd be talking about insanity in this trial? It's a pure fact of divine intervention that Macon Ponder happened to be searching that bridge when he did. Remember, he said he searched that bridge every two years and it just so happened on 17th March 2020 he was out there searching that bridge and he saw that suitcase.

Doctor Lewis says it was crazy to drive a suitcase across the country and dump it over a bridge in Florida. Was it really? Think about the divine intervention of Gannon's body even being found to get here to where we're at right now. And the effort and determination she took to hide his body. We're gonna talk about that quite a bit more as I go through my closing. What I'd like to do now is talk about the autopsy and his injuries. I'm not going to show you any pictures, I can tell you that right up front, I'm gonna use the diagram to describe his injuries because his injuries are relevant. They're not only relevant to the crimes that she is charged with but to her state of mind when she committed those crimes.

Doctor Ignacio testified and showed photos of each and every injury that Gannon had to his body. The first diagram depicts the stab wounds and the gunshot wound to his left chin area. Just by looking at these injuries, what does your common sense tell you, without Doctor Ignacio's testimony? Gannon was defending himself! He was fighting her off despite having hydrocodone in his system that made him lethargic he somehow was able to fight her off. The injuries to his fingers, his arms. 18 times. 18 times she took a knife and stabbed him. The locations of the stab wounds, what does that tell you? Use your common sense. It's not psychotic. It's strategic. The stab wounds are to the chest. As Gannon is fighting, the stab wounds are to his back. But it's not just stab wounds, you know that. She has to use judgment and reflection to get another weapon. What that weapon was... who knows? But she got a weapon and hit him in the skull four separate times.

I forgot to mention the strategic stab wound under his ear. The diagram doesn't do justice to the skull fracture that she caused, it completely obliterated his skull. The amount of force it takes to do that—judgment—reflection.

The next exhibit shows four separate strikes to his head. It wasn't good enough. It wasn't good enough for her. So, judgment, reflection. She goes and gets a handgun. She fires that handgun three times. I don't know how those bullets stayed in the pillow. We can rack our brain for ages. I don't know how those bullets stayed in that pillow. I don't know that, we will ever know. What matters is the bullet that went into Gannon. It matched the gun that she used that was still in the house. The one she attributed to Quincy Brown using, or Eguardo using, or whatever story of the day it was.

Judgment, reflection, location of the gunshot wound.

Let's talk about Macon Ponder a little bit. As she drives to Florida, she checks in at about 12:22 in the morning, just after midnight, at Candlewood Suites, Pensacola, Florida. Why did they drive all the way from Decatur in one night to get to Florida? Why does she wanna get rid of Gannon's body in Florida? Gulf of Mexico. If you drive this bridge at night as Macon Ponder testified to there's no lights on it. We know that sometime between 4am and 5am she's out there.

Look at the location where the body was found.

Look at the space she has to park this vehicle.

Why does she park there when there's plenty of room?

Because she can. 4 in the morning, there's no traffic out there.

Does she think there's water underneath the bridge? Is that illogical thinking as you're crossing a bridge, and you can't see anything? You cross a main waterway, the Escambia River, and you continue going until you find a place to stop? She probably had to wait so that there was no traffic to throw the body.

Did she ever think the body was gonna be found again?

You see the suitcase under the bridge. It was clearly someone who dropped it directly over the bridge. There was an imprint. They dragged it under the bridge not knowing its contents. More importantly, not smelling anything. This is important because Harley didn't smell anything. The body had been there since February 4th in the Florida heat. They didn't smell anything until the suitcase was open. This lends credibility to Harley being unaware of the suitcase in the back of the van and not smelling anything.

When they dump it out, they see the most horrific thing anyone can ever see in their lives. Gannon's body in the foetal position, decomposed, wearing the same clothes he was wearing on 27th January 2020 when she killed him. The sweatpants with a white stripe. Watch the video when they leave. You'll see him wearing sweatpants with a white stripe.

Let's talk about the law. Think about her mental states and sanity as I talk about the timeline. The first instruction I have up is the elements of murder in the 1st degree after deliberation. Most of these elements are not in dispute. The defendant, time, place, and date not in dispute. Culpable mental state is in question. To cause the death of a person other than herself: Gannon. Not in dispute. The insanity defence is the issue in the case. After deliberation, not only intentionally, but also that the decision was made after reflection and judgment concerning the act. Never one committed in a hasty or impulsive manner.

Now, some of you before you came into court, had never seen this definition and you're probably thinking about premeditation where people are planning something out and takes days to plan out the murder and then they finally do the murder. That's not what that definition says. It's just enough time to have judgement and reflection, to make decisions, to go from grabbing a knife, to go from grabbing a blunt force object, to go from grabbing a gun—is she exercising judgment and reflection?

It doesn't have to be good judgement. It doesn't have to be bad judgment. It just has to be judgment.

Is she making a decision?

A person acts intentionally or with intent when her conscious objective is to cause a specific result prescribed by the statute defined in the offense. It is immaterial whether or not the result actually occurred. Did she intend to kill Gannon when she did what she did to him? I would suggest that's not in dispute either.

We can now go to the next crime, murder in the first degree of a child under the age of 12 and the defendant was in a position of trust. This is just another theory of first-degree murder under the law. The mental state and age of victim are different. She was his stepmom; she was obviously acting as Gannon's parent at the time she did this. When a person acts knowingly or wilfully in respect to conduct or to circumstance described by statute defining an offense when she is aware that her conduct is of such a nature or that such a circumstance exists; a person acts knowingly or wilfully in respect to a result of her conduct when she is aware that her conduct is practically certain to cause the result.

To stab someone 18 times, hit him over the head four times, shoot at him three times, striking him once I think you might have an idea of what the result might be.

Let's go to insanity. These words mean a lot. This is not something you'll find in the

DSM-5. This is a legal definition not a mental illness. The law presumes everyone to be sane. They gladly accept the burden of proof.

What does insanity mean? The defendant was insane at the time of the commission of the acts if she was so diseased and or defective in mind at the time of the commission of the act, as to be incapable of distinguishing right from wrong with respect to the act.

Care should be taken not to confuse mental disease or defect with moral obliquity, mental depravity, or passion growing out of anger. Passion growing out of anger. If you lose your temper, you don't get to claim insanity. Revenge, hatred, or other motives and kindred evil conditions because when an act is induced by any of these causes the person is accountable to the law. You can't lose your temper and come in and say, 'I lost my temper, I wasn't myself'. We are humans—we have emotions.

In addition, diseased or defective in mind does not refer to an abnormality manifested by only repeated criminal or otherwise antisocial conduct. We heard a little bit about anti-social personality disorder, someone with antisocial personality disorder can have fun killing people, they lie all the time, have no sympathy or empathy. Those people don't get to claim insanity. Mental disease/defect is a severely abnormal mental condition grossly and demonstrably impairs a person's perception or understanding of reality not due to drugs or alcohol.

Do you think Harley would notice if the defendant had a grossly and demonstrably mental condition?

Do you think Al Stauch might have noticed?

You've gotta demonstrate it right? It's not something you snap your fingers and go into a different personality.

What about her brother? You think he might have noticed it?

Let's talk about the doctors. Doctor Niederhauser was really the first doctor to see her on 5th December 2019, and the 13th December for 30 minutes each time. It was a clinical evaluation where she relies on what the patient says. Letecia claimed anxiety. She was treated for anxiety and diagnosed with general anxiety disorder. That's not a severe and abnormal mental condition that grossly and demonstrably impairs a person's perception or understanding of reality. We all experience that.

In fact, you got to see her experience that on video on 29th January 2020 during her interview, she had to call the paramedics. She had exceptionally good vital signs. Think she might have been faking that to get out of the setting? Doctor Niederhauser also tells us she had no history of inpatient psychiatric treatment, or any other diagnosis of mental illness. No evidence of psychosis.

If she was experiencing psychosis in December 2019 the doctor would have had an obligation to commit her. That would be a severe illness. The timing of that visit, December 2019 it was so she could get a letter because she didn't want to work anymore. The second interview Letecia said she wanted to get out of her contract, so she needed a letter.

What else happens right before Gannon is murdered? She goes on a cruise in January. You think that might have something to do with not wanting to go to work based on what you know about her and the statements she's made? Doctor Mohr, a jail psychologist, evaluates people who come in who are charged with serious crimes, perhaps their first time in a jail. They evaluate to see if they are a danger to themselves or to others. She said it was a psychological evaluation. It was a clinical evaluation. They also want to know if there's any medication they may need. Letecia says she has anxiety, she didn't do the crime, not gonna be a problem. That was 5th March 2020. Doctor Mohr spent a lot of time with her from then until January 2021. 20th March she checks in on Letecia because Gannon's body was found. Letecia says, 'I was never in Florida.' She doesn't claim Maria Sanchez did it or ask Doctor Mohr for help with DID. Nothing.

Doctor Mohr told you there was no evidence during the entire time she spent with her that she had DID or any other severe mental illness that meets that definition. This was a little over a month after the crime. She reviewed notes from deputies that said, 'I'm gonna start acting crazy'. On 5th June 2020 she enters a competency issue into the court.

You know she read the police report and discovery and then all of a sudden, 'I'm gonna start acting crazy'. Is there another defence? No DID. Certainly, no Maria Sanchez during her entire time or visits with Doctor Mohr for that entire year.

The first competency evaluation is done at state hospital; the prosecution does not choose where she goes, or which doctors do the evaluation. This first competency evaluation on 15th July 2020; they have a two-week observation period. Nurses, employees watch her. She goes to a nurse and says, 'can you tell when someone's faking it?' Doctor Torres and Doctor Gray do a forensic interview on 4th August 2020. This is forensic, not clinical. We're not just gonna listen to what she has to say. We're gonna look at collateral information. We're gonna call Al Stauch, try to call Harley, try to call family members. They want to see if they can corroborate what she tells them which is that she has bipolar disorder, is manic depressive, she rambles. That's her mental illness. Nothing about DID, which according to Doctor Lewis she's had since a very young age. Nothing about Maria Sanchez. Doctor Torres' testimony about the competency evaluations, one of the questions was about multiple personalities. Doctor Torres asked her if she had multiple personalities? This is 4th August 2020.

She was diagnosed with specified personality disorder with borderline and narcissistic features. Does it meet the definition of severe, grossly, demonstrably? We know by her actions and how other people perceive her. Doctor Torres told you it's not a severe mental disease or defect. It's not something that affects her everyday life or her ability to make decisions. No evidence of psychosis during that evaluation either. No history of inpatient treatment. MMPI2. Remember that test? What did that test tell us? She exaggerates psychiatric symptoms to the point that even people hospitalized for mental illness don't answer questions that way.

You think she might be faking it?

Now we go to the second competency evaluation with Doctor Grimmett. Her defence at the time requested a second opinion, prosecution had nothing to do with that. 22nd December 2020. Think about how it has progressed. Now she starts talking about DID and bipolar. She says she has four distinct personalities. None of the 4 were Maria Sanchez.

Doctor Grimmett testified that she was creating these names, and that Jasmine was a Disney character. She talked about vampires, and Twilight, she even cited the characters from that movie. Doctor Grimmett said, 'wait a minute here, this is not DID this is characters from a movie'. She evaluated her for it anyway because that's what she is telling her. She didn't need to rule it out, it's not there. She also diagnosed her with other specified personality disorder with borderline and narcissistic features.

Jump forward to February of 2022. Some point before she pled not guilty by reason of insanity (NGRI) on 11th February 2022, counsel spoke with Doctor Lewis. She recommended she change her plea to NGRI. You think that put a little pressure on her? You plead NGRI and then I'll do the evaluation. Why didn't she do the evaluation right away? Why did she wait until November?

Doctor Gray and Doctor Torres knew the facts of the case. Insanity evaluation is a much broader evaluation. You have to look at everything. They attempted to talk to Harley and family members to see what had been going on with her. Now the defendant is saying that she's not bipolar, she has created more personalities as part of DID. Is it a coincidence she had consulted with Doctor Lewis prior to all this and now Maria Sanchez comes to play?

They found there was no credible evidence to conclude she has a condition conforming to the definition of a mental disease or defect. That's powerful language, no credible evidence.

What's also interesting, compared to Doctor Lewis's evaluation, is that in the March interview it was the defendant talking. They just let her go. In June they asked more questions. Doctor Torres asked to talk to Maria. Letecia said Maria doesn't just come out, you need a triggering event. That is what the DSM-5 says. She can't just summon Maria, but you saw on Wednesday how that happened, and it was magic according to Doctor Lewis. No severe abnormal mental conditions, no psychosis, no bipolar, no DID. Just other specified personality disorder with BPD and NPD features. Conclusion – Letecia Stauch was not legally insane at the time of the crime.

Credibility instruction. You may believe all the testimony of the witness, part of it, or none of it. This applies to every witness who testifies, including Doctor Lewis.

Motive. You didn't see motive in the elements of first-degree murder, but you see it here. Money is a strong motivator. Having shows on HBO—strong motivator. Having your son videotape evaluations on a first-degree murder case that's gotten quite a bit of publicity for perhaps another documentary is motive. You can't do a documentary if you say, 'she's sane, sorry, I did what I could—she's acting'.

Also look at her demeanour and manner while testifying. She wouldn't answer any of my questions. She wouldn't answer my questions because she didn't want you to know the answers. She wanted you to know what she wanted to say. She shows up to court late. Talk about narcissistic tendencies.

Manner while testifying. I think it speaks for itself how she testified. Especially when you compare Doctor Torres. Obviously, she would disagree with my questions, remember how many times she said 'it depends'. She's not our expert. She just happens to be the expert the state hospital chose to come in and do a neutral evaluation.

The truth. Doctor Lewis didn't know the definition of insanity in the state of Colorado. The whole reason she came in to testify. I'm not even sure what her opinion is anymore based on your questions at the end. Remember how she answered it about the MRI and EEG that she withdrew? My opinion is ongoing. What does that mean? Does that tell you that her opinion that she was legally insane at the time counts for anything? When you think about her preliminary report, late, she said she needs more information to make a decision but that didn't happen. She hands over a report saying she finds her legally insane - literally all she says. She didn't get the information that she needed. She had a third MMPI2 test. The results were the same. Exaggerating psychiatric symptoms to the point people who are hospitalized for mental illnesses would not answer those questions that way. That didn't seem to matter to her.

Facts of the case. It's important to look at the defendant's actions before, during, and after she killed him. Starting with the video of Gannon's burns. 26th January, 9:46pm. Why is she videotaping an 11-year-old who has burns? More importantly why does she stop videotaping a little boy, Gannon, who has burns? You think it might be because Gannon said, 'I'm just worried about my burns?' Think that was the purpose of that video? Do you think that's using judgment, and reflection?

The hydrocodone. I can't stand here and tell you how that got into Gannon's system. All I can tell you is there's only one person there who could've given it to him. Did she give it to him because of the burns? I don't know. But when she gave it to him, do you think that she used judgment and reflection?

27th January, 4:36am the decision was made for her to text Ms Hicks about her stepfather being killed. Doctor Lewis wants you to believe the texts about the stepfather is somehow tied to the killing of Gannon. She just didn't want to go to work that day. Could it possibly be that she knew what she was gonna do when she said, 'and tomorrow', in the video? Shortly after that she calls Gannon's school and says he's not coming in today. And she texts Al saying she's going to make up an excuse to stay home, which she does, and she says Gannon's not going to school because of his stomach. Judgment? Reflection?

At 8:14am and 8:16am she takes a picture of Gannon in bed. Why? Why did she text it to Al? 'Look, Gannon's alive. He's here. He's sick. He's in bed'.

We heard Al Stauch testify a little bit about Gannon. He has ADHD, he's hyper. But still at 8:14am and 8:16am he's asleep. Think he might be lethargic from the hydrocodone? Think she wants to prove he's still alive because she knew how much hydrocodone she gave him? Does that make sense? At 9:54am, she texts Al from her phone that she left her phone at the house. You think that's an indication she knew what was gonna happen? Is it that farfetched to think she knows Gannon had been poisoned and that something might happen to Gannon?

At 10:12am they leave in Al's truck. What the heck is she doing taking a sick kid out to go shopping for dog clothes? Narcissistic tendencies.

2:20pm they return. They stopped for 39 seconds. What are they talking about in that truck? Doors open, you see the leg drop, Gannon beelines right through the garage. You see the defendant going after him.

At 2:26pm you see the defendant come out and move the Tiguan into the garage. What was the need at that moment to back that Tiguan into the garage? Then she looks around. This is when the murder happens. There's no activity on her phone. She attacks him with a knife, not good enough. He fought when he was born, he's fighting now. He was born 1 pound 6 ounces. He lived through that. She's coming after him. She goes to get a blunt force object to crush his skull. Then she shoots him. That may not sound like rational thinking but it's certainly thinking.

That's the before and during. Let's talk about after. She stuffs him in a suitcase, drags his body to the storage room. Opens the large green suitcase. Somehow manages to squeeze him in there. Gets the blankets off the bed, wraps him up in that. Pillows. Picks up the shell casings, does something with the knife. Does something with the blunt force object. She sticks him into the storage room and throws boxes on him.

At 3:11pm Al texts and asks if she's sleeping. No response.

Laina gets home 3:15pm, she doesn't let Laina in the house. She makes her stay outside because she's got work to do. She's gotta clean that bloody mess in that room. She's gotta hide evidence. She's gotta tamper with things. Gannon's dad texts him at 3:35pm, 'hey buddy', having no clue what she did to him. No response to that, no one read that until 7:40pm that evening. 6:27pm Letecia texts Al that Gannon isn't home from a friend's house. 6:55pm she calls 911.

How can she do this?

How can she talk to Gannon's father like nothing happened? Is that the traits of an antisocial personality disorder? That you can have no sympathy, so cold and callous, and act like nothing happened? And she does it through the whole day. She calls Landen on Gannon's phone a couple times that night. Is that a trait of ASPD? Landen gets a call from Gannon? She knows he's missing and it's her!

The next morning 28th January 2020 6:22am the Tiguan leaves for ten minutes. Is it beyond the realm of possibility to see if she's doing a practice run to see if anyone is watching her because she's about to move the body? She comes back and backs into the garage like she never does. Then they leave - the defendant and Gannon's body. They go to the airport, leave the house at 8:13am, get there at 8:30am. She's made the decision to rent another car before she even left the house. Is that evidence of psychosis or of thinking things through? Al gets off the airplane, he's just worried about Gannon. Where's my son? You think at that moment he cared she rented a car? But she made a big deal about it. She never searched for Gannon.

They go to the interview at Starbucks at 1:30pm. Afterwards, she takes the rental car and disappears. No one knows where she's at. We do, because of Life360. We got her going back to the airport at 4:41pm, because there is a parking ticket found. She went into the airport at 4:41pm. She left quickly. She didn't need another ticket. The Tiguan didn't leave. Is it that crazy to think she's checking on Gannon's body in the back of the Tiguan? Does that sound like someone who doesn't know right from wrong? Does that sound like someone who's trying to get away with something?

At some point that afternoon Al searches French Elementary School for the Tiguan. A critical point in the investigation. When the Tiguan is not there, he now knows that his wife had something to do with the disappearance of Gannon. He does a second interview with police that night and tells them about the rental car and missing Tiguan. 5:25pm on the 28th Letecia tells Al they need an attorney.

At 7pm, she returns to the airport, exits at 7:03pm in the Tiguan. She manipulates her own daughter, tells her not to talk to the police. If she's manipulating Harley, do you think she was also manipulating Gannon and Laina? That video? 'We have to sell stuff, so the owner of the house isn't upset with us.'

She goes to the S Curve in Palmer Lake at 9:23pm. She's there for at least 5 minutes. The board with Gannon's blood on it was found there in mid-February based the Life360 data. Why there? Well, she can't keep it in the Tiguan. Did she know right from wrong?

At 12am, Harley picks her up. They leave the Tiguan in the parking lot. Al and Detective Bethel are trying to get in touch with her.

The next morning, they drop off the Kia keys. Is that rational thinking? Someone who didn't wanna get caught?

At 10:25am, she texts Detective Bethel, 'I'm on my way'. It takes her over an hour and a half to get there. The car is washed. In the interview, she plants seeds. The suitcase is critical. Eduardo also took a suitcase when he took Gannon. She knows where the suitcase is up in Palmer Lake.

30th January, Letecia's family arrives—Brenda, Debra, and Dakota. They hire a Nissan in Denver, go to Extended Stay Suites hotel in Colorado Springs. The next morning, they hire a van to get their belongings. Her suitcase, including the one with Gannon's blood on it that was recovered in South Carolina—pretty strong evidence. After they load things up, the suitcase was not there because the police were checking everything. Dakota saw the suitcase and she said she had softball equipment in it.

At 12:10pm the KKTV interview - they play the interview audio with photos of the bloody room and the board under a tree and other pieces of evidence. Every time she says 'was' about Gannon, *WAS* flashes on the screen. It ends with the photo of the suitcase under the bridge.

Is that evidence she might have some antisocial traits? To calmly talk to a news reporter like that. Amanda VanNest who was supposed to do the SANE exam was able to get a doctor to place a mental health hold but saw no signs of it being necessary on the 29th.

The GPS tracker shows her right back at the S Curve. She picks up Gannon's body and puts him in the trunk of the Altima, leaves the board, gets more dog outfits, and goes back to the hotel. She puts the suitcase in the van. That had to happen because Dakota saw it come out of the van in the morning. Do you think he felt manipulated by this defendant? She drives across the country with Harley, use their little scheme to check in as one person. Rational thinking? Possibly antisocial personality traits. Get to Florida on the 4th February. Another divine intervention, the power-up at 4:36am in between the hotel and where Gannon was found. It tells you when she dumped Gannon's body.

I want to talk about pretext phone calls. Eduardo, immunity, Quincy Brown, the bike accident, Uncle Matt. 'I'm so sorry Al for lying to you, I'm gonna tell you the truth. He wasn't in the car when I left Petco', fake pregnant lady with cash laundering money. She's arrested 2nd March 2020, now it's Angel the babysitter. The suitcase is found with Gannon's blood and her searches on her phone.

What do people who are truly legally insane do? They act like nothing happened. They don't move the body. They may even do the crime when someone is watching them because they don't know it's wrong. Do you think she would have done this to Gannon if someone was in the room with her? Of course not. They also don't lie, no reason to. They come in and say things like they thought they heard the devil—they had no choice. That's a severe mental disease or defect. The capacity to form intent or use judgment and reflection. Of Mice and Men. George is the smart one Lenny has severe mental illnesses. He likes to pet rabbits and is so big he doesn't even know his own strength, so he would pet rabbits to the point he would kill them. That is someone who can't form the capacity to kill. Not someone who gets weapons to kill with.

There's only one right verdict in this case. That's guilty to every single crime she is charged with.

Mr Tolini begins his closing statement for the defence.

The one thing they cannot answer, because there is no answer is motive.

Motive for why it happened. Motive for how we go from this picture on a hike—loving, kind, to less than 24 hours later, brutal rage. 18 stab wounds, 4 blunt force traumas, and shot.

This wasn't a pre-planned, calculated, killing for some gain. This was a psychotic break, fuelled by rage, attacking a demon from the past. They can't come up with motive because there is no motive that makes sense, ladies and gentlemen.

They have tried. They have spent hundreds, if not thousands of hours, going through phones, iCloud accounts, Facebook messages, interviewed everyone to try to find some motive. None of what they have done in the biggest investigation in the history of El Paso County has produced a motive. No one has said she had a problem with Gannon, no one said she was mean to him, done anything wrong to him until that horrible day when this happens.

That is the strongest evidence, to know this was not premeditated murder. This was a psychotic break. That is the only thing that makes sense. Pull yourself back and peel back the layers of the anger over the act, the deceit, his body being driven to Florida, and look at this rationally, the only thing that makes sense is a psychotic break. No other rational explanation to understand why this happened.

She was a special needs teacher her entire life working with kids with special needs. A mother to Harley, she did everything she possibly could. She was a wife to Al, and tried to be the best stepmother she could be to these kids. So much so she was left with the kids for very long periods of time. When Al went to Alaska, he left his two kids in her care. He was about as far across the country as you can possibly get, and he felt comfortable enough leaving his kids with her alone in South Carolina because he knew her, and he saw the relationship she had with Gannon, and he felt comfortable.

He felt comfortable enough to leave to go to Oklahoma. They had a loving relationship together until the evidence shows she had a psychotic break, that some mental illness from her past, got triggered and there's a temporary period of psychosis. That's the only rational explanation that has been presented. There is nothing else they can come up with as far as motive.

Does it make sense that she may have Google searched moving to Florida? Yeah. People have problems in marriages, they fantasize about getting away. How would brutally murdering Gannon, how would stabbing him 18 different times facilitate that move? It wouldn't. There's no rational basis behind the murder other than psychosis. One Google search out of thousands, "I don't like my stepson", that's not what I see there in that picture or the days leading up to this horrible tragedy. It does indicate - looking at the timeframe and reliable evidence- that somehow that fire triggered her. Maybe some type of trigger that had been disassociated long ago but we have her starting to meltdown right after the fire.

Doctor Lewis used the term wacky a lot. When something seems irrational, when it doesn't make sense, we have to consider mental illness and possible psychosis. That video you heard, listen to the tenor of her voice and what she is saying. She says she's freaked out and she sounds freaked out. She's saying irrational stuff like we have to sell the sofa, stuff to Gannon that makes no sense. We also see mania starting to set in when you look at this timeline.

At 4:36am she is still up texting. Even Doctor Torres does not doubt or dispute the abuse in her childhood. She is not sleeping. She is manic. She is texting throughout the night. 11pm, 2am, 4:30am, 5am, 7:32am. She is up the entire night and not sleeping. There is something going on in her head that is not seeming right.

They end up at PetCo. Mr Young has insinuated this is some big, preconceived plan, that she'd made some decision early on that she's going to kill Gannon. Does that make any sense? If she had decided at that point early in the day when everybody else leaves, Harley's left for work, she is alone with Gannon. If she made the decision to brutally murder him, why is she taking him in the car to PetCo to buy valentine's day outfits for the dogs. This pushes back the timeline to right before Laina got home. It makes no sense.

Hydrocodone, be very careful when they try to put facts in their opinion that was not provided by witness testimony. There was hydrocodone. Doctor Ignacio did not say whether it was a dangerous or inappropriate level, she just said it came back positive. It's Mr Youngs opinion that this is an overdose of hydrocodone. No basis for a brutal attack on an 11-year-old boy. Something is going on in her mind, something is there losing it, and something horrible occurs in the basement that causes a brutal attack.

The brutality of the attack I would say is the strongest evidence in this entire case of a psychotic break. That type of violence wouldn't be needed to kill an 11-year-old boy. Gannon weighed 80, 85 pounds, Not the biggest 11-year-old kid or the strongest. Not seeing this type of brutal horrific rage to kill him. No other explanation other than the psychotic break.

Laina comes home and look on that video, Laina wasn't pushed outside. She came in the house for 10-15 minutes and then went outside on her bike. The idea that Laina wasn't allowed inside was a fantasy and Mr Young's opinion. Harley went down into the basement, she changed out of her uniform, before going to the dollar store. Nothing that kept them out of the house, nothing preplanned that would keep the information away from them.

They don't know what is going on in her head. Mr. Young is trying to introduce antisocial personality disorder (APD). It has to be either DID where she has put this memory of this brutal attack of what she did to Gannon someplace she doesn't have access to, or APD that she's some type of psychopath.

Mr Young tried to interject many times with Doctor Torres about APD and Doctor Torres was firm. No, she does not meet the criteria of APD. No past criminality. Other people with APD are unempathetic and don't care about other people. She was a special needs teacher for her entire career. That is not a psychopath with APD. That could be someone with DID or someone with BPD with disassociate feature that has kept trauma in her past behind her and is trying to make the lives of kids with special needs better for them. That is someone with empathy.

The strongest evidence of disassociation going on here, look at the body worn camera of the sheriffs when they come in that night looking for Gannon. The horrible brutal attack has happened there, Gannon is in the house in the suitcase, this has all been reasonably covered up. She's there with her daughter and Laina, acting and presenting herself to these police, laughing, joking, being incredibly friendly just after this had happened because at that point in time, she has disassociated the horrible act she has committed. There is no other logical explanation for how she is doing that.

Going back and looking at these timelines, what is really important is the fact she is not sleeping at all. For this entire time period, she is doing things or using her phone all night long. She is in a manic situation and her mind is not working. We heard Doctor Lewis talk about irrational things she's doing that don't make sense. It makes no sense for someone who has preplanned for whatever reason, whatever motive, to brutally kill Gannon to then report him missing right away and then in a matter of 3 days later go into the police with a completely illogical, incoherent story.

You heard from different witnesses, Ms Stauch has above average intelligence. A smart woman. To come up with the ridiculous story of Eduardo days later is not the actions of a sane rational person. Even children know if you keep saying different stories, you're not gonna be believed. There is no reason for the story changes. She's not even planning to pay Eduardo, he intended to fix the carpet for free. That he is in the garage, takes her to the basement and rapes her for an hour. He then takes Gannon in a suitcase and leaves the home. That is not someone who is sane and rational. It is illogical to believe that that kind of thing can be believed.

Her actions continue to be irrational. She keeps changing her story. She keeps giving different accounts. Gannon is placed in the suitcase, driven all the way to Florida. She goes through all kinds of places where people are not around, deserted areas, long areas of desolation. Many places where that suitcase could have been hidden and never found and she goes all the way to Pensacola and drops it off in a dry space under a bridge right near a major city. Not the actions of a rational person trying to hide evidence.

She's then in South Carolina, googling for face transplants near her. Like she's gonna pop up and get an entire face transplant to change the way she looks. Not the actions of a sane and rational person. She was delusional.

Listen to all the pretext phone calls with Al. Listen to how her voice and tenor changes between phone calls, how her emotions switch rapidly, and how her stories switch rapidly that no sane rational person of over intelligence could possibly expect anyone to believe. She is freaking out and delusional and delusional in the thought anyone will believe all the variations she's trying to sell them. None of that is rational. None of that makes sense.

So, why?

What was going on?

What preceded this?

It's gonna end up in the mental health experts. Doctor Lewis is 85 years old. She has been doing research, treating, evaluating people with serious mental illness for over 60 years. She is one of the foremost experts in the country on DID. She has been published in peer reviewed journals well over 100 times, things that educates other psychiatrists and doctors she has authored and produced. She has an HBO documentary made about her. They don't go just to quacks to do documentaries. They did a documentary on her because she was groundbreaking in her field.

She has consulted on other stuff because she knows more about this subject than almost anyone else in the country. With her age, some of the minute things in the discovery got lost in her memory. What she has is the decades of experience with this, dealing with people with severe mental illness who commit heinous acts. She has that experience to rely upon, and she had 14 hours of interviews with her, notes from family members and other types of things. In her expert opinion Letecia is legally insane. She wanted the EEG and MRI to know if there was also organic brain damage or brain trauma contributing to the mental illness, but she did not need them to make the diagnosis of DID which she was confident on.

Do not discount her decades of experience or her expertise. To think a woman who has pioneered this, made her life on this, been peer reviewed, is willing to throw that away to come down here and testify at a substantially reduced rate is ludicrous and insulting. They pay their experts just as we do. Both sides hire and pay experts; they are not money grabbing liars. They come and testify; they charge a fee. She reduced her normal fee to come down and help with Ms Stauch and do the evaluation and she told you Ms Stauch of the hundreds of mentally ill people she has ever dealt with is one of the most mentally ill people she has ever dealt with.

She's not endorsing Maria did this or how it happened, but that Ms Stauch has disassociated the memory of the homicide because she can't bear to deal with it. Ms Stauch accepting the idea she committed this brutal horrible homicide in the manner it was done, smashing that 11-year-old's head in, cannot deal with it. To accept that fact in her mind would crush her. Would crush her soul, would crush her identity, and so she has come up with all of these delusional fantasies trying to come up with some other thing that may have happened.

She was hoping and believing it was somebody other than her who did this. The facts, we don't dispute that it was her, but she was not in her right mind when she did it and you heard Doctor Lewis state that. Look at the evidence and realize that is the only reasonable rational conclusion as to how this horrible thing happened was a psychotic break. Look at Dakota, when he realized his sister actually did this, he knew there had to be some type of psychotic break, there was no other explanation. Doctor Torres, Doctor Gray, and Doctor Grimmett – all agree there is some type of mental illness, but they disagree on what the illness is. BPD is a significant mental illness right on the border from full blown psychosis and neurosis, most significant of all the personality disorders. It is so serious because there are such prominent features of psychosis that go along with it—people hallucinate, become delusional, become irrational. It can come and go in people with BPD according to the DSM, according to Doctor Torres, according to Doctor Grimmett, when people with BPD experience high stress.

Doctor Niederhauser proved she was experiencing high stress and anxiety causing her to be unable to perform at work. The stress was mounting. Look at her Google searches. Her stress in life was becoming overwhelming, she felt underappreciated, she felt like running away, she felt like leaving, she felt like it was all too much on her plate, that there was nobody there to help her.

We heard from Doctor Torres how people with BPD feel stress differently and are more stressed by things others wouldn't be. The same things, the type of trauma where one parent who was molesting you and one parent who wouldn't do a damn thing about it, can cause DID or BPD. They both come from the exact same environment that Doctor Torres said Ms Stauch grew up in.

Something Dakota said: we don't know all the intricacies of the trauma and the abuse Ms Stauch suffered but Dakota talked about was how when she would visit, she would leave him with knives to protect himself from something or someone. You can conclude that as a kid Ms Stauch either had to protect herself with knives or fantasized about protecting herself and you have the connection with Gannon being stabbed with a knife.

You can't discount the fact that Doctor Torres readily admitted BPD can be a serious mental illness. People with this disorder can suffer from psychosis, can become irrational, and they can disassociate - which explains all of the crazy cockamamie lies. It's a fantasy from Ms Stauch to try to explain this. Whether you call it BPD or DID, look at the facts and realize this must have been some kind of psychotic action because normal people, mentally healthy people, do not one day go on a hike, take smiling photos, and the next day stab a kid 18 times for no apparent reason.

Mr Young would like her to have antisocial personality disorder, because it takes insanity off the table. None of the evaluators ever diagnosed with APD. It is always considered at the state hospital, but she did not meet criteria. APD talk is a smokescreen. The only thing that explains her conduct afterward is disassociation.

Mr Young would like you to believe the only time someone is legally insane is if they commit the crime and sit there saying yup it was me I did it for these reasons. Doctor Torres and the jury instructions from the court state someone cannot know right from wrong but still understand their conduct was criminal when it occurred. The covering up of a murder does not preclude insanity.

You have all the evidence. We are asking you to find her not guilty by reason of insanity. We're not saying set her free or don't hold her responsible. You've seen how it is at CMHIP - she is shackled fully, constraints, a locked facility. There are repercussions, but also treatment for the mental illness she has suffered from her entire life.

The other thing that is important is the burden of proof. Have they presented enough evidence before you that you can say without a doubt there's no way psychosis was involved here? I would put before you with all the different doctor's diagnosing her with some serious mental health illness, with their witnesses diagnosing her with a mental illness with transient periods of psychosis, with psychosis appearing to be the only rational reason and irrational behaviour afterwards, it all points to mental illness and in no way shape or form have they disproven that and it is their burden. If you believe it is possible this occurred in a state of psychosis, your legal duty is to find her not guilty by reason of insanity and that is what we are asking you to do.

Thank you.

Mr Allen begins rebuttal for the prosecution.

Ladies and gentlemen, the only fantasy in this courtroom is that this defendant, this stepmother who killed Gannon, had psychosis, that she was insane, on the 27th January 2020. That is the only fantasy that has been brought out into this courtroom.

They want to talk to you about motive. One thing the judge didn't read in the instructions is anything about motive. It's not an element of a single crime under Colorado code. We don't have to prove motive, and yet we did anyway.

This defendant hated Gannon. We know that because she searched it. 'I hate my stepson'. She has one stepson and she hated him. She was planning to leave Al Stauch and move back to the east coast. She wanted to hurt Al. She wanted to hurt Landen for that matter. She did, to the core. They will never recover from what she did to them, ever, and you know that. This was no snap in time, no instantaneous thing. This occurred over days.

She was planning to leave a week prior to Gannon's death when she killed him. Look at the searches. We know when she was looking to leave, we know she hated Gannon, we know she wanted out of a marriage with Al, we know she didn't like what Landen was up to because she would manipulate Gannon about Landen. We know this because of the evidence that we brought you. It proves motive.

Why did Al leave Gannon with the defendant on that weekend? Why would he leave and go to Oklahoma for two weeks of training if he knew there was a problem with the defendant? From psychosis? Al told you he would not have gone if he had seen some problem with the defendant. He said he would not have gone, and he did anyway, because she doesn't have psychosis. He never saw a single sign from her. What he didn't know unfortunately, he couldn't see into her heart. He couldn't see the hatred that she had for Gannon. The motive she had to leave and to hurt him to the core. He didn't know that it was all about her even though he had lived with her for some number of years. The defence wants you to speculate that the fire set off some sort of a trigger. You can't speculate, it's in the instructions and yet they're inviting you to speculate. Why would they invite you to speculate when they're talking about an 11-year-old boy who was brutally murdered? Because they want you to ignore the evidence that was brought into this courtroom. They want you to ignore this evidence and speculate on the other hand. You can't do it.

Saying she's freaked out in that phone call. Acting like she's freaked out. We all get freaked out sometimes. As Mr Young said, we're human. If you drive down the highway and see an accident you might freak out. You might have some rush of adrenaline and it kinda messes you up a little bit, that's human. Not psychosis. Further, that freaking out that she's supposedly doing is her acting. It's not psychosis. It's all about Letecia. It's all about this woman who murdered Gannon. Throughout the whole thing. The text to the school, to Leslie Hicks, that morning the 27th January. They want you to speculate again that that's some sort of a trigger. You know what it is. It's an unassailable excuse. You tell your employer that your stepfather, a member of your family, has just died in a tragic car accident, no employer's gonna make you come into work that day. She needed an unassailable excuse to not go to work. Because she knew what was happening later that day. She knew Gannon was done that day. That's why she calls Gannon out of school later. The timelines that we brought to you on Monday, her internet searches, tell you everything you need to know about her mental condition. She was calculating, manipulating, lying to everyone. Why? Because it's about her. Not about Gannon. Deflect the blame and make herself the victim.

Does it ever make sense when somebody kills another person? Can it ever truly make sense? Can it ever truly make sense when a parent kills a child? The answer to that is no. None of us in this courtroom, except one, has killed a child. That doesn't make it a psychotic act. That doesn't mean somebody's insane. Unfortunately, way too many people kill kids in this country. Why do they do it? Who knows. But it's not psychosis when this one did it.

Be very careful when people introduce facts. Mr Tolini got up here and wanted to introduce facts to you, inviting you to speculate. Be very careful about that. He tries to brush away the effect of the hydrocodone that was found in Gannon's system. First of all, Gannon should not have had hydrocodone in his system. Doctor Ignacio told you about that. It's not typically given to 11-year-old little boys. It's an opioid. It can cause people to get sluggish, lethargic, can lead to coma, can stop you from breathing, and can kill you. All of those things that hydrocodone, an opioid, can do to you, this woman did to Gannon. Why? Because she wanted to kill him.

Mr Tolini brought up the idea that the brutality itself proves psychosis. Is that true? Does the brutality itself prove psychosis from this defendant? The evidence has the answer for you. The defendant's own actions has the answer for you. The brutality of it speaks to the abject hatred she had for Gannon. And the pure determination she had to kill Gannon. This didn't start in one snap moment. When did this start? Sunday night. Sunday night with the candle. The candle incident that makes no sense according to the way that she describes it to people because she wants to make it Gannon's fault. Does that make sense? Mr Stauch told you the answer to that question. Harley told you the answer to that question. Gannon didn't play with fire. He would never go downstairs and just light candles randomly. He had a long history of having stomach issues where he'd get backed up and then have issues with it. And yet this day he poops himself and so he's gotta go burn a candle to mask the smell even though he'd never done it any other time in his entire life? Does that make sense? Or does it make more sense that this defendant burnt him?

That's the start of the attack, ladies and gentlemen. Sunday night. And it continues with the hydrocodone, a prescription for a full-grown man, is given to Gannon. That goes into the morning time. That's why he's lethargic. He can't get out of bed early like he normally would. He's walking slowly to the pickup truck at about 10:15 in the morning when they leave the house because he's under the influence of hydrocodone and then she drives him around, leaving him in the car. He's probably passed out in the car. It doesn't make any sense to leave an 11-year-old boy in a car unless there's something wrong. Something that she did to him. And this picture from Garden of the Gods, these two pictures that she sends Al Stauch that morning of Gannon in bed? Mr Tolini again is inviting you to speculate as to the reason for those pictures saying she's just a loving stepmother. What are those pictures? Think about that picture from Garden of the Gods in relation to the picture that she sends Al Stauch. They're proof of life pictures. They're pictures that she is sending out to prove to the world that she had nothing to do with what she's about to do. Why would she send pictures of Gannon in bed to Al Stauch except for a proof of life picture? A way to cover her tracks. And it starts early, right?

They want you to think this was some sort of a temporary snap. They said it on opening statements when Mr Cook dramatically walks out of the courtroom and says this is way too bad, we can't handle this, it's a crack in her psychosis, and then we hear it again today from Mr Tolini.

First of all, temporary insanity is not what our insanity statute is in the state of Colorado. Look at it. That does not apply here. Second of all, there's not a temporary insanity moment in this case. It starts from Sunday night and goes all the way through Monday evening. Almost 24 hours of horror that Gannon had to suffer at the hands of this defendant. What should have been the safest place in the world for Gannon to be.

People who live by stories, by telling tall tales, don't stop. Why would she stop doing that once this case started if she'd been getting away with it her entire life? Think about the manipulation that she carried out on everybody else in her life. Al told you about the manipulation. Everything this woman did in her life was manipulation, to cause chaos, to make her the victim and the focus of everything. Every single thing.

Harley didn't know how her own father died because she was lied to by this defendant. Why would she stop lying when the biggest thing that she's ever caused in her life is being drilled into by an investigation that is the biggest El Paso County has ever seen? That involves the FBI. That's who she is. She's a storyteller. Telling fantastic stories is not psychosis, it's who she is.

She starts looking up face transplant surgery centres. She says I need a new social security number. I need a marriage license; I need a replacement passport because El Paso County Sheriff's Office has mine. And she looks up fake polygraph. Why in the world would you need a fake polygraph unless you're covering your tracks, to have some sort of thing that you can anchor a legitimate story to that you didn't have anything to do with it. With this case. Why? Who thinks of that stuff except for people like this? I would venture to guess that not a single one of us in this room ever even knew a fake polygraph website existed before now. I know I didn't.

Let's talk a little bit about Doctor Lewis. She might be a world-renowned expert. She's the only expert that they could find to bring in here to tell you that this defendant had dissociative identity disorder. Not a single other doctor that testified here in this courtroom saw a single shred of evidence that she had dissociative identity disorder. Not a single one. And yet this doctor comes in and says she does have it. This doctor comes in and says she does have it and yet she doesn't even know what the definition of insanity in Colorado is. She starts throwing around words like McNaughten and other things that might apply in other states and she said sanity could depend on where you are, what state you're in, that kind of thing. Don't you think if she's gonna come in and tell you as an expert, this defendant is insane according to Colorado law, she should know what Colorado law is? And she couldn't do it. There were a lot of I assumes, I don't knows, deflections, stories about other cases. Any time she was pressed to justify her opinion she couldn't do it. You saw Doctor Torres in contrast to that. She could point to specific things about her evaluation of the defendant. Compare the two.

The instructions that you got from the judge are your roadmap for this case. They help you determine what the law is, and you're expected to follow the law. You apply that law to the facts in the case, to the evidence that's been piling up over the last several weeks. The presumption of innocence absolutely applies in every single criminal case. It applies in this case. Until you are determined that the charges have been proven beyond a reasonable doubt, she has the presumption of innocence.

We have the burden of proof. This system doesn't work if you don't hold us to our burden of proof. We expect you to hold us to our burden of proof. We welcome you to hold us to our burden of proof. Mr Tolini talked about proving it without a doubt. Proving this case without a doubt. You'll never see words like that in any jury instruction in the state of Colorado or in the United States. We don't have to prove cases beyond all doubt. We have to prove things beyond a reasonable doubt because this is after all a human function.

Nobody can ever prove anything 100%. Johnny Cochran after the OJ Simpson, in closing for the OJ Simpson case, if it doesn't fit you must acquit. What he's talking about is our burden of proof and he was absolutely right. If a case is not proven beyond a reasonable doubt, your jobs as jurors according to these jury instructions is to find a defendant not guilty and we expect you to do that. If we didn't prove the case, then hold us accountable and find her not guilty.

But if we did prove the case beyond a reasonable doubt, the jury instructions are also very clear on that. If we have proven the case beyond a reasonable doubt, the jury instructions tell you that you should find her guilty. If the crimes fit, you should convict! That's what the jury instructions say and that's the other side of the coin from Johnny Cochran's comment. If the crimes fit this defendant, convict her.

Deliberations are up to you. When you get back into the deliberation room, you get to control how that deliberation goes. The only requirements are that you all have to be together when deliberations are happening. You have to do it in the jury room. But you can take as long as you want, and you can be as fast as you want to come to a conviction or to a decision. Nobody's ever gonna second guess you if you take two weeks or ten minutes. It's up to you.

You should be able to find this defendant guilty based on the evidence. Not from what I say, or from what Mr Young says, or find her not guilty because Mr Tolini and Mr Cook say so. The evidence must guide you.

Let's talk about that question of sanity. That so diseased or defective in mind to be incapable of distinguishing right from wrong. Can this defendant distinguish right from wrong? The evidence and her actions tell you that she can. Why do all the things she did if she didn't know what she had done was wrong. Or if she suffered from a condition of mind caused by mental disease or defect that prevented her from forming a culpable mental state.

What is evidence of that culpable mental state? As Mr Young said it's in Gannon. It's on Gannon's body. The evidence that Gannon's body provides you, the story that that tells, about what she did, shows she has the ability and had the ability to form the appropriate culpable mental state. You don't stab an 11-year-old 18 times, 11 of which are on his arms and hands, as he's defending himself, unless you intend to kill him.

You don't then dispose of that knife that's never been recovered and hit him over the head with such viciousness four separate times that it cracks his skull open unless you intend to kill him. And that blunt force object is also never found. And then you don't retrieve a handgun, a 9mm handgun and squeeze that trigger three intentional times, hitting Gannon one time, unless you intend to kill him. That's exactly what this defendant did and that's how you know she can form the appropriate culpable mental state.

This woman doesn't have a diseased mind. She has no psychosis. Multiple doctors and longtime family friends and family members answered the question of psychosis for you. This defendant knew then, and knows today, the difference between right and wrong. Harley said it, Dakota Lowry said it, Al Stauch said it. Every single person that knew her knew she knew the difference between right and wrong. She was of sound mind and formed the culpable mental states required.

You learned about DID from at least two different doctors in this case. Extremely rare. Prevalence in society is roughly 1.4% but, most importantly, it's marked by severe behavioural health symptoms that would be noticeable by others. Other people like Harley Hunt, her daughter who lived with her every day of her life. Al Stauch, who was married to her for five years. Dakota Lowry who was her younger brother. These people would've noticed that she had something wrong with her. The forensic nurse examiner Amanda Van Nest at the hospital would have noticed it. This is two days after Gannon is murdered and the defendant fakes that panic attack in the sheriff's office and is taken to the hospital and given the opportunity to be examined for this supposed rape story that she had. And she splits.

Amanda Van Nest told you that she's dealt with people with severe mental health disorders. She's told you what happens when she deals with people like that. Called an M1 hold. An emergency situation where you put somebody in care for a period of time because they're a danger to themself or to others. Amanda Van Nest saw no signs that this defendant was anywhere close to justifying an M1 hold on 29th January. Doctor Niederhauser, about a month before Gannon was killed, the last medical professional to see the defendant before Gannon was killed. Also familiar with an M1 hold and saw no signs that would justify holding her against her will because she was a danger to herself or others. Because she wasn't. She didn't have psychosis.

Why blame others?

First, it's Gannon's fault, right? He pooped all over himself, started a fire, he's experimenting with drugs. Isn't that convenient that he's experimenting with drugs, he's curious about bath salts, and there's a Swisher Sweet planted in his backpack and he's got hydrocodone in his system. Isn't that convenient? Isn't that convenient concoction from this defendant?

Then she says he went to a friend's house and didn't come home. Is it because he loved his mom too much? He was a momma's boy. Is that the source of her hatred for Gannon? She knew she could never replace the love that Gannon had for Landen.

Then she concocts Eguardo/Eduardo, some random Mexican guy that works at the housing development. Just gives him access to the house through the garage code, he comes in to fix the carpet but in addition to fixing the carpet he rapes her. Bangs her head on the floor, no sign of injury on her. He curiously asked for boxes and a suitcase. Why did she have to introduce the suitcase? She had to explain away why Gannon was gonna be found in the suitcase she put him in. A suitcase that Al Stauch recognized when he was shown the picture. A suitcase that Dakota Lowry recognized this defendant struggling with before she drives off to Florida. She had to explain it away.

Next, it's Quincy Brown's fault. You heard special agent Jonathan Grusing, he talked about how he wishes he would've pushed her more on the Quincy Brown and let her expand on that character because this is the character she gave the most information about. He's a real guy. A guy that was published in the media. The most wanted people in El Paso County for sex offenses. Perfect fall guy for what this woman did.

She replaces Eguardo as the rapist, knew his name when his ID fell out conveniently and landed on the floor in front of her.

Then he turns into a guy up in Northern El Paso County selling a bike, or he's lying in the road as they're driving and gets into the car and forces them to come back home and he rapes her there. Or Gannon's test riding a bike, crashes, hits his head and then he takes off with Gannon.

Uncle Matt, the least descriptive person in any story this defendant had probably ever told. Boy she can tell some stories, can't she? Somehow Gannon knew him, and he was involved but we don't really know how.

And then it's the pregnant lady with the cash baby. Supposedly 8 months pregnant, involved with money laundering for Mexican restaurants. She gets into the car, starts pulling money out of her belly. Somehow, she's involved with what happened to Gannon. Pointing outwards, right? Pointing any way except for her. Except that in each one of these stories the blame for Gannon's disappearance is someone else and she's the victim in every single one of these stories. Figuring out a way to cast blame elsewhere and situate herself as the victim as to what happened.

It's a very calculated move.

Every single time she does it, she's doing it to explain away why pieces of evidence are found in the case. She knows about the suitcase that's gonna be found. She notices that we're searching up northern El Paso County, southern Douglas County, where the board is found. That's when the bike story comes in with Quincy Brown up in that area. She's gotta explain away why her GPS is gonna show her up in the area. Just up there innocently looking for a bike. But Gannon's blood is gonna be found up there, gotta explain it away.

It's Landen's fault. This is the most cruel of all right. That somehow Landen is responsible for Gannon because of her ex-husband? That somehow Landen is involved with Gannon ending up in Mexico? Why would she introduce the word Mexico? Because by the time she's saying this she's already pitched Gannon over that bridge in Florida thinking it's pitched over the Escambia River that flows out the bay and into the Gulf of Mexico.

It's Al's fault. It's his fault that Gannon is gone, and he should be investigated. Somehow, he contaminated the scene. Another cruel twist of the knife. Going after the people that Gannon loved the most and who loved him the most shows you the hatred that she had for these people. The hatred that she had for Gannon. And how she's going to use Gannon's horrific demise against the people that loved him the most.

Her stepfather, James, supposedly sexually assaulted her as a kid. It's his fault that she's the way she is. Except there's not a shred of evidence from anybody until she starts raising competency that there's any sort of ill harm by James. She never reports it to a single person for over 20 years and yet that's the trigger. Does that make sense?

It's a caped invader's fault. That's the last one, right? Standing on top of the bed wearing a cape. She then realizes it's Gannon, but she shoots him and stabs him and does all these other things to cover up for whatever. Does that make any sense or is this just another concoction? Another way to point outwards on blame and show herself as the victim.

And when she realizes those external sources aren't working, Doctor Dorothy Lewis comes into play. Before she looks at a shred of evidence in February of 2022, she's already said yeah you need to go with not guilty by reason of insanity. Dissociative identity disorder is the answer. She doesn't know a single thing about this case or this defendant in February of 2022. And so, what does this defendant do but start creating names? There's Taylor, Harmony, Christina, Jasmine—the frisky princess, little Lucia, and Maria Sanchez—the Spanish speaking Russian sniper who knows how to kill, kill, kill.

One thing we do know from this evidence, this defendant knows how to kill. Knows how to kill a defenceless little boy in his bed.

There's better words to describe this defendant and what she did. Unreliable. Every person that she's ever interacted with in her life can tell you that she's unreliable. That she tells tall tales. She hated Gannon. We know that because of the injuries that Gannon suffered. We know that she hated Landen and Al. Why take away their little boy the way she did and concoct the stories she did unless she hated them just as much as she hated Gannon?

She planned this. A week before Gannon goes missing, she's already looking at renting a U-Haul and places to live in Florida. Sometime prior to Gannon's death she searches 'I hate my stepson'. She premeditated this thing. We know that from the proof of life photos. Those two pictures that she sends to Al on the morning of 27th January. She's setting up her excuse. Portraying Gannon as experimenting with drugs when she knows that she's drugging him with hydrocodone.

She burned him on Sunday night when this all starts. Gannon didn't play with fire. He's not gonna intentionally burn himself. In that first story about the candle incident, she talks about taking the kids outside and having to go downstairs to get Gannon and they all pile in the truck and drive off. That never happened. This was just a story that she had to explain away because the fire didn't work. Gannon didn't die from the fire. Then, she poisoned him with the hydrocodone. That didn't work.

Remember Gannon was a fighter. 1 pound 6 ounce little boy when he was born. He overcame all the odds. He couldn't overcome this one, but he sure did try, didn't he? She attacked him, stabbing him 18 times. Like I said most of those are on his arms and hands because he's fighting back. She beat him over the head four times with some blunt object that's never found, cracking his skull like an eggshell. She shot him in the jaw, severing his spine and likely killing him instantaneously. She then manipulated the heck out of this investigation with her stories. Her stories and manipulations of this investigation caused it to be the biggest investigation in El Paso County History. We heard that from several different investigators involved in this case and it stretched from Colorado Springs all the way to Myrtle Beach, South Carolina.

She hid Gannon's broken, dead body in a suitcase in that storage room, she ran from cops when the circle was tightening. Remember that trip to Marshalls when the cops are going there to get cell phones and get the car that belonged to Harley? When they encounter her in the parking lot, she takes off running as soon as she sees those guys, she takes off running. Throws the keys across the parking lot, starts yelling at Harley, 'don't say anything'.

Why?

If she didn't know she had done something wrong, why?

Then she fled to Florida and then eventually South Carolina. To get as far away from this thing as she possibly could. That's why she's wanting to get a replacement passport, so she can escape the country.

She dumped Gannon's body over the bridge. Mr Young talked about this. Think about how divine intervention plays a part here. If Macon Ponder had been at that bridge a month and a half before then, Gannon's body doesn't get found for at least two years - if ever.

She murdered Gannon. On the 27th January 2020, she murdered Gannon. This little boy deserved so much more out of this defendant. He deserved protection, he deserved to live, he deserved to grow up and become a young man and someday have a family of his own. She took it all away.

Mr Allen plays the 911 call and non-emergency call Letecia made. It ends with Letecia being asked who the last person to see Gannon was. 'Uh, I guess me?'

Ladies and gentlemen, you're gonna go back into that deliberation room and start deliberating. Gannon deserves justice. This defendant deserves to be convicted based on the evidence that was presented in this case.

Gannon Jacob Stauch, 11 years old.

Find the defendant guilty of murder in the first degree after deliberation. Murder in the first degree, child under 12 in a position of trust. Tampering with a deceased human body and tampering with physical evidence.

Gannon deserves it. He deserves all the justice that you can give him.

Thank you.

The 12 main jury members take their final instructions and head into the deliberation room. The 5 alternates are released.

And now we wait.

CHAPTER 22

LETECIA STAUCH TRIAL – DAY 21 – VERDICT TUESDAY - 9TH MAY 2023

The jury has reached a verdict after deliberating for around 8 hours in total.

Letecia sat motionless as Judge Werner read out each of the charges followed by the jury's verdicts.

Count 1 – charge of murder in the first degree after deliberation we the jury find the defendant Letecia Stauch – **GUILTY**.

Count 2 – charge of murder in the first degree of a child under 12 by a person in a position of trust, we the jury find the defendant Letecia Stauch – **GUILTY**.

Count 3 – charge of tampering with a deceased human body, we the jury find the defendant Letecia Stauch – **GUILTY**.

Count 4 – charge of tampering with physical evidence, we the jury find the defendant Letecia Stauch – **GUILTY**.

The judge thanked the jury for their service and then released them from service.

Judge Werner said he needed at least 30 minutes before sentencing if that was what everybody wanted. The prosecution and the defence agreed they were more than ready for sentencing to go ahead.

After a short break victim impact statements were read out.

Nicole Mobley is the first person to make a statement. She thanks the judge and the prosecution on behalf of all the people who searched for Gannon.

Janey Cadenas also thanks judge Werner for making it such a fair and neutral trial. I have sat with the family for the last three years as a community member in Lorson Ranch watched the turmoil this has caused everybody in our community. We rallied together three years ago in a way most communities could never imagine. We did everything we could to find him because Gannon wasn't just a neighbour, he was everyone's little boy.

The entire community became afraid their own children could be next. I can confidently say this is the worst tragedy anyone could go through and every parent's nightmare. Justice has finally been served for Gannon.

Jeff Davenport, Gannon's great uncle, Al's uncle, tells how he has personal memories of the wonderful loving young man Gannon was. He wants to talk about the breadth of impact. The preciousness of an 11-year-olds life is beyond measure. This now convicted murderer did not just murder Gannon. She murdered all of the love and joy and encouragement and security he would have brought to everyone he encountered. She murdered his children and grandchildren. His prom, his career, his marriage, his retirement, his golden years, and it just goes on and on.

Because of her crime, all of our fragile trust in each other had been further eroded. It's not an exaggeration to say that millions of people throughout the world have heard of this crime and will become more suspicious of those who care for their children even if they have done it for years. Those who are truly mentally ill may receive more suspicion and may not receive the help they need.

The reverberations of her murder of Gannon will ripple throughout eternity and the impact of her crime is truly incalculable.

Veronica Birkenstock, Gannon's great aunt, Landon's aunt, says nothing in life prepares you for the murder of a child.

No one ever thinks this can happen to your family. Three years ago, I got that call and I have not left Landen's side for three years, even to all those hearings the defendant decided not to come to because she didn't think it was important.

As a Christian I must forgive even though I do not want to. God is the ultimate judge. I pray today that Judge Werner will give her what she deserves on this earth and will let God do the rest for eternity. I don't know if it's appropriate or not, but I would like to leave this Bible and ask that if you think it's okay, that it can be given to Letecia. I have sat here for six weeks and listened to the horrendous things she did to my nephew. I don't want the last memory of him to be what she did to him.

Our last memory of Gannon was one of fun, love, joy.

So articulate and, despite everything, he was gifted and talented. He wasn't supposed to live, the day he was born the doctors told us her had no chance. For months I saw Al and Landen pray over their baby.

One of the happiest days was the day he got to come home. He fought so hard to get there. His 11 years did have impact. I want us to remember who Gannon was, not what this evil deed did to his memory. He is our hero and will always be our hero.

Letecia tried to steal many things from my niece. She called her a drug addict. She called her homeless when she was in the hospital having her third child. She was there for months and months trying to save her life and her baby. She wasn't homeless. Landen is a good mother, and she loved her children. She loved Gannon and her only son was taken away by someone who was just ferociously jealous of my niece.

With all that said I pray you will give her a sentence she deserves, but also that God will forgive her if she repents for her evil ways.

Bob Rogers. He and his wife Patty are Laina and Gannon's grandparents. They never had the opportunity to meet Gannon in person. Laina is a beautiful child. She sings beautifully, she's talented. What she doesn't have is an older brother to stand beside her as she goes through her life. She still mentions Gannon quite often. We never want the spirit or memory of Gannon to be lost. I'm at a loss for words.

Deborah Pearce, Gannon's grandmother. She thanks judge Werner and everyone who has so carefully and impartially cared for this case and the loss of this precious child. I feel that if Gannon was here, he would say, 'Please protect my family and be concerned from the loss that they've had. Please take care of my family and make sure they're protected as time goes on and as life goes on'.

Landen Bullard, Gannon's mother. I miss you Gannon and I love you to the moon and back and back again. I know that every day you are with me and your sisters but that will never take away the ache that I have for you - to hold you, to hug you, to tell you how much I love you, and to see your smile and your innocence.

I remember all the pain your dad and I suffered with having children. It was never easy, and we were always fearful through the process. On 29th September 2008 our lives were forever changed. Our first biggest blessing came into the world weighing only one pound and six ounces. You fought all the odds and developed a personality and a smile that's larger than life. You become my hero that day. You forever changed my heart and my life and that will never change.

That is something that can never be taken away from me.

You came into this world fighting, and unfortunately, you left this world fighting. Your honour he fought against someone that he loved and trusted. Someone that myself and Albert both trusted and loved. Someone who could never understand what it means to love or trust anyone but herself.

For more than three agonizing years I've often wondered what I may say or if I would even be able to. For three years I have questioned every single possibility and scenario. For three years I have tried to forgive you, but I can't. I want to but no parent should have to bury their child. No parent should have to see or hear the horrific things you have done.

To the whole family, she has taken away the most precious gift in this world. Not just my family, not Al's family, but your own family. She destroyed dozens of lives, lives of people who never wanted to believe that she could have done this. She knew how special Gannon was and she knew what meant the most to me.

I in my heart can never understand her hatred and insecurities when it came to me. I did love her. Mother to mother I trusted her with my children while trying to survive a complicated life with my third child and she used every opportunity to write a narrative of my life to again to try to take pieces of my life when she already took some of it. That still wasn't enough. She searched so hard for love when all along she had it, but she took it for granted.

I didn't hold anger against her then. I still kept my heart open to her. She had so much love from Laina and Gannon. From Harley, her own daughter, that you willingly subjected to the chance of serving time for your crimes. Such an indicator of your inability to love anyone but yourself.

You had support, appreciation from me even when we couldn't see eye to eye because I valued you for helping me with our children when I physically couldn't. Even as I was fighting for my kids, and you wrote a false smear campaign against me and my children and also Al. For me, I still appreciated that they were loved by you - so I thought. You had everyone fooled. You projected abuse and addiction claims against all of us. Not just me. When all along you was the one harming innocent children. Anything to take the light off. Manipulating us, breaking my kids, and murdering my son.

I can't say that you ruined my life because that will be some form of sick victory for you because even through this process it's been a game for you. The people who listened don't know her style or her sly jabs she's even made at Albert and I. They don't know the significance of certain things she says or does. But we do. Instead of allowing her to take that power of hurting me further I wanted to tell you this. Let me tell you what Gannon has done, even to this day. Even after you murdered him and tried to taint any positive image of him. He has caused families and communities to come together, children and adults have given their life to Christ. He has called unity in times of trial. He is a hero.

She even tried to steal that away. A cape, huh? The one image of Gannon that was created for the world after it went on national TV begging for the return of my son. How dare you. How truly sick and cruel are you.

You stole so much from this world. Gannon's cousins, aunts, cousins, sisters, new siblings, grandparents, and friends are missing a huge portion of their lives without Gannon. Laina is missing her brother. Your honour I've never seen a bond between two siblings so close as theirs and she had to take that.

Why? I'm afraid we may never know that answer, will we?

I show his baby sister, Novah, pictures and videos of Gannon so she will always remember who he is because she stole him from us. He is not forgotten and never will be and it's so sad to face her - a person even Gannon loved. One that I know while she was attacking and killing him and fought for his life, he defended himself against her still loving her. A love she never deserved from him for what she has done. While she is too much of a coward to even come forward with the truth, she owes it to Gannon. But the lack of remorse and the lack of respect to Gannon through this trial, her lack of compassion shows me that we were all wrong.

She manipulated all of us and never loved Gannon, Laina, or Harley. I've sat here for over a month having to listen to her sick lies even as she tried to destroy who I was and Albert as a father. I've had to sit and listen and watch every reenactment of images no one wants left in their mind. You wanted to leave us with that knowing it would torture us. But you underestimated me. I am Landen. Gannon's mom. And that will never change.

Through my hurt, anger, and pain, I will never be the monster that she is. I can never be filled with the hate that her heart holds. I pray that we will never have to look at her face again. I will continue to hold onto my faith. Vengeance is not mine as I surely wish at some times but it's the Lord's. I have to trust in that.

Thank you, Judge Werner, for your compassion, your patience through this trial. I wanna thank the jury for their attentiveness and time they took for justice for my boy. To the detectives, officers, legal team for every single second they've poured out into Gannon's case. And to the community for your countless hours. Tecia, that was your biggest mistake. You underestimated this community and this defensive team. Lorson Ranch—they searched and fought for Gannon within hours, and they never believed your lies. From the moment they started. None of these people ever gave up on him. You never looked. All of these people I will forever hold close to my heart. Always Gannon Strong. My G-man forever. Justice has been served today.

Your honour, I pray that you just give her the best sentencing, the longest sentencing, you can. This will not bring my son back, but I can sleep soundly for the first time in three years knowing that this defendant can never harm anyone again. Knowing Gannon will always be a true hero in a cape. He will always be my son. That will never be taken away.

A recording of Gannon singing is played to the court.

Al Stauch, Gannon's father. I'm gonna start with something from my wife. Not to go out of order, but she didn't think she could make it through it, so. This is my wife, Melissa and these are her words.

'Some may say or think that I wouldn't be here if it weren't for Tecia. In part, that may be

accurate, and I would be okay with that, because then Gannon would still be here. I too know the pain of losing a child and there is no greater pain. We are now lifelong grief partners as this is a lifelong journey of pain with two sons waiting for us in heaven.'

I have some words from my daughter, Laina, I will address in the middle of my speech, but they're written in yellow so - leave it to a child.

Out of the night that covers me,

black as the pit from pole to pole.

I thank whatever God may be

for my unconquerable soul.

In the fell clutch of circumstance,

I have not winced nor cried aloud.

Under the bludgeoning of chance

my head is bloody but unbowed.

Beyond this of place of wrath and tears,

Looms but the horror of the shade,

And yet the menace of the years

Finds shall find me unafraid.

It matters not how strait the gate,

How charged with punishment the scroll.

I am the master of my fate,

I am the captain of my soul.

The poem I read is named Invictus. Translated from Latin it means Unconquerable. I quoted this same poem at Gannon's memorial here in Colorado Springs back in August of 2020.

Why August of 2020 when his body was ripped to shreds on 27th January? Well, as we heard testimony to, his body was found 1370 miles away. And then the process to identify his maggot infested remains withheld him from us until July 2020.

As I stated in my testimony on the stand Gannon was born severely premature and barely filled my two hands the first time I held him. At the end of his life, after his body was cremated into a pile of ashes, he was ultimately no bigger than the first time I held him.

As brutal as the weight became, I am thankful to God and the bridge workers for returning his precious body to Landen and I. I quote the poem Invictus again not to boast of my strength and perseverance, your honour, but to say to the world, I alone can control my actions and reactions.

Your honour, I refuse to allow anger to poison my soul and orient my life to a pursuit of vengeance. I refuse to allow pain to carry me through each day and promote the pursuit of medicinal retribution toward the offender. I refuse also to let my mind be clouded by inconsistency and emotion that deter me from the purpose of this life.

Your honour, the price I pay each and every day for this result, to only get pieces and parts of my son, consistently through time but the pain is too heavy and anger too overwhelming and the desire for vengeance too vexing. Instead, each and every day I pursue peace. I seek joy in my life and let the love I have for my wife and family flow in and out of me like a mighty wave.

As I told Tecia regularly at the end of our relationship my joy is mine alone and she cannot rob me of that. I will learn to experience G more and more as time goes on, but as I did my best to instil into his precious soul: love, joy, service, and kindness are the pathways to take in life.

This picture shows that in the fourth grade he already had a mind for service. Throughout these past three years since Gannon was beaten, and drugged, carved up, shot at point blank range, and discarded like yesterday's garbage, I've encountered many people that would figuratively do the same thing to me. I've been questioned, compared as Tecia did to my abusive father, and ridiculed for my approach to finding Gannon. I hope now that the world has seen that I was assigned the most arduous task of finding Gannon in the only place that was possible for him to have been - in the mind of a killer. Were my efforts fruitful? I believe so. But from the moment I did not see the Volkswagen Tiguan at French Elementary of that Tuesday evening, a clear direction for finding Gannon pointed directly and precisely at Tecia.

While others online - some who are even in the courtroom today - questioned my perceived lack of effort or concern. I stood still and stood firm in knowing that only one person had the information needed to find Gannon. Now I say woe to the person who questions a father's resolve when the safety and wellbeing of his children are at stake. I did not waver. I did not falter in the pursuit, nor did I allow the mentality of the mob to shake me.

But it was only by the grace of God that Gannon's precious body was finally found. In Mark 4:39 of the Bible in the middle of the storm, Christ arose and rebuked the wind and said peace, be still. In times of trial in my life, from seeing my father being taken away in handcuffs, seeing that sweet one pound 6 ounce baby boy, my first born son, being put into a Ziplock bag after he was born to help regulate his body temperature, and now searching for and never finding my son again, I have but one choice and that is in times of trial and tribulation to have that peace and be still.

As I alluded to previously that stillness does provide an easy target for many who do not understand peace, hope, and even faith. Some, including Tecia, feasted on my stillness, attacked, and yes left several scars. One of these scars come in the form of the financial and residential ruin that began in the early days of this ordeal. I'm just gonna skip this part 'cause I don't wanna make this anymore about me. I'm not seeking any restitution your honour.

For the $1.50 a month I receive from the defendant, Tecia, would just keep me connected to her for the rest of my life and I don't want that. So absolutely no restitution your honour. The murderer of which I speak was not always such.

When I met Tecia, she was beautiful. Extremely intelligent as many have testified to and a seemingly successful woman. A far cry from the nappy headed, murderous, narcissistic, and arrogantly flippant human being that sits in our midst today. Having a background in teaching, social work, higher education, certified babysitting, and endless amount of credentials that should render one trustworthy when it relates to the safety of children.

However, although she remains too much a coward to state the facts of what she did to Gannon, too much a lily-livered, self-centred, pathological liar to ask for forgiveness, and too much the facade of one who actually cares for others to have taken out their frustration on an adult or one that could defend themselves, she will one day give an account through her words or through her time.

Sending pictures of Gannon sleeping to Landen and I was telling, as the boy looked pale and absent of the energies that so defined him. This is what a happy, healthy boy looks like when he's sleeping in the next picture. That's what a little boy sleeping looks like. These pictures on the screen are of a happy, healthy little boy that's sleeping sweetly, healthily, where he lay. The impact Tecia had as a result of this heinous crime stretches far wider and far deeper than I could depict with my statement today.

Two other people torn to pieces as a result of this are Gannon's sister Laina and Harley. Speaking of Harley, I feel as though as I've lost two children as a result of this tragedy, one of which I will never see on this earth again and the other which I don't know if a relationship can ever be salvaged with.

Now for Laina. The video you saw as submitted into evidence, her bebopping down the street is actually an excellent depiction of Laina and her joy in life. She is very loving, trusting, and at times, way too social. Normally, you might be concerned by your little girl talking to the utility guy working in the front yard but in this case, it was the inside of her own home that was of grave concern. Nonetheless, her loss, Laina's loss, is like none I can even imagine. She lost her big brother, her only brother at the time. I still don't know if she has fully processed or fully understands the gravity of the situation but regardless has pressed forward and is thriving as best as she can. I am so proud of her, and these are her words. Once again they're in yellow so I'll do the best I can.

I asked her if she wanted to say anything to Tecia and this is what she said in her sweetest mind that she has.

"That you do not do that to people, especially your step kids and that it is never alright to do these things."

How sweet of a response can you get?

Now, for my precious, premature firstborn son, Gannon. I never in my wildest dreams would've ever thought you'd be in danger, buddy, or you know I would not have left you... (he begins to sob) ... at home with what turned out to be a murderer and the last person to ever see you on this earth. I'm so sorry.

(More sobs, he wipes his face)

Through a father's eyes, children are truly a gift from God. And among the best and most perfect creations God can make. Your honour, I do need to clear one thing up with the defence. It was said both in the opening statement and in the closing, somehow, Gannon has been compared to a demon. And I understand the process, I do, but if they wanna take the case up of Gannon being a demon, I will line people up from Alaska, to Denver, to Colorado Springs, all the way to South Carolina to testify against them. Gannon was nobody's demon. I don't care how much anyone was abused or anything he was not anyone's demon.

Gannon was truly my buddy. Very recently before he died the most alarming thing he did, was call me dad. Up until age 10 or 11 I was Daddy but in the last months of his life I was just dad. A signal that he was coming into those junior high, pre-teenage years. Another amazing thing that he finally started asking me regularly to play ball with him. He was never too much into sports for most of his life but that last 6 to 9 months he really started enjoying playing ball.

Some of the most memorable times were him running little 5-yard football routes in the street in front of our house. Most of the time he dropped the ball, but he kept asking, let's do it again, I almost had it that time Daddy.

Oh, and that Nintendo Switch. One of the most difficult pieces of evidence to give up was his Nintendo because that probably has the most of him on it. Knowing I may never see that again is truly devastating. For him, many of his games were not just games, but a challenge to overcome, as I made him beat specific games before I would buy him the next one. I remember not long before he died him beating the old school Zelda game he had. As he felt he was getting close to beating the final monster, he paused it ran upstairs and we sat at the kitchen island and he beat it right there, together with me. He was as excited as I ever saw him.

With all of that and all of the pain of only being able to see him play through the one YouTube video he was able to make, which I am about to play, I can sleep at night because the father I am and the son he is was culminated as always in our final embrace as he ran out of my arms and downstairs to watch Pokémon, I in his heart and he in mine.

The first part of Gannon's only YouTube video is played for the court.

That was one of the many he hoped to make and the only one he was actually able to make.

I do want to add something that I don't have in my speech that me and Landen already had a conversation about this, and I owe Landen an apology as well as she already gave me one, that we allowed Tecia to manipulate us and to some of the pain and disagreements we had between one another, and, Landen, I'm sorry.

But I will say this. Tecia was not the glue that kept everything together, she was not the answer, and this is not a jab Landen, okay, but Laina still lives with me. Tecia you were not the answer.

Now, your honour, if I have any influence on the final sentence for Tecia, first I asked to be stripped of my last name immediately. it's nauseating and infuriating to hear her called Ms Stauch these past three years.

Secondly, I ask that for every mile she drove Gannon across the country she spend 1 day in solitary confinement. I think that'd take us into 3 or 4 years. After that journey is complete, I recommend her sentence be equal to every year she stripped off of Gannon's life, which for the average male in America is 77, so that would give her 66 more years in addition to the 11 he lived. Lastly for every year of Harley's life that she abusively manipulated that child, she should have an additional year of prison. That adds 21 years to the total. I think without parole that should suffice.

I pray also that Tecia lives the fullest and happiest life that any inmate possibly can live. I also pray that every night before she falls asleep, her last breath before she drifts off sounds just like the breath that she described Gannon breathing as the life left his body and that all through her sleep she dreams of all the fun they had at Disney and other places we went throughout our time together and then every morning as she is about to wake the end of her dream, the last words Gannon spoke or screamed or cried, "Tecia stop! You're hurting me! Why Tecia? Daddy, help me! I want my mommy!"

(More sobbing).

Why couldn't you let him just be a momma's boy? It's all he wanted to be. He just loved his momma. I wish she would tell me what those words were so I would know. Then as he speaks those words the sound of a gunshot goes off and she wakes. Every day and night I pray she relives just those moments and wakes up to a nice warm and kosher breakfast.

In conclusion, I would like to share a picture of Gannon in his final state and final resting place and thank everyone that has had a positive impact on my family.

To everyone who has shared the positive impact Gannon has had on your life, from a proud and broken father, from the bottom of my heart, I thank you.

An image of Gannon is shown.

Mr Allen has a few sentencing comments.

The comments from the family and friends of the Stauch family said it better than I ever could about the impact this had on their lives. The loss of Gannon from his family and to this community will never be made right through this process, we all know that.

The defendant through her own actions tore Gannon's family apart, tore this community apart, and at the same time I've never seen a community come together the way this one did in the face of such tragedy—over an 11-year-old boy who most of us never knew.

The defendant manipulated this community, Gannon's family, the investigation. I've been a prosecutor for a long time, judge. I've seen a lot of cases, but I've never seen the kind of horror this defendant brought down on a community and a family. The torture that Gannon had to suffer in the last moments of his life are unspeakable. No matter what sentence you give us, it will never bring Gannon back, but it will go a long way towards healing. Healing this community. I hope healing Landen and Al. They're gonna live the rest of their lives second guessing every decision they made as it relates to leaving their children in the care of this defendant through no fault of their own.

Judge, on count 1 and 2, they merge, the only sentence available is life in prison without parole. As to count 4, tampering with the deceased human body, driving Gannon's body over 1300 miles away, hiding it from view, hoping it would never be found, I ask for the maximum 12 years and that it be consecutive to the life in prison without parole. Tampering with physical evidence is an F6, I ask for the max as well and run that consecutive. Judge, we do have that other pending case, 20CR 3170 hanging out there. In the grand scheme of things, although I would love to prosecute this defendant for that charge as well, in the interest of justice, I would like to see this defendant in department of corrections custody as soon as possible and so we are dismissing that charge.

Thank you, Judge.

Mr Tolini tells the judge Letecia doesn't have anything she would like to say to the court. The just needs to hear it from her and so he asks Letecia if she has anything she wishes him to consider—she says no.

Mr Tolini speaks up again to request she be placed in San Carlos. Judge Werner says he does not have that ability and is not going to make a recommendation one way or the other.

The judge apologizes, but says he needs to take some time to get his thoughts in order. He takes ten minutes."

Judge Werner returns for the sentencing.

"A parent's worst nightmare is getting a phone call letting them know that something has happened to their child. How much worse must that nightmare be when law enforcement asks not for a picture of your loved one but rather DNA and dental records. I've also heard it said that one of the worst tragedies a parent can experience is to outlive a child. I have known people both professionally and personally who have gone through that. It never leaves them, but the sharpness of the pain does diminish to some extent over time. I cannot fathom the pain Mr Stauch and Ms Bullard have experienced as a result of the defendant's actions. A sentence in a criminal case such as this will not change the fact that their son's life was taken from them and no sentence I impose and nothing I say will ever change that fact.

Ms Stauch, you betrayed the person you loved enough to marry. You told your husband lies and took away someone he loved. You took away every day that Mr Stauch or Ms Bullard could have had with their son.

When you take a life, regardless of how you do that, you forever alter the future. Neither

Mr Stauch nor Ms Bullard will ever see their son graduate from high school, go through the joy and the pain of that first love, or get married. They will never know what kind of impact their son may have had on the world if only he had lived to become an adult. And had Gannon's body not been found? They never would have known what happened to Gannon. They would always have had a lingering doubt about what happened to Gannon. And I cannot imagine the pain and sense of loss associated with that.

You betrayed your daughter Harley Hunt. I cannot imagine the emotional impact that you have had on her due to your selfish and calculated actions. This is a young woman that trusted you to put her interests above yours. This is a young woman who believed in you and believed you were innocent of this crime right up until the time that you pled not guilty by reason of insanity, and she still loves you. That's natural for a child and it doesn't matter how much older they get. You were supposed to protect her. I cannot imagine the guilt she feels or the therapy that she will need to address your betrayal. There is no evidence that she had anything to do with the murder or your coverup of it, but some people still think that she is somehow involved. She wasn't. The incredible strength of will and courage that it took for her to come in and testify is amazing to me, but she did it because as she said it was the right thing to do.

And while thankfully she didn't testify let's not forget about Laina. You betrayed her, too. You took her brother from her and forever altered her family dynamics. She will always wonder who she can trust and will always feel that loss. She was there the day you killed Gannon. His body was still in the house when she got back from school. At some point you even claimed this 8-year-old girl helped you move her brother's body from the basement to the back of your car. That's just simply not true. As she gets older Laina is gonna want to know more and she's gonna want to know if there was something that she could have done to prevent this. I hope she comes to realize that she has no fault in all of this.

You betrayed your stepson, and you took his life. You took away everything he was and everything he could ever become. I can't imagine the terror and confusion that he must have felt in the last moments of his life when he knew his life was being taken by someone he trusted to protect it.

Your attempt to raise the claim that you did this because of your adverse childhood is also a betrayal of people that have mental health issues. It Is no secret that there is a large part of our population that has mental health issues. It's also no secret that our country and our system could do a much better job addressing mental health issues than it does. However, the number of people with mental health issues who become violent is small and the number who become murderers is smaller still. Your claim that a mental health issue caused the murder in this case is a dis-service to all those who struggle with mental health issues every day.

This isn't the first case I have presided over in which sanity or mental condition of the defendant has been raised as a defence. I have had cases where the defendant's mental condition caused the defendant to act out in a certain fashion but even in those cases I have never seen conduct like this. I understand the claim of dissociative identity disorder. I have seen something resembling that and I have seen defendants with schizophrenic disorders. I can understand those. What I have seen is that the mental condition causes the person to act a certain way and when they realize what they did they are astonished by what happened or they have no memory of what happened.

Your claim is that it was another personality that murdered Gannon but there is no time during the minutes, hours, and days following the murder where Letecia came out and wondered, 'gee, why am I carrying a body around in my luggage?' That just isn't credible. You knew what you were doing. You made a number of clear and conscious decisions to cover or disguise what you had done.

Claiming a lack of motive is a common defence tactic and it can be a sound strategy. The truth is, however, that it only takes a moment to make a bad decision that results in disastrous consequences and oftentimes we never know why a defendant chose a particular course of action. However, that does not mean that they did not intend to undertake a course of action. Sometimes, as in this case, the likely explanation is anger. An 11-year-old boy with burns who feels that he's not being taken care of. An 11-year-old boy on the verge of being a teenager. Those of us who have lived through kids that were teenagers, we know how that is. It is not hard to imagine Gannon saying something - 'you're not my mom. I want my mom. I want my dad' and that would be enough to make you really angry, but anger is not an excuse. A defendant is responsible for the choices they made and the actions they undertook even though those choices arose out of or were motivated by anger.

It's clear that you hated and were jealous of Landen Bullard. You saw yourself as a better mother than she was. It's clear from the evidence that you had some resentment from being left with Mr Stauch's children. It's clear you had some resentment toward Mr Stauch because he travelled as part of his job. Some of that manifested as early as Al's assignment in Alaska when you made allegations against the people in his unit. That caused Al to have to return from Alaska. And in one of the phone calls that were played for the jury you talked about having to take care of his kids while he was away and what a good mother you were. It's clear you felt trapped. You wanted out. You were searching for a new job in a new location in Florida.

Mr Stauch had been gone on his new assignment for less than two days when the fire in the basement occurred, I can imagine that you saw your whole future consisting of taking care of Mr Stauch's children while he was off doing his thing and that's not the future that you wanted. I can imagine Gannon at some point after he sustained his burns telling you he wanted his real mom and how that comment would've made you angry. You took your frustration and anger for the marriage, the childcare, the absence of Al and even living in Colorado, you took all of that out on Gannon.

The evidence suggests you first stabbed Gannon repeatedly—18 times. Based on the number of defensive wounds he was clearly conscious for some of that. He was certainly gravely wounded. And chillingly, it would also explain how you were able to mimic the sound of Gannon breathing in one of your sessions with Doctor Lewis. Those were probably close to his last breaths. He was dying but not dead. The evidence could also lead one to conclude that he either fell or rolled off the bed where you shot him in the head and then beat him with the butt of a gun or a baseball bat. That would explain the blood found at different levels on the walls in Gannon's bedroom.

I'm also reminded of the look you had on your face when you slipped your handcuffs while being transported back to Colorado and attacked deputy James. I shudder to think that that was probably the last thing that Gannon saw before he died.

You have shown no remorse throughout this process.

Instead, you've made a conscious choice to build a web of lies. When you gave an interview to detective Jessica Bethel on 29th January 2020, you told her you lied to her about Gannon running away and that he was actually taken by a guy named Eduardo. When you explained that to Detective Bethel, you said you needed to lie because you didn't wanna face the consequences. You told her that you were trying to come up with a plan about what you should do and finally you told her you really thought you could fix this. I think that's true. You lied because you didn't wanna face the consequences. You needed to come up with a plan to fix this and that plan involved covering up what you had done. It involved lie upon lie. But you slipped up at various points and let kernels of truth escape.

In one conversation with Mr Stauch, you told him the FBI needed to close the borders of Colorado, needed to close I-95. I-95 doesn't go through Colorado it's an Interstate that runs along the entire eastern seaboard. It's also not far from where you dumped Gannon's body. When questioned by Detective Bethel, you told her that Mr Stauch might also make up some kind of story about you coming at him with a knife. You said you would never use a knife like that. Yet Gannon was stabbed 18 times.

Your actions in this case also show a very conscious attempt to avoid responsibility in this case. You started out with the story that Gannon had run away. You gave some hints that it might be related to bath salts or drug use by Gannon. You stayed with that story until you were called into EPSO for an interview. You knew they weren't gonna buy the story that Gannon ran away. Then you came up with the abduction. And you stayed with some iteration of that for a long time. But all of those versions had one thing in common. You were always the victim. In one you're beaten and raped and Gannon was abducted. In one, someone stole Gannon out of a truck in the parking lot. In another you let someone drive Gannon to a hospital to take care of a head injury that he had after falling off of a bike. In all of them, you could claim it wasn't your fault. You were just in the wrong place at the wrong time.

Then, you got arrested. You stuck to the story that it was someone else that took Gannon. During the hours you spoke with Special Agent Grusing, he told you he thought sometimes good people do bad things and sometimes it's an accident. Then they found Gannon's body. Then you saw the mountain of evidence against you. And this is a mountain the size of Everest. What was your position after that? Well, it was an accident and you, Letecia, didn't even do it. It was Maria Sanchez. You carefully crafted your new story to continue to avoid responsibility. It also allowed you to take advantage of the out that Mr Grusing and Mr Stauch suggested much, much, earlier when they asked you if this was an accident. Now it was an accident. Your Maria Sanchez personality shot Gannon by mistake because she thought he was an intruder in a cape.

Multiple personalities is not credible in this setting as regardless of how many personalities you have, you only have one body. I have presided over cases where a mental disease or defect prevented a defendant from remembering the course of events including the commission of a crime. Without exception, those defendants have been terrified when contacted by law enforcement because there was a period of time in their lives that they could not account for. Their body may have sustained an injury, and they don't know how it happened. They may have some new object in their house or on their person and they have no idea where they got it from.

We all have free will and we all make choices based on that free will. The people who suffer from the mental disorder you claim are terrified because their free will has been taken from them and they are being subjected to things and experiences they don't understand and don't have any recollection of. You didn't behave anything like that. One of the purposes is to impose an appropriate sentence for the criminal conduct that occurred. Another purpose is to punish an offender by imposing a sentence that takes into account the seriousness of the offense. Yet another purpose of sentencing is to prevent crime and promote respect for the law by providing an effective deterrent to others likely to commit a similar offense.

Anyone who's been in my courtroom before knows that I've said sentencing are the most difficult thing that I do. That's especially true in cases where someone has lost his or her life. Nothing I or the law can do will ever bring that person back. I have handled hundreds if not thousands of criminal cases over the years. I think in this point in my career I've presided over something like 200 jury trials. I've sentenced hundreds more defendants pursuant to plea agreements. This is not the first murder case that has come before me. This is not the first case I've presided over which involves harm to a child. This is not the first case I have had where a person who was in an unhappy marriage committed a crime.

Sadly, statistically there is a high correlation between violent acts including murders and family members. I have had a number of cases which have demonstrated one person's capacity for cruelty toward another human being. I can, however, say without hesitation that the facts in this case are the most horrific I have ever seen. Your conduct in this case deserves the maximum punishment that I can impose under Colorado law. As such with respect to the charge of first degree murder after deliberation I remand you to the custody of the Colorado department of corrections for the remainder of your life with no possibility of parole.

With respect to the charge of murder in the first degree of a child under twelve by a person in a position I remand you to the custody of the Colorado department of corrections for the remainder of your life with no possibility of parole.

Those two sentences will merge. If you have questions about that, you can ask your attorneys.

With respect to the charge of tampering with a deceased human body I'm also going to sentence you to 12 years followed by a 3-year period of parole. That sentence is to be consecutive to the life sentences that I've already imposed.

With respect to tampering with physical evidence I'm going to impose an 18-month sentence. That is also consecutive to the sentences for the murder changes I have imposed. I also understand with the consent of the prosecution and I'm assuming no objection from the defence that I will dismiss all the charges in 20CR3170, close that out subject to restitution, give the people 49 days for restitution, 14 days for response and if there's an issue, we will set it within the 90 days from today. I think that resolves all outstanding matters.

CHAPTER 23

SUMMARY

What can we possibly say that could sum up this case? Especially after the victim impact statements and Judge Werner's sentencing statement, there's not much at all.

Letecia Stauch, a manipulative, self-centred, calculated, evil woman, murdered Gannon in cold blood, inventing multiple scenarios in her twisted quest to evade justice.

Treated like nothing more than trash, she stuffed his broken body into a suitcase, before dumping it, hoping he would never be found.

Thankfully, Gannon now rests in peace, but that doesn't negate the fact that he suffered as no child ever should.

He deserved to live a full and happy life but died in a brutal prolonged attack, filled with fear and terror, robbed of his future by somebody he trusted—his stepmother.

During her trial, and there is no evidence to suggest before or after, that Letecia showed one shred of remorse for her unforgivable acts.

The only consolation is that she will most definitely die behind bars.

We can only pray that Gannon's family are able to move on from the devastating results of her evil actions and will eventually learn to trust again and to heal the wound Gannon's death left behind.

Rest in Peace Gannon Stauch.

ABOUT THE AUTHORS

Netta Newbound is the best-selling author of over twenty thriller novels/novellas to date including the Adam Stanley Thriller Series and the Cold Case Files. Her debut psychological thriller, An Impossible Dilemma, shot up the charts in 2016 in both the UK and US reaching #1 in several thriller and horror categories. This rapid success gained Netta a name for herself in the thriller genre. The Watcher also reached the top 20 in the US Amazon charts.

She has recently began focussing on the other love in her life, true crime.

Originally from Manchester, England, Netta has travelled extensively and has lived and worked in a variety of exciting places. She and her husband emigrated to New Zealand in 1998. They have three grown up children and four grandchildren.

Marcus Brown was born and raised in the North West of England in 1974.

What started as a hobby, has since turned into a full-time career.

He lives with his partner and a whole host of animals on the Wirral peninsula.

They have been working together for a number of years after establishing Junction Publishing.

Also by the Authors

Check out all Netta's books on Amazon.

Check out all Marcus Brown's books at Amazon.

Made in United States
Troutdale, OR
08/23/2024

22268140R00266